"In gold-laced veils of evening beautiful. . . ."* When Hollywood was Camelot and beauty was enough. Florence Vidor in Malcolm St. Clair's *The Grand Duchess and the Waiter* (1926).

*Baudelaire, "Epilogue" (Arthur Symons translation).

SAINT CINEMA
WRITINGS ON THE FILM
1929-1970

by Herman G. Weinberg

Preface by
Fritz Lang

SECOND REVISED EDITION
with 64 rare illustrations
and a note on this edition

PN
1994
W39
1973

DOVER PUBLICATIONS, INC.
NEW YORK

BY THE SAME AUTHOR:

Josef von Sternberg
The Lubitsch Touch
The Complete *Greed*

Copyright © 1970, 1973 by Herman G. Weinberg.
All rights reserved under Pan American and International Copyright Conventions.

Published in Canada by General Publishing Company, Ltd., 30 Lesmill Road, Don Mills, Toronto, Ontario.

This Dover edition, first published in 1973, is a revised edition (see "A Note on This Edition," page viii) of the work originally published by DBS Publications, Inc./Drama Book Specialists, New York, in 1970. The illustrations and index are entirely new features of the present edition. All the illustrations are from the author's collection.
This edition is published by special arrangement with Drama Book Specialists/Publishers.

International Standard Book Number: 0-486-22908-4
Library of Congress Catalog Card Number: 72-90629

Manufactured in the United States of America
Dover Publications, Inc.
180 Varick Street
New York, N. Y. 10014

In memory of Etta
my own true love

A NOTE ON THIS EDITION

They say, and I have said it myself, that there is nothing like first rapture. Like first love, it only happens once (that isn't quite true, but let it pass) and it has its own magic. But there are other magics as there are other girls (again, that isn't quite true and, again, let it pass). Recasting what one has previously written, which is to say, rethinking it in the light of sober reflection (for surely one was under a spell the first time and slightly heady with the euphoria of setting everything down for the first time—who knows what portions of it might endure?)—invariably results in second thoughts about what one once doted upon and now finds expendable in the light of clear day (shall I say "the morning after"?). At any rate, some portions of the text of the first edition are now deleted, as much to make room for the illustrations, which the first edition lacked, as for reasons of, well, "expendability." There is also some new text—and an index, which I'm told increases a book's usefulness immeasurably. In a way, though, it's like that old *jeu d'esprit*—"if one had one's life to live over again." Given the chance to have one's book to do over again is, perhaps, the closest one can come to that. The result is in these pages. It has also given me and the publisher a chance to correct all the typographical errors and *gaffes* of the first edition. As for the illustrations, I hope they speak for themselves. "What is the use of a book," thought Alice, "without pictures?" She had a point there. Remains the point of the book, which is about men and their work, and I have found it in Ecclesiastes: "Wherefore I perceive that there is nothing better than that a man should rejoice in his own works."

H.G.W.

Summer, 1972

Grateful acknowledgment is made to the following for permission to reprint copyrighted material:

Arno Press, Inc., for the "Foreword" to the reissue of *Close Up.*
Editions Seghers, Paris, for "A Tribute to Walt Disney."
Film Comment Publishing Corp. (1968), for "H. d'Abbadie d'Arrast—In Memoriam," "Greed" and "The Parallel with Georges Feydeau."
Film Culture, for "Touch of Evil," "Confidential Report," "Erich von Stroheim," "Coffee, Brandy & Cigars" and "Animal Farm."
Film Heritage, for "Thunder in the East."
Films in Review, for "A Farewell to Flaherty" and "A Visit with Hans Richter."
The *New York Times* Company (© 1950–1953), for "Von Sternberg Films the Anatahan Story."
The Seven Arts Feature Syndicate, for "My First Memories of Chaplin," "Grand Illusion," "Renoir Films the Voice of the People," "The Great Dictator" and "The Actors in Dreyer's *Jeanne d'Arc.*"
Sight and Sound, for "Von Sternberg Films the Anatahan Story."
Take One, for "Some Thoughts on Josef von Sternberg—In Memoriam" and "Triptych—Italian Style."
Variety, for "Some Footnotes to the Arts," "Coffee, Brandy & Cigars" (1960–1968) and "L'Envoi."

Wagner told Liszt that had he been happy, he would not have set down a note. One puts into one's art what he has been incapable of putting into one's existence. It is because he was unhappy that God created the world.
—*De Montherlant*

Memory is the one beautiful paradise from which we cannot be expelled.
—*Jean Paul*

We all have in us a Don Quixote and a Sancho Panza to which we listen, and though it be Sancho who persuades us, it is Don Quixote who compels our admiration.
—*Anatole France*

PREFACE
by FRITZ LANG

> ... *Yesterday is but a Dream,*
> *And Tomorrow is only a Vision*
> *But Today well-lived makes*
> *Every Yesterday a Dream of Happiness,*
> *And every Tomorrow a Vision of Hope.*
> —*from the Sanskrit*

One evening last fall—one of those cold evenings that often follow a warm day in Southern California—I was alone in my house. A fire of big eucalyptus logs was burning in the large fireplace.

There is no gas in my fireplace to keep it going. I like the real thing. A fireplace is a fireplace and not a gas stove.

I made myself a cup of coffee. Real coffee, not "instant." As I said, I like the real thing. No ersatz for me.

I carried the coffee to my comfortable easy chair in front of the fireplace, stepped up to the bar, poured a generous shot of Courvoisier into a snifter, enjoyed the oily traces of the liquid on the thin glass, and went back to my easy chair.

I had planned to read some back-number articles, to bring myself up-to-date about the student movement in Europe. I lit a cigar, thumbed through the first magazine, took a sip of coffee, a larger one of the brandy, put the cigar onto an ashtray, and started to read. . . .

But I couldn't concentrate.

The smoke of the cigar rising vertically, a steep straight line, gracefully spiraling at the top and finally drifting towards the fireplace, was mirrored in the brandy snifter.

Brandy . . . coffee. . . .

I reached for the coffee and stopped midway.

Brandy, Coffee & Cigars . . .

That reminded me of someone who detests substitutes as much as I do and whose whole life is a search for real values, the genuine.

I got up and walked into the library.

On three large shelves are magazines, books, pamphlets . . . all dealing with motion pictures. . . . I reached for the last edition of *Film Culture* . . . and there it was:

> COFFEE, BRANDY & CIGARS, (Things you never knew till now, and got on just as well without). By *Herman G. Weinberg*

I have known Herman Weinberg for more than thirty-five years. What immediately formed a bond between us was our mutual, incontestable conviction that film is THE art of our century.

I thumbed through different issues where *Coffee, Brandy & Cigars* appeared. . . . It was fun, great fun, to read—to give only one or two examples—that Orson Welles thought of Von Stroheim that: "His art is Jewish baroque," or that Ingmar Bergman is "emmerdant," whereas Herman Weinberg himself thinks that Bergman's films "are excellent Rorschach tests. . . ."

But Weinberg is much more than a charming, witty, and amusing raconteur.

In this book the reader will find film-reviews that are a veritable motherlode of deep insight into films.

Originally used as *Program Notes* for Harry Baur's *Golem* (1937), *Carnet de Bal* (1938), *Harvest* (1939), and *The Yellow Cruise* (1941), they are much more than program notes: they are deeply felt essays. What Weinberg writes about *Pepe le Moko* and Renoir's *La Grande Illusion* or of the actors in Carl Theodore Dreyer's unforgettable *Jeanne d'Arc* is simply must-reading for every film creator or aficionado.

Tolstoy once wrote: ". . . The film might be one of the mightiest means of spreading knowledge and great ideas, and yet it serves only to litter people's brains."

Herman Weinberg is a contradiction of the whole quotation, but the living example of what Tolstoy had envisioned film should be.

Proof:

His writings on the lives and works of Flaherty and Erich von Stroheim, or especially H. d'Abbadie d'Arrast, who died in 1968, the creator of "eight of the loveliest films ever made by anyone," but forgotten by almost everyone!

His films are lost forever, like many other films important for the art of the cinema and for its historians, because studio policies aimed at the destruction of old films printed on inflammable nitrate stock, but which same studios were "not above salvaging the few cents worth of silver which formed part of the cellulose base." (Erich von Stroheim)

One can read about this in an article by Weinberg called *The Lost Ones,* which regrettably was not included in this book.

I am sure that, having read the different collected essays, reviews, etc. of this book, the reader will agree that every article not only points out the obvious surface values of the described film, as the conventional critic does, but captures its very essence, its inherent real meaning, because Weinberg sees a film not merely with his eyes but with his heart.

And I am also sure that the reader's appetite will be whetted to learn more about the many widely published writings of Herman G. Weinberg, this Boswell of the art of our century: FILM.

*Beverly Hills
January, 1970*

CONTENTS

	PAGE
Author's Introduction	1
The Actors in Dreyer's *Jeanne d'Arc* (*November, 1929*)	11
My First Memories of Chaplin (*November, 1931*)	14
The Case of Pabst (*August, 1936*)	19
The Gods at Play (*October, 1936*)	27
Marco Polo—Modern Style (*November, 1936*)	31
A Mask, a Muff—and a Lady . . . (*December, 1936*)	33
The Golem (*March, 1937*)	36
Erich von Stroheim (*Spring, 1937*)	39
Un Carnet de Bal (*June, 1938*)	49
Grand Illusion (*December, 1938*)	53
Harvest (*June, 1939*)	57
Renoir Films the Voice of the People (*November, 1939*)	62
The Baker's Wife (*February, 1940*)	67
Time in the Sun (*September, 1940*)	69
The Great Dictator (*November, 1940*)	77
Pépé Le Moko (*February, 1941*)	82
The Last Will of Dr. Mabuse (*March, 1943*)	84
A Farewell to Flaherty (*October, 1951*)	85
A Visit with Hans Richter (*December, 1951*)	91
Von Sternberg Films the Anatahan Story (*February, 1953*)	95
Faust (*January, 1955*)	99
Animal Farm (*March, 1955*)	108
Greed (*Spring, 1955*)	113
Confidential Report (*1956*)	122
Erich von Stroheim (*April, 1958*)	127
Touch of Evil (*Autumn, 1959*)	134
Some Footnotes to the Arts (*January, 1960*)	137
Coffee, Brandy & Cigars (*Summer, 1960*)	143
Coffee, Brandy & Cigars (*January, 1961*)	147
Merry Go Round (*May, 1961*)	150
Queen Kelly (*Spring, 1961*)	155
Coffee, Brandy & Cigars (*January, 1962*)	162

Contents

	PAGE
Footnote to a Montreal Film Festival *(Winter, 1962)*	167
Coffee, Brandy & Cigars *(Spring, 1962)*	170
Coffee, Brandy & Cigars *(Autumn, 1962)*	174
Coffee, Brandy & Cigars *(Winter, 1962)*	184
Coffee, Brandy & Cigars *(January, 1963)*	192
Coffee, Brandy & Cigars *(May, 1963)*	197
Coffee, Brandy & Cigars *(Autumn, 1963)*	205
Coffee, Brandy & Cigars *(Winter, 1963)*	210
Coffee, Brandy & Cigars *(January, 1964)*	215
Coffee, Brandy & Cigars *(Summer, 1964)*	220
Coffee, Brandy & Cigars *(Autumn, 1964)*	225
Coffee, Brandy & Cigars *(January, 1965)*	232
Coffee, Brandy & Cigars *(Spring, 1965)*	235
Coffee, Brandy & Cigars *(Autumn, 1965)*	239
Coffee, Brandy & Cigars *(January, 1966)*	246
Judex *(May, 1966)*	251
Coffee, Brandy & Cigars *(August, 1966)*	256
Coffee, Brandy & Cigars *(January, 1967)*	259
Coffee, Brandy & Cigars *(Spring, 1967)*	262
Welcome, Fritz Lang! *(Summer, 1967)*	268
Coffee, Brandy & Cigars *(January, 1968)*	278
Thunder in the East *(Autumn, 1968)*	281
H. d'Abbadie d'Arrast—In Memoriam *(Summer, 1969)*	295
The Parallel with Georges Feydeau *(Winter, 1969)*	315
Foreword to *Close Up* *(Winter, 1969)*	319
A Tribute to Walt Disney *(Winter, 1969)*	323
Some Thoughts on Von Sternberg—In Memoriam *(Spring, 1970)*	326
Triptych—Italian Style *(Spring, 1970)*	334
L'Envoi *(Spring, 1970)*	350
Afterword	354
Author's Note	355
Index	357

LIST OF ILLUSTRATIONS

Florence Vidor in *The Grand Duchess and the Waiter*	Frontispiece
	PAGE
Two stills from *The Passion of Joan of Arc*	10
Chaplin directing *City Lights*	15
Léger's cubist portrait of Chaplin	16
Stroheim and Pabst in Hollywood, 1934	21
Two stills from *Amphitryon*	28 & 29
Three stills from *Foolish Wives*	42–44
Marie Bell in *Un Carnet de Bal*	50
Jean Renoir in Montreal, 1967	52
Orane Demazis and Gabriel Gabrio in *Harvest*	59
Still from *The Baker's Wife*	66
Eisenstein at Rivera's home, Mexico, 1931	71
Eisenstein and Tissé at a Mayan temple	72
Still from the Prologue to *Que Viva Mexico!*	73
Still from the *Sandunga* sequence of *Que Viva Mexico!*	74
Eisenstein and Tissé setting up a shot in Tetlapayac	75
Eisenstein and Tissé filming the carnival in *Que Viva Mexico!*	76
Chaplin and Paulette Goddard during the filming of *The Great Dictator*	79
Flaherty during the shooting of *Louisiana Story*	86
Still from *Moana*	89
Sternberg preparing a scene for *The Saga of Anatahan*	94
Still from *The Saga of Anatahan*	97
Werner Fütterer as St. Michael in Murnau's *Faust*	100
The Four Horsemen of the Apocalypse from *Faust*	101
Camilla Horn and Gösta Ekman in *Faust*	102
Stroheim filming *Greed*	112
A length of film from *Greed*	115
Michael Redgrave in *Mr. Arkadin*	123
Fay Wray and Stroheim in *The Wedding March*	128
Maude George, George Fawcett and Stroheim in *The Wedding March*	129
Norman Kerry in *Merry Go Round*	152
Dorothy Wallace and Sidney Bracey in *Merry Go Round*	153
Walter Byron and Seena Owen in *Queen Kelly*	156

xviii   List of Illustrations

PAGE

Still from *Queen Kelly* (cuirassiers and convent girls)	157
Two phases of Gloria Swanson's role in *Queen Kelly*	158
Fritz Lang, 1968	270
Lang and Karl Freund at work on *Metropolis*	271
Brigitte Helm as siren of the Yoshiwara in *Metropolis*	272
Gustav Fröhlich in *Metropolis*	273
Paul Richter as Siegfried	274
Rudolf Klein-Rogge in *Kriemhild's Revenge*	275
Inkijinoff and Charles Boyer in *Thunder in the East*	282
Boyer, Merle Oberon and John Loder in *Thunder in the East*	283
Harry d'Arrast and Ernest Vajda, 1928	297
Adolphe Menjou and Kathryn Carver in two stills from *Service for Ladies*	302 & 303
Ernst Lubitsch at the piano, 1928	316
Monte Blue and Marie Prevost in *Kiss Me Again*	317
Josef von Sternberg, 1939	327
Mauritz Stiller, Pola Negri and Erich Pommer	328
Ewald André Dupont filming *Love Me and the World Is Mine*	329
Paul Bern and Jetta Goudal	330
Jetta Goudal and Adolphe Menjou in *Open All Night*	331
Florence Vidor and Adolphe Menjou in *The Grand Duchess and the Waiter*	332
Old friends: Hans Richter (with Georges Méliès), Robert Florey, Chaplin, Jean Renoir, René Clair	348
Old friends: King Vidor, Fritz Lang (with the author)	349

AUTHOR'S INTRODUCTION

"What disturbs me most," once said Jean Renoir, "is the thought that films have such a short life. Techniques change, actors' styles change, and just as fashions become outmoded, films go into oblivion to join others that once moved us."

Indeed, this is so. Nothing dates so swiftly, is more transient, than yesterday's films, save perhaps yesterday's newspapers. There is something topical about every film, so devastatingly characteristic of the year in which it was made, something that mirrors its times (may I say *zeitgeist?*—the spirit of those times) so acutely, that the following year or two finds it already "old hat." This is both its strength and its weakness. It is the films' strength that they are such a trenchant (one might almost say psychoanalytical) mirror of their times, both influencing and being influenced by that time, and their weakness, because it is that very "moment of truth" (for better or for worse) that makes them prone to be so quickly cast aside when new values become the vogue. New truths for old! Like the "New lamps for old!" cry of the merchant in *Aladdin and the Wonderful Lamp*. And like the new lamps in that fable, their only value was their newness—of magic they had none.

This is a book about that magic.

And since in almost all its pieces the book makes a positive statement for the medium (I leave querulous observations and their whys and wherefores to my younger colleagues who have time on their side for such animadversions), gleaned from my first experiences with the films, which is to say, of course, from my first rapture with them, when the medium itself was still young and rapturous (and testing itself as well as its audiences), it is called, by reason of these modest tributes to some of the films' Olympian achievements, *Saint Cinema,* for, in a way, they are, by their very nature, offerings on the altar of the cinema muse.

That staying power that permits us still to speak of them

today, though some go back as far as forty years (the pieces as well as the films)—almost two-thirds the whole life of the cinema as an art, if we date its parturition from *The Birth of a Nation,* the film that started it all)—has given most of the films written about in these pages the status of classics and the artists who made them, the Giottos of the film, the nimbus of cinema immortals. A few exceptions to this are included to balance the whole picture.

But the young reader of these pieces today, today's moviegoer, what of him, what of those who have not bridged the two generations spanned by the history of the film? Here it is interesting to speculate on a statement by Pierre Louÿs in his preface to Claude Farrère's *Black Opium,* that exotic collection of short stories: "A good writer," he says, "belongs not to his own generation, but to the following one; and if it pleases him to take up anew the exposition of an old theme, it is for the reason that he desires to renovate that theme in such a manner that all known objections to it shall be no longer valid." Substitute the word "filmmaker" for "writer" and the statement itself is just as valid. Still, seeing these films (often for the first time) today, in revival or in the classroom, what do they mean to the film student? How does he relate them to his own experience, moviegoing or otherwise? I tell students in my film history classes to try to adjust their "time spirit" (in that felicitous German phrase), to get a sense of perspective, so that they will see the old film in the right light, as if they had overtaken the light years and were seeing the film at the time it first appeared, in its pristine freshness. I know that for young people this is for most of them all but impossible—yet I must say it so that they will understand what is involved in seeing a classic a generation or more after it was made. It won't do for such a film merely to look quaint, even charmingly quaint, and be tolerated or even liked for its charming quaintness. As the musicologist, Jerrold Moore, said in another context, about past traditions in music that time had burnished with a patina somewhat less than golden, "We inevitably lack the atmosphere of the time; an important factor, since their very staying power has perforce made them into period pieces. It is not really meant for us but for its own time. Half a century later, it has all the qualities of a souvenir, especially the compression of actual experience into that peculiar two-dimensionality which most subtly misleads the living memory."

So we have a seeming paradox: the film as inimitably a product of its time and the film artist invariably ahead of his time. The alert film student (I use the term in its broadest sense to include all aficionados) will have developed an historical sense, aware that fashion is a jade in films as in all things, and not be put off by her, thereby knowing exactly to what "f-stop" to adjust the lens of his mind so that he has the film classic in question set for brightest exposure and in sharpest focus. In that way and only in that way is he truly seeing what is on the screen before him. To look at such a film is one thing, to *see* it is another, the more difficult and, for that, the more rewarding.

So it is with the pieces in this book, they are reflections of their times; each is dated so that the reader is constantly aware of this. Thus we begin with the spectacular close of the silent era, follow with the pre-World War II sound era, notable especially for the florescence of the French film, then the feverish war years, closing with the post-war decades. The films examined (or rather, evoked) here were written about when they first appeared so that each piece represents a spontaneous expression of the time, as do those about the several artists included.

This then is the way "our daily bread of the movies" looked to one observer who was writing about it at the time and which he has now collated in this retrospective covering forty years. There were times when the movies were often not more than betel nut for the eyes, but those of us who grew up with the cinema, as it grew up, saw it through its various mutations, viewing its developments in turn with ecstasy and alarm, grew to have an affection for this daft art which had such a potential for noble work (and, alas, for also being so easily debased). In these pieces I have chosen to seek out this nobility in accordance with my as yet unwritten catechism of the cinema, one of whose tenets is that it is more important to speak of the good than the bad. Thus, again, *Saint Cinema.*

Another tenet is that because a film is old is not sufficient reason to venerate it. A mediocre violin, though made three hundred years ago, will always be mediocre, as a mediocre wine, however old its vintage, will not only always be mediocre but will get even worse. But a Stradivarius or Guarnerius violin will improve with age, as will a fine wine. While a film classic by definition is a film that was a sterling work to begin with—age has nothing to do with its merit, which is intrinsic, inherently in it, though time may even hallow it.

One thing *is* venerated above all else in these pages: the artist, because he is involved in the miracle of creation. "He (the talented creator) is the possessor of those gifts," concludes Louÿs, "which are commonly called native, but which are, on the contrary, so strange, those gifts which the poets are in the habit of attributing to the beneficent influence of invisible divinities, for the reason that the ability to create would seem to be a slightly more than human faculty."

Ave cinema gratia plena . . .

(In the early days of the French film, the coterie around René Clair invoked the protection of its patron saint, Notre Dame du Cinéma.)

Scattered among the articles, essays, reviews, that have been selected for this retrospective are installments of the column *Coffee, Brandy & Cigars,* of which some fifty have appeared during the past two decades. The inspiration for its title was a similar compendium by the Austrian raconteur and feuilletonist, Roda-Roda, *Der Schnapps, der Rauchtabak, und die verfluchte Liebe* ("Brandy, Tobacco, and that Damned Thing, Love"). The purpose of *Coffee, Brandy & Cigars* (so named because it comprised tidbits for after-dinner conversation) was to gather together little known facts and items, frequently bizarre or humorous, always revealing, sometimes satiric, sometimes illuminating, or startling even, peppered with the author's own comments on the passing scene—the whole constituting the raw material for an as yet unwritten history of the motion pictures *in extenso.*

In these "fillers" the reader will find, I hope, nuggets of real gold mined from the author's note-books. And if there are many items of a non-filmic kind it is because films do not exist in a vacuum but in the real world where other arts also flourish and of which the films are, for all their world-wide popularity, only a small part, despite the postulation made by Erwin Panofsky (in his essay, "Style and Medium in the Motion Pictures") that if all artistic endeavor in the world would suddenly cease, it would hardly be noticed by the great majority of the world's populace, but if there was a sudden cessation of movies it would be catastrophic. This is what I mean by "our daily bread of the movies" to which we preface, "Give us this day . . ."

Thus are the movies all things to all men, but they are still not the end-all and it is for this that scattered through these pages are the items reflecting the multi-faceted glitter of all the arts, particularly painting and music, the sister arts closest to the films. Indeed, the writer of these lines once, in a facetious moment to be sure, went so far as to hazard what he hoped was a *mot juste* when he suggested that with the advent of Saint-Saëns it was inevitable that the cinema be invented.

But the world of Saint-Saëns was a better one than today's. Being a world that flowered, and that's the only word for it, before the invention of the cinematograph began to litter people's minds, as Tolstoy put it, it was serene—a world in which that glorious burst of creative bliss, French impressionist and post-impressionist painting, blossomed. It was the world of Berthe Morisot's exquisite *In the Garden at Maurecourt*, which just portrays a little girl in a big straw hat sitting in a garden, a world in which Mme. Morisot (who was the sister-in-law of Manet) could say, "One dashes about and fusses; one no longer realizes that nothing is more important than a couple of hours stretched out on a hammock. Life is a dream and the dream is more than reality—there one is one's self. If one does have a soul, that is where it is to be found." Or a world in which Manet could write to Antonin Proust, "I remember as if it were yesterday the quick summary manner in which I treated the glove in your ungloved hand. And when at that instant you said to me, 'Please, not a line more!' At that moment I felt we were in such perfect accord that I could not resist the impulse to embrace you."

Does the reader of these lines wonder what all this is doing in a film book? Because I search for these eternal values in the films—and sometimes I find them, as when Dreyer's Joan asks, as she is being readied to burn at the stake, "Where will I be tonight?" Or sometimes outside the films themselves as when René Clair tells me that once, when Josef von Sternberg came to Paris, he sent a bouquet of roses to Clair as a prelude to their first meeting. You didn't know that, did you? No one knew it—that's why *Coffee, Brandy & Cigars* came into being, as a repository for such items against the day when they could all be corralled, sifted and sorted out, placed in their proper categories and slotted into their positions in that "as yet unwritten history of the motion pictures *in extenso*." Similarly, *Saint Cinema* is primarily about eternal values, cinematic or otherwise, especially otherwise, because that's what the subjects of the films are about. *The subjects of the films are non-filmic* (except on the rarest occasions) so that the book addresses itself to their content as well as their form.

"The life I have chosen," wrote Winslow Homer to his brother, "gives me my full hours of enjoyment for the balance of my life. The sun will not rise, or set, without my notice or thanks."

That's what it's all about (note how he echoes Mme. Morisot), to do work that brings that kind of satisfaction, that kind of serenity, in or out of the cinema. This, then, is a book about some aspects of the human condition in the guise of a film book.

Remains the matter of the current license permitted the screen, or say, rather, licentiousness, as being practiced today by the current medicine men of the movies . . .

The flagrantly explicit depictions of sex and violence so far beyond anything ever depicted before (not even sparing us the sudden frenzy of cannibalism) among even some of our best current directors, like Godard, Fellini, Pasolini and others, is surely a reflection in the cinema of a growing pessimism about the future of mankind and the absence of ideals or myths on which to peg a more constructive horizon. It is, of course, also pitiful evidence of the abysmal contempt with which today's film producers hold their public, for whom the theatres have become so many troughs. The stage, too, has become infected and, like the motion pictures, claiming the rights of "free speech," flaunts its defiance of all morality, ethics, and sensibility. Will not our sports arenas be given over to spectacular displays of sex next? Didn't Aldous Huxley once predict it when he said sex would eventually become a spectator sport like ice-skating? "Thus," commented Harriet van Horne in a New York Post column reviling the wave of boorish sex that has engulfed our times, "thus do we fulfill the nightmares of our prophets."

Note that under censorship, which enforced subtlety on the artist, the great body of all that constitutes the glory of the cinema was accomplished. Under censorship the art of Griffith, Stroheim, Eisenstein, Chaplin, Lubitsch, Sternberg, René Clair, Dreyer and the rest of that hallowed company, whose names constitute the pantheon of the cinema, flourished. I never thought I'd some day be defending censorship until I saw what the absence of censorship led to, the total erosion of all grace.

The true artist does not succumb to his own stimuli. He holds himself aloof from his subject matter and never loses control of it or himself. I once wrote, in another context, that the still young cinema had such a potential that the really great artists had, perhaps, not yet appeared, despite the formidable array of names one could already cite. The present appearances, I said, might be only the half-gods, the Davidic Messiahs, before the genuine advent. I no longer believe this. I think we've had it, as the popular expression puts it, and the purpose of this book, if I may be so bold, is to make an offering toward consolidating that position in terms of some of the best work that was achieved.

It may be that I am as premature in my judgment of the new "permissiveness," as I was in 1929, the year sound came to the screen, when I similarly viewed with alarm the demise of the silent film in a piece called (paraphrasing the writing on the wall at the feast of Nebuchadnezzar), "Mene Mene Talkie Upharsin." But this time I don't think so. For over forty years I have watched the screen and thought about it and have few illusions as a result as to what constitutes "progress." In 1895, the year Auguste Lumière invented the cinematograph, he lost no time in predicting, "The cinema is an invention without a future." There must have been something about that rattletrap mechanism he concocted that "didn't smell right," if I may be forgiven the mixed metaphor. Depending on how long your idea of a reasonable future is, he may not, or on the other hand he may very well have been proved to be right.

For the most part today's new films have for some time now neither illuminated life for us nor guided us—they only diverted us, when they managed to do even that. And divert has two meanings—to amuse and to lead us off the right path.

For a mess of tainted pottage (what else can you call the present screen pornography?) we have sold the cinema's birthright. Film-making today has become a grim, joyless thing. Even Hollywood, once the world citadel of screen glamour, has lost all interest in itself and is up for sale—back to the real estate interests which first founded it and made of a cow pasture a kind of Cythera in our time, not to mention its status as the seat of a great industry with world-wide ramifications.

In the process, we have lost certain values. It is to recall those values that I have evoked some of the films and artists that imparted those values to it. The films themselves are evoked rather than reviewed in the conventional sense, the task of reviewing them having long since had that office performed for them by my colleagues. More than anything else, and despite the sometimes tart critical asides, the purpose of this book is to evoke the cinema paradise we have lost.

Hollywood . . .

Suppose it *were* only a dream, like Paul Morand once envisioned the end of New York, "a prodigious attempt, an avatar, a fleeting renaissance, a superb purgatory?" And will the Pacific waves return to break on the California shore that once knew a place called Hollywood and one day will know it no longer "when silence lies unbroken over a world that once knew a brief moment's agitation"?

I don't like unhappy endings, even in forewords. I know that sometimes they are inevitable, but just the same, if one could do something about it, like the wry "happy-end" Carl Mayer and Murnau provided for *The Last Laugh,* why not? So I, too, would like to end on a happier note, a more ardent one, as a tribute to those ardent days of the cinema's youth, the days of its innocence and charm, as in the proud toss of the head of D'Artagnan, kneeling before his King, Louis XIII, in Douglas Fairbanks' *The Three Musketeers,* that ineffable last close-up of Doug before the camera irises out—or the mad ecstasy of the cream-separator sequence of Eisenstein's *Old and New—*or the adorable final shot of Clair's *14 Juillet,* the abandoned taxi and flower girl's cart in the deserted street as dawn breaks over Paris. I recall those blithe days because they were full of such exultant flights of the spirit and because it is this very ardency, this bravado, as exemplified in the following jest which may make it possible for me to close this foreword with my own wry "happy end."

It is an anecdote James Joyce was fond of telling (he swore it was true) about a medic friend of his, a distinguished physician from Harley Street, who though noted for both his medical skill and high fees was also, alas, addicted to spirituous liquors, especially Scotch and Irish malt whiskies. He and Joyce were riding through London one fine day in a cab that was suddenly stopped by a crowd gathered in the middle of the street. "What's up?" asked the good doctor, already deep in his cups, though it was scarcely noon. "Accident, guv'nor," replied the cab-driver, whereupon the doctor slowly got out, followed by Joyce, and made his way unsteadily through the crowd to where the accident victim lay. "I'm a doctor," he proudly announced, with a hiccup that made Joyce and even the doctor himself wince. They all gave him room. Bending down over the victim, he listened to his heart beat, took his pulse and gave him a brief once-over. "Well," he said, getting up and proceeding to remove his jacket, and once more hiccupping, but with pride shining in his eyes for the deed of derring-do he was about to accomplish, "The man's dead," he announced, "but I'll see what I can do."

Epilogue

Q. "What kind of a happy ending do you call that?"

A. "You see? It's no use—this foreword can't have a happy ending."

"Portraits burnt in copper, bronze . . . obviously no aura of quattrocento gold and gold dust and fleurs-de-lys in straight hieratic pattern. . . ."* Dreyer's *The Passion of Joan of Arc* (1928).

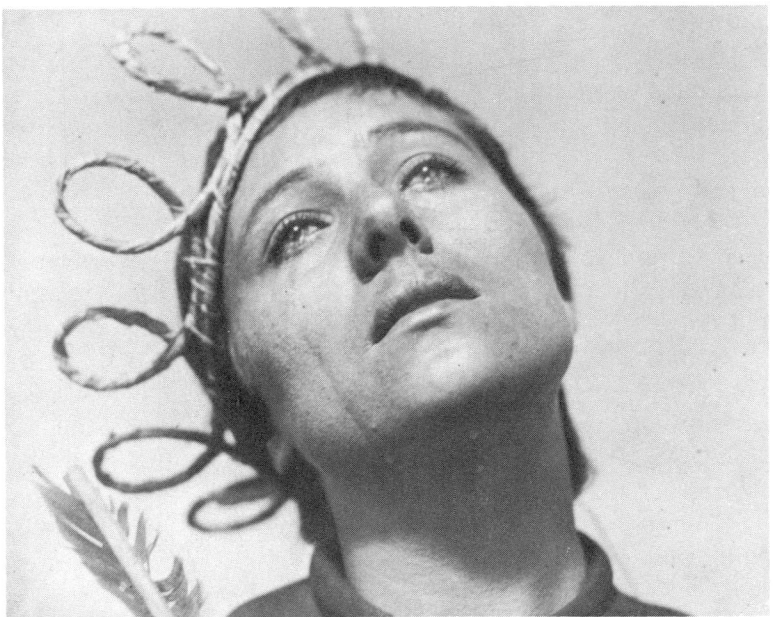

"Superbly, almost mediumistically portrayed by Mlle. Falconetti . . . no weakening incense as Fra Angelico gold and lilies of heavenly comfort. . . ."* Falconetti as Joan.

*H. D. (Hilda Doolittle), in her review of *The Passion of Joan of Arc* in *Close Up*, July 1928. Reprinted by Arno Press, New York, 1971.

THE ACTORS IN DREYER'S *JEANNE d'ARC*

To Lucie Derain

La Passion de Jeanne d'Arc (France, 1928) (Silent) Scenario by Carl Dreyer and Joseph Delteil from the book by Delteil. Directed by Carl Dreyer. Photography by Rudolph Maté and Kotula. Design: Hermann Warm, Jean and Valentine Hugo. With Maria Falconetti, Sylvain, Maurice Schutz, Antonin Artaud, Ravet, André Berley, Jean d'Yd.

A film was born—a real film where in a mass of celluloid, lies sincerity, intelligence, faith. . . . Carl Theodore Dreyer's *Jeanne d'Arc*.

I have seen the film. One is bewildered by so much beauty. And also by the truth, by the simple realism with which Dreyer interprets Joan's last hours. That is one of the chief factors that give *Jeanne d'Arc* so much force and bravery, the expressive vigor of which carried away the players.

Think of it—for more than four months, forty-five artists had been stripped of their modern personalities to be no longer of this century but monks of the fifteenth century, mystic, ignorant, and cruel—the monks of the Middle Ages.

And you, Sylvain, you were no longer the actor applauded by French audiences in your interpretation of Tartuffe. No—you were Bishop Cauchon himself, with his ferocious wheedling, his prying eyes, his deep hatred hidden beneath a mask of kindliness —you were Bishop Cauchon—and you burned Jeanne.

And you, Schutz, you became a criminal monk—tall, slender, rigid-faced, deep-wrinkled, sharp-eyed—you trapped your victim, you deceived her, and now while she burns, you're moved. My word! A tear comes coursing down your ruffled cheek. It's remorse, isn't it?

There is also the infamous d'Estivet and Jean de Maistre, the inquisitor, and Houppevelle, who paid with his life for his move of pity for Joan, and many other monks with flowing robes and shaven skulls, eyes, now hateful, now tender, now contemptible. These faces, which the will of Dreyer "uncivilizes," seem as if they were painted on cloth. These perfect faces, glittering, wrinkled like crumpled parchment, where not a bit of color weakens the harshness, the imperfections, or catches the "life spirit," are in themselves masterpieces of composition.

The names of those who make up the astonishing tribunal of Dreyer's *Jeanne d'Arc* (for one must give them their due) are: Sylvain, Schutz, Ralleu, Dacheux, Berley, Mainay, Ravet, Jean d'Yd, Antonin Artaud, Nikitine, Jacques Arnna . . . their names . . . but of what avail . . . they are marvelous!

For four months, giving proof of their artistic conscience without parallel in the history of the screen, shaving their heads to have a real tonsure bathed in an atmosphere of silence and moral corruption where each one felt his modern personality leaving him, these artists in *Jeanne d'Arc*, the monks and the soldiers, thought, worked and played in the *zeitgeist* of the fifteenth century which was inculcated in them by their director, Dreyer. Every hour of every day, the actors in *Jeanne d'Arc* assumed their roles as monks—not as one puts on a doublet and vest—but as one gets underneath another's skin, heart and soul. It is this which is beautiful, great and true; it is this which is strong and brave and an imperishable honor to the troupe of artists who play in and are directed in this exceptionally fine camera painting by Carl Dreyer.

Dreyer's method of directing his players is extremely personal and very tiring. He pretends that once the actor is chosen by the casting director, he has no more to suggest, in the way of playing a scene, to him. He pretends to believe that the actor knows what is expected of him and Dreyer leaves him alone, in absolute silence surrounded by hissing arc lamps which seem to search into his breast to root out his heart. And it is not long before, in this meditation, the nervous tension and sharpened sensibility produce the expected (to Dreyer, anyway) miracle: the actor takes the personality of the being he undertakes to portray, he incarnates it, he no longer belongs to the mechanical world, he is what the director wanted him to be. From now on Sylvain will forever think of condemning Jeanne. Dalleu will be the eternal prosecutor; the executioner will dream, as in life, of rolling needles, and Artaud with his fixed eyes will have in life hallucinations of the corpse of a saint burned at Clamait (the name of the studio where *Jeanne d'Arc* was filmed)—pardon, at Rouen.

Oh, yes! The actors of *Jeanne d'Arc* during all their hours at the studio were not a little obsessed by their roles. And returning to their homes in the modern fashion, the harshness of their adopted personages pursued them still. It has been for them the most difficult screen work of their careers. Dreyer is inaccessible to pity when he is directing. And this person, charming, shy, becomes at the studio The Master, who literally casts a spell over his actors.

I have voluntarily kept the name of Falconetti for the last. That this artiste was able to endure such dread, such moral and physical fatigue, is almost incomprehensible. She who was in nearly all the scenes, she who during four months, with shaved head, sandaled feet, was not more than a tortured human creature—all heart and soul, her white face showing marks of the greatest suffering, she who identified herself so fully with Jeanne that she cried and trembled after certain preliminary scenes—she who was Jeanne, a simple girl, wise, prudent, mysterious, good, and sad, she who was also nothing but a woman who cried, prayed, and feared, who carried her crucifix until the end and found the end of her passion in an overwhelming crescendo.

She, Falconetti, as Jeanne d'Arc, magnificently human, gave the greatest example of artistic and vibrant faith. She was, perhaps, an actress . . . but more than this, Jeanne, a woman, a saint—hers was an anguish that bleeds. . . .

November, 1929

Leaves From The Diary
Of A World Famous Clown

MY FIRST MEMORIES OF CHAPLIN

Translated from the German of Adrian Wettach, who was Grock, the internationally famous clown.

To make the world laugh—that is the task of the clown. Always this has been his function, from the time when he was but a traveling mountebank. He must know how to make a crowd laugh with a single voice, how to strike the responsive chord that will make a hundred or a thousand throats emit a single peal of hilarity.

To achieve such merry unison, the clown must make the audience feel that it is his ally. He must convince it of his utter sincerity. That is his art; the clown must believe in his art and in his ability to impart to his audience a genuine sympathetic appreciation of that art. He must take his work seriously, keep in perfect trim, both physical and mental, practice constantly the business of his performance. Of course, even clowns don't work all the time—even clowns have their moments of relaxation, when they drop the gravity which makes others laugh, and indulge in a smile or two themselves. Yet even these smiles have in them something pensive, wistful.

Not all comedians, however, grow gay after hours. Take, for instance, that master of the craft, Charlie Chaplin. He seldom laughs or even smiles, for he is always thinking of his work, busy inventing a new quirk. An artist through and through, he cannot dissociate himself from his artistic outlook. That is why he is the greatest clown in the world.

Quite different is his brother Syd. Of a jolly temperament, full of youthful enthusiasm, this other Chaplin has none of the wistful melancholy of Charlie. It was Syd whom I met first, years ago, in London, where he was then appearing in Fred Karno's *A Night in a London Music Hall*. His role, that of a drunkard, provided an excellent vehicle for his unique talents, and brought

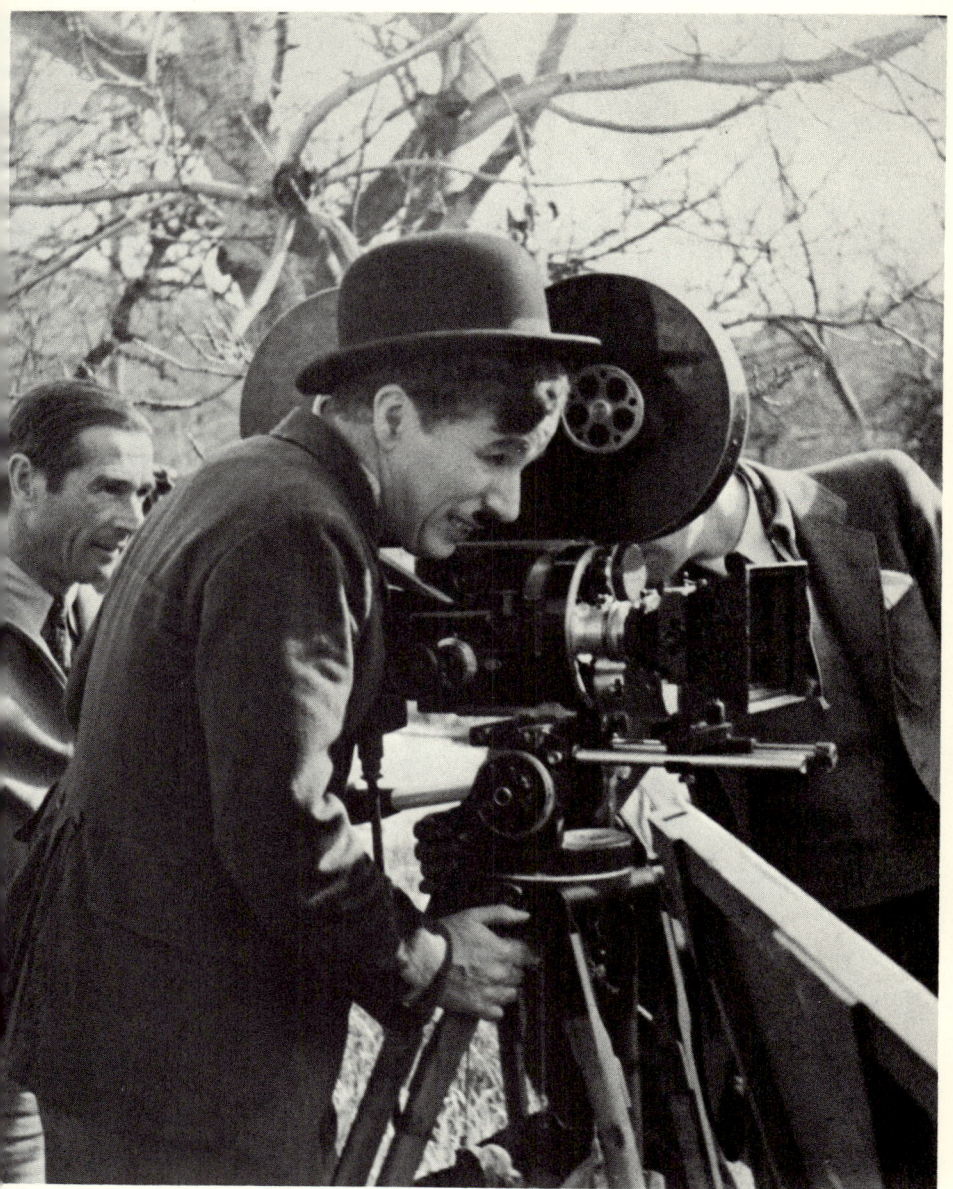

"The Great God Pan"* at work on *City Lights*.

*Title of Robert Payne's book on Chaplin, Hermitage House, New York, 1952.

A cubist portrait of Chaplin by Fernand Léger created in 1921 for his film *Charlot cubiste,* which remained unfinished, later being used by him in the *Ballet Mécanique* (1924). A string in back actuated the arm, which raised and lowered the little derby.

him almost instantaneous success. The name of Chaplin became famous.

Some years later, while on tour in South America, I found that one of the variety halls in which I was scheduled to appear was also showing *A Night in a London Music Hall*. Among the performers was listed the name of Chaplin. This was something very unusual—running into a fellow performer in a distant clime after the vicissitudes of years have blotted out the memory of a thousand friendships made during hurried visits and performances, at hundreds of dinners and hotels. Only rarely do such friends meet again in the same country, the same city, the same theater, billed together on the same program. But the name of Chaplin was not one to be forgotten.

I was very glad to see Syd again, to listen once more to his account of his experiences. No success could erase from his mind those half-forgotten fragments of his youth, which seemed to take him back to his early boyhood, with its poverty and privations.

Among other things, Syd told me that Charlie was playing at another music hall in town. At once I rushed over and asked for him.

"There he is," I was told. I stood agape. That couldn't be Charlie! A small, insignificant-looking man, very shabbily dressed. The "little fellow" saw me, rushed up to me and cried:

"Grock! Grock! My brother has told me so much about you! I am Charlie Chaplin."

I saw at once the contrast between the brothers—Syd so exuberantly gay, Charlie so sad and pensive.

One winter Charlie and I appeared on the same boards. Charlie was silent nearly always. Although he could draw the most spontaneous applause from any audience, he was one of the few humorists who kept a very serious and, at times, tragic countenance, whatever success might come.

Once—I remember it well—the "little fellow" was excited. We had been talking, in our dressing room, of what future we might expect in our craft. I told him my plans. I wanted to become famous, successful, to earn a great deal of money.

"You?" cried Chaplin. "You? Never, never in your life! Have you ever heard of an artist making his own career? It happens very seldom. Luck is everything. You can't make success certain by working hard—in this you are just as powerless as I am."

And then Chaplin smiled. The smile reminded me of a childhood incident. I had once remarked to my mother that I wanted to become richer than the richest man in the world; my mother beat me. When Chaplin smiled it hurt as much as that beating of long before.

Twenty years passed. Chaplin gave our generation true insight into the heart of the clown—more than that, into the heart of all browbeaten humanity. He taught us all how to smile, how to laugh. He had received the adulation of the world, the living, piercing reality of which he understood only too well. This he gave over to his unlimited audience, which understood him because he forced it to.

We met again.

"You, Grock!" he said. "Still we aren't famous—still not big. We'll have to fight further, to work on. When at last we do achieve success we'll be old."

And then he smiled again, that same wistful smile.

He, the greatest of comedians, the greatest of tragedians—Chaplin, whom adoring millions have made a millionaire!

Perhaps, when he hears that I have retired from the vaudeville stage to make my first talkie, he will exclaim: "Poor, poor Grock!" Perhaps he will think that I did not achieve my aim, that I didn't become as "big" as I had dreamed of becoming. That is possible.

I do wish, though, that Chaplin might see this film some day. I would want him to judge it seriously, not to smile or laugh at it.

But that may not be possible, because Charles Spencer Chaplin is the most discerning critic I know.

November, 1931

THE CASE OF PABST

Among the great artists and men of science who formed the flower of German culture after the war, and who were uprooted in the Nazi "purge" of January 1933 and during the dark days that followed, one of the leading figures was the genial Georg Wilhelm Pabst, *cinémarégisseur* extraordinary of the Ufa and Nero studios. A voluntary exile from the land of his adoption, that land which nourished his art, whose soil was once so fertile for the creative efforts of such men as Reinhardt, Lang, Pommer, Jessner, Feuchtwanger, Wassermann, Brecht, Weill, etc., Pabst floundered about the studios of France and Hollywood without being able to adjust himself to the terrible nightmare of this shocking reality, namely, that the integrity of the artist was a myth so far as the world is concerned, that art is not universal, nor above the bickerings of politicians and dictators, that money rules all, and that this is pretty much the worst of all possible worlds. How else to explain the abortion made in Hollywood which carried his name as director (*A Modern Hero*), and to realize that this was from the man (apparently, though one refuses to countenance such a fact, and one sets it down to studio supervision or hopeless indifference on the part of Pabst) who made *Die Dreigroschenoper?* The two are irreconcilable.

Confined in a Belgian prison camp during the war, Pabst began turning his mind towards the theater, which is to say, the dramatization of human beings under emotional stress. Postwar Vienna provided a deeply moving theme which, with its grief-laden days and the pall of human misery and sorrow in which the once lovely Austrian capital lay shrouded, served as Pabst's first bid for recognition in the film world. *Die Freudlose Gasse* (The Joyless Street) attacked not only the bourgeois merchants who, with police protection, were fattening on the once blooming flesh of the rosy city, but attacked the war profiteers and the gaudy and obscene spectacle of their frenzied orgies while Vienna en masse starved and died.

This was the first manifestation of Pabst's intense social feeling, his almost Shakespearean regard for the human being as the protagonist, which was later to show itself in the lyrical *Liebe der Jeanne Ney,* the psychoanalytical *Secrets of a Soul* (based on a case history of Freud), the psycho-pathological *Box of Pandora* (after Wedekind), through the more complex social irony of *Die Dreigroschenoper* and the fiercely internationalistic *Westfront 1918* and *Kameradschaft.* In all of them, no matter what wizardry he accomplished with the aid of his cameraman, Fritz Arno Wagner, Pabst illuminated the individuals as protagonists who stalked through his cinematic dramas with significant overtones which kept shooting off the gross material. The genial Communist commissar of Vladimir Sokoloff in *Jeanne Ney,* the fabulously endowed nymphomania of Lulu in *Box of Pandora,* the antisocial mockery of Mackie Messer in *Die Dreigroschenoper,* the sullen passion of Karl in *Westfront 1918* —all remain vivid and ineradicable in the memory even to this day.

It is because Pabst has been so successful in delineating the psychology of the individual that he was able to utilize a few individuals in *Kameradschaft* to symbolize a mass of people. *Kameradschaft,* which won the League of Nations gold medal as the best picture of the year to promote world peace (an award subsequently given to Milestone for *All Quiet On The Western Front* and Vidor for *Our Daily Bread*), revolved around workers of different countries symbolized by the miner who, east of the political frontier speaks one language, and west speaks another. "Ethical, not esthetic values make up the significance of this film," said Pabst, and he proceeded to show how purely artificial are the barriers of political boundaries. The story developed the ideal of international comradeship which, when the need arose, proved stronger than nations, mightier than the individual nationality. Its plot, as is well known, was based on the Courriers mine tragedy of 1906, on the Franco-German border, when 1400 French miners lost their lives in a gas explosion and onrushing flood, and the German miners over the frontier went to the rescue of their French comrades. The time was moved up to the present. Ignoring political formalities, the rescue party breaks through the post above, while the remainder tear down the dividing frontier bars below, bearing the significant words:

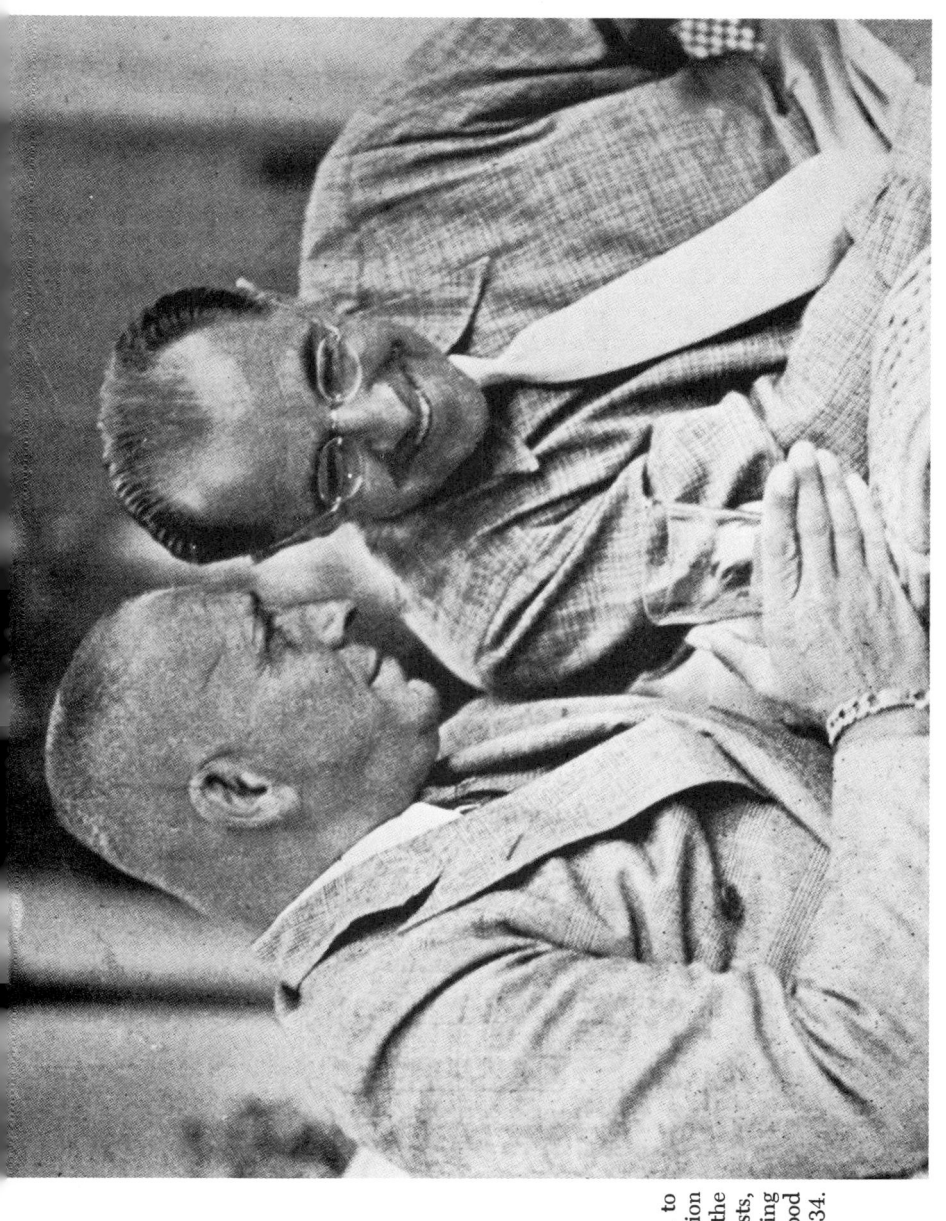

"You know what she said to me?" A rare confrontation of two *monstres sacrés*, the screen's two supreme realists, Stroheim and Pabst, during the latter's visit to Hollywood in 1934.

22 Saint Cinema

"Frontier 1919," and succeed in rescuing their comrades.

"Why do we hold together only when we need each other?" asks the Frenchman, in returning thanks to the German miners, "Why not always?"

Cheers and hosannas spring up from the German-French crowd waiting on the borderline for the return of the wounded members of the German rescue party as they greet the men who clamber down from the trucks and embrace each other. One of the rescued French miners springs up on the truck and a sudden and intense silence prevails.

"*Comrades!*" he shouts in his native French, "We are all miners together and because we are all of us miners you have brought us up from down there; because we are all miners together, our comrade Caspar has broken down the iron frontier grill. He has done it because we all have only two common enemies—gas and war! I am telling it to you now—and never forget it! We are all miners together. Thank you, comrades. I won't say goodbye but au revoir. *Au revoir! Auf wiedersehen! Auf wiedersehen! Auf wiedersehen!*"

The crowd roars its approval until one of the German rescue party, his arm in a sling, asks again for silence and speaks in German:

"*Comrades!*" he says, "I did not understand what the French comrade said, but we all understand what he meant. Because it is all the same, French or German. We are all workers, and a miner is a miner. The coal belongs to all of us, whether we break it on this side or the other. We stick together because we belong together. *Long live our French comrades! Good luck!*"

That was Pabst....

In the original version, Pabst showed the French and German miners putting back up the barriers that were knocked down during the catastrophe and rescue—under police and military surveillance. This ending to *Kameradschaft* was ordered removed by the censor in Germany and was not exhibited in this country. The film ended with the fraternizing of the miners.

To give the story greater present-day meaning and to allow the film's ideology an immediate application to the ominous world unrest today, Pabst shifted the action of the events pictured (originally occurring in 1906) to the present day. *Kameradschaft* was less hysterical than *Westfront 1918*, therefore a work of greater artistic integrity (even though *Westfront* must be set down as one of the most uncompromising of the antiwar films). In its depiction of a state of suppressed terror it is equaled only by that other great "poster" film—*Potemkin*—and like *Potemkin* it ends on a note of jubilation. *Kameradschaft* is a record of nobility and self-sacrifice, which is to say, a record of human experience. It is a great peace film.

It was, therefore, inevitable that Pabst should make *Kameradschaft* a great social film, one for which his early psychological dramas prepared him. Setting the action of the story after the war gave the film an irony this story otherwise would not have had. Pabst's realization of this, his refusal to produce just a sensational dramatic film centering around an isolated incident without stressing the social inference, deserves the highest praise. (Compare *Kameradschaft* to Gaumont-British's meretricious *Transatlantic Tunnel* with its bellicose talk of uniting the two English-speaking peoples, England and America, against the threat of the "Federation of Eastern Powers.")

It is reputed that Pabst said, upon completion of *Kameradschaft*, "I am through with the social film." However this may be, and for whatever reasons he made this statement, of which we are not aware, this did not prevent him from making *Die Dreigroschenoper*, the greatest social satire in films to date. It was an adaptation of the Brecht-Weill play with music which startled Berlin in 1928–29. "Brecht's work may well be looked upon as the epitome of that violent and bitter flowering of the German drama and literature which took place a few years after the inflation, when foreign loans had helped to stabilize a crazy currency and subsidize reckless and fantastic plans for economic recovery," writes Eric Walter White in the current issue of *Life and Letters* (London). "That short period of illusory material prosperity was accompanied by feverish activity and extravagant experiment in the arts, much of which had already caught and recovered from the post-war infection of expressionism . . ." *Die Dreigroschenoper* was an outgrowth of this period. Remotely derived by Brecht from John Gay's *The Beggar's Opera*, its central motif served Brecht to draw a parallel between the ageless corruption that existed in high places with the hopeless poverty of that other half of the world that lies eternally enshrouded in darkness. It had none of the revolutionary optimism of, let us say, Gorki's *Mother*. It was defeatist in tendency and in execution. But it was bitter and it cut deep.

Brecht and the Nero company, who acquired the film rights, quarreled over the conception the film transcription should take. The Nero Company (headed by Seymour Nebenzahl) had bought the rights of a popular stage success and wanted to make as literal a screen translation as possible. Brecht was opposed to such literal transliteration and wanted to reshape the material and readapt it for its new medium. The film, as ultimately produced by Pabst, who was caught between two fires, lay halfway between the Brechtian ideal and commercial necessity.

But that did not prevent it from being a great film in its own right—and, to this observer at least, Pabst's masterpiece. Unfortunately, the version shown in this country was mutilated by censorial cuts (just as the original stage version had several of its more trenchant songs deleted by the management of the Berlin Theater am Schiffbauerdamm in 1928), but enough remained to delight us with this most subtle and beautiful of all the Pabst films.

Gay's *Beggar's Opera* is so well known as to hardly warrant a synopsis of *Dreigroschenoper* here. Suffice it to say that the dialogue is studded with such Villonesque lines as:

> *You gentlemen who teach us how to conduct our lives*
> *And steer clear of sin and crime,*
> *First you must give us our daily bread,*
> *Then you can start your preaching.*

Full of helpless anger and pity, *Die Dreigroschenoper* (stage version) made many in the audience feel uncomfortable and caused them to leave the theater before the end of the performance.

Peachum's speech on beggary, for instance:

> But I have elicited the fact that those who inherit the earth may cause misery but cannot bear the sight of it. Even though they have sufficient food to the end of their days and can smear their floors with butter so that even the crumbs that fall from their tables become sopped with fat, they cannot with equanimity see a man collapse from hunger, especially when he has to choose their very doorstep to faint on.

Upon the completion of *Die Dreigroschenoper*, Pabst was invited by Mussolini to make a film in Italy. Pabst said he would if he were allowed to do the only story that interested him, so far as producing a film in that country went. They asked him what the story would be. Pabst replied: "Spartacus, the slave leader." Pabst never made a film in Italy—naturally.

Then came *L'Atlantide*, from the Benoit novel, a fantastic thing dealing with the "lost continent," which one group of archaeologists holds lies buried somewhere under the desert wastes of the Sahara. A sort of Hearst *Sunday-American* Supplement story, full of vague and delightful improbabilities, but touched with mystery and romance, it became a case of material, in itself unimportant, made glamorous by the fires of a great talent. Pabst went to Africa for the exteriors and Erno Metzner, his scene designer, did sets in the Berlin studios of Nero, after photographs of ruins, arches, etc. taken by Pabst in Africa.

And what of those other Pabst films, that reveal other facets of this great director's extraordinary faculty for telling a story with camera? His insight into human character, his knowledge of reflex actions that cause people to act the way they do, his worldliness and sophistication, his rare charm, and delightful intimacy? What of *The Joyless Street*, a thing of deep shadows and pale, distraught faces, made unutterably sad in the glare of white light; *The Box of Pandora*, in which the male, destroyed by sex, succumbs, laughing, forgiving, before the devastaing onslaught of physical voluptuousness as expressed in the character Lulu— the child-woman—who is, alone, unconscious of her allure; *Crisis*, an acute psychological marital drama, that foreshadowed Lubitsch's later experiments in this genre; *Skandal um Eva*, perhaps the least of the Pabst films, but gay and intimate and full of honest laughter and quiet humor; *Secrets of a Soul*, almost as important a film as *Dr. Caligari* in its probings of the unconscious; *The Treasure*, Pabst's lone excursion into the stylized treatment of telling a film story, one of the finest and most simple and direct of the German screen tragedies; *The White Hell of Pitz Palu*, which he co-directed with Dr. Arnold Fanck, transforming a mountain film that, under Fanck, would have been full of German mysticism (like Fanck's own *Heiliger Berg*) into something worthy of forming a chapter of its own out of Mann's *The Magic Mountain*; *Jeanne Ney*, which in its uncut European version was one of the most charming and beautiful pieces of cinema craftsmanship ever made . . . its lovers parting in the rain, in the war-torn Crimea . . . the gentle, lyrical scenes in Montmartre . . . the feverish activity at the boat . . . the amazing opening scenes in which the perambulating camera ferrets out a score of telling details—a more remarkable traveling shot than even Alexandrov's highly-touted five-hundred-foot glide in *Jazz Comedy.*

"The world of the bourgeoisie in which we live and work," wrote Pabst to the Soviet director Friedrich Ermler, congratulating him on his film *Peasants,* "insists that the film must not be a means of propaganda. Of course, by propaganda they mean— opposition. Every attempt to use the film as a forum for the discussion of the burning issues of the day runs up against the 'morale.' Today, every living problem is declared outside the 'morale.' The world, by this prohibition, proves both its weakness and its knowledge of that weakness. It has dragged down to the level of the peep-show the finest instrument for the cultural advancement of humanity since the invention of the printing press. No regard is ever paid to the vulgarity and barbarousness of the film so long as it maintains the present order—the profit system."

That was Pabst. . . .

What have we to look forward to now from this extraordinary talent? The future is full of uncertainty. The world is again full of unrest, and rearming for lord knows what. After a long period of silence in which we heard nothing about Pabst, or his plans, in the midst of general world upheavals as reported by the press, and the onslaught of commercial talking films, that had little or no relation to the golden age of the cinema as Pabst and his illustrious contemporaries knew it, there appeared a small item in the newspapers one day, that a film company was being formed in New York to bring Gounod's opera, *Faust,* to the screen in a new color process and that one, G. W. Pabst, was assigned as the director.

Since then, nothing.

August, 1936

Amphitryon (*Les Dieux s'amusent*) (Germany, 1934) French version of Günther Stapenhorst production for Ufa. Scenario by Reinhold Schuenzel and Albert Valentin. French adaptation supervised by Raoul Ploquin. Directed by Reinhold Schuenzel. Photography: Fritz Arno Wagner. Design: Robert Herlth and Walter Roehrig. Costumes: Rochus Gliese. Music by Franz Doelle. Lyrics and dialogue: Serge Veber. With Henri Garat, Marguerite Moreno, Jeanne Boitel, Armand Bernard, Florelle.

THE GODS AT PLAY

The fables of antique mythology must have contained in them an irresistible allure to have kept their luster for us these two thousand years. The gods of Olympus have become as familiar to us as the most famous deeds in history.

Jupiter, Juno, the Muses, Satyr, Venus, Mercury, Neptune—they are as well-known to us as Joan of Arc and Napoleon. At every turn, especially in the arts, we come across works and symbols that bring to mind the memory of these gods and goddesses and the enchanted world in which they lived.

At a recent exposition in Italy, we saw a tableau entitled: "The Birth of Venus." In the old palaces of the French kings we find: "The Pavilion of Flora," "The Galleries of Apollo," "The Salon of Hercules." Even in your drawing room, after dinner, you will play a game wherein the guests try to remember the names of the nine Muses. All this proves that twenty centuries of Christianity have not been able to eradicate the persistence of this pagan religion, the creation of the most marvelous of poets, the ancient Greeks.

Among the fables of this charming mythology, those which have inspired artists and poets most, have been the tales of love between the gods and mortals, their delightful metamorphoses, their fabulous disguises . . . which invariably accompany these romances.

There was Narcissus, who changed into a flower; Syrinx, who became a reed; Echo, who became an echo; not to mention the thousand and one little stratagems invented by Jupiter to

(Freely after the original score by Franz Doelle)

The women of Boeotia, famous for its music, greet the return of their victorious Grecian warriors in song. From Reinhold Schünzel's satiric operetta *Amphitryon* (1934).

approach his not-too-willing ladies. Did not the master of all the gods and men metamorphose himself into a bull, that he might seduce the beauteous Europa? Into a shower of golden rain, to win the chaste Danae? Into a beautiful swan, for Leda? And so on. . . .

After having inspired poets, painters, sculptors, choreographers, and musicians, why shouldn't these perennially beautiful legends and poetic ideas serve equally to inspire the newest art—the cinema?

Granted that the antique age has already been interpreted on the screen, from *Ben Hur* to *The Private Life of Helen of Troy*, this is the first time that authors of a film have dealt, not with mortals, but with gods.

And so, directors Reinhold Schuenzel and Albert Valentin have dared to place, for the first time, Olympus and its inhabitants in a motion picture. Of the thousand and one myths, each amazing, each eternal, which came out of ancient Greece, there are few which have furnished a subject for so many works as Amphitryon. From Plautus to Molière and Giraudoux, the Amphitryons are innumerable. In fact, one *can* count them. The one by Giraudoux is the thirty-eighth. The one by Schuenzel and Valentin is the thirty-ninth—and the first for the screen. *Amphitryon*'s subtitle, *The Gods at Play*, is apt, and well put. The Greeks must have been a happy people for whenever their gods wanted to have fun they visited Sparta or Athens. "They came down from Olympus," Mark Twain reminds us, "and had wonderful times with those hot young blossoms." The film is utterly Parisian in spirit, from beginning to end, recalling such examples of the classical opéra bouffe as *Orpheus in Hades* and *The Beautiful Helen*, with its swooningly beautiful songs, such as "Nuit et Jour." As for the direction of *Amphitryon*, it is among the most remarkable feats yet achieved in the cinema.

Three gods—Jupiter, Juno, Mercury—three thousand players, and five stars—Henri Garat, Odette Florelle, Jeanne Boitel, Armand Bernard, and Marguerite Moreno, have chanced to find themselves in a film dealing with the gods at play—a hazardous undertaking, but one which promised great rewards. This divine picture, and I use the word divine in every sense, proves that they have emerged victorious.

October, 1936

La Croisière Jaune (France, 1934) A document of the Third Citroën Automotive Expedition from Beirut to Peiping, sponsored by André Citroën. Directors of the expedition: Georges-Marie Haardt, Louis Audouin-Dubreuil, Victor Point. Directed by Alexander Sauvage. Continuity and montage by Leon Poirier. Photography by Morizet, Specht. Music by J. E. Szyfer, C. Delvincourt, M. Mirouze. Staff artist: Alexandre Yacovleff.

MARCO POLO — MODERN STYLE

Knowledge is cumulative, hence some fifty or more centuries of civilization can be said to have gone into the preparation of the Citroën-Haardt-Audouin-Dubreuil Expedition across Central Asia. That knowledge is power was also proved in the splendid lesson in valor vouchsafed us by the members of this expedition who drew upon their wisdom and courage to see a heartbreakingly difficult journey through to its victorious finish.

There have been men as courageous before. Marco Polo traversed pretty much the same route six hundred years ago. In Haardt, leader of the expedition, and Audouin-Dubreuil, his associate, was the same lust for adventure and distant horizons mixed with a dash of economic penetration that characterized the Venetian merchant, Polo. Both came back with fabulous tales of the East—Marco Polo laden with silks and spices, rare jewels, and fantastic tales of strange lands which none knew existed; Haardt (who did not come back, but broke and died under the terrific strain of the expedition) left as his heritage a tale as fantastic as the most incredible stories of Marco Polo—a film, *La Croisière Jaune*, "The Yellow Cruise." Whereas Marco Polo was not believed, Haardt most certainly is. For in his beautiful, moving, and tragic film, is imprisoned for posterity the log of his journey and the strange things he saw on it. The Chinese have a proverb: "A picture is worth a thousand words." Poor Marco Polo may have had to burst his spleen to convince his compatriots that he wasn't lying. Haardt, even if he is not with us, is believed through the eloquence of his pictures which speak more profoundly than anything we can say about them in awe, in admiration and in breathless astonishment.

Not only did Haardt show us pictures to substantiate the stories once considered incredible by Marco Polo's listeners—he let us hear the sounds of the great Orient, through the magic of the photoelectric cell. He has blown the breath of life into his images by recording the calls and cries, the kaleidoscopic tumult of their daily lives. Murmurs of strange tongues, snatches of even stranger songs and folk melodies, groans and screeches, whistles and clanking, dull rumbling of carts and animal cries, chantings of the Koran, the wail of Chinese infants, the song of a Mongolian princess, the skirl of a Highland pibroch at Khyber Pass, the street noises of the bazaars, the machine-gun fire across the barren wastes of Sinkiang during a rebellion, the shells falling in Shanghai during the Japanese invasion, the scurry in the streets, the grateful blast of trumpets at the French Legation in Hanoi, effusions, smiles, handclasps, congratulations—they merge, swell, and sway like a great wave breaking over the strand, they become a veritable babel, a cacophonic symphony . . . they are the very stuff and pattern of life.

Truth is indeed stranger than fiction. "And nothing," said the newspaper *Gringoire,* in Paris, of *The Yellow Cruise,* "is so beautiful as the truth." Is it because of its straightforwardness, its almost aloof presentation of the most incredible things, that the film reaches such heights of poignancy?

November, 1936

Maskerade (Austria, 1937) Original scenario by Walter Reisch. Directed by Willy Forst. Music by Willy Schmidt-Gentner. With Paula Wessely, Adolf Wohlbrück, Peter Petersen, Hilde von Stolz, Walter Janssen, Olga Tschechowa, Julia Serda, Hans Moser.

A MASK, A MUFF — AND A LADY . . .

Vienna—1905. . . .

The accumulation of twenty centuries in the art of living. . . .

Around the hub of the *Stefanskirche* the gay metropolis on the Danube turned in perennial festive gaiety, like a ferris wheel in the Prater, to the waltz rhythms of Lanner, Strauss, and Lehar. . . .

It is the year of the premiere of *The Merry Widow* at the Theater an der Wien.

The *heurigen* wine flowed, the Prater blazed with lamps glowing amid the trees and was made tumultuous with laughter and song from a light-hearted people . . . and a popular artist of the day sketched a lady in a mask and a muff and nothing else!

Even frivolous Vienna was shocked. Scandal. Everyone knew the lady's name—the muff gave her away. She had won it at a grand ball attended by the *haut monde* of Vienna. As for the lady's husband, well, there would be the very devil to pay!

So they made a film of this factual incident, with **Olga Tschechowa** as the woman scorned, Adolf Wohlbrück as the artist, and Paula Wessely as the innocent pivot of the fireworks-triangle. And it was in the latter, in Paula Wessely, that a new and great artiste of the screen was discovered. "Duse!" cried the critics. "Bergner!" At any rate, *Maskerade* ("Masquerade in Vienna," for so the film was called), precipitated the young lady into overnight fame. She became one of the biggest names among actresses in Europe.

This was her debut.

It was also the directorial debut of Willy Forst, heretofore known as an actor of considerable wit, polish, and charm, as vide his well-remembered performances as Nikki in *Two Hearts in Waltz Time,* the dance master in *Merry Wives of Vienna,* the impecunious student-artist in *Theft of the Mona Lisa.* But no one ever dreamed that beneath that bland exterior lurked a directorial strength, a laughing irony, and an ability to wring from players such performances as they never gave under less gifted directors. In this, Forst utilized essences of the alchemy of Erich von Stroheim for his prodigious effects. For there are prodigious moments in *Masquerade in Vienna*—perhaps the most consummate of these being the veracity of the atmosphere he has reincarnated for the Vienna of 1905.

This is not the trumped-up gaiety that Hollywood imagines prewar Vienna to have had. It is not even the typical Continental (London-Paris-Berlin) idea of what things were like in the days of Franz Josef.

This *is* the Vienna of 1905! To those of you who were there, the picture will be fraught with nostalgic memories, so brush away your tear for a Vienna and a period that is no more. For those who were not, and to whom this glamorous period is but a legend, director Willy Forst has miraculously filled an important gap in your lives with his delightful film of frivolity tinged with intrigue, immorality with grace, and reminiscence—with regret.

Masquerade in Vienna is based, as we have been told, on an actual occurrence, a *scandale amoureux,* during a *Fasching* in Vienna in the years of its prewar florescence. The prototype of the film's protagonist—Heideneck, the artist, who sketched a lady in a mask and a muff and nothing else—was Recznicek, a popular artist of the day, who embellished the covers of the semi-risqué

A Mask, a Muff—and a Lady . . . 35

illustrated periodicals of Vienna with cynical drawings of sophisticated Viennese society.

The title: *Masquerade in Vienna* is, perhaps an ominous one to those who remember how often the music of Strauss has been the only authentic Viennese note in so-called "Viennese" films before this. Willy Forst, the film's director, has been beguiled by the music of Vienna before, but in this film he recaptures the spirit of Vienna of the early days of this century with very little help from the Vienna Philharmonic Orchestra, which is there, nonetheless, to back him up with its cascades of tonal spendor. The settings are impeccable, the air with which the cast carries itself has just the right mingling of carelessness and responsibility, and the contretemps which forms the basis of the plot is deliciously of the period.

A lady is painted in a mask and a muff for decoration and thanks to the carelessness of the artist and the mistake of a servant, the portrait appears in a magazine. The scandal is immense. Heideneck, the artist, is distraught and all of fashionable Vienna is an elegant mark of interrogation. At the last the artist gives, or rather, seems to give the secret away and the blameless companion of a Countess finds herself the object of an attention she cannot understand. Paula Wessely takes a naïve part and plays it with a naïveté which deepens into emotion when she finds herself falling in love with Heideneck. So far, director Forst has kept the colored, trivial balloon of his story bouncing gaily in the Vienna air, but suddenly it is punctured by the revolver shot of a jealous mistress. Heideneck falls wounded, and the audience realizes that well over an hour has passed and that an irresponsible anecdote is to be buried with full rites and a formal tying up of loose ends. However, so absorbing has the film been up to this point that it would take a master, indeed, to provide an anticlimax that would send an audience away gurgling with delight as Forst does with his ironic dénouement. In the midst of the explanations, we are vouchsafed an opportunity to hear Caruso's voice—an exquisite pleasure no matter how far removed it is from nature—singing *La Donna è Mobile* from *Rigoletto* during a performance at the Theater an der Wien at a moment when to be reminded that "woman is fickle" is to smile, succumb, and forgive. The happy ending helps us to drink this subtle cup of balm without realizing that director Forst and author

Reisch have indicted no one in a comedy that brilliantly indicts an entire frivolous society. Added to which we are allowed to appreciate the full versatility of Paula Wessely and Adolf Wohlbrück, as Fräulein Dur and Heideneck, and Olga Tschechowa as the jealous and extremely lovely Anita.

December, 1936

Der Golem (Germany, 1920) (Silent) Scenario and direction by Henrik Galeen and Carl Boese. Photography by Karl Freund. Design: Hans Poelzig, Rochus Gliese. With Paul Wegener, Albert Steinrück, Ernst Deutsch, Lyda Salmonova.

Le Golem (Czechoslovakia-France, 1936) Scenario by A. P. Antoine and Julien Duvivier from the novel by Gustav Meyrink. Directed by Julien Duvivier. Photography by Jan Stallich, Vaclav Vich. Design: André Andreiev, S. Kopecky. With Harry Baur, Germaine Aussey, Roger Karl, Roger Duchesne, Jany Holt, Marcel Dalio, Carette.

THE GOLEM

Of the many myths and legends which have fired the pens of poets, one of the more enduring is that of the Golem, which originated in the tortured, twisted ghetto of medieval Prague. Its archaic quality has persisted these three hundred years, and even Gustav Meyrink, in his famous novel *Der Golem*, says: "I really do not know what the origin of the Golem legend is, but that somewhere, something which cannot die haunts this quarter of the city [Prague] and is somehow connected with the legend, of that I am sure."

In *The Golem: Legends of the Ghetto of Prague,* Chayim Bloch explains that:

> Men who live amidst mysticism are at pains to prove that the exalted Rabbi Loew and all those saints and sages before him, to whom is attributed the creation of a Golem, understood, thanks to their profound knowledge of the Kabbala, how to employ the *Shem, ha-me, forasch*—the preeminent name of God, so as to endow with life a shape formed by them. Those, however, who do not believe in and deny any justification for the mystical and the occult, aver that we have here to deal with a symbol, the allegorical meaning of which has been forgotten, because of the clearness and vividness of the symbol itself, which has consequently come down through the centuries with a sort of independent life of its own in the shape of a legend.

The Golem was formed of clay, it served its master dutifully and loyally; ultimately, however, it became mad and ran amuck, so that its master had to turn it back again into earth which he did by taking away from it the *Shem,* the sacred word, the life principle. (The letters engraved on the forehead of the Golem were: *aleph, mem, soph,* the Hebrew characters for "Truth." The Golem was returned to dust by erasing the first letter, leaving the word for "Death".) But, as the legend goes, the Golem is not yet dead—even from its "corpse," which is still preserved in the attic of the synagogue in Prague, emanates fear and dread.

This idea has intrigued the well-known writer, Egon Erwin Kisch, to the bold undertaking of ascending into the attic of the Altneu Synagogue of Prague to look for the "corpse" of the Golem. In *Der rasende Reporter* he tells us that he did not find the Golem, but he pursued another clue which took him to the burial grounds of Galgenberg, on the outskirts of the city, where the Golem was reputed to lie buried. Kisch thought it extraordinary how the dates of time and the place agree with historical reality.

Prague then was a seething caldron of the black arts. The court of the Emperor, Rudolph II, drew to it all the quacks, magicians, astrologers and alchemists of Europe. Here was fertile ground for them to distill their witch's brew for a king half-crazy with fear; and horoscopes by the stars, mandrake roots, and similar hokey-pokey were the order of the day. Occasionally, really learned men, like the astronomers Kepler and Tycho Brahe, or the scientist and Kabbala student, Rabbi Loew, were admitted to the court. But between obsession with parasitic charlatans and the oppressive influence of his ruthless and vainglorious chancellor, Lang, poor Rudolph, suffering from a hereditary illness anyway, was doomed. Rudolph and Rabbi Loew were great friends—but Loew died in 1610, and Lang took this opportunity to poison Rudolph's mind against the Jews of Prague by frightening the emperor with the Golem, which at that moment was abandoned, returned to an inanimate state, in a deserted attic of the old synagogue. Hence, Rudolph's fear of the Golem, and his passion to have it destroyed. But it destroyed him and his corrupt court, and brought Rudolph's brother, the Archduke Mathias, to the throne. History records Mathias of Bohemia as a kindly king.

This, then, is the story of the Golem, a mixture of fact and fancy, yet where fact begins and fancy ends, no one knows. All that remains is the prophecy of Rabbi Loew: "The Golem partakes of the everlasting belief; and will rise again at the end of all human existence, but in quite a different form."

March, 1937

Variations on a theme by Maurice Bessy.

ERICH VON STROHEIM

When Eisenstein visited America he was asked what, in the American cinema, he admired most. He replied: "Chaplin, Von Stroheim, and Walt Disney."

As for Chaplin and Disney, they have had accolades enough showered upon them, by native and visiting celebrities alike. Our concern is with Stroheim, whose unhappy art flowered for a decade, then withered and died, plucked by the hands of the money grubbers and the fake morality tutored by the Haysian regime in Hollywood. Stroheim's uncompromising realism struck a sympathetic chord with Eisenstein, and it is natural that the two should have admired each other's work. But whereas Eisenstein was working in a Socialistic state, where the movie was regarded as something more than an innocuous diversion, Stroheim worked in the hothouse atmosphere of that great citadel of reaction—Hollywood. Eisenstein shelled a decadent capitalistic society from the vast plains of the USSR, which served as a stand from which he could hurl those projectiles—*Potemkin, Ten Days that Shook the World, Old and New*—shattering the hypocritical complacency of a Europe which confused its death rattle with its crunch of tanks, its thud of regimented hordes, and the megalomaniacal screeching of its dictators. Stroheim bored from within, and, while Eisenstein knocked off Europe's armor plate, he dissected an aristocracy in its last stages of sophisticated decay with the precision and effectiveness of a surgeon's scalpel.

Stroheim revealed the great festering wound which was eating away the heart of this society. *The Merry Widow* and *The Wedding March*—not projectiles, surely, but subtle and insinuating cups of poison. Kings, queens, princes, great barons, wealthy industrialists, the glittering *haut monde*—locomotor ataxia, haemophilia, nymphomania, satyriasis, perversions, gluttony, rape. This was Stroheim's "high world." His brief war scenes in the lamentably unfinished *Merry Go Round* had all the terrible indictment of those in *The End of St. Petersburg*. In *Greed* he ripped the last shreds of "respectability" off man as an animal, and cried:

"For shame!" The spectacle he revealed was shameful enough, but the disclosure only made him enemies, and his eventual studio ostracism was sealed with the mutilation of this film—a mutilation that endeavored to lessen the shock of this whining, pitiful creature that God was supposed to have created in His own image, and which Stroheim revealed so mercilessly through the ironic translucent crystal of his lens. But Stroheim disowned the adulterated version of his masterpiece (as he had disowned every one of his preceding and succeeding works, all of which were similarly mutilated—save *Blind Husbands* and *The Devil's Passkey*), just as Eisenstein, years later, was to disown the adulterated and perverted version of his great epic of the Mexican people, *Que Viva Mexico!*

In truth, both men had much in common.

But Eisenstein's art persists in its growth, fostered by a new society. Stroheim's was ferreted out and uprooted by a vicious clique that answered all guarantees of "freedom of expression," "integrity of the artist," etc., with a sardonic smile.

Once a rumor penetrated that Stroheim wished to go to Russia. What happened about this, no one seems to know. But now, thanks to an unexpected inheritance and the help of several friends, word comes that we will once again hear from Von Stroheim. Perhaps he will film his novel, *Paprika*, a gypsy prose rhapsody published here last Fall. Let us hope it is true.

Yet, what strange destiny for a man!

Is his name really Erich von Stroheim? Is he really a former lieutenant of the old Imperial Austrian Guard, the son of a great Bohemian nobleman? Is he not, rather, a creature from another world, marvelously possessed of a mysterious spirit, caparisoned to mystify the throng?

This much we know: He lived in Vienna at the height of its dying imperial splendor, before the hounds of Europe brought her to bay, a graceful wounded stag. Stroheim lived in the Vienna of dainty carriages with their rigid lackeys, horses trotting along with carriages on their light springs, making their carefree way to Schönbrunn; the Vienna of the aristocracy and of a thousand glistening lights flickering in the Prater, lighting up the gaiety at Sacher's, reflecting its sparkling brandy in the dark eyes of its gypsy demimondaines. . . .

Saber-scarred and monocled, hearts filled with chivalry,

souls filled with poetry, the young Uhlan officers lived, danced, and loved. When the war came, they left, forgetting to pay their tailor bills—but they did not hesitate to fight and die brilliantly at the Piave. One could see them near the Stefanskirche in 1918, asking for alms in the Graben. Black glasses covered their burning eyes, and in the hot swirling dust they dragged their poor, tattered, military rags, still clinging to their withered frames, from which dangled torn epaulets. . . .

Others of the old upper class, more fortunate, or maybe less fortunate, became gigolos, confidence men, or forgers . . . and then, when the artificial years of inflation collapsed, they, too, collapsed, and wound up in prisons. . . .

Only one among them knew how to turn defeat into glory—into millions. Only one among them knew how to, phoenix-like, recreate the Imperial Court of Vienna out of the ashes left by the awful years of holocaust.

The Imperial Austria of old! Shattered by defeat, it returned more brilliant, gayer, and more glittering than ever—in the films made by Erich von Stroheim in Hollywood.

Into the heavy, wholesome diet that the American movie public consumed before his advent, he subtly poured a few drops of venom.

First came *The Pinnacle* (changed to *Blind Husbands* by Carl Laemmle, its producer, who claimed that women wouldn't go to see a film about card playing), then *Foolish Wives*, that subtle and perverse sexual comedy which was exploited by Universal as "The First Million-Dollar Picture," with an electric sign on Times Square changed daily as the production cost sheet mounted, which shenanigans were subsequently to boomerang against Von Stroheim and gain him an unwarranted reputation for insane extravagance.

In *The Pinnacle*, Stroheim, himself, portrayed a little weasel of an Austrian officer on a holiday in the Tyrol, with just enough energy to attempt to seduce every woman he met. Eventually, he falls from a high cliff through a jealous husband's treachery. The title was a symbolic one, nor did the symbolism run to an esoteric deck of cards somewhere in the film.

In *Foolish Wives*, Stroheim again played a similar (Russian) officer on a holiday, this time in postwar Monte Carlo. For his seductions he winds up with a knife in his back and his body

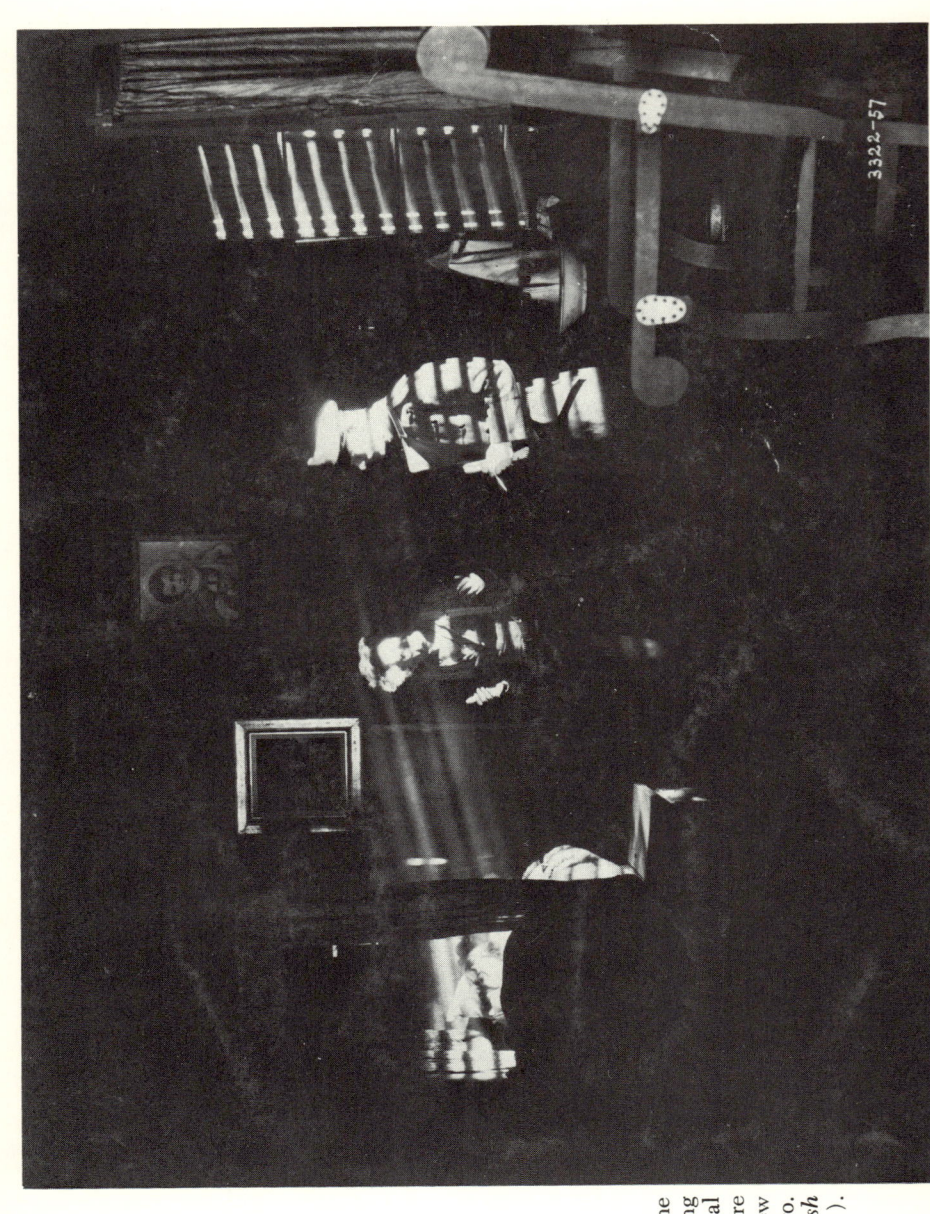

The *morbidezza* of the scene is heightened by its being played in almost total darkness. Long before Sternberg, Stroheim knew the power of chiaroscuro. From Stroheim's *Foolish Wives* (1921).

Karamzin (Stroheim) receives an early visitor (Maude George). Note the helmeted skull by the single flower on the chest of drawers (right) with the white glove peeping out—a characteristic "Breughelian" detail of the director. Cut from *Foolish Wives*.

"Perhaps this earth will never be the place for one [Berlioz] whose orchestra, to be complete, called for the trumpets of Judgment Day."*
The bogs and marshes of the storm, the bogs and marshes of the mind. An agitated moment cut from *Foolish Wives*.

*James Agate, *Around Cinemas* (Second Series), Home and Van Thal, London, 1948. Reprinted by Arno Press, New York, 1972.

thrown with that of a dead cat into a sewer. Retribution has always run riot in the Stroheim films. They were the most moral things imaginable. The villain invariably got his at the end, in the most unsavory manner Stroheim could devise.

Thanks to him, the women and young girls of America learned to prefer the slick, insolent archdukes, whose kisses burned like the lash of a whip, to the bucolic American heroes. Stroheim was the true creator of a sophisticated cinema. But the art of the sophisticated cinema was degraded, corrupted and commercialized by others.

Dilettantes appeared, with all the surface polish and superficial tricks which Stroheim could not or would not have. It is true that his technique was frequently distressingly static for a motion picture, but his individual scenes were so heavy-laden with thought, so beautifully prepared, lighted, and composed, that one easily forgave him a lack of movement, pace, and camera angles. Stroheim always had something to say, and knew how to say it, which was more important.

And then Stroheim did the thing that suddenly made him great—he broke the rules of an art which he created.

When he had gained all that he wanted, when he had lost all taste and feeling for money, he suddenly began to know anguish and despair. Torment followed.

He made *Greed* (from Frank Norris' *McTeague*), into which he poured all his soul. Flying in the face of the box-office, he made a film that was the negation of what the entire motion-picture industry in America had been built upon. He not only flew in the face of the box-office—he spat in its eye. For once the screen would tell a measure of truth, even if it killed Von Stroheim to do it (and it did—the mutilation of *Greed* snuffed out the divine spark that kindled in the artist and left a broken and bitter man).

Greed was the apotheosis of the ugly, the sordid in human beings. The film opened with:

> *Gold, gold, gold, gold,*
> *Bright and yellow, hard and cold,*
> *Molten, graven, hammered, rolled,*
> *Hard to get and light to hold,*
> *Stolen, borrowed, squandered, doled.*

In the original, the epigraph read:

> *O cursed lust of Gold! when for thy sake*
> *The fool throws up his interest in both worlds—*
> *First, starves in this, then damn'd in that to come. . . .*

From that opening title to the last shot in the desert of Death Valley, with the bewildered McTeague, handcuffed to the body of the dead Marcus, going insane from thirst, with a few yards off, a bag of gold coins spilled out futilely on the scorched terrain, Stroheim told a story of greed that struck home so deep in the hearts of all who saw it that many hated the film (in Berlin they hissed it off the screen), and it was reputedly a box-office failure, according to Metro, but that's another story.

It was dedicated: "To my mother."

The very photography stank of the squalor it sought to depict. But *Greed* was beautiful, as truth is beautiful.

The fake morality of Hollywood would not let Stroheim have his masterpiece. They cut it. From forty reels it had been reduced, grudgingly by its creator, to twenty reels—beyond that Stroheim would not cut it. They called in a hack who brought it down to the regulation ten. Its elements of greatness were only partially discernible in the version released to the public. Whole episodes, upon which he had labored for weeks and months, were lopped off, and swept away on the cutting-room floor. Stroheim disowned it, just as he was subsequently to disown the released version of his sly comedy, *The Merry Widow,* in which he sought to depict the decadence in the old royal family of Vienna. Those who saw the original version of Stroheim's *Merry Widow* said it was a shrewd and sardonic thing. The version shown was still better than the usual Ruritanian operetta stuff—it had infinitely more verve than Lubitsch's version which, though witty, was so Americanized that the glamour and witchery of the original were lost. (Lubitsch sought other values.)

In *The Wedding March* (and its sequel, *Marriage of the Prince*) Stroheim strove to become the Goya of the films. Necromancer of the spirit, he now liberated the instincts which he had repressed so long. . . .

It was these instincts that gave us those twisted, tortured candelabras whose translucid flames were agitated by the wind; those nightmarish lights, from behind which emerged an ebony crucifix; the weather-beaten faces of soldiers, the horrible, grimacing, laughing faces; the exotic foods, chaotic visions mixed with orgies and cemeteries . . . the rape in the butcher's shop with thick blood oozing all around and a pale little girl struggling on the stone floor . . . and another girl, the pathetic little cripple in a wedding gown, with horror-stricken eyes, prostrating herself on the stones in a deserted chapel before the Madonna. . . .

Then America got angry.
It pronounced Stroheim a madman.

You cannot defy a young and healthy nation with impunity—its people are not interested in lecherous, demented worlds.

The Wedding March, although beautifully cut by Sternberg at Paramount's request, was released without benefit of its sequel, which carried the story to its logical conclusion. Paramount was through with Von Stroheim. So were they all through with him. So was MGM, Universal, and Pat Powers (who backed *The Wedding March*). No one would have anything to do with a director who could not discipline himself to tell a film story as everyone else did, in the regulation eight or ten reels and in such a form as would not require the inevitable wholesale censorial deletions which characterized every Stroheim film to date.

But the winning personality of the man was not to be downed even yet. He persuaded Joseph P. Kennedy, then a Wall Street financier, to give him financial backing for an original story, *Queen Kelly,* set in Potsdam and German East Africa. It was to serve as a starring vehicle for Gloria Swanson. After a reputed $850,000 had been spent on it, three months had elapsed, and Stroheim was just getting started, sound came in, and producer Kennedy opined that the worst talking film would make more at the box-office than the best silent film. And so production on the silent *Queen Kelly* was stopped. Stroheim was out of a job again. A talking picture which he made, *Walking Down Broadway,* was caught in the middle of a feud between two producers involved with it and was remade by another director, the original version having been "too gamey" for the producer, who had his way.

This was the end of Von Stroheim. The dizzy decline of the idol followed. He was reproached for his megalomania, his arrogance—his wanton spending, brought about chiefly because of an almost fanatical insistence on realism and fidelity of detail. The producers resented his insolent demeanor, the eternal monocle stuck in his eye. They tore up his contracts. They ruined him financially. Alone, he lived in thirty immense, cold rooms, from which his creditors had removed furniture, rugs, sculpture, books. He sought refuge in a hotel—he drank heavily. To make a living, he accepted bit parts in absurd films. He wrote bad articles which he filled with blunt pornography. The man was cracking up—and no wonder! One felt ashamed and squirmed in one's seat watching Stroheim, broken and defeated, playing a "fanatical director," an analphabetic caricature of himself devised by cinema illiterates, in *The Lost Squadron*, directed by a man who had not a tenth of Stroheim's talent.

A spring had snapped—he did not recover.

His own son, a youth of eighteen, brought him a summons for nonpayment of his wife's alimony. At a hearing before the judge, Stroheim confessed that his worldly goods consisted of but eight dollars.

America turns a cold shoulder to those who dare to frighten her. . . .

But here he is again. He returns!
To say what? To do what?

He will film his novel, *Paprika*, they say. *Paprika* is purposely scandalous, exaggerated, heavily erotic; slang mixed with Germanisms becomes uncouth; but occasionally from its depths there comes a cry, bursting like a flash of lightning—a flash behind which we see the old Stroheim.

Will he succeed? We can doubt it or not. The world of 1936 is a different world from the one that witnessed the birth and development of Stroheim's inspired art.

But he no longer seeks death. It is life he now seeks.

And this phantom who returns among us, dressed in an old cashmere dressing robe burned full of cigarette holes; this phantom who comes back with his blasé, tired look—still wearing his monocle; is he not a more touching, more vital figure than those happy men before whom the road of life passes straight and clear?

Spring 1937

Un Carnet de Bal (France, 1937)
Original scenario by Henri Jeanson, Bernard Zimmer, J. Sarment, and Julien Duvivier. Directed by Julien Duvivier. Photography by Agostini. Music by Maurice Jaubert. With Marie Bell, Harry Baur, Pierre Blanchar, Raimu, Fernandel, Louis Jouvet, Pierre-Richard Wilm, Françoise Rosay, Robert Lynen.

UN CARNET DE BAL

A story, cynical, moving, enchanting, and disenchanted, of lost youth and first love deliberately re-encountered.

A widow of thirty-four or -five finds, among her late husband's papers, the dance program of her first ball. Its memory, clothed in illusory idyllic romance, decides her to seek out the half-dozen men whose names are written there, and who, nearly twenty years before, had sworn to love her all their lives. She sets out, and finds what one might expect. The first is dead. He had, in fact, committed suicide when she made her ambitious but ill-judged marriage to another man. But his mother, played with the discreetest and most dreadful hint of madness by Françoise Rosay, still lays his place at the dinner table, still puts fresh flowers in his room, with its boyish untidiness, its twenty-year-old calendar, its half-burnt cigarette, and still awaits his evening return.

The second, a young lawyer, is now proprietor of a dubious sort of nightclub and is about to serve a second term in prison. Louis Jouvet stamps his own ironic personality mordantly on this scene.

The third, once a distinguished musician, she finds in a monastery, reasonably happy as a boys' choirmaster; a portrait ruefully drawn by Harry Baur, not the white and sickly "aquarelle" one might fear, but authentic, rich and mellow.

The fourth, an unquenchable optimist from the Midi, who was going to be President of the Republic, with a huge fortune and an unlimited choice of beautiful women, found that "the sun

Christine (Marie Bell) contemplates the dance program of her first ball. Duvivier's *Un Carnet de Bal* (1937).

came out," and he lingered on the road to his ambitions; but he is mayor, nevertheless, of his little town, President of everything except the Republic—of the bowling club, of the local band, of the Society of ex-Presidents; and he is about to marry his cook, does, in fact, conduct the ceremony himself, and reads himself an extempore congratulatory address into the bargain. Raimu, true son of the "Midi," can be trusted with this richly comic scene.

The fifth man, tracked down in a dreadful apartment on the Marseilles waterfront, is a broken-down doctor with a dubious practice, wracked by epilepsy, and nagged by a hideous shrew of a mistress whom, at the end of an exacerbating but discreetly contrived scene, we see him preparing to murder. It is a part suited to Pierre Blanchar who incarnated the neurasthenic Raskolnikov so acutely.

The final anticlimax is the young widow's return to her home town, where the sixth man, now a domesticated and unpretentious little hairdresser, takes her to another ball, and confronts her idealized memory with the cruel and absurd reality. Fernandel invests this gay sequence with irresistible charm and humor.

Sufficiently disillusioned, the young widow (Marie Bell) returns to her Italian villa, and finds on her doorstep the solution to her problem—the son of the man among them all she loved most, but who is now dead. She will devote herself to this young boy—now she has a purpose in life. She takes him to his first ball.

"A first ball," she tells him, as they leave together, "is as important as a first cigarette—but no more."

June, 1938

Nana, The Little Match Girl, La Chienne, Madame Bovary, A Day in the Country, The Lower Depths, Grand Illusion, The Human Beast, The Rule of the Game—Zola, Andersen, Flaubert, Maupassant, Gorki—a roll of honor such as few screen directors have unfurled. Jean Renoir at the 1967 Montreal Film Festival.

La Grande Illusion (Grand Illusion) (France, 1937) Original scenario by Charles Spaak and Jean Renoir. Directed by Jean Renoir. Photography by Christian Matras, Claude Renoir, Bourgoin, Bourreaud. Design: Lourié. Music: Joseph Kosma. With Jean Gabin, Pierre Fresnay, Erich von Stroheim, Carette, Dalio, Dita Parlo.

GRAND ILLUSION

It is, perhaps, just as well that Jean Renoir, the director of the French antiwar film, *Grand Illusion,* has not the capacity to hate, despite the fact that two of the things he hates most in the world are fascism and anti-Semitism. Like his father, Auguste Renoir, the great impressionist painter, the son is a gentle soul, all kindliness and good humor. And this shows in his work. *Grand Illusion,* though it attacks war and the imperialist war makers, and preaches against the unnatural boundaries between class, race, and creed that government and society have set up, is really the quietest film imaginable. There is no ranting, raving, or tearing of hair in it. There is not a moment's bitterness. Rather it is like a man who draws up before a fireside with you and tells you a story of a series of events that once happened to him, and you believe this story because it has the ring of truth in it.

Because there are things in *Grand Illusion* which you can't invent—they are too simple, too artless, too lacking in guile for that. Renoir, himself, was an officer in the French army during the war. The impressions of his prison-camp days stuck with him all these years. The result is this story of men made useless to life and to themselves—the French prisoners and their German captors—both victims of the war.

What is the "grand illusion"? It is, says Renoir, the idea that one can continue to have faith in worn-out social systems. Two of the principal characters in the film are a French and German career officer, respectively. Each stems from the aristocracy, from a group that had long since reached its zenith, and whose doom was sealed at Sarajevo. The war was to wash away all the old prewar values, and the French and German aristocrats knew this and were resigned to it. There is, for example, a scene wherein the aristocratic German officer invites his French colleague and prisoner into his private quarters. They smoke and chat amiably, reminiscing about the "good old days" when suddenly the French officer says, "Why did you invite me to your private quarters and not my two fellow officers?" (Maréchal and Rosenthal, fellow prisoners with the French officer).

The German commandant smiles—"A 'Maréchal' and a 'Rosenthal'—officers?"

De Boeldieu, the French officer, answers, "They are good soldiers."

Von Rauffenstein, the German, replies, "A nice present from the French Revolution."

A bit later he says: "De Boeldieu—I don't know who is going to win this war, but whoever does, the days of the Rauffensteins and De Boeldieus are over."

Almost the whole philosophy of the film is in that brief scene. Maréchal is a man of the people, a mechanic raised to the rank of lieutenant. Rosenthal is a Jew. To Rauffenstein they belonged to an "inferior" class. De Boeldieu, on the other hand, was regarded by Rauffenstein as a man of his own class, a career officer from an ancient and noble family, like himself, despite the fact that he was a Frenchman and, at the moment, an enemy. How strong were the bonds of class! This explains the machinations and connivings between the "haves" and the "have nots" not only in the arrogant days before the war, but even today. The World War turned out to be a class war, after all. The French and German imperialists were as interested in prolonging the war as their troops were in having an end to it, since the former had everything to gain by it, while the latter had nothing to gain. "Soldiers of the world unite against the common enemy—war" might have been the slogan in 1914.

So today, Jean Renoir hates fascism because it breeds war— and he hates anti-Semitism, too, because it is as unnatural as fortified boundaries. There is a scene of great humanity wherein Maréchal and Rosenthal, Gentile and Jew, having escaped from the German prison camp, are stumbling, half-starved and frozen, across the countryside towards the Swiss frontier. Rosenthal hurts his leg, which impedes his progress. The nervous tension between

Grand Illusion 55

the two men rises and snaps. Maréchal accuses his comrade of slowing them up—they will be captured again by a German patrol if they don't make better speed, whereupon Rosenthal says, "Is it my fault that I hurt my leg?"

This is too much for Maréchal.

"So when a German patrol overtakes us, you'll tell them that you hurt your leg, that's why we couldn't go any faster, and then they'll let us go?"

Rosenthal's bitterness wells up in him. Before they both realize it, they are reviling each other and Maréchal, weary, hungry and cold (as is Rosenthal, to be sure), can't stand it any longer and he shouts, "Besides, I never liked Jews anyway!"

"It's a bit late for that," answers Rosenthal, "don't you think?"

Maréchal goes on by himself, and leaves his comrade with the bad leg to shift for himself. Rosenthal pretends indifference, tries to sing a gay song (which Maréchal sings, too, to prove his indifference) but he finally breaks down and weeps. He feels someone standing by his side and looks up—it is Maréchal. "Come," the latter says. "I'll help you—let's go." He takes Rosenthal's arm and, smiling, joking, with new courage, they go on—together.

This is taking the whole problem of anti-Semitism out into the light, looking at it, and disposing of it with a neatness of dispatch that is one of the most heart-warming things it is possible to imagine. The Christian has acted like a Christian—a disciple of Christ. He has been true to himself, therefore he could not be false to any man.

Above all, this is a film about peace.

In the face of their common enemy—war, and the war makers, both Jew and Christian are united. That is why *Grand Illusion* was banned in Germany and Italy. In Vienna, on the day that the Nazis moved in, *Grand Illusion* was taken off the screen in the middle of a reel by the storm troopers. Renoir regards this as a signal honor—as a decoration. He says: "This incident fills me with pride. At the risk of becoming a bore, I repeat it on the slightest provocation. I cannot restrain myself. For I do not consider this a military decoration, but a moral one; and I will not return it to Der Führer as HenryBernstein returned to Il Duce the Cross of St. Maurice and Lazarus."

Indeed, I am tempted to let Renoir speak for himself at this

56   *Saint Cinema*

moment. You must know that he says:

> The appalling atmosphere of war is again upon us. Between shots of *La Bête Humaine,* which we are now filming, the cameramen, electricians, stagehands and actors, bewildered, look at each other, shake their heads and shrug their shoulders. If Mr. Hitler knew how much he was annoying us, I am sure he would be vastly pleased. Personally, I refuse to give him the satisfaction. I do not mean that I ignore Der Führer. But at no time do I permit my animosity for him to get the better of me, I feel that it has become a personal matter between Hitler and me. If millions of men, like myself, were to consider this menace a personal problem, the scourge of war would not again descend on man.
>
> Because I am a pacifist, I made *Grand Illusion.* To my mind, a true pacifist is a true Frenchman, a true American or a true German. Among right-thinking men the day must come when there will be a common ground of understanding. Cynics will say that my words, at this moment, reveal a certain amount of childlike trust. But why not? However annoying that Hitler may be, he has in no way modified my opinion of the Germans. From my earliest childhood I loved and esteemed this people. To illustrate: If from my boyhood I were the inseparable companion of a friend, and one day he contracted syphilis, this would not seem to me sufficient reason for withdrawing my affection. With all my heart I would try to find means of restoring him to health, as quickly as possible.
>
> In *Grand Illusion* I attempted to show that we, in France, have no hate for the Germans. . . . In the war, we had no hate for the "enemy" either—they were just as good Germans as we were Frenchmen.
>
> It is my conviction that I am working for an ideal of human progress in presenting on the screen an undisguised expression of the truth. For example, by portraying, in *Grand Illusion,* men who were sincerely fulfilling their duty as society decreed, within the framework of established institutions, I believed I was making my humble contribution to the peace of the world. I wanted a German who saw my film to say to himself, "These Frenchmen are nice

people. They eat, they drink, just as we do. They require love and—above all—friendship." That is what the French people who saw the film said about the Germans. But, unfortunately, the Germans were not permitted to see my film. In my heart this distresses me. What disturbs me most, however, is the thought that films have such a short life. Technique changes, the actor's style of playing changes, too; and just as fashions are outmoded, our films go into oblivion to join others that once moved us. Now, at a time when this film might do the most good, *Grand Illusion* has been banned in Germany.

It may be that tomorrow I shall have to take my old uniform out of camphor and go back to making a distasteful march eastward from Paris. It will be a great comfort to think that some Americans will know that, if I do this, it is done in firm conviction, but without a shadow of hate. . . .

December, 1938

Harvest "Regain" (France, 1937) Scenario by Marcel Pagnol from Jean Giono's "Un de Baumugne." Directed by Marcel Pagnol. Music by Arthur Honegger. With Gabriel Gabrio, Orane Demazis, Fernandel, Le Vigan, Rollan, Edouard Delmont, Henri Poupon, Odette Roger, Paul Dullac.

HARVEST

Harvest is a filmed tone poem in three movements: the tragic aspect of winter's solitude, the awakening of spring with its renewed desire, the fecundity of summer—life in blossom, fruitful, lush under the weight of the Provence sky. . . .

In soft, almost hushed cadences, it parallels the changes wrought in the lives of two people, a man and a woman, with the miracle of the seasons. Out of their regeneration, achieved against a counterpoint of the life cycle in nature, emerges a simple grandeur—the godhead in man, eternal woman, the good bountiful earth, all three rooted in each other, so that,

> ... *Thy will be done, on earth,*
> *as it is in Heaven.* ...
> *Give us this day our daily bread.* ...

But men left the village of Aubignane. Now there remained none to sow wheat in the good soil, none to impregnate the earth's great womb with the seeds of a new harvest, none to drive the ploughshare deep into the rich, dark, earth so that the spring rains would find the tender green shoots to nourish and send them sprouting up until the horizon was made rapturous with grain swaying heavily in the great summer winds. None, that is, save Panturle, whom a life alone had made half savage, who poached on small game in the forest for sustenance, who trod dumbly, blankly, the grassgrown path to the village.

Up along the path on a spring day comes Gedemus, the knife-grinder, with his wife Arsule who, like a beast of burden, pulls his grotesque cart with a leather thong across her strong, young body. They rest the night in the deserted village.

In the morning, Arsule is gone. Gedemus, discovering blood on the threshold of Panturle's abode, hurries to the police, but so incredible is his story (and so ambitious for promotion is the sergeant) that they arrest him.

Arsule, of course, is not dead; the blood was that of a trapped fox. Arsule is living happily, in their first spring, with Panturle.

There follows an idyll of the hunter tamed. This great thing that has happened to him and which has given life a fuller and richer meaning, this has enfolded the life of Panturle with beatitude. And Arsule, too, has completed her life as a woman. She loves him, she will bear his child. But Arsule cannot live on meat alone—she must have bread. Bread is made from wheat, and wheat means plowing, sowing, gathering the harvest, the real symphony of life, the clamorous and exultant deux à deux between man and nature. ...

And Gedemus, the knife-grinder? He admits, to Panturle,

Before the screen ran amuck. Orane Demazis and Gabriel Gabrio in Marcel Pagnol's seraphic *Harvest* (1937).

that a wife to him is worth only the price of a donkey, while to Panturle she is beyond all bargaining, for she has revealed to him the true meaning and beauty of life. So begins once more the cycle of life in a tiny village which holds the secret of the world.

Those who tasted the grapes that grew in the village, before they went away, did not see the vine leaves hanging there.

The following is translated from the French of Jean Giono

Civilization doesn't always mean progress. For years, men all over the world had left their farms and villages for the wars, for the lure of great cities. The villages decayed and went to ruin, the farms became overgrown with weeds and wild grass. A heavy silence hung like a pall over what, once, had been thriving and happy communities. The story of *Harvest* is the story of one such village, a story of Provence, in the Basses-Alpes, where I was born and where I have lived all my life.

The village in *Harvest*, which I have called Aubignane, is known as Redortiers by its inhabitants. Time and the migration of its young men have taken their toll of it. It is as terrible to look upon as a face ravaged by beasts.

One bright morning, Marius, our master mason, had climbed the belfry of the church that we had constructed, to fix a crucifix into the crumbling gable. From there he could overlook the great windswept plateau. Suddenly he perceived a man approaching. Although this man was still some distance away, the wind carried the sound of his steps to us with a sharp crispness. The man's step was solid and sure, the step of one who was accustomed to this land. He belonged here.

Marius descended and came over to Pagnol and me. "Did you see?" he said. "There's one of them arriving now."

When the man approached, we saw that he was old but hardy, with a tough tanned skin like the bark of a tree. His mouth was straight, a little cruel and ironic. It was silent like the mouth of a man who has lived long in solitude. He looked about him, scanning the houses we had built, deliberately, one by one. Then he spoke.

"What is this?" he asked.

"Aubignane."

"Aubignane . . ." he repeated.

"What is Aubignane?"

"A village."

"A village?" he said, repeating it several times, while he continued to survey the strange new landscape. "But," he said, looking squarely at us, "there's never been any village up here, friends. Well, now, what do you say to that? I know this place. I can tell you. For forty years I have herded sheep down there" (he pointed to the valley below) "and I have been looking at this hill for forty years and there's never been any village on it. Don't tell me any fairy tales."

"We're not telling you fairy tales," intercepted the mason. "We're building a village."

The man repeated once more the magic words, "A village!" Then he asked, "And what did you say the name of this village was?"

"Aubignane."

"It's not a name of these parts."

"The name is in a book."

"Then it shouldn't be in the book," he said.

"It's really only the name we've given to the hill."

"But you have built ruins," he said.

"That's true," answered the mason. "But, after all, we're only telling a story—a story about a village on a hill—and this village is in ruins. The story is about a village that was dying, as you see it now. And then a man made it live again—with his labor and his love, and what was a desert became again a flourishing village."

"I understand," the old man said. Then he added, "I smelled your soup cooking. That's what brought me here."

"You can have some with us," said the mason, "if you care to."

"I won't say no," said the man without a change of expression. "But you must finish those walls and make a village. You must tell your story right up to the end, comrades. On this very hill, you must show me an entire village, when you are through. As long as you want to tell a story about a hill and a ruined village."

"Yes," said the mason. "Well, you see, that's just it. A hill, a village in ruins, and a man who looked like you."

June, 1939

La Marseillaise (France, 1938) Original scenario by Jean Renoir, Carl Koch, N. Martel, J.P. Dreyfus. Directed by Jean Renoir. Photography by Bourgoin, Douarinou, Maillols. Design: Léon Barsacq, Wakhévitch, Jean Perrier. Music by Joseph Kosma, Sauveplane and 18th century songs. With Pierre Renoir, Louis Jouvet, Escande, Clariond, Jacque Catelain, Gaston Modot, Carette, Lise Delamare, Jenny Hélia, Irène Joachim, Nadia Sibirskaïa. Produced by popular subscription of the people of France.

RENOIR FILMS THE VOICE OF THE PEOPLE

Even in school, the French Revolution was painted in lurid colors for us. With popping eyes we read about the half-savage Danton, the cunning Robespierre, of the murder of the ugly Marat in his bath by the beauteous Charlotte Corday—all of which had all the thrills of a Sunday supplement such as our less conservative newspapers give us each seventh day to atone for their dullness the other six. At any rate, we grew up with preconceived notions of the Revolution as a terrible thing fomented by the bloodthirsty populace; our hearts were wrung with pity for the sad and pale Marie Antoinette who was to offer her pretty little neck to the guillotine, and we even felt a measure of compassion for the weak and helpless Louis XVI, who couldn't realize why the people of France hated him so.

When we were old enough to go to the movies, the situation had hardly changed. The French Revolution was still depicted as a "Roman holiday" of the people who were let loose to despoil the very flower of France. In films like *Orphans of the Storm, A Tale of Two Cities, The Scarlet Pimpernel,* and most recently, *Marie Antoinette,* it was all too, too sad—I mean about those handsome aristocrats. Indeed, it would seem that the people of France were no better than those horrid Bolsheviks who dethroned Czar Nicholas II, and then caused the downfall of Kerensky.

Only the French people, themselves, had never made a film of their historic struggle for liberty which was for them exactly what our own war of independence was for us. And so, one day the people of France formed a coordinating committee which was placed in charge of production, and they embarked on a film of the French Revolution called *Marseillaise*. Jean Renoir, who had previously made *Grand Illusion*, that most untheatrical of all films about the World War, was appointed director. At last, the world would be shown what the French Revolution really was like, not as it had been glamorized and romanticized for, lo, these many years. The production cost was financed by popular subscription on the 150th anniversary of that historic event. Each person contributed two francs, for which he got a receipt which entilted him to a two franc reduction in the price of admission to see the film when it was released. The then existing Popular Front government of France, under the leadership of the Jewish socialist, Léon Blum, officially sponsored the picture, and placed the entire archives of the period at the disposal of director Renoir.

Six months later, *Marseillaise* was finished. Renoir issued the following statement:

> The physical action of *Marseillaise* is but a means to an end, a spiritual expression of the French Revolution. I have not tried to make an historical film, but a simple, human story. I have tried to film an idea—quite simply and without fuss, one of the greatest periods in our history. I have not tried to film the revolution in terms of "Let them eat cake!" the storming of the Bastille and the harangues of Danton and Robespierre.
>
> I do not regard *Marseillaise* as an historical film at all, but as a modern film. "The romance between liberty and the people," of which one of the characters in the film speaks, is as applicable today as it was then and as it has always been. I was not interested in history in terms of the costume film. The heroes of *Marseillaise* are not the bewigged protagonists, but the events of the time, not its representative figures.
>
> As a substitute for "modern" and "historical," I prefer "realistic." As in *Grand Illusion*, so with *Marseillaise*—I was

interested solely in the capture of the mean and construction upon it. In *Marseillaise*, I have constructed the modern ideal of democracy upon events that occurred 150 year ago. *Marseillaise* is a film of contemporary ideals. It does not stop with being a fictional or historical film, if you insist on these terms. It is not concerned either with fiction or history—it is concerned only with problems of the present day. I do not have to remind you, after the Austrian *Anschluss*, the annexation of Czechoslovakia, and the annihilation of Poland, what those problems of the present day are. You can mention the word liberty to an Australian bushman and he will know what you mean.

Above all, I am interested in human beings. During the weeks of casting *Marseillaise*, I was delighted to find the exact types I had visualized for the various roles. It seemed as if I had recognized them at once. I was immediately seized with the desire of letting you know about them and I hope you will admire them as much as I do. That would be my greatest reward.

That is Renoir—and the spirit of the democratic ideal which actuated the filming of *Marseillaise*. Children who see it (and they should see it) will learn, perhaps for the first time, that the men and women who overthrew the feudal regime of Louis XVI were not the grandiloquent puppets that bourgeois history records, but normal, intelligent, congenial, and amiable people. It is the French Revolution told in terms of the man in the street. Many adults will also, perhaps, be learning this for the first time. That is why the people of France contributed their two francs each—so that the whole world should know this.

Renoir has not caricatured the enemies of the people in *Marseillaise*. Marie Antoinette is still pale and sad, and Louis is still a pathetic and bewildered figure. But the real heroes and heroines of the film are the people themselves. The wag who scrawls "Here lies the Bastille!" on a placard over the fallen gates; the jovial Bomier, who cannot learn the words to the new song, *Marseillaise*, because they are too difficult; the three weary soldiers on the march to Paris who discuss the best way of wrapping up one's feet so that they don't get sore on the long journey; the fat, jolly lieutenant, Javel, who becomes alarmed at seeing a friendly priest talking to one of the soldiers, and who insists that "there goes the advance guard of reaction," and has to be told by his comrade that just because a priest wears a frock it does not necessarily brand him a reactionary. All these and many more are characteristic of the great humanity with which Renoir has again, as in *Grand Illusion,* imbued *Marseillaise.*

At a time like this when enduring values are in jeopardy, when the nations of Europe are again pitting themselves against each other in a war of annihilation, proving once again (as if further proof were needed) the futility of war as an instrument of national policy, the film *Marseillaise* boldly states the democratic ideal of a free people. *Marseillaise* is more than a monument to the struggle for independence of the French people—it is a monument to the Czechs and Austrians, the people of democratic Spain and the innocent victims of the German, Italian and Japanese juggernauts everywhere. What *Marseillaise* has to say about liberty is eminently worth repeating, though it has been said before, notably by Hugo in *Les Misérables* and '93 and by those who fought in the Paris Commune of 1870 and in the American Revolution of 1776.

At the end of the film, one of the characters mutters something about the death of a soldier of the people having been in vain. The army of the people is outnumbered. Victory against such odds seems hopeless. But another answers him: "The people once faced liberty like a lover before his sweetheart to whom he has been forbidden to speak a word. Suddenly, thanks to us, he is able to approach and speak his mind to his beloved. Of course, they are not yet married and the end of the romance is not yet in sight but now at least they know each other and they will find each other again."

This is the voice of the people and, as the saying has it, *Vox Populi, Vox Dei,* "the voice of the people is the voice of God."

November, 1939

Return of the errant and contrite wife. From Pagnol's paean to the indomitable spirit of the Midi, *The Baker's Wife* (1938), in which Raimu triumphed so brilliantly.

La Femme du Boulanger (France, 1938) Scenario by Marcel Pagnol after "Jean le Bleu" by Jean Giono. Directed by Marcel Pagnol. With Raimu, Ginette Leclerc, Charles Moulin, Charpin, Robert Vattier, Delmont, Blavette, Maupi.

THE BAKER'S WIFE

Both *Harvest* and *The Baker's Wife* deal with bread as the fundamental need in our every-day application of "life, liberty and the pursuit of happiness"—the former in terms of poetic drama, the latter in terms of mordant comedy. Both are from the same pen.

In *The Baker's Wife*, the author has substituted, for the quasi-epic utterances of *Harvest*, Olympian laughter. His fable of the baker's wife who ran off with the handsome shepherd and was made to come back by the villagers, not because they felt sorry for the grief-stricken baker, but because he wouldn't bake any more bread until she did come back, is the sort of theme Aristophanes would have loved. The author of *Lysistrata* applied the same idea to war two thousand years ago. Giono has flavored the Attic wit of Aristophanes with the Gallic zest of Balzac (is this not a "droll story" in the best tradition of the *Contes Drolatiques?*) and De Maupassant, his spiritual progenitors. As for Anatole France, whose cloven hoof peeps out throughout *The Baker's Wife*, and whose deathless satire is the eternal glory of French letters, he would have kissed Giono on both cheeks for this delicious comedy.

But here the story is the thing, and not its inspirational sources; how the reactions to the baker's serio-comic plight is tempered by the characters in the story according to that which each has to lose by the baker's wife running off with another man. The simple villagers are concerned only with the loss of their daily bread; the marquis is concerned only with the loss of his prize horse, on which the two impetuous lovers rode off; and the village curate is concerned only with saving the baker's soul. He urges him to meditation and prayer, as remedies for his misfortune. To which the baker answers, "Prayer? That is good when one has sinned, but have I done wrong? Because God has suffered my wife to run away with the shepherd, is it I who should ask forgiveness? I respect God, but from now on he is my debtor!"

That night, the errant wife returns, tearful and contrite. The baker receives her with tenderness in a scene of such savage irony as the screen has seldom before known. But before that, he has said to the assembled villagers: "If you bring me back my wife, I will make you bread the like of which you have never before tasted. I shall mix rosemary with the pine-wood that I use for heating the oven. I will not take my eye off it a minute while it bakes. I will make bread so good that people will not say 'I have eaten cheese on bread' but 'I have eaten bread under some cheese.' I shall give five pounds of bread every day to the poor and in every loaf I make for you there will be part of my friendship and of my gratitude."

Giono has disarmed us and rendered us helpless against such bursts of tenderness by his irrepressible humor. When the baker, still refusing entirely to believe "the worst" about his wife's sudden disappearance, goes on a drunk as a result and delivers a hilarious epic monologue on the frailty of women, he suddenly bursts into tears, falls to his knees and in despair asks, "Why did she go away like that, why? Do you think she went to her mother?" "Why not?" answers the marquis, to console him.

"But," replies the baker, "would she have gone to her mother on horseback?"

February, 1940

Time in the Sun (Mexico-U.S., 1939)
Edited by Marie Seton and Paul Burnford from footage shot by Eisenstein-Alexandrov-Tissé on their Mexican expedition 1930–31 for *Que Viva Mexico!* Scenario based on Eisenstein's original scenario. The project, *Que Viva Mexico!*, remained unfinished.

TIME IN THE SUN

"The story of this film is unusual. Four novels framed by a prologue and an epilogue, unified in conception and spirit, creating its entirety.
"Different in content.
"Different in location.
"Different in landscape, peoples, customs.
"Opposite in rhythm and form, they create a vast and multicolored film-symphony about Mexico.
"Six Mexican folk-songs accompany these novels, which themselves are but songs, legends, tales from different parts of Mexico, brought together in one united cinema show."

Thus Sergei Eisenstein described his conception of *Que Viva Mexico*—this was, in essence, the scenario, this the shape of his heroic epic of the Mexican ethos, a cinema ballad in the great folk-song tradition of the *Volsung Saga*, the *Iliad*, and the *Mahabharata*.

"Four novels framed by a prologue and an epilogue...."
Ancient Yucatan, in the days of the flowering of the Mayan, Aztec, and Toltec civilizations, before the Spanish conquest, before the coming of the Conquistadores. The ritual of death (echoed with sardonic gaiety in the epilogue) is followed by the ritual of life. Softly and tenderly ends the prologue.

Into this hushed beatitude a strange new symbol appears —a new god to dethrone the old gods, the fair-skinned (so unlike an Indian's!), tear-stained figure on a crucifix, who is to supplant the ancient gods, Teoyaomiqui and Mitlanceutli, and the sacred Plumed Serpent, while His mother succeeds Tonatzin, "mother of the gods." And with Him, the white conquerors from

Spain bring a disease that only gold can cure. So Cortez flayed about him, laid waste the soul of the Indian and enslaved a whole people for the greater glory of Spain. The religious dances of many tribes tell in dance form the story of the Spanish conquest. And the pilgrimage re-enacting Christ's journey to Calvary reveals the deep effect of Christianity, so imposed, on the Indian mind. On the ruins of the old temples, built from the same stones, glittering cathedrals rose. On the dark, broad base of the old Indian culture, the frenetic Spanish life settled. To the insinuating music of the *paso doble*, the arrogant matador laughed at death in the bull ring. Ends the first novel.

Survival of the ancient matriarchy of Tehuantepec, fertile, languorous valley, where life flowers, abundantly, flowing along the stream of its ancient *dolce far niente*. An idyllic little intermezzo in the great clangorous symphony that tells the story of this ancient people.

It is 1906. Mexico, though separated from Spain, is still ruled, under Díaz, by the system of peonage instituted by Cortez. On a day of Corpus Christi is told a story of brutality and exploitation that is only one of a thousand such stories. No longer will the peon drown his angush bitterly in the pulque from the maguey. The spark of revolt is fanned into a wild, angry flame. End of the third novel.

The fourth novel, the revolution, was not filmed. It was to have paralleled the birth of a child to a *soldadera* with a battle between the revolutionary and the government. The exultant cry of new-born Mexico. In 1911 Díaz fell and the Indian began to absorb his masters.

Epilogue. In which all the ribbons of the preceding novels are tied together into a gay bow. "Calaveras," or "Death Day," gay and satirical holiday! Into the traditional festival of All Souls' Day the Indian humorously inserts his contempt for death. The laughing children, the candy skulls, the grandiose politicoes and magnificoes who are nothing but skeletons underneath their grand raiment! And the merry-making at the tombs of the dear, departed ones! Drink and feast and make love! See the ferris wheel of life slowly turning in the sun behind everything that goes on. Life shall be reborn in endless reduplication! In these laughing faces, young Mexico has found its strength at last.

Thus has *Time in the Sun* told Eisenstein's story. Told it as

Two proteans of twentieth-century art—Diego Rivera and Sergei Eisenstein—meet at the former's home before Eisenstein and his *équipe* (Alexandrov and Tissé) embark on their film epic of Mexico. Frida Kahlo Rivera is on her husband's right. (1931)

"The intoxicating perfume of work."* Eisenstein at the viewer of Tissé's camera at one of the ancient Mayan temples. From the Prologue to *Que Viva Mexico!* (1931-32).

*Peter Balbusch, from notes made on the sets during the filming of Sternberg's *Shanghai Express*. (Balbusch subsequently collaborated with Hans Dreier and Richard Kollorsz on the décor of *The Scarlet Empress*.)

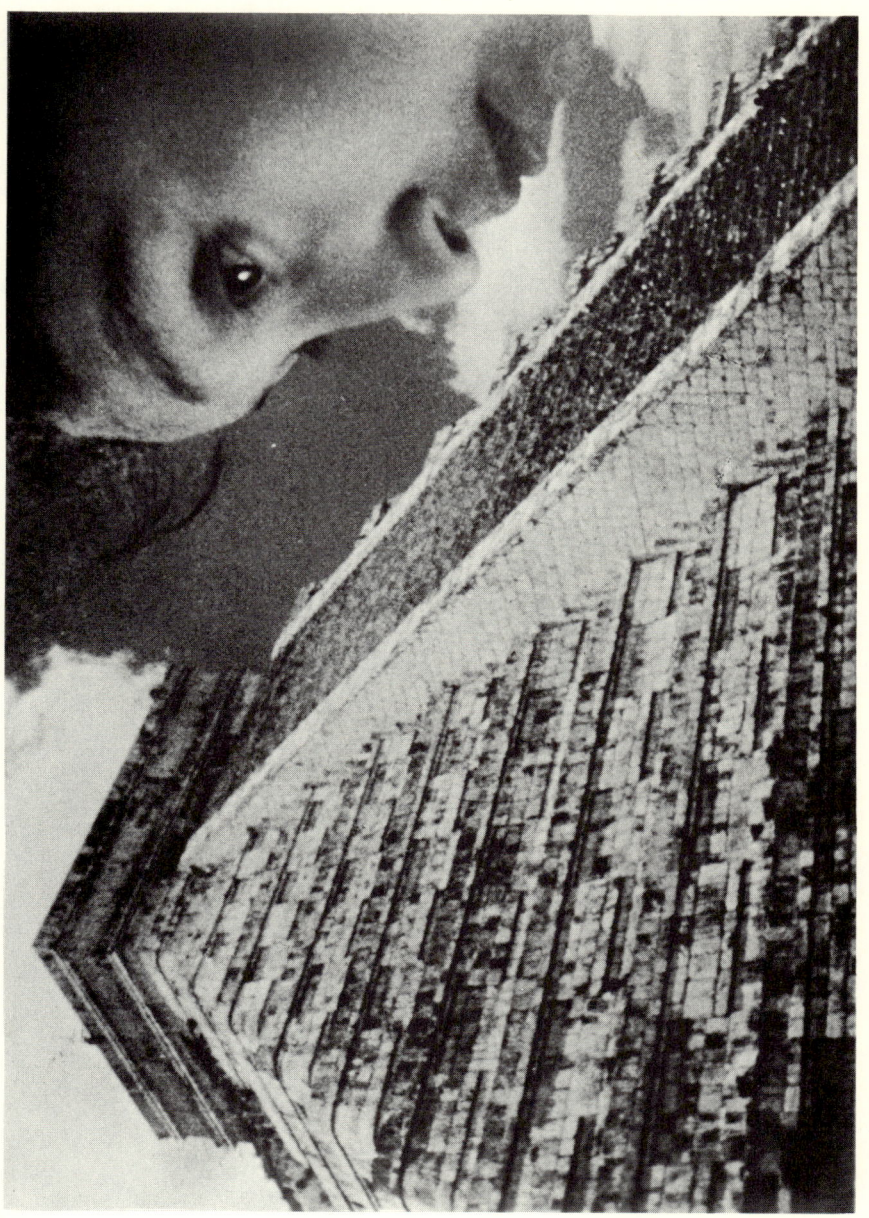

"Time in the prologue is eternity."* Dwellers of Yucatan have conserved the characteristics of their ancestors. *Que Viva Mexico!*

*Opening line of the Prologue to the scenario for *Que Viva Mexico!* by Eisenstein and Alexandrov.

"Portrait of a Young Man" by Eisenstein and Tissé, from the *Sandunga* sequence filmed in Tehuantepec, a matriarchy, where the chief function of young men is to become the fathers of more Tehuanas. *Que Viva Mexico!*

A typical Eisenstein set-up for a shot. Filming anti-clerical material in Tetlapayac. The director, in beret and white ducks, watches Tissé, that most sublime of all cameramen, get his range. *Que Viva Mexico!*

"See the ferris wheel of life slowly turning in the sun. . . . Life shall be reborn in endless reduplication!" From the carnival pageant, *Calavera,* closing sequence of *Que Viva Mexico!* (Tissé at the camera and Eisenstein in pith helmet at right).

a love story, of the love of a people for the land, and of the sun for the people.

September, 1940

The Great Dictator (U.S., 1940) Written and direced by Charles Chaplin. Photography by Karl Struss, Rollie Totheroh. Design: J. Russell Spencer. With Charles Chaplin, Paulette Goddard, Jack Oakie, Reginald Gardiner, Henry Daniell, Billy Gilbert, Grace Hale, Carter De Haven, Maurice Moscovitch.

THE GREAT DICTATOR

The Great Dictator begins and ends on a note of terror. Starkly it opens on that fateful morning of November 11, 1918, somewhere on the western front. The earth shakes with paroxysm, coughs, strangles, and vomits its gorge as the screaming shells plow into it, burst and send the hot iron shrapnel flying in all directions from the roseate irises of foul black and red, like poisonous flowers laughing hysterically in their death agony, rising slowly in putrescent grandeur, infecting the sweet, cool morning air with its gangrenous vapor. (Elsewhere, the knife-glitter of the surgery ward, the torn flesh on the beds of pain, cotton soaked in ether, the clotted blood, twisted faces and mingled stink of sweat, tetanus, and carbolic acid.) Behind the cold, gray opening of *The Great Dictator,* etched sketchily in charcoal blacks and whites of a gun here, a bursting shell there, and men scurrying like rats in a trench all around, is Latzko's *Men in War* and the hatred of war of the artist who begins here to make his plea for universal brotherhood.

When the camera swings swiftly by "Big Bertha," the

obscene product of a diseased imagination, a little man, cog number "x" in the horrendous war machine now got out of control, stands ready to pull the lever-cord that will send a shell hurtling seventy miles to Paris on the Cathedral of Notre Dame. What an achievement! What a thing is man, indeed! But the little man by the big gun is Charlie Chaplin and so with an exquisite pas de seul he pulls the lever-cord and the shell spits out of the gun to land on a nearby outhouse, with a boom and a splintering crash, and a "pshaw!" with a disappointed snap of the fingers from Chaplin. From this moment on Chaplin ridicules war. The spectator's horror has turned to bitter laughter. Chaplin struggles with a hand grenade that has fallen down his sleeve into the recesses of his uniform. "Take the pin out, count ten and throw it!" he was warned. But with the pin out it is now sputtering somewhere in his clothing. Frantically he tears at his uniform as the precious seconds tick off, locates it, tosses it quickly away and it explodes. With a sigh of relief, he faints. This is not war as the dictators teach it to their youth.

So Chaplin begins *The Great Dictator* by reviling war and showing his contempt for it as a thing of vast and horrible imbecility.

Wounded, he spends the next fifteen years in a hospital, emerging to find his fatherland held in thrall by a dictator heading a political party that has terrorized an entire nation into whimpering submission. He returns to his little barber shop, to take up life where he left it, but the street has now become a ghetto and the other Jews live in constant fear of the storm troopers. It seems that Jews have become the special butt of the new regime and his first encounter with storm troops who paint "Jew" over his shop windows leads to a fight and a realization that something terrible has happened while he has been away.

Then we see what it is that has happened. Before a great throng, against banners with their ridiculous arbitrary insignia (Chaplin humorously substitutes the double-cross for the swastika), the great dictator himself. Again, Chaplin—the dictator, who had the misfortune to look like the little Jewish barber. (None of the reviewers of the film have commented on the beautiful logic of this resemblance in Chaplin's scenario; how it is borne out in real life that the world's most hated figure is indicted by the world's most loved figure.) Then follows a dev-

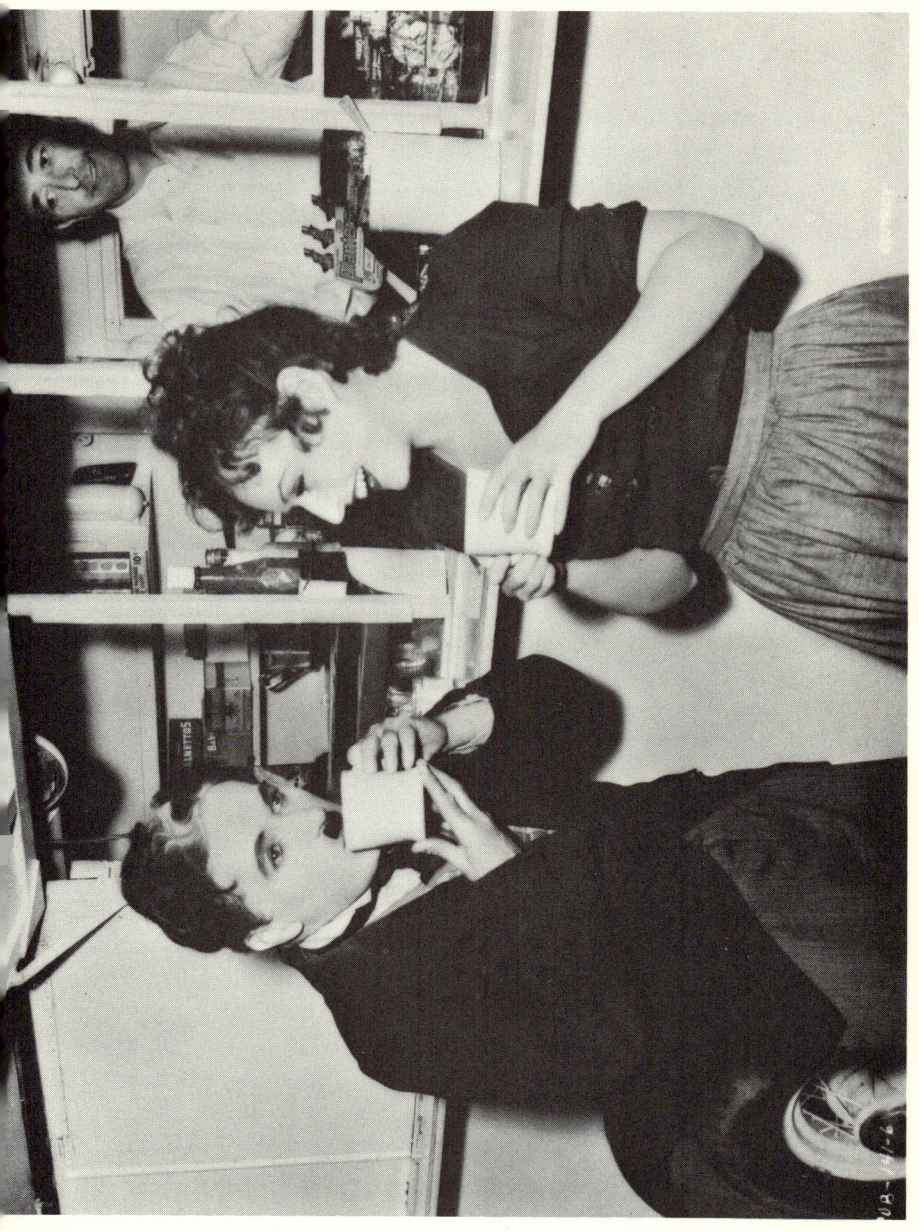

Chaplin and Paulette Goddard take a coffee break during the filming of *The Great Dictator* (1940).

astating parody of Hitler having a seizure, in other words, giving a speech. The psychopathic sobbings, breast-beating, contemptuous exhortations for sacrifice which the fatherland demands and all the assorted razzle-dazzle and pure, unadulterated sheep-dip, have been scrambled by Chaplin into such a towering edifice of hilarious nonsense that at his conclusion, when the great dictator has shouted himself dry, Chaplin makes his final crushing comment on the whole paranoiac performance. The dictator gulps down a drink of water and then . . . but perhaps you had better see for yourself how deliciously Chaplin puts across one of the things he thinks is the matter with Hitler. ("My speech makes as much sense as his do," commented Chaplin recently.) Subsequently, there is another bit with the dictator again having shrieked himself hoarse, raising the glass of water spontaneously to his ear, but, suddenly realizing that what he regarded up to now as his *Sitzfleisch* was really only a hole in the ground, brings the glass down to his mouth. (But if you think Chaplin lets it go at that, you just don't know Chaplin, nor, for that matter, do you know the very funny story of the lunatic and the Queen of the Netherlands that refugees brought over in recent weeks. If you know the story, you'll know what I mean when you see this episode in the film.)

"Originality and truth are to be found only in details." said Stendhal. If I dwell on the details of Chaplin's great fresco, it is only because in them truth is revealed in all its splendid incandescence; in these seemingly insignificant details are Chaplin's sharpest observations and, by far, his greatest originality. Such as, following upon an auto-erotic tête-à-tête with his minister of propaganda who envisions for him a beautiful, blonde aryan world ruled by a brunette dictator whom this race of supermen and superwomen would worship as a god, the great dictator leaps in ecstasy across the room and up a drapery, where he remains, for a moment poised and transfigured. In what way is this merciless observation of Chaplin's different essentially from the mystic of Berchtesgaden, perched in his armoured aviary on a high crag of the Bavarian Alps, there brooding on the *Götterdämmerung* he has unleashed on the world? ("I hear a beating of wings!" said Herod. "I do not wish to hear it! It is an omen of death!" Oscar Wilde would have understood Hitler, as Freud did. But the beating of wings is the R. A. F. and they understand him, too, as do now even his former appeasers and as soon everyone will understand him.)

The dictator slides down the drapery, he is alone. He approaches a terrestial globe, lifts it—and flings it rapturously into the air. A beatific smile plays upon his mouth. Against soft, shimmering music out of Wagner by way of a good aryan pogrom, the great dictator does a bubble dance with the terrestial globe. The *morbidezza* of this scene, the profundity with which Chaplin, with shocking suddenness, has realized the essence, not only of his own film, but of what is happening to the world today because of the aberration of one man, is apocalyptic. It is not only the most intense lyrical moment that Chaplin has ever touched, but one has really to go back to Shakespeare and Goethe to find passages that will equal it in its febrile glow.

The rest of the film's story, of how the little Jewish barber, after a series of misadventures, comes to be mistaken for the "Furore" and is called upon to speak before a massed throng come to "celebrate" the fall of Austria, is too well known by now to need detailing here. The critical boys and girls of the metropolitan press have had their field day with this passionate summing up by Chaplin of how he feels about the spectacle of humanity being kicked around. But Chaplin, himself, has answered his critics better than I, or anyone, could do. "May I not be excused in pleading for a better world? . . . It was a very difficult thing to do. It would have been much easier to have the barber and Hannah disappear over the horizon, off to the promised land against the glowing sunset. But there is no promised land for the oppressed people of the world. There is no place over the horizon to which they can go for sanctuary. They must stand and we must stand."

Listen to the closing words of Chaplin in *The Great Dictator*, that bitter four minute speech in which he says, "I should like to help every one, if possible, Jew, Gentile, black man, white. We all want to help one another. Human beings are like that. We want to live by each other's happiness. . . . In the 17th Chapter of St. Luke it is written: 'The Kingdom of God is within man'— not in one man nor a group of men, but in all men. You, the people, have the power to make this life free and beautiful, to make this life a wonderful adventure. . . ." Listen to these words and then contemplate the crowning irony of the National Legion

82   *Saint Cinema*

of Decency's statement that they are not recommending *The Great Dictator* for children because: "Unrelated to plot or characterization, Chaplin utters a seemingly gratuitous and personal remark suggesting his disbelief in God. In view of the star's following, this utterance in its possible harmful effect on audiences is deplored." (Hannah, played by Paulette Goddard, asks the barber if he believes in God, and the barber thinks for a moment and begins, "Well . . ." but she interrupts him and goes on to tell him an incident apropos.)

I say here and now that every child in America should see *The Great Dictator,* that God is not the special concern (nor the private property) of the National Legion of Decency, that Chaplin's God is as good as theirs, that the god-head in man is a more real God than the detached Being that any individual or group of individuals can summon according to what axe he has to grind. Why did the Legion of Decency make no statement about the godlessness and bestiality of the Nazi film, *Feldzug in Polen,* which played for two months to packed and cheering houses in the German quarter of New York? What kind of "decency" is that?

In the Talmud it is written that there are things on earth which make even the angels in Heaven weep.

November, 1940

Pépé le Moko (France, 1937) Scenario by Inspector d'Ashelbé (of the Paris *Sûreté*) and Henri Jeanson. Directed by Julien Duvivier. Photography by Jules Kruger. Design: Jacques Krauss. Music: Vincent Scotto, Mohammed Ygerbuchen. With Jean Gabin, Mireille Balin, Lucas Gridoux, Line Noro, Gilbert Gabrio, Dalio, Saturnin Fabre, Charpin, Gaston Modot.

PEPE LE MOKO

"Heavy, heavy hands over thy head, Fine or superfine?" —Old Saying

"It is a tale of love and lovers that they tell in the lowlit Causeway that slinks from West India Dock Road to the dark waste of waters beyond. In Pennyfields, too, you may hear it; and

Pépé Le Moko

"I do not doubt that it is told in far away Tai-Ping, in Singapore, in Tokio, in Shanghai, and those other gay-lamped haunts of wonder whither wandering people of Limehouse go and whence they return so casually. . . ." Thus does Thomas Burke begin his story of *The Chink and the Child*. Change the setting to the Casbah of Algiers, that vertiginous maze of terraces stepping down to the sea, and you have the mood of the strange and blazing story that d'Ashelbé has woven around "le Moko," a fellow from Languedoc, in Provence, who drifted here to escape the police.

This teeming Berber native quarter of sad-faced children and lacquered whores, black, yellow, white, and brown, refuge of the hunted, the outcast, backwash of the whole world, human flotsam cast up from the Mediterranean onto this pile of barbarous steps, the names of whose streets are notorious and from the depths of whose hovels and dim-lighted cafés spirals thin music, strange cries, the babel of a thousand tongues; an ant-heap raucous and clamorous under the hot African sun by day; a labyrinth, mysterious and bewitching, under a phosphorescent moon by night. Over all the cry from the muezzin, "*Allah . . . il Allah . . . Mohammed rassoul Allah. . . .!*"

Pleasure and crime . . . for two years Pépé has made the Casbah his hideout. And when a girl from the outside world comes, and they reminisce about Paris, which is in the blood of both of them, the two years of the Casbah turn to ashes in Pépé's mouth—the honeyed kisses of his native mistress, and those of "the three hundred widows who would mourn at his funeral." "Patience cannot abide in the heart of a lover," says an old Arab proverb. And so when Pépé realizes that he is in love with this girl, he announces to his friends, who have already begun to betray him, that he will go down from the Casbah and risk the police drag-net lying in wait for him, to return with her to Paris. But another loved him, too, Inès, the Algerienne, and she could not bear Pépé in the arms of the white woman. And so if she cannot have him, no one else will have him—only the police, to whom Pépé pleads, "I can't slip away now. Let me look at the boat that is taking her away. I would like to see it leaving." Silently, his eyes scream her name as he watches through the iron grill of the dock-gate. "Gaby!" A long, mournful blast from the departing liner drowns out his last despairing cry. "Forgive me, Pépé!" sobs the other one, to whom love was strong as death.

In Pépé's head, as in the head of a *kif*-smoker, "little birds are breaking dry sticks. . . ."

February, 1941

The Last Will of Dr. Mabuse (Germany, 1932) Nero Film. Original scenario by Thea von Harbou and Fritz Lang. Directed by Fritz Lang. Photography: Fritz Arno Wagner. Design: Karl Vollbrecht, Emil Hasler. With Rudolph Klein-Rogge, Otto Wernicke, Gustav Diesel, Oscar Beregi. Vera Liessem, Camilla Spira, Karl Meixner, Theo Lingen (original German version).

THE LAST WILL OF DR. MABUSE

In every age, violence has been used by gangsters and demagogues to terrorize a mass of people. Thus was power attained by Attila and Tamerlane, by sultans and czars, medieval robber barons and and "secret societies" like the Inquisition in Spain, the Ku Klux Klan here, the Mafia in Sicily, the Black Dragon in Japan, and, in our own time, Nazism in Germany.

This film was made as an allegory, to show Hitler's processes of terrorism. Slogans and doctrines of the Third Reich have been put into the mouths of criminals in the film. Thus the director hoped to expose the masked Nazi theory of the necessity to deliberately destroy everything which is precious to a people so that they would lose all faith in the institutions and ideals of the State. Then, when everything collapsed and they were thrown into utter despair, they would try to find help in the "new order."

The distorted world in which the madman in *The Cabinet of Dr. Caligari* lived, revealed to us through the broken planes and surfaces of that film's decor, finds its direct descent in the unreality of the glass room and the superimposition of distorted lines on Hofmeister's asylum-cubicle in *The Last Will of Dr. Mabuse*. Both, in essence, are mystery films—not till the end of *Caligari*

The Last Will of Dr. Mabuse 85

did we know that this was a tale told by a madman; not till the end of *Dr. Mabuse* do we know that this is a tale of two madmen. But whereas the deranged narrator in *Caligari* rationalizes his plight, transmuting the saintly Dr. Caligari into a monster, Prof. Baum, in *Mabuse*, rationalizes an avowed madman, transmuting the monstrous Dr. Mabuse into a saint. This odd twist to *Mabuse* has its psychiatric aspect in the allegorical nature of the story as set forth by Fritz Lang in his screen foreword. The premise of *Mabuse* i.e., the "hypnotic" influence that one brain can exert upon another, is also the theme of the recently published *Donovan's Brain* by Curt Siodmak.

Lang is the High Priest of the psychological film. From the megalomaniacal Dr. ("I am the State!") Mabuse in his early film, *Mabuse, the Gambler,* through the coldly psychotic master-criminal, Haighi, in *Spies,* the nymphomaniacal robot woman and her demented creator, Rotwang, in *Metropolis;* the lust-murderer in *M;* the blood-lust of a mob in *Fury*; and now the paranoiac Prof. Baum in *The Last Will of Dr. Mabuse,* Fritz Lang has dissected several of the most important aberrations that sometimes afflict the human mind. He has an uncanny genius for invoking terror out of the simplest things, as for instance, a child's balloon caught in high tension wires (*M*) or the wheezing drone of a printing press (*Mabuse*). The lawless in his films are either psychopathic or anarchistic and it is a logical development of his unique art that his most recent film, *Hangmen Also Die,* concerns itself with the Nazi arch-criminal, Heydrich.

The Last Will of Dr. Mabuse was made by Lang as a warning and a prophecy—out of the Mabuses come the Heydrichs, Himmlers, and Hitlers.

March, 1943

A FAREWELL TO FLAHERTY

And all I ask is a merry yarn from a laughing fellow rover,
And quiet sleep and a sweet dream when the long trick's over.
JOHN MASEFIELD: *Sea Fever*

It was to be a "going away" party.
In a week, or a little more, Robert Flaherty was to start

"He was only an eye," said Cézanne of Monet, "but what an eye!" Flaherty at the viewer of Leacock's camera during the shooting of *Louisiana Story*, framing the composition of a shot.

around the world by air with a battery of new, three-dimensional color cameras, to film and record the sights and sounds of the earth. It was to be a veritable "film symphony" of the world.

The sponsor was Mike Todd, the theatrical producer. He had invested in a new film process and Flaherty was to try it out, full scale. Walter Ruttmann's *Melody of the World*, made for the old Hamburg-America Line, was the only precedent for what Flaherty intended.

But what the creator of *Nanook* and *Moana of the South Seas*, the director with the most gracious camera-eye of them all, would do with such an opportunity, was sure to be unprecedented, and this project had been the film world's most exciting news of the year. *Louisiana Story* had proved, were proof still needed, that the master poet of the camera for thirty years, the Herman Melville of the lens, had not lost the touch that had enthralled two generations.

Flaherty was in high spirits that night. When I arrived, escorting a dark-eyed damsel with whom he was then working on another project, he threw his arms around her and gave her a hearty kiss. Releasing her from his bearlike grip (he was, of course, enormous), he looked at me and said laughingly: "Don't tell me I have a rival—already!" Then he noticed we had no drinks and galumphed off to tell the waiter.

The setting was the Coffee House, his favorite retreat in New York, an unbelievably quiet nook just off Times Square.

In a few moments we were all seated at a large round table (Flaherty was never happier than when playing host). There was his daughter Monica and her scholarly looking husband; a Russian girl who resembled a character in a novel by Claude Anet; the effervescent wife of a celebrated radio commentator and her daughter; a French writer; and half-a-dozen others. Beaming at Monica, the lucky possessor of a lovely English-Irish complexion, Flaherty asked proudly: "Isn't she pretty?"

At first of course, the talk was of the forthcoming journey. Everyone wanted to know about the new cameras—were they *really* three-dimensional, etc? Flaherty did his best to explain, but his heart wasn't in it. "Oh, it's a lot of technical stuff . . . you can only show the picture in one theater at a time . . . costs too much to equip all theaters with the special screens and so forth that's needed . . . or something like that." Anyway, they were going ahead, undaunted, and make the picture. The wine flowed freely.

"You know why I'm *really* going?" Flaherty suddenly interjected, and shook with laughter at what he was about to say. "When we stop off in Arabia I'm going to get myself lost in one of those harems and they're not going to find me for two weeks!" Daughter Monica laughed at the grotesquerie of her father's boast.

"Anthropological research?" I suggested.

"That's it!" Flaherty cried, amid new peals of merriment, "Anthropological research! No second hand observation for me!"

Someone got the hiccups from laughing.

By the time dessert and coffee were passed around so were risqué stories. The radio commentator's wife told some hilarious ones, and her daughter contributed two or three of the demure kind. One of them reminded Flaherty of a couple *he* knew, and these were the most innocent, the most fragile and evanescent, risqué stories I had ever heard. How like his character they were! I felt that I had always known that were Flaherty to tell a risqué story, it would be *just* like the ones he told that night. I remembered this feeling when, some time later, I came across Winsten's observation in the New York *Post* that of all the people he had ever met, Flaherty was the only one who looked like a saint.

Then the dark-eyed damsel thought the atmosphere ready for her Boccaccio style. Emboldened by her virtuoso performance, I tried to think of some choice ones, but could remember only the savagely bitter one told by Eisenstein about the two men shipwrecked on a desert isle. Since I haven't ever been able to tell that while sober, I dismissed it from my mind. Need I add that my incredulous ears soon heard, over the table's hub-bub, the very same story, being told by a man of whose presence I had not until then been aware?

Flaherty hospitably laughed at them all. But after the story I had refrained from telling was told, Flaherty switched the flow back to another of his sun-flecked idylls, the kind that make you smile inside before you smile outside. He always told them as though they were personal experiences—until the tagline. Then my dark-eyed damsel let go with with her bilingual one of the Italian tourist-guide who misunderstood the reason the American tourist wanted to see the Queen or the Pope.

The eye of Flaherty... the Samoan maiden, Fa'angase. "Here," said Henry Adams of the South Seas, "is rustic Greece of the Golden Age, still alive." "Critical jingling sounds tinny before the simple languid beauty of *Moana*," wrote Ted Shane in *The New Yorker*. *Moana* (1926).

"Let's all go over to Monica's!" said Flaherty. We piled into several cars and headed east for Beekman Place, where Monica and her husband have an apartment overlooking the East River. Upon arrival everyone had their second wind, and the stories started anew, at least in my corner. We had divided into small groups, and each had its own subdued interests. Flaherty went from one to the other, a fine, jolly man, as young in heart as the youngest.

How often I had marveled at the zest of this man of sixty-eight, who played Corelli and Mozart on the violin for relaxation, who used to lumber up the stairs of Lopert Films to ask about *Louisiana Story*, which they were distributing. "How're we doing?" he would ask, and then, invariably, to me: "Come on, let's have a drink!" Or dinner. (Finnan-haddie was one of his favorite dishes, but he would eat or drink anything edible or drinkable.)

He was usually in a contemplative mood when we were alone, and sometimes spoke wistfully of films he had wanted to make in Japan and China, and of one based upon the medieval festival staged each year in Siena. How often he had said, when reminiscing about the many difficulties he had encountered in trying to achieve his ideal in films: "Film is the longest distance between two points."

I then told him that once, when Pabst complained that if he hadn't been so choosey about the scripts offered him, he could have directed many more than twenty films in some twenty-five years, I had remonstrated that Flaherty had made only six films in thirty years, and that Pabst had shot back: "But what films!"

It was getting late. Flaherty suddenly begged to be excused and announced he was going home.

In the doorway he paused, glanced at each of us in turn, and smiled a collective farewell. We and he had exchanged the "merry yarns of laughing fellow rovers." May he find "quiet sleep and a sweet dream" now that the long trick's over.

October, 1951

A VISIT WITH HANS RICHTER

I visited Richter recently in his walk-up studio-apartment on East Sixtieth street. The steep climb winded me and I asked him why artists have to live in eagle's nests. Is it because Parnassus and Olympus were so lofty? He laughed. "Certainly not! If you were on Mount Everest you would hardly be any closer to the stars than if you were in the Carlsbad Caverns. Is the coffee too strong? Wait, I'll make some more."

While he was at it I scanned the paintings by him that cover his walls. They had the logic of mathematical problems, a graceful and patrician balance of design. Their coloring was vivid and sunny—each canvas seemed, in the surety with which it was blocked out, like an apothegm.

I thought of his films, blocked out like his canvases, in "cinematic weights and measures," especially the delicately balanced *Film Study* (1926), the dream-like fluidity of which was interrupted rhythmically with percussive shocks—the film's own "heartbeats." And his *Everything Turns!* (1929), a satirical cross-cut of carnival life, all of which was like watching an acrobat balancing precariously atop a column of swaying chairs. In his films, as in his painting, there was a preoccupation with balance, an extension in art of his logician's mind, of his penchant for an ordered philosophy of life in which there are no surprises, and everything ends with *quod erat demonstrandum.* I could not help thinking that he was a kind of solitary.

"What made you turn from painting to film?" I asked, when he brought the coffee.

"The research Eggeling and I did made me aware of dynamic problems that couldn't be solved on canvas," he replied. "If there had not been film, I would doubtless have been satisfied to extend the scope of scrolls, which are a kind of extension of canvas. Or maybe I would have invented the film—who knows?" This last with a smile, as he added:

"If an Egyptian Pharaoh could think of having figures

painted on the columns of his palace in a progression of postures, so that, when racing by in his chariot, he could watch a 'moving picture,' I might have come up with some such idea, too. At the risk of repeating myself: who knows?"

Then:

"Film was not invented for the purpose of helping the painter solve dynamic problems, however. But film does serve the artist in this respect.

"In the cinema of today the place of the experimental film—I hope that phrase will soon be supplanted by 'film poetry'—is exactly the place occupied by poetry in literature. You ask what is the value of the experimental film today and what has been its influence on the so-called commercial film. To a wrong question you cannot get a right answer. The value of the experimental film isn't in its influence or lack of influence on the commercial film. It exists for its own sake, as poetry does. That doesn't mean that commercial films cannot have poetry—very often they do. A poet like Cocteau has proved it. I'm not sure whether his *Orpheus* is purely commercial or purely poetic. I think it wavers between the two, but his earlier *Blood of a Poet* is pure poetry. No doubt about it."

At this point I asked who, of present-day American experimenters, he admires most. "The Whitney brothers and Fischinger," he said. "They are not speculators. Also Francis Lee, McLaren, Len Lye and Stauffacher." He went on to say that there were some who misused the "sensations so easily obtainable in the medium of the experimental film," and that surrealism not infrequently was "a blanket excuse for the exhibition of a menu of personal inhibitions."

And the future?

"The experimental film will have as definite and recognized a place in the future as the documentary film has today."

I rose to leave.

"Anyway," he added, "I've done exactly what I wanted to do." Wherewith he brought out a bottle of brandy and we had a nightcap.

"We're all lineal descendants of Georges Méliès," Richter said as I again got up to go.

"He was the first to know what the cinema was for—not because he invented the trick film, but because he instinctively knew what the main esthetic of the film is. Wait, I'll walk with you a bit."

"Well," I said at the top of the stairway, "going down will be easier than coming up."

"Isn't that always the case?" he smiled. "In everything?"

When we came out into the cold night air, I made the usual reference to the brass monkey.

"You think *this* is cold?" he laughed. "You should walk across Red Square in Moscow on a frosty January night. An icy wind that probably started somewhere in the Urals cuts your face. You can hardly breathe!"

We walked westward toward Central Park. Richter was busy with the great theme of his life. "It's still too early to talk of a tradition," he said. "This year is but the thirtieth anniversary of a movement in an art that is itself only thirty-five years old."

He began to speak of his next project. He wanted to tell the old Greek legend of the Minotaur in terms of today. "Each of us is in a labyrinth, in which he fights a Minotaur of his own," he said. "The thread that led Theseus out of the labyrinth also bound him to Ariadne. Amid the terrors of the labyrinth, of the unknown, this thread is a fragile thing, but it's all we have."

He stopped, as though what he had just said was his ultimate declaration, as though there was nothing more to say. "I'll turn back now," he murmured.

I thought of some of his other unrealized projects, of his modernized *Candide* (1934), in which Candide's optimism, set against the onrushing tide of barbarism in Europe, seemed less excusable than ever. I thought of his thirty years' unswerving fidelity to an ideal. He was, indeed, a solitary of the cinema.

I looked back at him slowly wending his way homeward, his tall silhouette a deeper shadow in the night. Then, like an abstract pattern in one of his films, it vanished.

December, 1951

"Semba was 19, with the beard of a man and the brain of a grasshopper. He was next in line for Keiko's favors. . . . Keiko found a parachute, which meant elegance for us instead of clothes made of tree-bark. . . . Semba, our friend the lady-killer, found a ring, the easy way to a woman's heart." From Sternberg's narration for *The Saga of Anatahan* (1953).

The Saga of Anatahan (Japan, 1953) Scenario and narration by Josef von Sternberg from a book by Michiro Maruyama. Narration spoken by Von Sternberg. Photographed and directed by Von Sternberg. Design: Kono. Music by Akira Ifukube. Starring Akemi Negishi.

VON STERNBERG FILMS THE ANATAHAN STORY

In a man-made jungle cluttered with electric cables and junction boxes, in the ancient Japanese capital of Kyoto, Josef von Sternberg is currently filming the celebrated Anatahan story, a weird footnote to the last war. Far from Hollywood, the director of *The Blue Angel, Morocco,* and *Shanghai Express,* among others, has converted a large industrial exhibition hall in Kyoto's Okazaki Park into a studio. Here a South Sea island jungle has been built, complete with ferns, palms, underbrush, thatched huts and a derelict boat. This will be Anatahan, a verdant dot among the Marianas in the South Pacific, where thirty Japanese men and a single woman held out for several years after Japan's surrender in the last war, refusing to believe in Japan's defeat, and putting up a vain resistance against American occupying forces. To make things that much tougher for themselves, the men fought over the lone woman and several were killed in these frequent skirmishes.

This item, reported in *The New York Times* last year, inspired the film but, contrary to expectations, the Von Sternberg version of the Anatahan incident will be completely independent of the actual occurrences on the island.

"The story as told by the survivors is a sordid one, and I am not interested in it," the director declared. "I am creating, instead, a sympathetic picture of those people." The film, which is being made for the international market, will be an "ambassador for Japan," according to Von Sternberg.

"We hope to open the eyes of the world to the great wealth of art in Japan," he remarked. "What is known publicly about the subject is not in my mind. In fact, I would have been pleased if the subject was not known to the world." And, indeed, when the real heroine of Anatahan was in Tokyo, the director said he had little interest in meeting her, because he was *not* going to produce Kazuko Hika's biographical incidents, but an artistic film *based* on this episode.

For his screen heroine, the discoverer of Marlene Dietrich found a nineteen-year-old dancer, Akemi Negishi, an unbilled member of the Nichigeki Dancing Team. Interviewed during a recess in her act, Miss Negishi engagingly told reporters, "I don't understand why Mr. von Sternberg picked *me* for the part."

Not a single shot will be filmed in the actual locale. There will not even be any process shots by which actual backgrounds are "grafted" on to the foreground action. The entire development of the story will be photographed in the improvised studio jungle set. According to Von Sternberg, there is no need to shoot films in their actual locales—contrary to much current Hollywood practice. Because, he states, film reality and actual reality are fundamentally different. "Shooting at the actual locale does not necessarily result in an artistic production. The artist's primary attitude is to understand the *essence* of the reality he seeks."

To the question of production cost, the director caustically replied, "What difference does it make how much it costs? Certainly it won't be more than it gets back."

Asked to comment on Japanese films, he said, "I did not

"Next in line was the ex-cook of the *Heiske Maru*—Yoshiri. He aspired to Keiko—the goal of his ambitions was not very lofty. We are driven by forces about which we know nothing."* The director discusses the scene with Jun Fujikawa (Yoshiri) through an interpreter, as Akemi Negishi (Keiko) looks on. *The Saga of Anatahan.*

*From Sternberg's narration for *The Saga of Anatahan*, written and spoken by the director. While the attitudes are always his own, the director speaks the role as one of the survivors, Michiro Maruyama, from whose account of this incident the film derived.

come here as a teacher but as a student. It would be awkward, indeed, if I surrendered my rôle of movie director for that of a movie critic."

The language problem is a formidable one. "I have a hundred Japanese working for me and it's not easy to keep them well informed and organized." For this reason, the director has devised two methods to overcome the language barrier: (1) a unique diagram showing all characters and their interrelationships by way of color lines in each sequence, and (2) a set of about thirty drawings to show each sequence pictorially.

Other innovations include the mounting of a Mitchell camera (the only American piece of equipment on the set) on a ten-foot-high cylinder in the fashion of an X-ray camera, which can be moved up and down and clamped at any height. This is said to be far more desirable than the conventional tripod mounting because it enables quicker changes of camera levels.

The chief problem remains a language one, not a technical one. The latter is easily enough mastered by a man who could re-create in California a North African desert outpost so well that the Pasha of Marrakech refused to believe that *Morocco* was not actually filmed there. Since few in the cast of *Anatahan* understand English, everything the American director says must be translated on the spot. Hence, invariably 10 or fifteen seconds, if not more, elapses before an actor comes to a halt after Von Sternberg shouts, "*Hold it!*" This can get very enervating after a while. "The language barrier is tremendous," sighs the director. "The strain is worse than physical—it's *all* mental."

Anatahan, as the film will probably be called, is an enterprise of Daiwa Productions, represented by Yoshio Osawa, a Kyoto financier and one-time president of the Toho Film Company, Nagamasa Kawakita, president of Towa Films, Inc., and Von Sternberg, who invests his services.

It is not Von Sternberg's first visit to Japan. He was there some sixteen years ago, during a world tour—promising his many admirers (his films are very popular there) that he would come back some day to make a film.

He is supremely confident of his first film in Japan. In a recent letter to the writer he said, "It is shaping up beautifully... I intend to set a standard of visual excellence with this picture." As an indication of what can be expected from the director who has already set standards of visual excellence in his past work, notably *Docks of New York, Shanghai Express, The Scarlet Empress* and *The Devil is a Woman,* it is most revealing that, in the above quoted passage from his letter, he crossed out the typed word *"picture"* and wrote *"film."* There is a difference. In that difference lies the history of the art of the motion pictures.

February, 1953

Faust (Germany, 1926) (Silent) UFA production of Erich Pommer. Scenario by Hans Kyser, after Marlowe, Goethe, and old Germanic legends. Original subtitles by Gerhart Hauptmann. Directed by F. W. Murnau. Photography: Carl Hoffmann. Design: Robert Herlth, Walter Roehrig. With Gösta Ekman, Emil Jannings, Camilla Horn, Yvette Guilbert, Wilhelm Dieterle.

FAUST

All things corruptible
Are but a parable;
Earth's insufficiency
Here finds fulfillment;
Here the ineffable
Wins life through love;
Eternal Womanhood
Draws us above.
—GOETHE: *Faust*

Mendelssohn writing his music for *A Midsummer Night's Dream* at seventeen, or Eisenstein directing *Potemkin* at twenty-six (let us not even speak of Keats, Raphael, Mozart, and such), do not make any the less incredible the fashioning by Murnau, at

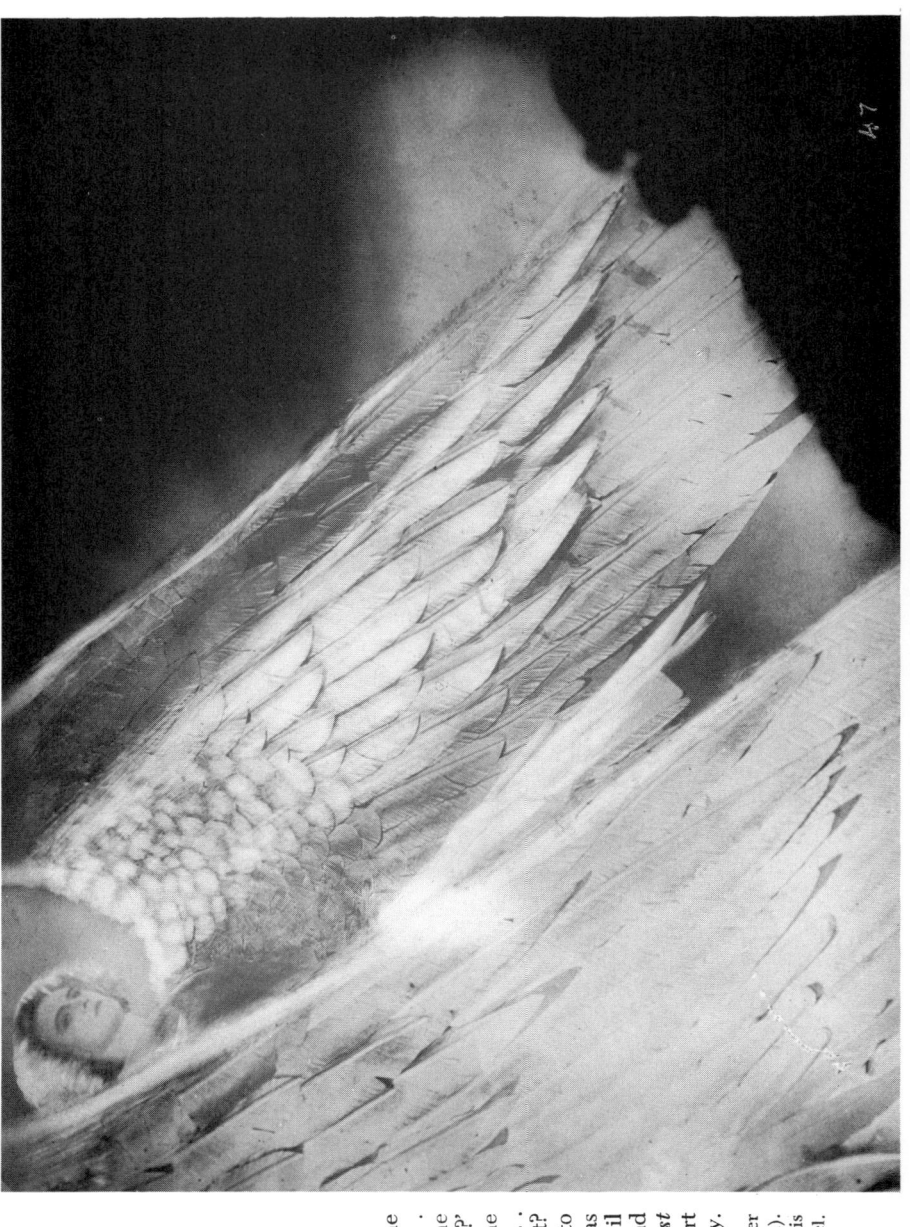

Painting with light, using the screen as a vast fresco. . . . *"Prologue in Heaven."* The Lord: 'Do you know Faust?' Satan: 'The doctor?' The Lord: 'Aye, my servant.' . . . Satan: 'What will you bet? You will lose him yet to me.'"* Werner Fütterer as St. Michael addressing Emil Jannings as Satan (and Mephisto) in Murnau's *Faust* (1926), derived from Part One of Goethe's tragedy.

*Goethe, *Faust* (Walter Kaufmann translation). In the film, the Lord is represented by St. Michael.

Murnau beats Albrecht Dürer at his own game. The Four Horsemen of the Apocalypse (Rev. 6: 1–8)—War, Famine, Disease, Death—a stunning conceit of the director, as it is not to be found in the Prologue to the Goethe drama. From Murnau's *Faust*.

Murnau's lovers in *Faust*— Camilla Horn as Gretchen and Gösta Ekman as the young Faust.

thirty-seven, of this visual poem which in 1926, the year of its release, was called the "most beautiful film ever made." Almost three decades later the judgment still stands. The best passages in *Siegfried, Earth, The General Line, The Passion of Joan of Arc, The End of Saint Petersburg, Moana,* and others of that hallowed company, equal, perhaps, even the best of *Faust*—and, certainly, every frame of Murnau's earlier *The Last Laugh* is exquisitely composed—but never before or since was there such a prodigy of "best passages," nor, for that matter, such an exultant flight of the cinema spirit. Alongside *Faust,* even the masterworks named, even *Potemkin* and the art of Chaplin, yes, even *The Last Laugh* and *Moana,* are "literary works," polemics, semi-documentaries, or pantomimic tours de force in comparison, for all their own flights of the cinema spirit which were, indeed, considerable.

What Murnau achieved in *Faust* is without parallel on the screen. It was as if he undertook to paint a vast fresco with light and shadows. His canvas was the whole of the medieval world—his brush was the camera lens, hovering over the innocent young lovers, as Mephisto cynically watches their gambols in the garden; darting up and down the twisted streets of the old town in the night as Mephisto, after he has slain Valentine, cries out "Murder!"; soaring over the earth as Mephisto takes Faust on a journey to show him the ways of the world during which flight kingdoms fall, orgiastic rites are performed, people are born, live, and die; love is an eternal perfumed garden of erotic delight; love is a night with the ravishing Bianca, Duchess of Parma, during the festivities of her wedding night, when Mephisto makes it possible for Faust to enjoy "le droit de seigneur" in a silken alcove surmounting the many-terraced structure, which unfolds upon a riot of dancing maidens, of streaming waters and gleaming fires, of snow-white elephants bearing bridal gifts, gigantic and bejeweled. . . . Thus is the venerable scholar, Faust, rejuvenated through his pact with the devil, swept beyond the horizon of his unlived youth. Here I could do no better than did Katherine Zimmerman, a critic of the period whose pulse beat with that of the film when she described:

> Jaded with wickedness and prodigality, we see Faust turn to memories of his rural home where sloping rooftops and slanting stretches of wall merge in fantastic angles, and

where the shy, flowerlike beauty of Marguerite is supreme. And here Murnau has forged into the snatched moments of true love's romance a sly and mocking parallel of amatory indiscretion between Aunt Martha and the Devil. It is a gay unstudied touch that stays for a light moment the plunge into the pangs of hell. The shame of Marguerite and the remorse of Faust soar from the quivering depths into a plane of beauty that leaves all beauty pain. The Prince of Darkness shadows sable wings to claim his wager, when through the tremulous mists true love rains forth her beams and Satan is overpowered.

And what of the incandescent prologue in Heaven in which Satan wagers the Archangel that he will win the soul of Faust? What of the cathedral scene, which is the quintessence of the Gothic spirit? What of the Brueghel-like scenes of the village fair? The sulphurous and scorching scenes of the plague that are out of the Book of Doomsday? Or the peripatetic Mephisto slyly mocking the aged scholar, Faust, doffing his cap to him in "homage." Who, indeed, is the "cher Maître" here? What of such an image as Satan's monster wings closing like a great thunder cloud over the town? And the exquisite moment, for the briefest moment it is, as it should be, of the discovery by Marguerite's mother of her daughter's shame? And the excruciating catharsis, Marguerite's burning at the stake by the outraged townsfolk, what paroxysm is this as the thistles of flame join suddenly to make the word "Love"—an ending so harrowing and of such beauty that the emotional havoc wrought by the whole presentation is made complete.

In this lay the uniqueness of *Faust*—that, while superficially it might be called "paintings in motion" (first mentioned by Munsterberg and Bloem) it transcended that dubious appellation by being the purest and truest creation in a medium all its own— cinema, which does not need painting as a source of inspiration, though it follows the same rules of balance and design. For Murnau's film was primarily a pictorial *Faust,* not the lyrical one of Marlowe or the philosophical one of Goethe, and it owed as much to old German legends lost in the mists of antiquity as did Lang's *Siegfried,* which is the only film to which it can be compared. It was the purpose of both *Siegfried* and *Faust* to overwhelm the spectator with the pictorial splendor of their images in which the most vivid and eloquent metaphors that words could convey found their equally expressive transmutations on the screen. That both achieved lyricism, too, is a tribute to the ecstasy with which they were made, in which every movement, every line, plane or surface, every countenance, tree or cloud, stone, house or wall, every gesture, grouping, reaction, was shaped to fit poetically and dramatically in the whole context as if a film were not composed of many thousands of separate images but of one single image. Here we are back to our alliteration of *Faust* undertaken by Murnau as if it were a great fresco painted with lights and shadows.

There were criticisms of *Faust* at the time, nonetheless, minor carping criticisms, as if the arrogance of Murnau in presenting what seemed to be a near-perfect work of art was not to be countenanced. Perfection was not for mortals to achieve; that was something reserved for the gods. (The "only-God-can-make-a-tree" school.) They said it was "almost too beautiful. . . . One becomes a bit cloyed and longs for an ugly, strong, masculine composition." (John S. Cohen, Jr. in the New York *Sun*.) And another: "If the gorgeous, artificial prettiness of *Faust* palls after five-and-a-half reels, it is because mankind cannot bear artificial beauty for a long period." It was accused of lacking vitality and vigor. In some esoteric quarters it was attacked as "tawdry and bombastic."

Be that as it may, two films of the size and opulence of *Faust* and *Metropolis*, both produced by UFA in a single year, 1926, were enough to deplete the cash reserves of that great German film trust, and by December of that year, UFA was on the financial rocks, on the verge of bankruptcy. It had spent the whole of the $4,000,000 borrowed from Paramount and Metro-Goldwyn-Mayer only a year before to reorganize its production and distribution facilities in an international merger known as Par-Ufa-Met, by which the two American film trusts were to exchange product and distribution facilities with the German company. Only $16,600 remained in Ufa's treasury. The *Deutsche Zeitung* interpreted Ufa's difficulties as the death of the German film industry and a corresponding triumph for American motion picture producers. (Ufa itself was part of the Dawes Plan, being responsible for 5 percent interest on approximately $357,000 worth of Dawes industrial debentures as a part of Germany's post-World War I reparation annuity.)

Erich Pommer, production head of Ufa, was naturally bitter when Murnau decided not to wait to see whether Ufa would weather its financial storm and, with a print of the completed *Faust* in his luggage, set forth for America and Hollywood. There, at the MGM studios in Culver City, he cut and edited the film for its American premiere, since MGM had already selected *Faust* as one of its "quota" releases here. He accused Murnau of ingratitude and all the rest, leaving Ufa in the lurch, just when they needed him most, etc. But by this time, Murnau was far more than a director of notable German films, he was a world figure, internationally acknowledged as one of the screen's greatest artists, one who would gladly be given carte blanche by any studio in the world to make whatever kind of film he chose. Who could resist such an offer? And what more logical place to go than to "the golden land"—America, which is to say, Hollywood? Already the tide of emigrés to Hollywood was in flux—Lubitsch, Dupont, Jannings, Pola Negri, Lothar Mendes, Conrad Veidt, Camilla Horn, etc. So, while Ufa was being reorganized by reducing its capitalization and floating a new loan among its stockholders, Lang formed his own film company, Fritz Lang Film G.M.B.H., for which he made *Spione* and *Frau im Mond*. In Hollywood, Murnau made a deal with Fox to do *Sunrise*, completed the following year. In 1928, he did a second film for Fox, *Four Devils*, and in 1929 a third, *Our Daily Bread*. Neither of the latter two pleased either Murnau or the public and there was so much studio interference in his production of the last that the director finally decided to call it quits. For two years he was inactive until, in 1931, he and Flaherty, also a victim of studio interference, decided to pool their resources, buy a yacht, sail around the world, making pictures together. The two supreme poets of the screen—what a beautiful dream! "Murnau-Flaherty Productions"! Their first stop was the Polynesian islands where, in Tahiti and Bora-Bora, they made the now memorable *Tabu*. More Murnau than Flaherty, *Tabu* went on to become a world success but Murnau did not live to enjoy it. Shortly after his return to Hollywood, he was killed in an automobile accident. The beautiful dream of Murnau and Flaherty was over. The yacht, *Bali*, on which the two had sailed, was wrangled over by lawyers, appraisers, auctioneers, in the settlement of the Murnau estate.

What presentiment was there in the early work of Murnau, beyond a rather better than average film talent, to foreshadow the supreme artist who was to make *Faust?* He began his film career as director in 1919 but it was not till 1922 that he produced his first major work, *Nosferatu.* Where is the bridge between this macabre work and the rhapsodic *The Last Laugh,* that came three years later? Save in a few furtive experiments by Leopold Jessner (*Backstairs*) and Lupu Pick (*New Year's Eve* and *Shattered*), there were no indications that a cleansing rain was to wash away a decade's accumulation of hit-or-miss film making (with several obvious exceptions, of course). The advent of *The Last Laugh* was like Peter the Great opening the windows of his palace to let the "fresh air of Western Europe in and blow away the centuries' accumulation of asphyxiating ideas of the old order in Russia." This film, with its unbroken sheet of glistening photography from beginning to end, uninterrupted by a single title, had, with *Greed, Variety,* and *Potemkin,* an enormous influence on film making throughout the world. The following year came *Tartuffe,* and the year after that, *Faust.*

What remains? Only this, that my appraisal of *Faust* has been made on the basis of the complete version, of a print struck directly from the original negative, retaining the full spectrum of subtle gradations of this miracle of black and white photography, from the frostiest of whites to the silkiest and most velvety of blacks, its original titles by Gerhart Hauptmann, and its original silent projection speed. (And no Gounod in the music score, please!) For anything less than that, this essay does not apply. However, realizing the problems faced by a film society in 1955 attempting to duplicate as much as possible that old magic which was ours who saw *Faust* when it first appeared in all its pristine glory in 1926, this note may have a kind of historic interest.

Hell-scarred, like the visage of Dante, *Faust,* withal, is full of raffish humor in the vivacious playing of Jannings and Yvette Guilbert. Nor was Dante's song to Beatrice more seraphic than Murnau's to Marguerite in the person of Camilla Horn. All this was made fluid and malleable in the creative imagination of the quintet of incomparable artists who worked as one in fashioning this true "poem in pictures" as the film modestly calls itself. When today we are enthralled with the beauty of Castellani's *Romeo and Juliet* and the Japanese *Gate of Hell,* as much for their use of color as for the delicacy of their compositions, let us not forget what was once achieved more than a quarter of a century ago, in black and white, in the witchery of Carl Hoffmann's photography, the apocalyptic visions of Murnau, in *Faust.*

January, 1955

Animal Farm (England, 1954) Scenario by Lothar Wolff, Borden Mace, Philip Stapp, John Halas, Joy Batchelor, from George Orwell's allegorical novel. Directed and animated by John Halas and Joy Batchelor. Photography: S. G. Griffiths. Music: M. Serkes. A Louis De Rochemont production.

ANIMAL FARM

A Socratic Dialogue:

In truth, I do not understand your objection to the drama that was performed in the forum today. You say it is against Sparta, yet do they not perform similar dramas against us?

Certainly, or so I am told. At least, I have not seen them. Let us suppose they do. That does not change my feeling toward it.

Why not?

Because I object to it on grounds that have nothing to do with whether they do or do not issue polemics against us. These are on the grounds of esthetics and ethics. A breach of the former would be enough. Compounded with a breach of the latter, it becomes insupportable.

What is the esthetic breach?

The drama pretends to be a fable, but it is fable without a moral; it is a fable, or allegory, in which human actions are presented in the guise of animal actions. But how can this convince any intelligent person who knows that animals don't act that way? Aesop was far cleverer. Granting them the power of speech, all the literary license Aesop needed, his animals act as animals. And it is acting a way not contrary to their nature that they make their valid points to us. Thus, the tales of the dog in the manger, or the fox and the crow, the fox and the stork, the fox and the grapes, and all the rest of them, are as sharply observed from the standpoint of the animals as from that of human beings. Thus, being credible in their motivations, they are valid in their morals. What has been gained by disguising human characters as animals in the drama in question, however? Nothing but an over-simplification into one facet of an idea that has many facets. Is this a gain or a loss? Are we children who cannot be trusted with the whole truth, with all the facets? If Sparta does the same thing, it is wrong, too, but that doesn't make us right in also doing it.

I'm afraid your esthetic grounds are beginning to interlock with your ethical grounds.

You see? How can you avoid it? The ethical grows out of the esthetic. A bad craftsman will not fashion a vase of noble symmetry, no matter how good are his intentions. Nor will a poet, whose alliteration is false, fashion a valid drama, also for all his good intentions.

Then you do not object to his intentions—that is a great deal.

In itself it is nothing. I mistrust so-called "good intentions." History is the chronology of tyrants who have claimed for themselves "good intentions."

That goes for Sparta, too.

Yes, it goes for Sparta, too. I would almost say that to govern at all is to be unjust. The only purpose for which power can be rightfully exercised over any member of a civilized community against his will is to prevent harm to others. His own good, either physical or moral, is not a sufficient warrant. Alas, it is, perhaps, only too true that Sparta has adopted the dictum of the tyrant— *"Oderint dum metuant!"*—"Let them hate me, if only they fear me!" You see, I am cognizant of the failings of Sparta, and, above all, of the salutary dream of a "better society" that was perverted by the new masters, but the anti-Sparta drama we witnessed told us nothing we did not already know. Facile slogans are as dangerous for us as they were for Sparta. Demagogues with "good intentions" are similarly as dangerous for us as they were for Sparta. Pigs are pigs, no matter what their nationality is. The psychology of a pig makes him act the way he does. Have the Athenians no pigs? Now that's the heart of the matter. An allegory which would expose all pigs—whatever their nationality—and for all time, that would have a meaning for us. But if I were to compose a drama about Spartacus and state that after he led the revolt of slaves against their cruel Roman masters he was succeeded by one of the freed slaves who became a tyrant just as cruel as the old masters, what would I prove with that? That revolts are bad and never accomplish anything? Do not we Athenians owe our existence as a nation to a revolt? And were the circumstances not much the same? The drama we witnessed even concludes on the verge of another revolt. Revolt is the *catharsis* of that work. "Progress is the result of change," one might say. "Eternal change, so long as each change is a step forward." Why are you smiling?

Forgive me, but now you are arguing on my side.

Am I? I was not aware of it. You cannot confuse me with your sophistry, my friend. Besides, I do not necessarily wish to win a debater's victory over you, but to clear the atmosphere of false and irrelevant definitions. Only the broadest vision can make this possible. Such a vision, for example, as our teacher, Socrates, has expounded with such lucidity, with such charity, I might add, at the Academy or the Lyceum, namely, that men aim at the good, that no man voluntarily chooses evil. To do evil or to choose evil is a matter of lack of insight. The central virtue, therefore, turns out to be knowledge. Health, wealth, beauty, all these are good insofar as they are well used. And a good use of the goods of life demands knowledge of their appropriate enjoyment. "If we knew how to convert stones into gold," said Euthydemus, "they would be of no use to us unless we also knew how to use the gold." Similarly, it is not enough, as the drama we are discussing reasoned, to hate evil; we must also love good. And this the drama failed to set forth. And so, a work which is actuated solely by hatred falls of its own weight, defeating its own purpose, however salutary that purpose. If there is love in the work for an ideal, the author of it is a bad poet, for he did not communicate it to me, tho' you, apparently, may not necessarily require it of a drama. But, for me, only a work actuated by the love for that which we have the courage to call good, if we think it is good, is light enough to soar. It may have its sombre glints, for love and hatred are opposite sides of the same coin. But the coin must have a certain value and it is in the world of values that ideas matter. Thus does Plato shine in implacable, eternal beauty, constituting a metaphysician's dream of order amid the harassing and perplexing confusions of the world of experience. My friend, you should not absent yourself so much from the discourses at the Academy and the Lyceum. The search for Truth, Justice, and Wisdom, can be as edifying as the eyes of the harlots by the fountain of Panops or outside the Temple of Venus.

You do well to chide me, but I confess that for the moment I find the eyes of Bilitis, a true daughter of Olympia, more edifying. I have set her up in an apartment by the Ilissus, where she is today in the company of her dearest friend, Lais. Now this Lais combines the beauty and mind of Aspasia, and I thought that perhaps you would . . .

Come, Lysis, let us to the baths and then pay our respects to the fair ladies as behooves true scholars and gentlemen!

March, 1955

A dream comes true—Stroheim films *Greed* (1923–24).

GREED (U.S., 1923-24) (Silent) Goldwyn Productions, MGM release. Scenario by Erich von Stroheim from the novel, *McTeague*, by Frank Norris. Design and direction by Erich von Stroheim. Photography by Ben Reynolds, William Daniels, Ernest Schoedsack. Edited by June Mathis. With Gibson Gowland, Zasu Pitts, Jean Hersholt, Tempe Piggott, Chester Conklin, Sylvia Ashton, Dale Fuller (and, originally, Cesare Gravina).

GREED

One late evening in 1924, three men (accompanied by a silent and brooding fourth) staggered from a projection room where they had been viewing a single film for the previous ten hours, and unanimously declared that they had just seen not only the greatest motion picture ever made, but one that would probably never again be equaled, let alone surpassed. The three men who made this statement were Idwal Jones, a San Francisco journalist (who still contributes occasionally to *The New York Times* and who has since written several books on California), Harry Carr, ex-foreign correspondent and scenarist, and Rex Ingram, director of *The Four Horsemen of The Apocalypse, Mare Nostrum*, etc. The fourth was Erich von Stroheim, the director of the film they had just seen. The film was *Greed* in its entirety, some forty-odd reels.

This film was the realization of a vow Von Stroheim had made many years before, shortly after he arrived in the U. S. He was living, practically destitute, in a ramshackle hotel in New York City and happened to find a copy of a book called *McTeague* by Frank Norris on the dresser in his dingy, room, probably left there by the preceding tenant. What a thing is chance! In such an accidental way the seed of *Greed* began to germinate in Stroheim's mind. He read the book that night only because it was there and he had nothing better to do. As the book advertisements are fond of saying: "He couldn't put it down." He read the thing through at white heat and it was this story, after he had finished reading it, that decided him on a career in motion pictures. This was before the First World War and films weren't very much then, being still little more than a novelty for the penny arcade and the nickelodeon trade. To have such a vision then, of filming this great naturalistic novel by one of America's then foremost writers (frequently referred to as "the American Zola"), was to have vision indeed, and a remarkable sense of prophecy, unconscious or not. That the movies could ever grow up to become a medium wherein such a story could be filmed—and what is even more, that he, a young penniless immigrant lately come from a stint in the Austrian army to seek his fortune in a new world, could make such a film himself without even any training in the theater, let alone what little training anyone could have had in those days in the film—was to have a vision for which "daring" is too mild a word. It was, perhaps, unprecedented. When intellectuals and anyone with the slightest artistic pretense had contempt for this ingenious toy, the "kinetoscope," here was a man with a wonderful vision of what this contemptible gadget could do. (It is, perhaps, not without irony that we can observe today how this has been completely reversed: how the "gadget" has now become such a miraculous instrument and the films turned out by it so frequently contemptible.)

But the dream to film *McTeague* was put aside, and lay dormant for the decade ahead, in which the necessity to earn a living at any kind of a job was always pressing. A singer of German lieder in a New York rathskeller, a flypaper salesman in the Southwest ("where it was so hot the flies didn't have the energy to fly high enough to reach the kind of flypaper I was selling—the long spiral kind that hung down from chandeliers—so I had to find something else."), a lifeguard at Lake Tahoe, who couldn't swim, a riding master (he *could* ride), a rail-worker—all of which doubtless was to give him a good insight into the seamy side of life on which he was subsequently to draw when he actually did become a film director. He also served for a while in the American army in the Mexican campaigns.

His early years in Hollywood as extra, assistant director, technical consultant, etc., are too well known to detail here. He sold Carl Laemmle the idea of letting him make his first picture, *Blind Husbands*, which was such a success that Laemmle

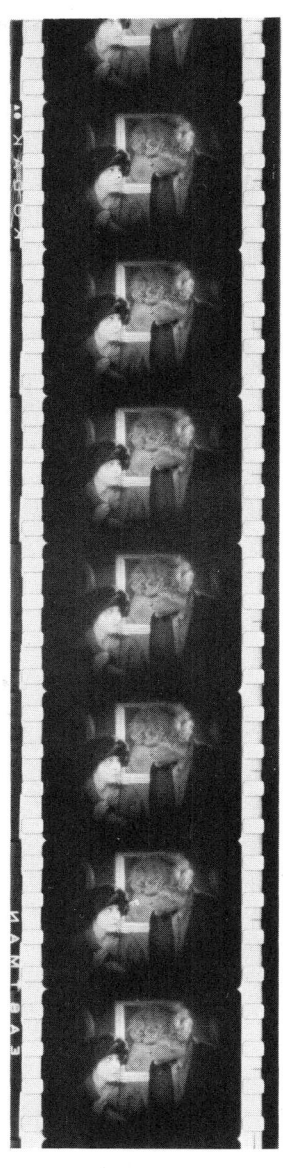

The film of the world unreels "like a ribbon of dreams" (Orson Welles)
. . . a fragment of the 42 reels of *Greed*.

let him make a second directly afterwards, *The Devil's Passkey*. This, too, was a success and by this time Stroheim could have anything he wanted. He embarked on a spectacular production, *Foolish Wives*, the film which made him internationally famous and of which Renoir said that it had induced him to abandon his career in ceramics for that of the cinema. "If such a thing were possible in films, then I wanted to work in that medium, too," said Renoir. That was in 1922. With three hits behind him (including considerable controversy over moral aspects of his last picture which sent the censors, official and self-appointed, scurrying for their scissors), Stroheim was riding the crest of the wave and could film any subject he wanted to under his own terms and conditions. In Hollywood there were then only two others with the same power: Chaplin and Griffith. Most other directors in such a position would not have jeopardized this position of wealth, power, and fame. They would have played it safe. Not Stroheim. When he felt himself psychologically ready to obtain his demands (even after the abortive *Merry Go Round*, which followed *Foolish Wives* and which was taken from him early in its production and turned over to another, because of a difference of opinion between him and Laemmle's production chief, Irving Thalberg), Stroheim felt that now was the time to realize the ambition of his first precarious days in America—to film *McTeague*.

He was out of Laemmle's company, Universal, so he approached the Goldwyn Company and sold them the idea. That they let him embark on it at all must be set down as a first miracle, since it was in direct opposition to everything movies had been up to that time, at least in America. The story of five people destroyed by greed in a small suburb of San Francisco was hardly the kind of story people would rush to the box office for. Movies were very much an escape medium (as they still are, of course), and only Stroheim's powers of persuasion could have overcome any producer's natural resistance to such a pessimistic work.

What was the movie world like at the time Stroheim began to make *Greed*? He had nothing to draw from, no precedent for what he was about to do; he was like a lone explorer setting out into a trackless jungle or an arid waste. It could cost him his professional life, but he didn't care. Armed with just a "compass," Norris' book, he wrote his own script in collaboration with June Mathis, he cast it himself (no casting director was ever on a Stroheim-directed film), and chose the sets himself. One uses the word "chose" aptly for no sets were built for the film. All exteriors were shot in the streets and suburbs of San Francisco and, of course, for the final sequence, in Death Valley (not the Mojave Desert, as the Museum of Modern Art foreword for this film still states), and all interiors were interiors of actual houses in San Francisco and suburbs, which the film company rented. As a matter of fact, Frank Norris' book having been based on an actual murder case that had taken place in San Francisco, Stroheim went out of his way to rent the very building in which the murder had taken place. To add still more realism, Stroheim had his actors stay in these same buildings during the shooting period, "to get into the feel of it." Although Stroheim only got paid for actual shooting time, and was not given any extra salary for all the other activities mentioned here, he was so set on having this film turn out just the way he wanted it, that he was ready to forego the financial returns which by right were due him. He felt that true realism could not otherwise be achieved. His fanatical quest for more realistic portrayals sometimes led him to extremes, and Jean Hersholt tells the story of the filming at Death Valley, where Stroheim actually drove his actors frantic until they were in such a state of wrath that they had no difficulty in playing the scenes of the fight at the end of the picture. Stroheim is said to have told them to look at each other with hatred, as if they were looking at him.

Cesare Gravina, who already had appeared in two films under Stroheim (*Foolish Wives* and *Merry Go Round*), was recalled by Stroheim from South America, where he was accompanying his wife, a singer, on an opera tour, to return to Hollywood for the role of Zerkow, the junkman. Unfortunately, all his scenes were later cut out by MGM. Dale Fuller, who had also served under Stroheim in *Foolish Wives* and *Merry Go Round*, was recruited again for the half-demented Maria Macapa. Gibson Gowland, who was in Stroheim's first picture, *Blind Husbands*, was to play McTeague (and was called from England to do so), and Zasu Pitts was rescued from idiotic comedies in which she was then appearing to make her debut as a tragic actress as Trina—another of Stroheim's daring innovations. Jean Hersholt, an anonymous screen extra at the time, was chosen as Marcus. They were all part of the "Stroheim Stock Company," as they were facetiously called, all, with the exception of Hersholt, having appeared in two or more Stroheim films. Other members of this "stock company" were Maude George, Mae Busch, George Nichols, George Fawcett, Sidney Bracey, Hughie Mack.

When Stroheim sought an insurance policy to cover the players and crew who were to go to Death Valley, it was refused him, but he went anyway. It must be remembered that the Death Valley of 1922 was not what it is today—there were no sleek automobile roads, no hotels or inns, no gasoline stations, no water—just a lot of the most desolate, hot, miserable nothing on the whole continent. There were tarantulas, scorpions, snakes, and other such fauna. It was so hot, and there was so little water, that a shuttle of trucks was instituted between the locations in Death Valley and the nearest town, one hundred miles away, carrying out members of the crew that collapsed daily. When the shooting was finished in Death Valley, which are the final scenes in the film, Jean Hersholt spent weeks in a hospital suffering from an internal hemorrhage induced by the heat. ("It was 140 in the shade—and no shade," as Stroheim put it.)

The picture was finally completed at a total cost of under $500,000, which by standards then or today was a low budget. Since Stroheim's contract called for him to be paid only while directing, he had to cut the film without salary. This he would have been only too glad to do, had they let him cut it, but they didn't. The version he showed his friends, Idwal Jones, Harry Carr (with whom he was later to collaborate on the script of *The Wedding March*), and Rex Ingram, was the complete first rough cut, and ran for ten hours, as we have stated. Stroheim, realizing that no film could run that long, cut it himself to twenty-four reels (four hours), beyond which he said he could not take out another foot. When MGM threatened to cut it down themselves to marketable length, he sent it to his very close friend, Rex Ingram, to reduce further. The latter cut it down to eighteen reels and warned him that he would never speak to him again if he cut out another foot. By this time, MGM lost patience and took the film away from Stroheim to cut themselves. ("It was cut by a hack cutter who had nothing on his mind but his hat," was the way Stroheim refers to that painful episode.) When it emerged from the MGM cutting room, it was down to ten reels, which is the version the world knows as *Greed*. Here was, perhaps, the only film in history in which more was missing than was contained in it. The version you see today is about one quarter of the first rough cut version and less than half of the one Stroheim was satisfied to compromise with, his second version, the twenty-four reel one. So even of this second "compromise" version, there is more missing than you see. (The funeral during the wedding was not in the book but is a touch added by Stroheim.)

What is missing? Those who have read Norris' book and have seen *Greed*, needn't be told. They know, for everything that was in the book was originally in the film. For those who have not read Norris' book, the following are the principal scenes missing:

(a) The entire secondary story between Maria Macapa and Zerkow the junkman. Maria Macapa is seen only in a few brief scenes as the slatternly Polish servant girl who sells Trina the lottery ticket which starts the woeful chain of events that destroys them all. But her relation to Zerkow, the Polish junkman, to whom she relates fabulous tales of golden service plate her family used to have and who drives the little man, greedy with lust for the golden vessels, until he kills her when she can't produce them and then throws himself into San Francisco Bay—all this is out. Not a foot of film showing Cesare Gravina in the role of Zerkow is left in the film.

(b) A third parallel story, the romance between the nice little old lady and the nice old gentleman, which flourishes in the same house where McTeague had his dental parlors, and where another romance, that between McTeague and Trina, begins to decay with the acquisition by Trina of the $5,000 won in the lottery.

(c) All the scenes of the Sieppe family, of Trina's parents, brothers, and sisters, in their home in the suburbs, including the scenes where the family has to move out because the miserly Trina no longer will send them any money.

(d) The transition of Trina from McTeague's sweet and loving wife to a miserly shrew after she wins the $5,000 from the lottery. Innumerable details are missing, like the scene where Trina goes to the bank to cash her $5,000 check and asks to be given it in gold pieces. The character of Trina's uncle is omitted entirely, too. He kept Trina's money for her and let her draw on it whenever she wished. This explains why McTeague knew Trina had all her gold pieces with her that night at the children's school, because he went first to her uncle who told him she had drawn the entire balance.

(e) The entire sequence after the murder of Trina by McTeague between the time he kills her and until his arrival in Death Valley, where he goes to escape with the gold pieces, including his wanderings around San Francisco.

(f) Innumerable scenes of long, bony hands voluptuously fondling gold coins and gold vessels (only a few remain, inserted haphazardly and not as a refrain as originally intended). All the nightmare scenes of Zerkow dreaming of unearthing Maria Macapa's golden service plate in a cemetery where she said they were buried, amid twisted crosses and open graves. The hallucinations of Trina in which the bloodied Maria Macapa, after she has been knifed to death by Zerkow, comes to haunt her with "Wanna buy another lottery ticket?" The smiling corpse of Maria Macapa twines itself around Trina. "Wanna buy another lottery ticket?" This happens at a time when the pitful Trina realizes her life has been ruined by the lottery ticket, but she is helpless against her own lust for her beautiful, shining gold pieces. It is when she goes to visit Maria Macapa that she finds the servant girl already killed by Zerkow in exasperation.

(g) Many close-ups and other shots characterizing McTeague's attitude towards Trina before and immediately after their marriage. The whole idea of the film, that the inexperienced and uncouth McTeague, by his sheer overpowering sex lust, frightens the timid Trina into seeking an outlet for her frustrations in her lust for gold, is insufficiently developed. Only the scene where Trina sleeps with gold coins strewn all over her naked body, remains.

(h) The entire opening of the film. How McTeague came to be a dentist is told in flashback, not chronologically as in this version. This flashback begins with the McTeague family in a small mining town. Every Saturday night, McTeague's father, a congenital alcoholic, turned himself into a drunken, raging beast in a miners' saloon, with its blowzy "hostesses," who took whatever was left of the miners' pay that didn't go for drinks. In this version, there are no scenes of McTeague's father at all, and all scenes of the saloon are missing. There was a terrific scene of delirium tremens in this sequence, where McTeague's father sees a snake slowly coming out of a whiskey bottle at him. It is because McTeague's mother doesn't want him to become a drunkard among the miners like his father, that she persuades him to take up a profession like dentistry, actuated by the chance arrival in town of Dr. "Painless" Parker, an itinerant dentist-charlatan.

(i) Many shots of Death Valley which gave the sense of the day-by-day, slow, inexorable breakdown of McTeague's spirit as he realizes he has trapped himself in this desolate waste—long before Marcus catches up with him.

It should be stated in closing that the actual incidents on which Frank Norris' book is based, took place in San Francisco just before the century's turn. It should also be stated that the so-called "box-office-flop" of *Greed* was engineered by MGM (according to Von Stroheim) for tax purposes, and the story of the bookkeeping end of this film is as long and harrowing as the film itself. It should further be stated that Stroheim has disowned the butchered version of *Greed* you see, and that although despite its mutilation it still remains an uncommonly powerful work, he feels toward it as one would feel toward a man lacking one leg, an arm and one eye. He is still a man and can still function, after a fashion. *Greed* (the name given the film by June Mathis, it was originally to be named *McTeague*) is still a film and can still function in that respect, also after a fashion. But a man is born whole, as *Greed* was also born whole. Would anyone attempt to justify the mutilation of a man by saying "War is War!!"? As well attempt to justify the mutilation of *Greed* by saying "Business is Business!"

Even if it were a case of "Business is Business," it is shameful and inexecusable on any grounds that the negative of the original *Greed* was not saved for posterity. (Hope springs eternal in the true archivist's breast and a print of the complete *Greed* is the holy grail in his life . . .) This would have harmed no one, as saving the complete negative of Eisenstein's *Que Viva Mexico* would have harmed no one. It would have enabled us to see the full extent of the genius of these two great masters of the film like nothing else they had ever done. That is the irreparable loss. The world can afford to lose some of its "businessmen"—it cannot afford the loss of a single artist or work of art. How idiotic is Joyce Kilmer's "Poems are made by fools like me, but only God can make a tree." There are billions of trees in the world—there is scarcely a handful of great poems.

Spring, 1955

Confidential Report (Mr. Arkadin) (Spain-France, 1956) Original scenario and design, Orson Welles. Directed by Orson Welles. Music by Paul Misraki. With Orson Welles, Patricia Medina, Robert Arden, Akim Tamiroff, Paola Mori, Mischa Auer, Katina Paxinou, Michael Redgrave, Gregoire Aslan, Peter Van Eyck, Suzanne Flon.

CONFIDENTIAL REPORT

For all the cant that the eighth art, cinema, is a collaborative art, the inexorable rule does not change even for the cinema: it is, like its sister arts, primarily an art which also depends on the individuality of the artist. Were this not so it could not even be considered as an art. We constantly spout the names of Griffith,

The crocodile in the background is a typical Wellesian comment on his characters, this time the Dutch fence, Trebitsch (Michael Redgrave), shown here in his curio shop. Here they are all predators. Detail from *Confidential Report (Mr. Arkadin)* (1956).

Chaplin, Stroheim, Sternberg, Lubitsch, Murnau, Eisenstein, Clair, Gance, Pabst, etc., because they had individuality as artists, their work was recognizable as such, and their collaborators, talented as they might have been, rarely contributed to work of equal stature when they collaborated with artists of less individuality. In the vanguard of the second generation of film artists who have grasped and held high the torch of the unique art of cinema, lit by the first generation's Giottos of the film, is Orson Welles.

If the financial Kubla Khans of moviedom take any pride at all in their medium, it is for the luster given it by its creative artists, the "legion of honor" of fine films that saved the motion pictures from being dedicated solely to profit and the movie moguls' financial aggrandizement. And the basic attribute of a fine film is that it is indigenous to its medium, i.e., it uses its medium creatively, originally, sans concessions to all popularly accepted canons of movie-making and movie ideologies, sans pleading to be liked as most films plead to be liked—often the more spectacular they are the harder they must plead, because of the huge investment at stake. Sans fear of censorship of any kind, and, above all, sans knuckling under for whatever expediency, for the easy buck, whatever way that easy buck might be attained . . . stars, best-sellers, current vogues, "don't-say-one-word-or-show-one-thing-that-could-offend-anybody," violence, catch-penny sex with its patina of hypocrisy to get it by, conformism in every facet of life from the cradle to the grave, and all the sand-in-the-eyes of color, big screens, etc. It is because *Confidential Report* flies in the faces of these shibboleths, because it dares to go "against the grain" of the popular conception of what constitutes a motion picture in 1956, because it is such a relief from the literalness of most pictures with their a-b-c progressions from word to word and scene to scene, because it is not prechewed and predigested and because the spectator cannot sit back and relax, but must meet the film at least half-way to try to figure out what the hell is going on practically every second or he's lost. Stated positively, this latest film of Welles' is yet another example of the wild joy he takes in movie making. Using as a springboard the mystery surrounding the disappearance of a fabulously rich tycoon like the late Lowenstein (who disappeared in a plane over the English Channel), or such "mystery men" as Zaharoff and Krueger, he lets go with a kaleidoscope of swiftly drawn, acidly limned sketches of the moral chaos of Europe in the period covered by two world wars. Mr. Arkadin (played by Welles) pretends to his daughter's suitor, a busybody American drifter, that he does not know who he is and sends him on an assignment to find out, dig up his past, for which he pays him well. But Mr. Arkadin knows very well who he is, and it is an unsavory past, indeed; what Mr. Arkadin really wants to find out is: who else knows who Mr. Arkadin is? One by one, as the now scattered members of the old Arkadin gang are turned up (in Milan, Copenhagen, Tangiers, Amsterdam, Paris, the high seas, Mexico, Munich) they are rubbed out by the long arm of Arkadin—all so that his daughter (who is the only thing he loves besides the power that money can give him) may not ever learn, by the slightest chance, the sordid basis of her father's fortune. By an ironic twist of fate, Arkadin loses the race with time and all his millions cannot save him. The ending is neither happy nor unhappy. It's like the reverberations of a bell that has ceased ringing. And during the ninety minutes of unreeling of this film, *Confidential Report* does, indeed, sound with the clangour of a multitude of sounds, from the chanting of the *penitentes* in Spain to the frenzied jazz at one of Arkadin's sumptuous masquerade parties; from the wheedlings of the Dutch fence turned "antiquarian," Trebitsch, delightfully played by Michael Redgrave, to the perfumed confidences in the Paris nightclub of the Baroness Nagel, ex-police spy; from the pathetic German street musicians to the glinting drops of sorrow uttered by the tubercular Jacob Zouk (superbly played by Tamiroff), last of the gang, holed up in a Munich garret; from the rills of a pipe spiralling upward in Tangiers to the banshee wail of a near-East *hora;* from the bitter-edged resignation of Sophie, ex-*entraîneuse* (magnificently played by Katina Paxinou) to Arkadin's voice booming desperately over the radio . . . sound and image have been made fluid and malleable in the creative imagination. Like Stroheim, Welles has a love of the baroque—in this style he has found the world in microcosm not only in his preoccupation with decadence (vide *Citizen Kane, Lady from Shanghai,* etc.) but also in the involutions of his cinematic style. He disdains telling a story chronologically, he must "back-track" on himself, past and present are like a great fugue, intermingling. Keeping up with Welles' furious pace is Paul Misraki's febrile musical score which has caught Welles' contagious paroxysms. It is a feverish thing, this film, told in percussive shocks; it stamps, it boils, it flaunts the most outrageous human visages before the stunned spectator. Its metaphors of word and image in a script whose literacy and sophistication make most film scripts seem jejune by comparison, and which is streaked with sardonic humor, keep you constantly guessing their significance (the credits are superimposed over bats wheeling in the dark). Arkadin, with his "eye of a basilisk," is quietly underplayed by Welles for maximum effectiveness. A Stroheimesque *morbidezza* infuses the whole, and even if the whole is somewhat less than the sum of its best parts, being imperfect as a fully realized work of art, Confidential Report is still that *rara avis* among films—the intensely personal expression of a highly gifted artist, intoxicated by the creative possibilities of the film medium, and who imparts something of this prodigality of joy in the medium to us. Would that this infectious spirit were contagious enough to be caught by other directors, including some of our best current names, *hélas!*

1956

ERICH VON STROHEIM

> *There's rosemary, that's for remembrance: pray you, love, remember . . .*
> Shakespeare: *Hamlet*

Being some personal reminiscences of Von Stroheim, recalled from memory . . .

To the Countess Maeterlinck, "I never took myself very seriously as an actor; as a director, yes—as an actor, no."

Driving up Fifth Avenue on a rainy night—the long ribbon of green traffic lights suddenly changed to red, like a necklace of emeralds become one of rubies, reflected in the glistening asphalt. "That would make a nice shot in a film."

After sitting though all three acts of the play *Arsenic and Old Lace* in stony-faced silence while all about him were laughing their heads off, "Oh, you know me—I don't find anything funny anymore."

To the query why he spoke his lines in French films so slowly and meticulously, "To stay on the screen longer."

"Did you ever read Charles Fort's *The Book of the Damned?* You should—it's a remarkable book, all about natural phenomena the scientists can't explain. There are lots of things we have no explanation for. I believe in extrasensory perception and all that, I absolutely do."

Trying to get him to deliver a promised article by press time for Klaus Mann's magazine, *Decision,* while touring one-night stands in *Arsenic and Old Lace* in the Midwest, "Unless the Holy Ghost comes down and writes the article for me, which, as you informed me, must be in Klaus Mann's hands in a week, I won't be able to contribute for the next number. That issue will greatly suffer through it, but it can't be helped."

Of Von Sternberg: "A very cultured and intelligent director."

Of Lubitsch: "Lubitsch shows you first the king on his throne, then as he is in his bedroom. I show you the king first in his bedroom so you'll know what he is when you see him on his throne."

At the "21" club in New York, Chaplin catches his eye—they smile, nod, hesitate . . . who will defer to whom? As if there had

"Then Nature mourned . . . the birds were hushed . . . and it rained and rained and rained . . ." (title). Nikki makes a farewell visit to Mitzi on the eve of his loveless marriage to Cecelia. Fay Wray and Stroheim in *The Wedding March* (1926–27).

"*Pro Gloria Dei, Patriae, et Familiae.*"* Nikki and his parents *chez soi* following the death of Cecelia. He is shocked at the cynicism with which his mother takes their new situation, which has given them Cecelia's munificent dowry and Nikki his freedom again. From *The Wedding March*. (Maude George, George Fawcett, Stroheim)

*"For the Glory of God, Country and Family," motto of the House of Wildeliebe-Rauffenberg. "Especially the family," remarks Prince Nikki sarcastically. From *The Wedding March*.

never been any question about it, he gets up, excuses himself to us, and rushes over to Chaplin's table.

Whose work did he especially like in Hollywood? (The year is 1940.) "Milestone, Ford, Victor Fleming, Capra, Lubitsch."

In Europe? "Renoir, Pagnol, René Clair, Eisenstein."

What American pictures? "*The Informer, Stage Coach, Of Mice and Men, Grapes of Wrath, Gone with the Wind, Mr. Deeds Goes to Town, Ninotchka, Our Town, The Biscuit Eater, Dead End.*"

European films? "*La Bandera, Les Bas-Fonds, La Chienne, La Grande Illusion, Sous les Toits de Paris, La Kermesse Héroïque.*"

What projects would he like to do? "*The Diary of a Chambermaid* by Octave Mirbeau, *Les Civilisés* by Claude Farrère, *God's Little Acre* by Erskine Caldwell, certain stories by Maupassant, *Paprika* by myself."

What happened to *Walking Down Broadway*? "Sol Wurtzel, one of the chief moguls at Fox, did not understand the story or the picture. After it was finished he had it rewritten, remade, and rebaptized. It came out as *Hello Sister!*—a 'B' picture. Sol Wurtzel wanted to prove to Winnie Sheehan that his (Sheehan's) judgment had been wrong in engaging me to direct during Wurtzel's absence. I happened to be in the middle of a feud between them."

He detested the German military roles of both world wars that economic necessity forced him to play. (There was one exception, that of Von Rauffenstein in *La Grande Illusion*.) He found it ironic that between the two world wars he should have made an auspicious career as a director only to wind up playing the same antipathetic German officers he started out with, as if *Blind Husbands, The Devil's Passkey, Foolish Wives, Greed, The Merry Widow,* and *The Wedding March* had never happened.

When he threw a party, it was a real party—not a few miserable canapés, second-rate rye, and potato chips surrounded by a group of simpering, gushing hypocrites. I recall one in New York replete with caviar, champagne, and sweetmeats galore to delight Heliogabalus, and a guest list as succulent. (Only Tom Curtiss, of the Paris *Herald-Tribune*, his long-time friend, mentor, and everything else good, including "father-confessor," outdid him once in this respect by throwing a party at the old Astor designed to bring Stroheim and Thomas Mann together as a prelude to discussions which he hoped would result in Stroheim's filming *The Magic Mountain*. This was a wing-ding out of a Stroheim film, indeed.)

A picture post-card from Niagara Falls, during a visit there, inscribed, "So much water and no whiskey!"

A chain letter, "I am sending you this chain letter because I believe in Paul Kohner, my agent, and the guys listed ahead of him, Joe Pasternak, Robert Z. Leonard, etc. (as you can see, the sucker-list is pretty melodious), . . . and because I believe in you. . . ." (Someone must have broken the chain as he predicted it would be broken—but hope sprang eternal in those wonderful days. . . .)

He wrote "Poto-Poto," his African story, with Dietrich in mind to play the role of "Roulette" Masha, a flashy blonde who works the boats plying the Red Sea, taking on any gambler, staking herself against the cold cash of her partner. She loses a particularly high stake once to a degenerate African trader, who takes her back with him as his mistress to a steaming little green hell up river on the East African coast. An expanded French translation of this story was recently published in Paris. Stroheim directing Dietrich—what a missed opportunity!

He directed a practical joke once on a young doctor friend who went calling on his girl, only to be met by another girl in his fiancée's apartment who disclaimed all knowledge of the medico's inamorata, insisting it was *her* apartment. The strange girl, playing it straight-faced, had her sinister aspects, certainly, under the circumstances, but what gave the situation its most bizarre touch was the fact that, save for a pair of slippers (and smoking a cigarette in a long cigarette-holder), she conducted the entire conversation completely in the nude.

"R. H. Cochrane, vice-president in charge of publicity at Universal, after I finished *Foolish Wives*, thought its production cost of $735,000 was so close to a million that he decided to call it, for publicity purposes, the first million-dollar picture. Universal had put up an electric sign on Broadway, changed weekly as the production cost 'mounted.' They spelled my name in lights as '$troheim.' A lot of good that did me!"

He treasured a gold cigarette case that the cast of *The Merry Widow* gave him when the picture was finished, inscribed with all their signatures as an expression of their love for him.

Returning to France at the end of the war, a farewell party

was held on the deck of a nondescript French freighter on which he was to voyage across, the big liners being not yet returned to passenger service. Turkey leg in one hand, bumper of Scotch in the other, he grimly regarded a snarled coil of rope on the deck, a flagrant violation of one of the cardinal rules of the sea. "Just look at that," he said. "That would never happen on a German boat. Well, if you don't hear from me anymore, you'll know why." But he loved France and had only contempt for German junkerism.

How can one reminisce about Stroheim and not also recall the role played by Denise Vernac after his first trip to France, when he was called over to appear in *Marthe Richard?* She came as a journalist to interview him and remained as secretary, majordomo, and ministering angel, cushioning him against the "slings and arrows" of the world. Rarely, I think, has a woman exhibited such selfless devotion.

He could think of the most startling things. "Did you ever make love in a steaming stable on a hot summer afternoon?"

By 1921, when the movies were still a wilderness, he had already directed three of the most sophisticated films ever made— *Blind Husbands, The Devil's Passkey,* and *Foolish Wives.*

"What were the lengths of your films as cut by you for their final versions and the actual lengths in which these films were released to the public by the producing companies?"

Answer:

Blind Husbands	9,000 ft. released in	8,000 ft.
The Devil's Passkey ..	12,000 ft. released in	12,000 ft.
Foolish Wives	21,000 ft. released in	14,000 ft.
The version at the Museum of Modern Art is		7,000 ft.
Greed	24,000 ft. released in	10,000 ft.
The Merry Widow	12,000 ft. released in	11,000 ft.
* *The Wedding March*	14,000 ft. released in	14,000 ft.

He never won an Academy Award in Hollywood, either as actor or director, but France made him a Chevalier of the Legion of Honor.

---

* Stroheim was being generous—actually, according to the original script, there was more shot. The bordello scene alone was at least 1,000–2,000 feet longer than the released version. Also, this represents only the first part.

His last screen role was as Beethoven in Sacha Guitry's *Napoleon*—fittingly, too, for what Romain Rolland once said of the master of Bonn was as applicable to Stroheim: "Beethoven would not have been what he was were it not for his excesses."

Plagued by illness; doing one-night stands of *Arsenic and Old Lace* ("I, who never could be sure of remembering two consecutive lines of dialogue!"); following up leads everywhere for a possible film role here, a possible directorial post there, most of which led up blind alleys; writing scripts, articles; beset by personal anxieties that would have tried the patience of Job—he nevertheless maintained touches of optimism glinting through the somber pessimism to which he had been brought by the chicanery that kept tripping him up. Despite that . . . he could close a letter jubilantly, as he did to me once, "*Vivat . . . crescat . . . floreat!*" Live, create, flourish!

He wanted to show that the whole world was kin, that there was good and evil everywhere, and not always where we would expect to find them, and sometimes in the most surprising places. Human nature was compounded of contradictory attributes, which Dostoevski realized so trenchantly, and no Stroheim character ever ceased for an instant to be a credible human being, whether cast in the role of hero or villain. A complete human being himself, with the wide latitude that this permits, he observed human frailty as he would observe it in himself, with irony or compassion, depending on the circumstances, but never losing his sense of humor, which was prodigious and, more often than not, withering.

Round and round went the eternal game of lust that fascinated him as a scientist is fascinated by the developments in research he is undertaking . . . lust for the things men lust for, the lust for money, for love, for youth, before which borderlines of nationality and caste crumble. Like Asmodeus, he soared over the rooftops of the world and peered into the windows, and what he saw there is partially discernible in the pitifully few fragments that were permitted to remain of his work by those whom he angered or made afraid. But he loved life, and it was this that the buffoons who tried to "put him in his place" did not understand, for how could they know that a man can have wings and rejoice only in the flight of his creative spirit?

April, 1958

Touch of Evil (U.S., 1957) Scenario by Orson Welles from a novel by Whit Masterson, *Badge of Evil*. Directed by Orson Welles. With Orson Welles, Charlton Heston, Janet Leigh, Joseph Calleia, Ray Collins, Akim Tamiroff, Mercedes McCambridge, Joseph Cotten, Marlene Dietrich.

TOUCH OF EVIL

This is only "accidentally" a Welles film, the story having been imposed on him by the studio which threw him a sop when he made it a condition that he would act in another film for which they wanted him if they'd let him direct a picture. They had this story-property, anyway, and said, in effect, "All right, do this." The modifications made in it by the studio without his knowledge, after he completed it, were not very serious, according to Welles, and were not a tenth of the changes that *Mr. Arkadin* (also known as *Confidential Report*) suffered. Four brief scenes between Charlton Heston and Janet Leigh (particularly one in the hotel) were neither written nor directed by Welles, but they total scarcely more than a minute of projection. The cuts, however, were more considerable—though none of the scenes of violence were tampered with, only those making "moral statements." Also, the credit titles were originally at the end of the film, superimposed over the last scene of Dietrich disappearing in the night. The present position of the credits, at the beginning, over the opening action, interferes with the spectators' view of the movement of the automobile and the actors which kicks off the story.

Although no American directors have been more experimental than Welles, he has declared that he addressed his film to the widest possible audience, of all social categories, all ages, all horizons. He believes it is the duty of the *cinéaste* to do this. "Whether I achieved this or not is another matter," he stated. "I want to make films that will seduce people away from their television sets to go to the theaters, but in the case of *Touch of Evil*, this wish of mine was reduced to nothing, as the film got very little distribution in America." When asked if he would have made *Touch of Evil* any different in France, for instance, he replied, "No . . . I had carte blanche in its actual filming. If I'd had a percentage of the receipts, instead of working for straight salary on it, I'd have wanted to participate in the European exploitation of the film because I think it's more European than American by the very nature of its subject matter. This wasn't intentional—it just turned out like that."

Detail: "I don't know how they got the title, *Touch of Evil*, or what it's supposed to mean."

Question: "It is generally stated that film is a collective art, a collaborative one. What do you think?"

Welles: "Absolutely not! One needs assistants, collaborators, of course, it is a collective effort, but essentially it is a very personal kind of work, much more so than the theater is, in my opinion, because film is a dead thing, a ribbon of celluloid, like a sheet of paper on which one writes a poem. A film is something which is written on celluloid. The theater, on the contrary, is living, it is a collective experience, almost religious, in which everyone participates."

Which brings us, finally, to *Touch of Evil* as a characteristic work of its creator. It is not major Welles, but even minor Welles is better than most other films, so few are the really creative directors the cinema has nowadays. *Touch of Evil*, for all the tampering that has been done with it, emerges as recognizable Welles, which in itself is a great deal in a time of stupefying banality and meretricious pretensions with which the current American cinema is rife.

If we take *The Birth of a Nation* as the beginning of film as an art, that makes about forty-four years of achievement in the motion pictures with which experience one approaches a new film today. Not to mention the great backlog of art in Western culture which spans some five thousand years or so. The more pretentious the film, the greater the challenge it faces, not only from other films, but from the vast experience of art itself. The serious observer does not, therefore, see a film in a vacuum, but sees it as it utilizes its medium, as it obeys the inexorable laws of art, and as it blazes new paths. It has a dual stature, in comparison with other films (greater and lesser), and in comparison with works of art in other mediums. Only in that way is it properly put into focus . . . all personal prejudices aside. Few films emerge with any stature at all, measured by this. Those of Welles have stature. And *Touch of Evil*, though no great shakes as a story, is full of fascinating details and, as Stendhal reminded us, "Truth is to be found only in details."

I remember feeling, when I saw the opening sequence of the film, "Oh boy, here we go!" The rhythmical ticking of the time bomb, which guides us into the parallel rhythm of a mambo in the nondescript little Mexican border town on the night the story opens, is pure cinema, utilizing image and sound marvelously to establish an immediate effect. It is fluid, restless, visceral, dynamic—everything film should be and so seldom anymore is. Nothing is left to chance, every move has been artfully contrived for its maximum effect. Every face has been shrewdly chosen. The dialogue has that elliptical quality with which people naturally speak. The camera has an ever-present sense of the grotesque. Though the exteriors were shot in Venice, California, they have the absolute veracity of Los Robles, a Mexican border town. It is not necessary to go to actual locales, as everyone is doing today, for "authenticity," if you understand, as von Sternberg once put it, "the essence of the reality you are after." A Stroheim going to Death Valley for *Greed* in another thing. His was the ultimate essence of reality and he certainly understood why he had to go there and nowhere else.

I should like to remark, before closing, on the swiftly drawn image of a low-down Mexican brothel, as laconic in its few details as Ozep's in *The Yellow Pass*. It is presided over by a brunette-wigged Marlene Dietrich as a cigar-smoking madame who receives the drunken American cop, Quinlan (Orson Welles), with good-humored tolerance even though it's "after hours" and the only thing available are "movies"—you can imagine what kind. I could do an essay on how you can tell a director's style by the way he portrays that hardy institution, the brothel, because here is a test of the director's taste and discretion versus harsh reality, and woe be to him who pussyfoots here or who gets mealy-mouthed or squashes about in an erotic swamp. It is a test of a director's esthetic equilibrium. As with the rest of the film, there is no bourgeois complicity here, no hypocrisy, no bowing to virtue and walking away. I think I like that about *Touch of Evil* most.

Autumn, 1959

SOME FOOTNOTES TO THE ARTS

"Le bon Dieu est en le détail."
—Cézanne.

Gleanings from a diary of personal reminiscences, collected over the years:

Fernand Léger's delight with the unexpected metaphor when I told him his paintings were to me "clangorous in red and black, like new fire engines." To the query, what fascinated him most in New York, he replied, "The drugstore windows!" (They made pleasing geometric patterns to him.)

When I asked Alexander Woollcott if his chapter on a French circus poodle he had once seen and described in *While Rome Burns* was not a thinly disguised pen-portrait of Harpo Marx he chucklingly admitted it.

The atonal composer, Edgar Varèse, on one of the many differences between Europe and America: "In Europe, when a rich woman has an affair with a conductor, they have a baby. In America, she endows an orchestra for him."

Thorold Dickinson on violence in the films: "The sentimentality of brutality."

Robert Flaherty, sighing over the difficulty he had getting backing for his films: "Film is the longest distance between two points."

When G. W. Pabst similarly complained of the relative paucity of his output, some fifteen or twenty pictures in thirty years, I remonstrated that Flaherty had succeeded in making scarcely five or six in the same period. Whereupon he exclaimed, "But what films!" (One of Pabst's favorites was Josef Von Sternberg's *The Scarlet Empress*, which, he said, always left him "ga-ga" with its pictorial extravagance. "Whenever I hear it's playing somewhere, anywhere, I drop everything and go to see it again!")

I did a foreword to the French version of Fritz Lang's *The Testament of Dr. Mabuse*, drawing a parellel between Mabuse and the Nazi megalomaniacs. "Exactly right," said Lang. "Let it stay." Then he told me how Goebbels, a great admirer of *Metropolis* and *Siegfried*, had offered him the post of film *gauleiter* of the Third Reich. "This," said Lang, "I realized was the kiss of death. I got the hell out of Berlin the same night and fled to France."

Ernest Boyd and Tom Curtiss exuberantly singing "I'm Going to Maxim's" from *The Merry Widow* one night at the Barbery Room at a dinner party for Erich von Stroheim. (Nothing like two Irishmen singing in German!) Boyd, translator of the complete works of Maupassant, didn't recognize the existence of airplanes or the intellectuality of women. "The only mental effort a woman should have to make," he said, "is to see that the seams of her stockings are straight."

Jed Harris' hilarious imitation of two taxi drivers who had just bumped into each other, getting out of their cabs and arguing whose fault it was—as it would sound in New York, London, Paris, Cairo, Ankara, and Naples. (Their references to each other's zoological antecedents were awesome in their virtuosity.)

Piet Mondrian, the Dutch abstractionist painter—the gentlest person I ever met.

The difference between an artist and an illustrator: When I asked Georg Grosz what he thought of Arthur Szyk, he replied, without answering, "Next question?"

To my query if he had any plans for a new film that he, himself, would direct, Ben Hecht answered, "There's a lot of palaver about independent production these days, but I don't see any differences between the so-called independent and—I suppose you'd call them—"dependent" films. It's still just as hard as it ever was to get backing for a truly independently made film."

Jimmy Savo told me that Fellini once wanted to do a film with him from his original story called "The Golden Flea"—a fantasy like *Harvey*.

Valeska Gert, the German actress and mime, also told me about an original story she had written for the screen, but could get no one to back it. A story of twin sisters, one good, the other bad—who reverse their characters as they grow up, the "bad" one becoming a paragon of virtue and the so-called "good" one becoming truly evil. (The theme was that one had to look beneath the surface of people for their true characters.)

Von Stroheim on Jean Renoir: "The only man who can outdrink me." (At a drinking bout between Stroheim, Renoir, and novelist Joseph Kessel, Kessel suddenly started chewing his wine glass. When he had seemingly disposed of all but the stem of the glass, he tossed it away. "You shouldn't have done that," the awesomely impressed Renoir deadpanned to Kessel, "That's the best part!")

Stroheim once recalled his start in Hollywood when he, "Bull" Montana, and Lon Chaney used to walk each day to Universal City, seeking extra work. "Because of our combined overpowering handsomeness we were known as 'The Three Graces.'"

Asked why he invariably wore an armband of mourning in films in which he acted, he replied with a heavy sigh, "I don't know . . . *Weltschmerz,* maybe." Erwin Piscator once described Von Stroheim's *The Wedding March* to me as being like a novel by Balzac. "He is the best novelist of the films," he said.

Some memorable screenings: Watching the full version of Pudovkin's *Storm Over Asia* (with Russian flash titles) with Ernst Lubitsch. "What a picture! What a director!" he exclaimed. Watching the mutilated version of *Greed* in the Museum of Modern Art projection room with Von Stroheim who said he was seeing it that way for the first time. "I need a drink after this," he said. "Two drinks!" Looking at *Dr. Caligari* with Han Janowitz, co-scenarist of the film. "You know, Carl Mayer and I never intended it like this. We didn't have a frame story, originally. That was Fritz Lang's idea." A screening at the old Lloyd's of Dreyer's eerie *Vampyr,* with the film's star, Julian West, in the person of the almost equally eerie Nicky de Gunzberg, present. Seeing *U.F.O.* (Unidentified Flying Objects) with Willy Ley, the rocket expert, and Fritz Lang, who antedated the current science-fiction vogue with his remarkable *Woman in the Moon* (Frau im Mond) in the late 20s. "I'm not so sure," said Ley, "that it's a matter so much *where* they're from as of *what* they are. We have by no means exhausted all the natural possibilities." Watching Von Sternberg's *Macao* with him in the RKO projection room as he gazed, in stonyfaced silence, at the reshot, reedited, almost completely remade version of his original film. As after the screening of *Greed,* we went to the nearest bar to recover.

In answer to my confession that I always have had a secret

yen to be a beachcomber, Von Sternberg replied, "Why don't you have a go at it, and observe how a noble rock becomes first a round pebble, then sand, and finally mud."

The most exciting theatrical first-night in my memory—*What Price Glory*, with Louis Wolheim and William Boyd (and lovely Leila George) at the Arthur Hopkins Theatre; the most exciting movie first-night—*The Big Parade* at the Astor; the most glamorous, in the old, long-since-forgotten sense of the word, movie first-night—Stroheim's *The Merry Widow* at Gloria Gould's rose and *intime* Embassy Theatre (now become a "schlock" house, like so much else on Broadway).

One of America's foremost sexologists, Gershon Legman, has become one of the world's foremost authorities on the ancient Japanese art of *origami* (paper folding), second only to the Grand Pooh Bah of the art, Yoshizawa of Japan. (Some day I'm going to quote some of his devastating critiques on the movies from the psychiatric point of view, in letters received from him over the years.)

Said an old-time director to me once anent the custom of Stroheim and Griffith sometimes having had credit lines reading, "Personally directed by . . ."—"Look, man, my hat was always off to those two but, what the hell, did they think the rest of us directed by mail?"

The paintings of the Jackson Pollock school, those "mud-in-your-eye" effusions of de Kooning, Still, Rothko, Kline, etc., remind me of what the critic, Victor Llona, once said of James Joyce's *Finnegans Wake*, "I don't know what to call it, but it's mighty unlike prose."

Apropos an Orson Welles picture that has never been shown publicly in America, *Mr. Arkadin* (also known as *Confidential Report*), because no distributor could be found to take it, herewith an excerpt from a letter from Welles to me: "By long practice I generally refrain from reading reviews of my own movies or plays. Through the years I've found an uncomfortable majority of my critics to be the opposite of encouraging, and I have a weakness in this matter: I tend to be very impressed by almost any reasoned attack on my work which may get into print . . . I have never been able to take a good review quite as seriously as a bad one . . . What really pleased me was not so much that you liked *Mr. Arkadin,* but that you liked it for what I take to be the right reasons. This, of course, is the ultimate compliment."

All the talk (currently revived anew via the American-Soviet "cultural exchange" of films) about movies being the best international good-will ambassadors, to make for mutual understanding between nations, sounds fatuous indeed in the face of history's two greatest wars during the film's brief lifetime, not to mention all the rest of the assorted bloodlettings that have soaked the earth since the parturition of the cinema. Don't look to the movies to save the world.

Ah, the movies, the romantic movies! Max Ophuls peopled the bagnio of Madame Tellier with as delectable a bevy of houris as one could wish in his *Le Plaisir,* but when a contemporary caricaturist, Steinlen, depicted them in a drawing "Chez Mme. Tellier," they were a lot fatter, homelier and less appetizing. However, an actual photograph (in Francis Steegmuller's *Maupassant: A Lion in the Path*) of the Madame (whom Maupassant immortalized in his famous story, "Mme. Tellier's Excursion") and her flock shows them in reality to have been brutish enough in their ugliness to have frightened Dracula.

A letter from Marlene Dietrich from Berlin (1929) asking me to send her the New York reviews of *Three Loves,* her first film to be shown in New York (it was silent) before *The Blue Angel,* introduced her officially to the world and brought her her first real fame. She was anxious to know what impression she made on Americans. The reviews were already an augury of things to come.

A letter from Darius Milhaud about doing a film together, *My New York* (i.e., Milhaud's New York, he'd just arrived in 1940, a refugee from occupied France). He was to give a sophisticated Frenchman's impressions and write the musical score. The film wasn't made but he wrote the music anyway and called it *A Frenchman in New York.*

Although Alexander Korda bought the film rights to Thomas Mann's *The Magic Mountain,* and Zoltan Korda was supposed to direct it, nothing ever happened. Some years before, at a sumptuous dinner party thrown by Tom Curtiss at the Astor, designed to bring Thomas Mann and Erich von Stroheim together and which he hoped might result in the filming of this book (to have been financed by Gifford Cochrane), I asked Dr. Mann what he thought of the project. He replied, "I am fascinated by the idea, of course, if Mr. von Stroheim and Mr. Cochrane are willing, but do you *really* think it is possible to film that kind of a book?" (I didn't.)

Meeting Alexander Kerensky during luncheon at a Madison Avenue restaurant, very genial, and a "dead-ringer," even a generation later, of the actor who played him in Eisenstein's caricature of him in *10 Days That Shook the World.* Dave Fine tells me that the erstwhile head of the short-lived Provisional Government of Russia in 1917 used to visit the old Stanley Theatre often to keep up with the new Soviet films.

Eugene d'Ormandy-Blau, concertmaster of the Capitol Theatre symphony orchestra during the silent movie era, playing Sarasate's *Gypsy Airs* twice a day for a week as soloist with the orchestra under the conductorship of David Mendoza. Subsequently he was to become Eugene Ormandy, the present conductor of the Philadelphia Orchestra.

Walking down Broadway on a somnolent warm June night in 1926, dresed in my white linen suit and very thin white felt hat, following Adolphe Menjou, similarly attired (that was the vogue then) into the Rivoli Theatre (they were showing Mal St. Clair's *Are Parents People?* with Menjou, Florence Vidor and Betty Bronson) where Hugo Reisenfeld, the orchestra's conductor, introduced him from the stage . . . and we were vouchsafed that winning Menjou smile of the blithesome 1920's.

January, 1960

COFFEE, BRANDY & CIGARS

What a pity . . . The film might be one of the mightiest means of spreading knowledge and great ideas and yet it serves only to litter people's brains.

—*Tolstoy*

The current flurry over Ingmar Bergman would come with better grace if all who showered such an accolade of praise on him had similarly recognized his great predecessors. But never in this country has there been such an extended period of extravagant acclaim over the appearance of a new film artist as in the case of Bergman—it's as if no one *really* knew how to make films until Bergman came along. His preoccupation with morbid things, the violence and hysteria with which his films (even comedies) are rife, seem, however, to fill a want at the present time, which is certainly an age of anxiety and neuroses. He litters his films with such a hocus-pocus of dark surmises from beginning to end that the mind reels from such a farrago of morbid *chic*. His actors are never universal types, they are Swedes, they *look* Swedish, they *react* Swedish ("Bergman has a nice situation in that alcoholic little country of his," said Wolf Mankowitz recently. "Swedes are great at getting sloshed and killing themselves."). "*Bergman est emmerdant,*" said Orson Welles quoted in an interview with Jean Cau in the Paris weekly *L'Express*. Paraphrasing Pablo Casals on modern music, which he called art, not music, I would say that Bergman's films are art but not film. I also think they are excellent Rorschach tests.

Welles on Stroheim in the above-mentioned interview: "Bavarian . . . baroque. His art is Jewish baroque . . . very beautiful. The 'new wave' is Alexander Dumas, *fils* . . . the imbecile end of romanticism. I prefer Murnau to Stroheim. I detest that which is *chic*, the picturesque and exotic. Today everything is *chic* . . . I'm not sure the cinema is an art, not at all sure, because there's no one today who can say, 'Here, here is *my* film . . . here is a film which I, myself, have made.' *Citizen Kane* was made by me. *The Magnificent Ambersons*, the first five reels . . . as for the rest. . . . *The Lady from Shanghai* wasn't edited by me. . . . Most films I see give me the impression that I hear the sound of the clapper on the set before each take. A good film for me is when I don't 'hear' it. . . . All 'scopes' are zero. . . . Cinema will disappear, killed by television. The films we still make today are the last dinosaurs before the post-Pleistocene age. Soon they'll disappear altogether, leaving only the small, inexpensive films . . . that's the future. . . . I am obsessed with death. . . . America and Russia want to suppress death but they're killing life. . . . One should read the Christian mystics, Shakespeare, Montaigne. . . . Montaigne was one of the greatest Frenchmen. Proust is 'chic'—not Montaigne, nor is Alexander Dumas, nor the Hugo of *The Man Who Laughs*, nor Molière. Just the same, I read Proust; I admire him but I don't like him. . . . Do I believe in God? I won't answer that. . . . There is death. . . . But I detest protestantism, puritanism. Protestantism is vice without charity. . . . I once wrote a scenario for Chaplin and Garbo, *The Loves of D'Annunzio and Duse* . . . two crazy monsters, degenerate hyper-romanticism . . . a ridiculous and theatrical passion . . . but neither would do it."

Von Sternberg's *Anatahan:* I commend it to your attention as the most deeply felt work of one of the supreme artists of the screen. It is one of the increasingly rare examples of Somerset Maugham's "(an) art not of self-indulgence or self-complacency but an art of right action."

Re big screens: it is not size but *scale* that matters. The smallest physical image can become monumental once this is understood. The big screen for spectacles is, therefore, redundant. "A dew drop can reflect the universe," said Dovzhenko.

Wistful was it to see King Vidor try to recapture a passage of visual poetry from his early *Bardelys the Magnificent* in *Solomon and Sheba,* and fail. (The low-hanging branches of a willow tree brushing the camera's lens as it passes slowly in a boat carrying the lovers.) But the old magic was gone. Eleanor Boardman and John Gilbert were not there, nor was Vidor's heart, only his mind, remembering. . . . Love wasn't there, either, love for what he, Vidor, was doing . . . and for the lovely, fragile beauty of Eleanor Boardman, his inamorata at the time.

Our current crop of directors are eclectics, picking from others what they can use. Vidor picks from himself, being one of the "old guard" who originated film imagery, but Ingmar Bergman in *Wild Strawberries* went back a decade for the old doctor who sees himself in a coffin—an exact counterpart of which appears in Kurosawa's *Drunken Angel,* made almost ten years before. And Kurosawa's shadow of a doll dancing to a music box in *Drunken Angel* was antedated yet another decade by a similar scene in Von Sternberg's *Dishonored.*

A few months before he died, the Cinema Museum of Turin asked Giovanni Pastrone, director of the historic *Cabiria,* to record his voice for their collection. "You can have all my mementoes," he answered sadly, "but not my voice—not my voice of today. You should have heard me bawling out orders in 1910. You should have taken my voice then."

Christopher Fry shouldn't really care that he didn't get screen credit for his work on the screenplay of *Ben-Hur.* He's in good company. Michelangelo didn't get any either in the film for his Sistine Ceiling which was used as the background for the film's credit titles.

The double flute designed by Eisenstein for the victory celebration in *Alexander Nevsky* can be found in Rubens' "The Triumph of Silenus." Rubens' flute player looks just like Harpo Marx and his Silenus like Santa Claus. Try making something out of that.

The grotesquely speeded-up coach driven by Dracula and bearing Jonathan Harker to the castle in Murnau's *Nosferatu* was presaged almost a century before in Sheridan Le Fanu's* *Carmilla,* where a dizzily speeding coach carries a female vampire to a castle, for the same reason.

The entire plot situation of *Our Man in Havana* (from a Graham Greene novel) stems from one of Somerset Maugham's Ashenden stories called "Gustave."

The gag in Buster Keaton's *The Navigator* where he and his girl, floundering in the sea, are suddenly raised from the water by a surfacing submarine, was first used by Jules Verne in *20,000 Leagues Under the Sea.*

For all its sophistication, Billy Wilder's *Five Graves to Cairo* falls back on a corny touch that was old even when Ouida used it in *Under Two Flags.* In *Five Graves to Cairo,* a French canteen girl (Anne Baxter) sacrifices herself for her American soldier

---

* Author of Through a Glass Darkly from which Dreyer made *Vampyr.*

(Franchot Tone). In *Under Two Flags,* a French canteen girl, named Cigarette, sacrificed herself for her British soldier.

It's getting tougher every hour to be original.

When it comes to cockeyed opinions about films, it was invariably the non-film people who had the blind-spots that were verily as wide as Mercutio's church-door, as witness the American playwright, Arthur Laurents, delivering himself, anent *Greed,* of the following: "Unintentionally one of the funniest films ever made." And the late American novelist, Nathanael West, writing of *Potemkin*: "One of the most confused pieces of direction I have ever seen." George Pratt reminds me that Robert E. Sherwood also thought *Potemkin* confused. I could cite three dozen equally fatuous opinions of equally sacred icons of the film hierarchy by film and non-film critics alike. No wonder *Ben-Hur* won eleven Oscars this year. It follows.

The anti-intellectual attitude of much American film criticism is echoed again by Buster Keaton in his recent autobiography wherein he accuses Chaplin of having "his head turned by the critics" after their avalanche of praise for *A Woman of Paris,* following which "the divine clown tried to behave, think and talk like an intellectual." As if that were an esthetic crime and the resulting body of his work after that epochal film, therefore, inferior to what preceded it. Such critics live in the "never-never" land of Peter Pan, the boy who never grew up.

After praising Sternberg's *Woman of the Sea,* commissioned by Chaplin but never released, Robert Florey writes, in a recent letter: "But it wasn't as striking as the first four reels of *The Masked Bride* that Sternberg had previously directed for MGM and which no one ever saw except L. B. Mayer and his gang, plus myself. The same goes for the marvelous first version of *The Exquisite Sinner* which Sternberg also made for MGM. If this one had been kept intact at Metro, it would still be showing in ciné-clubs today . . . it was a masterpiece. . . . I think he is one of the few geniuses of the movies. . . . Too bad they butchered *Macao* and *Jet Pilot.*" Later he says: "I was not astounded by *Black Orpheus.* You should have seen the twelve reels Orson Welles shot in Rio, during the carnival, for Howard Hughes about ten years ago, in color. They never did anything with this magnificent film and Hughes never let Orson finish it."

If this were the best of all possible worlds, one bounty we

would have been vouchsafed was a film with Elizabeth Taylor directed by Von Stroheim. She has real beauty and intelligence (only Dietrich, before her, radiated that rare dual quality, vis-a-vis von Sternberg) and the result could have been epochal, alas, alas! And while we are indulging in chimeras:

Twentieth Century Fox should have permitted von Sternberg to launch Mai Britt in his adaptation of Shelby Foote's stunning sex-shocker, *The Temptation of Luther Eustice* (ex-*Follow Me Down*), and they would have had a new star, instead of the disastrous remake of Sternberg's *Blue Angel* under another director who desperately tried to copy "that old black magic" of Sternberg that made the original version unique and inimitable.

"We are living in a culture and in a time that encourages the faceless," said the musicologist, Leopold Mannes, recently. "Naturally this tendency infiltrates, among other things, art, architecture, music, etc. The smooth surface, free of blemish, free of risk—as free of bad taste as it is of any taste—finds its way into performance as well as into creation. True art is for those who dare risks—not necessarily technical ones, but risks of the spirit . . . it stands ever ready to betray anyone who brings to it too little adventure of the soul."

Summer, 1960

COFFEE, BRANDY & CIGARS

COLLOQUIALLY YOURS

One of the season's biggest unintentional laughs occurs in *Song Without End* when Liszt, greeting a group of visiting friends at his home, among whom are Chopin, George Sand, Liszt's manager, etc., sticks out his paw at George Sand and exclaims, "Hello, George!"

MISTRESSES

There used to be an ultra-exclusive private club in pre-World War I Budapest that had a small, discreet sign over the cloakroom: "Members may not bring their mistresses as guests unless they are the wives of other members." (I think it was the Club Pagagaly. Anyway, it was a whole Lubitsch comedy compressed in one sentence. Which reminds me of what Melchior Lengyel, the playwright-author of *Ninotchka*, once said: "Kissing a woman's hand is never the right thing to do; it is either too much or too little." Ah, those Hungarians!)

A PREMATURE MOSLEM

Hugh Griffith, the Arab horse dealer in *Ben-Hur*, exclaims at one point, "By the beard of the Prophet!"— despite the fact that the Prophet he refers to, Mohammed, did not appear until some six hundred years later. There was no Mohammedan religion at the time of Christ.

CHAPLIN AND DEBUSSY

Few people know that Chaplin and Debussy once met. Chaplin was visiting Paris with the Fred Karno Co. where he did a turn dressed as a little dog. In the audience was the great French composer, to whom Chaplin was later presented at the composer's request. Debussy kissed him on both cheeks and told him how delighted he was.

SPEAKING OF FEATS

One of the great musical tours de force of our century was that of Darius Milhaud, the French avant-garde composer now teaching in California. He wrote a double string quartet, which can be played separately as two individual string quartets or together as a string octet.

FAMILIAR REFRAINS

Erich von Stroheim once ruefully commented that "in Hollywood you are known by the last thing you've done," unknowingly echoing what Oscar Wilde said to André Gide after being released from prison: "The public is so dreadful that it never knows a man except by the last thing he's done."

ORIGINS

The recent Manhattan appearance of Marcel Marceau in his pantomimic drama based on Gogol's "The Overcoat" recalls Dostoievski's statement about this memorable short story. "We all came from under Gogol's overcoat." (Sudden thought: could this have been the genesis of Carl Mayer's story for the famous Murnau-Jannings film, *The Last Laugh?*)

IF YOU KNOW SOURCES

There is little new under the movie sun: The plot, such as it is, of the Marx Bros.' *Duck Soup* was first told by R. L. Stevenson in *Prince Otto*, and that author's stories about King Florizel of Bohemia were the genesis of the "kick-off" for Chaplin's *A King in New York*. And there was even a real-life counterpart for Tennessee Williams' Sebastian Venable, the rich young homosexual of *Suddenly Last Summer*, flinging money to a bevy of street arabs, in Oscar Wilde similarly comporting himself on a visit to North Africa. Even so original a film artist as von Stroheim took his masked musicians in *The Merry Widow* from Casanova's description of a fancy bordello he once visited, and the incident of the girl who loses her underpants while watching a parade, in *Queen Kelly*, from Carl Sternheim's play, *Die Hose* ("The Pants"), written a generation before.

MALRAUX ON HOLLYWOOD

André Malraux' one word description of Hollywood's "rediscovery" of realism: "Neon-realism."

CONUNDRUM

During the time when *The Lovers* and *Private Property* were simultaneously on view on N. Y. screens, the ads for *The Lovers* quoted one review as saying, "As close to authentic amour as is possible on the screen." While the ads for *Private Property* quoted another review saying, "More realistic and incisive than *The Lovers.*" (Reminds me of a passage in one of Schumann's piano sonatas marked, "As fast as possible," which is followed a few bars later with the admonition, "Faster.")

STRANGE COINCIDENCE DEPT.

Sean O'Casey doesn't have to crib from anyone, being our most incandescent playwright, but how account for this curious coincidence? In his play, "Bedtime Story," Angela says to Mulligan: "Angela's bright eyes, her scarlet lip, fine foot, straight leg and quivering thigh have lost their charm for Mr. Mulligan..."

Now hark to these lines from Shakespeare (*Romeo and Juliet,* Act II, Scene 1):

Mercutio: *I conjure thee by Rosaline's bright eyes,
By her high forehead and her scarlet lip,
By her fine foot, straight leg, and quivering thigh...*

January, 1961

Merry Go Round (U.S., 1922) Silent Original scenario by Erich von Stroheim. Direction begun by Von Stroheim and completed by Rupert Julian. Photography: Ben Reynolds, William Daniels. Design: Richard Day and Stroheim. Production Supervisor: Irving Thalberg. With Mary Philbin, Norman Kerry, Albert Conti, Dorothy Wallace, Sidney Bracey, Cesare Gravina, George Siegmann, Dale Fuller, George Hackathorne, Maude George, Anton Wawerka. A Carl Laemmle Universal-Super-Jewel Production.

MERRY GO ROUND

After three box-office successes in a row (*Blind Husbands, The Devil's Passkey,* and *Foolish Wives*), Von Stroheim announced he would next do a story set in pre-World War I Vienna. Universal, which had achieved the status of a major company by virtue of these films, approved Stroheim's original screenplay, and elaborate sets called for in the script were built. Shooting started August 25, 1922. The script called for 1500 scenes, of which Stroheim had shot 271, totaling 83,000 feet at a cost of $220,000 when filming was stopped by Irving Thalberg, then production head of the company. The reason was a quarrel between Thalberg and Stroheim over matters of detail in the shooting. This is the same Thalberg who approved the truncation of *Foolish Wives* and who, when he was subsequently moved over to MGM, approved the truncation of *Greed*. Rupert Julian was called in to finish the picture and he started October 7 of the same year. Julian claimed later that the length of the original script plus censorship problems was responsible for the sacking of Von Stroheim. Julian discarded the original script and "from day to day built a new story and characterizations for the film as it now stands. The love story, as it is now presented is absolutely original . . . and in the film, with the exception of approximately six hundred feet at the beginning, was directed by me. The introduction of Norman Kerry riding in the coach with Franz Josef, the banquet sequence, and the elopement of the Countess with her groom, Sidney Bracey, was not by me." Julian finished the picture January 8, 1923. He stated that he spent $170,000 to finish it.

"In the original script by Von Stroheim," Julian said, "there were four thousand feet of titles alone. Ten reels is the most a film can have to be a commercial success. The film as envisaged by Von Stroheim would have run to 20,000 feet. Of course, I do not mean to imply that Mr. Von Stroheim might not have made a successful picture, even a complete one, from his script. I do say, however, and undoubtedly Universal felt that way, that it would have been a tremendously expensive picture. The point upon which I wish to lay especial emphasis is the fact that the film now being shown is my work, with the exception of a few hundred feet, as described."

For all the talk about Stroheim being a realist, he was essentially a romantic. The theme of loveless marriage (so rife in the world) runs through all his films, even in *Greed*. It is, perhaps, best summed up in the dedication of *The Wedding March*—"To all the true lovers of the world" and its sub-titled theme stated at the beginning, "O love—without thee marriage is a sacrilege and a mockery!" Indeed, it was in *The Wedding March* that Stroheim tried again to tell the story that was denied him to tell in *Merry Go Round*. A study of both original scripts shows this. Many of the scenes, later to appear in *The Wedding March*, first appeared in his script for *Merry Go Round*.

But *Merry Go Round* was more than just a love story, it was to have depicted the last days of the Austro-Hungarian empire's

Count Franz Maximilian von Hohenegg ("Franzi") (Norman Kerry) in mufti with his friends on a spree in the Prater. From footage directed by Stroheim and retained in the version taken over and completed by Rupert Julian. The scenes by Stroheim, like this one, inevitably are bursting with life. *Merry Go Round* (1922).

Countess Gisella von Steinbrück (Dorothy Wallace), fiancée of the Count, with her groom (Sidney Bracey). From footage directed by Stroheim and cut from Rupert Julian's version. *Merry Go Round*.

monarchical grandeur and the end of an implacable feudal system. (Years later, Stroheim was to have revived this theme in *La Dame Blanche*, which remained unfilmed.)

The original script reveals, for all its illuminating detail, a discretion in the exploitation of "realism" that is always the mark of the true artist. No roll of drums, no useless waste of film footage is employed in depicting gigantic sham battles in the war episodes. We see the Austrian legions leave for the front and then we see them again, in defeat, wounded, beaten, weary and disillusioned, creeping back to an inflation-ridden Vienna. Something of this concept of depicting war has been retained in the present version, as much of the original script's atmosphere, ambiance, setting and basic plot has been retained, through considerably watered down.

So strong was Stroheim's personality and original conception of this film that even scenes done by Rupert Julian have been taken by many to represent Stroheim's work. But those who recall the sharpness and bite of *Foolish Wives*, even in its several truncated versions, will quickly see that the syrupy *Merry Go Round* is a far cry from the brutality of that earlier masterpiece of Balzacian realism and psychology.

One has only to compare anything else directed by Rupert Julian to see the difference between Julian plus Stroheim and Julian alone. One has also only to see Julian as an actor (he played Prussian officers, too) and compare him with Stroheim, himself, as an actor to also realize, crushingly, that one knew what he was doing and the other did not. Julian was a hack who got a lucky break at the expense of another and far greater man and artist.

That *Merry Go Round* still emerges as an interesting work owes, of course, far more to its original conception by Stroheim than it does to what Julian actually accomplished himself. When the picture was released, the screen credits said the picture was directed by Rupert Julian. No credit for either story or direction was given to Von Stroheim.

Stroheim left Universal and sold the Goldwyn Company the idea of letting him make *Greed*. There is a distinct relation between *Foolish Wives* and *Greed*—but none between *Merry Go Round*, as it now appears, and *Greed*. In that fact you have the answer to the whole matter.

So *Merry Go Round* remains what it has always been from its initial release, an interesting curiosity of film history, definitely worth seeing for that reason, but not to be confused for a moment with a film by Von Stroheim.

The difference between the "realism" of the present *Merry Go Round* and that of *Foolish Wives,* say, or *Greed,* is the difference between the realism we encounter in life, itself, and that of motion pictures. Let us recognize the difference between artists of whatever medium who know what the world is and those who don't. Stroheim was to the cinema what Goya was to painting— and Rupert Julian was to the cinema as Anthony Hope was to literature.

May, 1961

Queen Kelly (U.S., 1928) (Silent) Original scenario and direction by Erich von Stroheim. Photography: Paul Ivano, Gordon Pollock. Design: Harry Miles. Produced by Joseph Kennedy. With Gloria Swanson, Walter Byron, Seena Owen, Tully Marshall, Wilhelm von Brincken. Unfinished. Released version edited by Gloria Swanson.

QUEEN KELLY

This is a fragment of a film which only intermittently gives indications of Stroheim's intentions. The portion shown here was put together by Gloria Swanson in an attempt to salvage something out of the debacle from the material shot for the film's prologue which represents only one-third of the picture. Out of this one-third she attempted to make a whole film by shooting an "ending" herself . . . the suicide of Kitty Kelly with the Prince kneeling at her bier. As the film is now, there is no reason for the film's title, *Queen Kelly,* because only in the original script by Stroheim did she get the nickname.

Stroheim forbade the showing of the film in America because

For Langlois, Eisner and Sadoul this was Stroheim's farthest excursion into the realm of neurotic sensuality. Perhaps he could be summed up in the dictum posed by the sage who said, "If you don't lose your mind over certain things, you have no mind to lose." Prince "Wild" Wolfram (Walter Byron), beloved *enfant terrible*, and his cousin and fiancée, the mad Queen Regina I of Hessau-Nassen (Seena Owen), in *Queen Kelly* (unfinished, 1928).

Contrasts were the spice of life for Stroheim, usually opposing the sacred and profane, like Rodin's *The Kiss* vs. the Queen and her drunken fiancé in the previous still—and the squadron of cuirassiers on maneuvers vs. the line of convent girls herded by their nuns here. Nothing is overlooked, not even the wayside shrine in an arbor of apple blossoms and the prie-dieu before it—and the dazzling whiteness that binds them all together. *Queen Kelly*.

And still the ironic contrasts . . . . Gloria Swanson as Kitty Kelly, novitiate at a convent, and as "Queen" Kelly when she inherits her aunt's brothel.

it was never completed. The sudden advent of the sound-film brought shooting of this silent film to a halt when producer Kennedy told Stroheim, "Now the worst talking film will make more money than the best silent film." Originally, it was a pre-World War I story set in one of the old Prussian states of Imperial Germany and in Dar Es Salaam, German East Africa. The entire prologue and the introductory African material was filmed. The original story, in an outline prepared by Stroheim, is as follows:

> The life history of a young girl, Kitty Kelly, brought up in a convent-school in one of the Duodec States of Imperial Germany. . . .

The cousin of the Queen, the beloved enfant terrible, Wild Wolfram—and the Queen's fiancé—is punished by her for one of his escapades with some extra duty with his escadron of cuirassiers outside of the little capital where he encounters the convent girls herded by their nuns. As the girls curtsy before the Prince, one girl's panties fall to the ground. They are Kitty Kelly's. He laughs, to the dismay of the girl who in her rage throws her pants into the Prince's face. He keeps them as a souvenir. He falls madly in love with her. He kidnaps her from the convent, brings her to his apartment in the palace where he is surprised by his cousin, the Queen. She puts him under arrest and whips the girl out of the palace. After an unsuccessful attempt at suicide, Kitty is brought back to the convent where a cable awaits her. It is from her aunt in Dar Es Salaam in German East Africa, who has paid for her niece's education and who suffered a stroke. Kitty is shipped back to Africa. On her arrival she finds that her aunt is the proprietor of a saloon-bawdy house. At the deathbed of her aunt, she is married to an old but very rich degenerate and inherits the establishment. After the death of her aunt, she declines to live with her husband but takes charge of the house. On account of her regal ways and carriage everybody nicknames her "Queen Kelly." The Prince had been sentenced to Custodia Honesta and on his return from the fortress finds out the whereabouts of Kitty. He has himself transferred into the Imperial German Schutztruppe in Africa. He meets Kitty in her saloon but finds that she is married. After harrowing experiences during which the husband dies, he marries Kitty. The Queen, meanwhile, has been assassinated and he is recalled to ascend the throne. He refuses to come unless his wife, a commoner, would be accepted as Queen. She is accepted and Kitty becomes now really "Queen Kelly," residing in the palace from which she had been forcibly ejected.

As can be seen from the foregoing sketch of the original plot, there was considerably more to *Queen Kelly* than the excerpt that survived. But even this excerpt survived, if that's the word, in a form bearing little resemblance to the way Stroheim would have cut it. All the present scenes are too long, stretched out to make a full feature out of what was intended only as a brief prologue to the main story. Some stills are extant of the African material shot up to the point where Kitty Kelly is introduced by her aunt to the rich degenerate (played by Tully Marshall). They show the sleazy African bordello with its complement of blowsy white and black "merchandise." Tully Marshall (the Baron Sadoja of Stroheim's *The Merry Widow*) is here seen in a dirty white tropical suit and panama hat, a six-shooter in a holster strapped around his waist, a quart of whiskey in his jacket pocket, chewing on a cigar—and is on crutches. Stills also exist of Kitty Kelly as the Madame of the bordello, complete with long slinky black silk gown, black feather boa, black "picture hat," orchids at her shoulder, a long dangling rope of pearls and harsh make-up, a sardonic commentary on all the Madames of history.

The character of the Queen, Regina I (Seena Owen), is archetypal of Stroheim's incisive probing into that all but vanished "world oppressive with heredity, where a society had become imprisoned by the threads woven to safeguard it, stagnant, a perverse world, crueler than that of de Sade, more overwhelming in its moral misery than that of Sacher-Masoch" (Henri Langlois). Out of this world, Stroheim evoked these phantoms who once more go through their grisly "danse macabre" in the infernal machine of his hell-scarred plots which, in themselves, were but pretexts to show the decay of this society. The assassination of Archduke Franz Ferdinand at Sarajevo in 1914 suddenly sounded the death-knell of this world amid the dying screeches of the double-headed eagle. In *Queen Kelly* we were again to penetrate that "incestuous universe with its solemn boredom, its degeneracies and absolute power, its complacency and unpunished complicities—a universe evolved for the creation of monsters, psychotics, victims, slaves, lackeys. . . . Never had Stroheim gone so far in dissecting the anatomy of the Central Powers and the 'divine right of kings.' Never before had he pushed so far his taste for ostentation with those highly polished wax parquet floors, marble pillars and walls, staircases of porphyry, chandeliers of crystal reflected to infinity in mirrors . . ." (Henri Langlois). "Never before had he gone so far with the voluptuousness of his material in his baroque art, an art of iridescence . . . his images lull our senses, playing on the white uniforms of the cuirassiers, the white headdresses of the nuns, the white robes of the convent girls, the white apple blossoms in bloom . . ." (Lotte Eisner).

What remains of all this can be caught in a few fleeting images of this mortally wounded film. Doubtless, we should be grateful to Miss Swanson for making at least this version, her personal print, available to film societies today—else it would never have been seen at all. It is not her fault that the film was never completed by its director. But it no more represents a Stroheim film than does *Thunder Over Mexico* or *Time in the Sun*, put together by others from footage shot for *Que Viva Mexico*, represent films by Eisenstein

Every true artist is always retelling the same story he has evolved as a pretext to make his statements, constantly refining it to reveal ever new facets. With Stroheim, beginning with *Merry Go Round*, it was the old Cinderella story or the Prince and the commoner, which went through several evolutions, in *The Merry Widow, The Wedding March, Queen Kelly*, and his novel, *Paprika*. Even the African milieu of *Queen Kelly* was repeated in even more harrowing form in his novel, *Poto Poto*, and there exists the unfilmed scenario by Stroheim of what was to have been the swan song of his films on Middle European royalty, *La Dame Blanche*, with its tenuous "valse triste" mood, a last salute to the end of a world.

"There is no New Wave," said Claude Chabrol, "there is only the sea." Every wave is a new wave, and what are waves but the surface manifestations of the sea? The art of the true masters is the currents below the surface, immutable and eternal.

Spring, 1961

COFFEE, BRANDY & CIGARS

In Marlene Dietrich's A.B.C., a "philosophical dictionary" patterned after those of Ambrose Bierce and Voltaire, she says, "*Whatever aging people say to the contrary, we all regret our youth once we have lost it.*" Another actress, Sarah Bernhardt, once put it another way when in her later years an old admirer came to visit her in her apartment high over Paris. Climbing all the stairs he asked her breathlessly, "Why do you live so high up?" To which she answered, "Dear friend, it's the only way I can still make the hearts of men beat faster."

AGAIN, WILDE SAID IT FIRST

In the French film, *Life Begins Tomorrow*, Jean-Pierre Aumont says to André Gide, "May I ask you an indiscreet question?" To which Gide replies, "There are no indiscreet questions, there are only indiscreet answers." Very nice, only Oscar Wilde said it first. (Apropos Wilde, the idea of "Odorama" was presaged by him in his original stage directions for "Salome" which indicated "Braziers of perfume should take the place of an orchestra —a new perfume for each emotion.")

PRECEDENTALS

The "Marriage" sequence by René Clair in *The Frenchwoman and Love* was antedated by a short story, "Here We Are," by Dorothy Parker a generation ago (1931 to be exact). And the climactic scene of *The Virgin Spring* (the miraculous appearance of a spring on a site where virtue is crushed by violence, as a sign of divine recognition of the incident) was first used by, of all people, Douglas Fairbanks in *The Gaucho* over thirty years ago.

The highly-touted Carnival in Rio scenes of *Black Orpheus* were not only antedated but far surpassed by those shot by Orson Welles for his unreleased film for Howard Hughes, *It's All True*.

Coffee, Brandy & Cigars (January, 1962)

Grigori Kozinstev in the Soviet *Don Quixote* shows a little naked boy in a peaked sombrero running up a road between two men conversing, for no special reason save that it made for a charming touch. It would have been more charming if it did not recall its original use (far more enchantingly) by Sergei Eisenstein in that portion of his unfinished *Que Viva Mexico!* salvaged by Marie Seton in *Time in the Sun* where he had an adorable shot of half a dozen little naked boys, all in peaked sombreros, running up a flight of street steps like a flock of birds suddenly taking off.

Jean-Luc Godard's *Breathless* has an exchange of dialogue: "You oughtn't to wear silk socks with tweeds." "No? I like the feel of silk." "Then lay off tweeds." You will find it in Dashiell Hammett's *The Glass Key*, written very much earlier.

The entire jewel robbery sequence in *Rififi* was outlined in the novel, *Alexanderplatz, Berlin*, by Alfred Döblin, published in 1929.

VON STROHEIM AND ZINNEMANN

In 1927, Erich von Stroheim wanted to release his Viennese epic, *The Wedding March*, in two parts. It was denied him as being "uneconomic." Today, Fred Zinnemann, wanting to do the same thing with his Hawaiian epic, *Hawaii*, from the vast Michener book, finds himself against the same impasse and for the same reason. (George Stevens justified the three-hour lengths of *Giant* and *The Diary of Anne Frank* by saying, "I believe in giving audiences something for their money. Then they'll tell their friends." Stroheim used the same argument in 1923–24 for his masterwork *Greed*, and was called "crazy.")

THE SADO-MASOCHISTIC UPDATE

Aficionados of *Ben-Hur*, new version, ought to see the old version by Fred Niblo with Ramon Novarro and Francis X. Bushman. No miniatures were used in the sea battles as in the current one, nor did it resort to the trickery of painted-glass "sets" as this one does. Nor have they been able to improve on the chariot race of the first one. They did leave out all the sex of the original version, however, and substituted for it brutality. *O tempora*, etc.!

If you have seen *Crack in the Mirror* with Orson Welles and Juliette Greco, read Somerset Maugham's story, "A Woman of

50," and be surprised. (And for that matter, with memories of Ingmar Bergman's *The Magician*, if you still have them, recall or try to see again at some film society, Leni's *Cat and the Canary* and see how it was all done before and with better ambiance too.)

Even so original a director as Chaplin couldn't *always* be 100 percent original as witness his wild party scene in *A Woman of Paris* (1921) where a girl is unpeeled of the drapery in which she is swathed till she is left nude. The same incident occurred in the late Paul Claudel's scenario for his ballet, "L'Homme et son Désir" (music by Darius Milhaud) written in 1917. (Not to mention Chaplin's reworking of the conveyor-belt scene in René Clair's *A Nous la Liberté* for his *Modern Times* and the lottery-ticket chase into football scrimmage of Clair's *Le Million* for the "chicken-football" also in *Modern Times*. But as René Clair said, he owed so much to Chaplin that he was flattered.)

RE HUMAN STEEDS

In one of the *La Dolce Vita* orgy scenes, Marcello Mastroianni is shown riding a girl on all fours on the floor, a reductio ad absurdum of Von Stroheim's drunken officers, also on all fours on the floor, being "ridden" by girls cracking whips in the bordello scene of his *Wedding March* thirty-five years ago. And Mastroianni flinging feathers from a pillow in the same scene was merely echoing what Roy D'Arcy and his drunken companions did in a wild party scene in Stroheim's *Merry Widow* in 1925. (Only Stroheim turned it into a quasi-poetic thing by having his debauchees fling the feathers out of the windows so that the street below looked in the gray dawn of the next day as if it had been snowing. Where, indeed, are the snows of yesteryear?)

After two screen versions of *Rain* (Gloria Swanson and Joan Crawford) in which no spoken reference was made about the weather, it being taken for granted, comes a third with Rita Hayworth, in which a soldier says to Sadie Thompson, "Let's go before it starts to rain"—*Sic semper cinema!*

FOR THE RECORD

There were two *Potemkins before* Eisenstein's (in France and England), a *Greed* (called *McTeague* with Fania Marinoff and Holbrook Blinn) before Stroheim's, and even an *Intolerance* before Griffith's—by Georges Méliès in Paris, *La Civilisation à travers les âges*.

And, if only for the record, Murnau's *The Last Laugh* (1925) was not the first silent film which had no subtitles, as is generally supposed. Alex Tairov's *Death*, from a novel by Camille Lemonnier, antedated this stunt by ten years, in 1915, which itself was antedated two years before, in 1914, by Max Reinhardt in his film *Venetian Nights*, from a scenario by Carl Vollmöller. (How *recherché* can you get?)

Doug Fairbanks in *The Thief of Bagdad* threw powder from a magic box with which to create an army in that memorable fantasy. Did he or did he not know that Jason's army, in the old Greek legends, sprang up from dragon's teeth sown in the ground? Or that stones were thrown by Deucalion and Pyrrha to repopulate the earth in the Greco-Roman flood myth? Zoroastrianism has it that this was how man was created, by angels throwing stones over their shoulders and where a stone fell there a man appeared, which is to say that man is no more than a thing of chance.

The Spanish government has not only banned Buñuel's *Viridiana* but threatened to boycott any country's films (with which it had reciprocal agreements) if such countries show it. France has already acceded. The U. S. is apparently not involved, on a technicality. But this is old stuff with Spain. In 1937 they not only banned Von Sternberg's *Devil is a Woman*, but demanded that Paramount destroy the negative.

Apropos *Viridiana*, it's a searing film but Buñuel (the original angry young man) said it all and much stronger in his 1930 *L'Age d'Or*, banned practically everywhere. Compare Fellini's juxtaposition of Christ vs. the girls in bikinis at the beginning of *La Dolce Vita* with the scene of Christ and the girl at the end of *L'Age d'Or*. (There's a print at the George Eastman House in Rochester.)

"On the set they call me Mr. Meticulous," said Ross Hunter, producer of *Flower Drum Song*. "I want everything to be real.... People are much more aware of what they see on the screen today ... they can tell the real from the artificial." Said by Von Stroheim forty years ago.

"New York is becoming more and more like Sodom and Gomorrah—anti-natural," remarked Hans Richter, the pioneer film experimenter, recently. "Those arrogant skyscrapers going up everywhere ... there isn't a mountain on earth with such sheer walls, even Everest. Their heights are not attained by a natural grace but are arbitrary." Which recalls Rodin's dictum, "All art that has not its roots in nature is false."

Little, indeed, is new under the sun. . . .

Listen to Ravel's *Ondine* and then to the last third of Schelling's *Nocturne à Ragusa*. (Who remembers that one?)

Recall the last scene of Milestone's *All Quiet on the Western Front*, which was Karl Freund's idea, where Lew Ayres reaches from his trench for a butterfly, the famous scene with the soldier's hand (played, incidentally, by director Milestone himself), and then remember still further back (some six years before that) when Vidor first did it with John Gilbert reaching for a flower in the shell-hole scene of *The Big Parade*.

Who would have thought, for instance, that seven years before *The Blue Angel* there was a German film in which both Emil Jannings and Marlene Dietrich appeared: *Tragoedie der Liebe*, directed by Joe May. (Miss Dietrich, of course, had only a bit part then.)

"I'll never sell *Wuthering Heights* for a remake," said Sam Goldwyn. "To me it is the perfect movie, and I won't have it tampered with."* Which echoes what Willa Cather once said about her stories when she set a blanket refusal for their filming by anyone. And ditto, J. D. Salinger.

And the producing company of Orson Welles's still unseen here *Mr. Arkadin* (a bizarre and fascinating film in its original version), which complained in a suit against the celebrated actor-director that his "excessive drinking on and off the set" put a great strain on everybody and ran a ten-week job into sixteen months, reminds one of what Lincoln answered to complaints of General Ulysses Grant's drunkenness. "Find out the brand he drinks," said the President, "and see that all my generals are well supplied with it."

To all cults of obfuscation, I would remind them of Shaw's "No great artist uses his skill to conceal his meaning."

"Strange how potent cheap music is."

—Noel Coward, *"Private Lives."*

January, 1962

---

*He has since sold it.

FOOTNOTE TO A MONTREAL FILM FESTIVAL

A caprice by Gretchen on a theme suggested by me.

Moon over Montreal . . .
In a little black Volkswagen driven by Norman McLaren through the evening drizzle to the Isle St. Hélène for the party after the gala opening at the Loew's Theatre of François Reichenbach's *Un Cœur Gros Comme Ça*, a *film gros comme ça,* which inaugurates the third annual film festival here.

Also in the car are Guy Glover and Dad. I tell Norman of John Grierson's recent lecture at the Museum of Modern Art, after which, during the question and answer period from the audience, Dad was tempted to ask, "What are The 39 Steps?" but resisted it. I told Norman of Grierson's discussing the composing by Auden of the memorable narration for *Night Train*. "This is the night train," I began, "crossing the border. . . ." And Norman picks it up as we turn to cross the Jacques Cartier bridge over the St. Lawrence . . .

> *Carrying the mail and the postal order . . .*
> *Letters for the rich, letters for the poor,*
> *Letters for the boy and the girl next door . . .*

We are on the little island in the middle of the river and Norman rolls down the car's window so we can smell the wet grass.

The St. Hélène Restaurant, where the festival celebration takes place each year, used to be a gunpowder magazine. Nevertheless, we raise our glasses of Montrachet and Dad offers a toast, the one Léa proposed in Morand's *Open All Night:*

> *To our health which is dear to us all,*
> *And which is so necessary to us,*
> *Because with health we can earn money,*
> *And with money we can buy sugar,*
> *And with sugar we can catch flies!*

The contingent from New York includes the Schlossers from the Carnegie Hall Cinema, Rudi Franchi, Marshall Lewis, Michael Burton, Robert Breer, Arnold Eagle and Bill Starr of the AFFS. Louis Marcorelles, just over from Paris, asks Dad, "Do you know Jonas Mekas? Eugene Archer? Andrew Sarris?" It's his first trip to North America and he's glad, he says, to find it just as big as he thought it would be. The festival is officially launched by Canadian actor, director, and recent Vancouver festival juror, Claude Jutra, the Sarasate of the Twist, doing his "Sacre du Festival" dance with a dusky nymph (the star of his first feature).

The evening is the usual *succès fou:* the orchestra weaving garlands of music endlessly around the dancers, the Montrachet flowing from bottomless magnums, the guests crowding the gigantic buffet as at one of Trimalchio's feasts. Dad and I stand in awe before a magnificent, ravishingly garnished whole Nova Scotia fresh salmon, at least a yard long. This is the second year we've looked at one like this one here and next year we hope to get up enough *savoir faire* to command the waiter behind the buffet to cut off a slice. Later, in a corner, over their plates, the ciné-buff group of Marcorelles, McLaren, and Dad discuss the eighth art far into the night, broken only by intermittent excursions to the buffet for coffee. (Brandy and cigars are in plentiful supply.)

Dad is on a panel discussion taped at the National Film Board for a television film on the new experimental cinema which the CBC will show this Fall and which New York may also see. While there, McLaren showed us around the Film Board, including his own work room: a work-table with rewind, colored inks and pens, and a frosted glass square in the center (which lights up) covered with multi-hued patterns of paper in all manner of shapes. All around were bins and racks of film lengths, and a large bulletin board covered with souvenirs of his world travels and drawings by his friends, including two of my own, one a succession of vignettes of Norman during an interview, the other a "coq d'or" inscribed to him, "A rara avis for a rara avis." We meet Evelyn Lambert, Norman's genial assistant. The room is absolutely gay with its multitudinous colors and designs. "So this is where it all starts!" exclaims Dad. "Exactly the way I thought it would look." In the commissary afterwards we are joined by the two Guys—Glover and Côté—and interest runs high among the Canadians (Arthur Lipsett, of the incisive little anti-world madness film, *Very Nice, Very Nice,* comes over too) about the American "new wave," the Charles Theatre and the salutary work it is doing for new young filmmakers, and all the sudden filmmaking activity in New York.

Montreal—a Russian's idea of what New York is like. Rudi Franchi describes it: "All those gigantic smoked meat places!" Indeed, every second place is a restaurant along the main boulevard, most announcing the merits of their smoked meats, the local specialty. Garish neon signs set St. Catherine Street ablaze at dusk while at night, dominating the scene, a large neon cross on Mount Royal shines high and beneficent above the city.

A one-week festival's events come thick and fast: Besides the thrice-daily showings of new films at the festival theater, there were fringe screenings midnights at the Elysée for the New York group, including amusing shorts made by the French *nouvelle vague* bunch in their pre-feature days; the exposition of film posters from the world over at the Place Ville Marie, Montreal's stunning new skyscraper (right out of *Metropolis*), at which we awarded our own first prize to the Czech, Jiri Salamoun, for his superb drawing of Erich von Stroheim as Rauffenstein in *La Grande Illusion;* the nightly sessions, after the festival showings, at the Kino Club in the stately Hotel Windsor where the buffs gathered to eat and drink, dance and talk till two A.M.; the quasi-surrealist incident of three workmen trying to enter the fifth floor hotel bedroom of Mrs. Schlosser when the lunchtime whistle blew and they found themselves right outside her window ("Peter! Peter! Get those men out of here!"); the candle-lit tables at the Kino Club on the night when the lights went out at one A.M., a mystery that remained unsolved to the end; the showing of the complete *Earth* by Dovzhenko, preceded by Mme. Dovzhenko's touching greeting to the festival read by a spokesman; the Russian *Peace To Him Who Enters* with its lusty ending that brought spontaneous laughter and applause from the audience; Brazil's *O Pagador de Promessa* ("The Given Promise") which made them gasp; Dan Drasin's *Sunay,* which left them in bewildered silence until I started applauding, which "opened the dike" to the flood of applause that followed. Over all, Germain Cadieux and Pierre Juneaux, festival heads, hovered over merriment and mishap with equal aplomb and with cool, patrician equanimity.

But on the surface, at least, all is serene. Claude Jutra dances the festival out each night at the Kino Club, and it rains almost every day. But, *tant mieux*, as they say here, it will "soften the ground" for next year's festival.

Winter, 1962

COFFEE, BRANDY & CIGARS

"If you chase after the taste of the public, you don't see their faces, only their backs." —MAX OPHULS

Did you know that in the last days of the Russian attack on Vienna before they captured the city in the last war, they chased Nazi soldiers through the famous amusement park, the Prater, and killed many who took refuge in the House of Mirrors and who were confused in their escape by the endlessly reflecting glass? (Just like the climactic scene in Welles' *Lady from Shanghai*.)

Apropos the current vogue for "profound" films with "hidden meanings," I recall Fritz Kreisler's "Simplicity in art is the hardest thing to achieve. Technique can be learned." Echoed by Murnau: "Real art is simple but simplicity requires the greatest art." Apropos the current vogue for going all over the map for "authentic locales" in film-making, I recall Frederick Loew (composer of *My Fair Lady*) saying, "I don't believe in authenticity at all—the effect is all that is necessary—as long as you give the effect." Apropos so many pretentiously intellectual films with their labyrinthian involutions which mean whatever you think they *might* mean without actually being sure (whatever happened to directors who had an attitude and made that attitude perfectly clear and which once used to be one of the *sine qua nons* of a good film?), I recall a painting I saw at the Museum of Modern Art by a Belgian, Van Hoeydonck, *sans* title, consisting of nothing but a few off-white strokes on a white canvas. If Rembrandt's "Aristotle Contemplating the Bust of Homer" is worth $3,400,000, what is M. Van Hoeydonck's little art diversion worth? And yet it masquerades as art. Or I am reminded of that sardonic Hungarian who gave a recital in London during which he premiered his music-less piano concerto, not only a concerto *sans* orchestra but *sans* a single note played on the piano throughout. The concert was applauded and reviewed in all seriousness as "something new in music." And, finally, apropos the current screen vogue of erotomania in which both the "art" film and the strictly commercial film are so often equated with who can get away with the most brazen salacity short of the *polizei* descending on all concerned, the anaphrodisia of the bulk of them is pitiful. And the public which flocks to them, and whom the censors, "those guardians of the dirty little secret" (D.H. Lawrence), try to protect from what they *really* want to see, keeps coming back for more. . . . "Maybe next time . . ."

Sudden thought: How wonderful Laurel and Hardy would have been in Beckett's *Waiting for Godot*. In memoriam: Eduard Tissé, Eisenstein's cameraman, one of the all-time great cinematographers and, for *Que Viva Mexico*, even in its unfinished state, for me the greatest . . . which reminds me of the Bicycle Corps joining the workers' revolt in *Ten Days*, with its ravishing phantasmagoria of spinning wheels . . . Kozintsev and Trauberg's *The New Babylon* (1928) on the Paris Commune, with its prodigality of sarcastic energy in terms of the most stunning Renoiresque imagery. . . . The original *Four Horsemen of the Apocalypse* by Rex Ingram with Rudolph Valentino, seen again after almost forty years and as moving and beautiful as ever (especially in contrast to the remake abortion by Vincente Minnelli). . . . Did you know Harpo Marx once played the piano in a bordello? . . . Although such *oeuvres* as *42nd Street, Ben Hur, Exodus, Vertigo, Bigger Than Life, Never Give a Sucker an Even Break* and other such *Meisterstuecke* made the all-time ten-best lists in the recent *Sight and Sound* international symposium, there was not a single vote for such epochal films as *Siegfried, A Woman of Paris, Foolish Wives, The Marriage Circle, Broken Blossoms, The Big Parade, Variety, The End of St. Petersburg, A Nous la Liberté* (I could extend the list ten-fold).... Why doesn't some enterprising producer tackle two fascinating and extremely filmable subjects: Paganini* and Diaghilev? ... Re-seeing the Leyda-edited footage from *Que Viva Mexico* recently reminded me that Eisenstein had filmed the flower boats of Xochimilco in exactly the same context with which a decade before Stroheim had filmed the flower boats of Monte Carlo in *Foolish Wives*. ... And seeing the idyllic Tehuantepec scenes of Eisenstein's heart-breakingly beautiful footage also reminded me that E. once wanted to make a film in Polynesia, to make up for the *Que Viva Mexico* debacle, an idea that was rejected by the Soviet film powers. ... If ever a film was made with love it was *Que Viva Mexico*. The best work is always done with love. ... That same purity of creative passion is to be found in Vigo's extraordinary *Zéro de Conduite* and *L'Atalante*. Truth with the velocity of light. And as a study of a decaying society (what Vigo called "*Point de vue documenté*," i.e., social documentary) his *A Propos de Nice* antedated *La Dolce Vita*, *L'Avventura*, *La Notte*, etc., by thirty years, far more clearly and, as a result, far more piercingly. And ten years before even Vigo, Stroheim had antedated him in pillorying the idlers at Monte Carlo (and exposing its backstreets) in his historic and endlessly fascinating *Foolish Wives* (original twenty-one reel version).... "I don't know whether it (*A Propos de Nice*) will be a work of art," said Vigo, "but it will be cinema." Echoed a generation later by Pablo Casals on the subject of modern music: "It may be modern, but it's not music." ... "The anarchic fury of Vigo ... the enormous liberating force of its quasi-nihilism" (James Agee on *Zéro de Conduite*).... They mutilated *L'Atalante* while Vigo lay dying (at twenty-nine) just as *Lola Montès* was mutilated while Ophuls lay dying. And did not the tragic end of *Que Viva Mexico* kill Eisenstein, as much as anything else did? (He wanted to commit suicide when he learned how his labor of love of 17 months was going to be disposed of.) Let us not even mention what the mutilation of *Greed* (another labor of love, of two years) did to Stroheim.... But the Minnellis and

---

*There was an early German silent film with Conrad Veidt as Paganini (good casting) and a later English sound film with, of all people, Stewart Granger (bad casting).

the Bergmans and the Logans and the Premingers and others of their ilk, everywhere, never have any trouble working. . . . In the bull-fight footage of *Que Viva Mexico,* a bull tormented with banderillas sticking in him, pauses to look down at a flower-festooned banderilla fallen from the picador's hand; for a moment it is like a toy, until the picador snaps him out of his little idyll, goading him on to charge so that he can get two more banderillas stuck in him. I wouldn't trade this "moment of truth" for nine-tenths of all the films currently around. . . . I liked also the scene in De Seta's *Banditti a Orgosolo* where the shepherd boy, after the death of his flock, cannot bear to leave his shepherd paraphernalia which he has been so used to carrying, even if he no longer has a flock to carry them for. This, too, brushes the edge of pain. (Don't explain to me the match-game in *Marienbad* or whether Mr. X did or didn't lay Miss Z there last year.) . . . "As no other art can, the cinema can stupefy. The great majority of today's films seem to have exactly that purpose. They thrive in an intellectual and moral vacuum. They imitate the novel and repeat over and over again the same stories." (Luis Buñuel) . . . "Everyone wants to think of me as a dedicated intellectual but, truthfully, I don't really like making films." (Alain Resnais) "It is too late to play cross-word puzzles and plastic anagrams with life. We have first to preserve some part of it, to demonstrate that part of it is worth preserving." (Joe Regina in Scenario Magazine) Good old soft-focus photography (à la Arnold Genthe) of the "good old days," which limned an effulgent nimbus about the taffy harlots and gilded coxcombs of the screen . . . what sins were committed in its name! . . . I confess that Welles' *Lady from Shanghai* holds an endless fascination for me. . . . The shot of Rita Hayworth running down from the hills to the town at dusk in a little Mexican seaport is enchanting and the dialogue is a joy. . . . Finally, an observation by the prince of abstract film animators (and astringent satirist), Norman McLaren, "If I find a film dull, I find it infinitely more entertaining to watch the scratches."

It is a thought that haunts my nights.

Spring, 1962

COFFEE, BRANDY & CIGARS

The Talmud says: the deeper the sorrow, the less tongue it has. So this epigraph will be brief. She wanted to play Grushenka in THE BROTHERS KARAMAZOV but they jeered her and gave her junk instead. With unconscious irony her last picture was called SOMETHING'S GOT TO GIVE. Poor butterfly . . . she gave in the fullest possible measure . . . broken on the wheel of Hollywood. Arthur Miller dedicated a volume of his collected plays to her out of love. Come, you writers everywhere, dedicate something to her for the same reason. She aspired like you to do good work. This is no one's private sorrow. I dedicate this column, from its first installment to the last, to the memory of Marilyn Monroe.

A whoosh of roman candles, fire-balloons, catherine-wheels, rockets and bengal-lights in honor of MM . . .

All the cant and hypocrisy unloosed by the amorous carryings-on of Elizabeth Taylor during the filming of *Cleopatra* is not only, of course, envious but stupid to pass all understanding. Why did Fox pay her a million dollars? Because she was Elizabeth Taylor—not any one of a dozen other pretty and less "temperamental" stars whom they could have gotten for much less—and they wanted her for the vivid image the public (which made her into the No. 1 feminine box-office star) has of her. Only a star who knows her own worth, and knows with whom she's dealing, could ask that kind of money—and get it. Why, then, shouldn't she know her own mind too? And whose business was it save those involved? Fox need only have worried about making a good picture; a Cleopatra on the set who acts like Cleopatra off the set can only be all to the good for such a picture. (I refer, of course, only to the moronic public's overwrought imagination of who Cleopatra was, from previous movie images they have had of her from Theda Bara and other lurid practitioners of the rites of Isis.) It wasn't Taylor who skyrocketed the cost of the picture to an appalling thirty million dollars. What was "extra-curricular" on the production budget of *Cleopatra* was not Taylor's peccadilloes but Fox's fat-headedness in all the mistakes that were made that could be compiled into a lexicon titled, *How Not To Make A Film*. Besides which, Elizabeth Taylor gave *Cleopatra* at least a million dollars worth of free publicity throughout the globe, thus reimbursing her generous employers for all that lovely money they paid her, even before the film has gone into release. I hope, for the future stability of the human race, that it's not only a good picture but makes lots of money. I'd hate to live in a world where *Cleopatra* was a flop, an utter disaster. The reverberations would doubtless eventually affect everyone, adversely I'm sure, and the yowls of Fox would reach to the moon. I don't want to be around when Darryl (White Fang) Zanuck has to alibi this fiasco to the stockholders. No, *Cleopatra* had better be a success, for all our peace and quiet. With Taylor and Mankiewicz, two virtuosi, it has that chance.

The story (it's a quasi-legend by now) of Cleopatra and her asp is old stuff. Not only has it been perennial grist for the movie mills but even such artists as Shakespeare and Shaw have had their go at it. While waiting to see the new film version (remember what I warned you about in the preceding paragraph, so you'd better go) I suggest you read the chapter, "Anthony and Cleopatra," in Edgar Saltus' *Historia Amoris* (Sisley's Ltd., London, 1906). Everything you need to know about that slippery nymph of the Nile, that slue-footed, sloe-eyed piece of cloven Egyptian catnip, is vividly described in its nine reeling pages. If the movie manages even half its frabjous razzle-dazzle —oh boy!

Say what you will, Nabokov chose a corny title for his *Lolita*. The polysyllable girl's name with its two l's is such old stuff by now one wonders why so deft a wordslinger as he is felt he needed it as an additional enticement to the public. It dates back to Lilith, that female demon of early Semitic folklore, and has since then been reduplicated in one variant or another endlessly, the most recent being Wedekind's Lulu, Lola Montez, Heinrich Mann's Lola Freulich (later Lola-Lola of *The Blue Angel*), Lola, the devil's emissary in *Damn Yankees*, and now Lolita . . . sirens all, but one wonders how any intelligent man could have been taken in by any of them.* All he had to do was notice the name, which was like a label—"Danger, 1000 volts" —and he'd have given them the widest possible berth.

The films shown at the Montreal Film Festival this past summer were of as high an average as is usual with film festivals of major rank. Reichenbach's *Un Cœur Gros Comme Ça*, alleged to have been filmed with hidden cameras and sound recorders, followed a genial Negro boxer through his preparations for a fight in which he loses, and its philosophical aftermath. Humorous, touching, and dramatic, it paints as warm and affectionate a portrait of a human being as you could wish for. The point is, with today's movie hits resembling more and more case histories of Krafft-Ebing, does anyone wish for this sort of thing? The Brazilian, *O Pagador de Promessa* (The Promised Payment), prizewinner at Cannes earlier this summer, reconstructs a supposedly true happening of a peasant's simple faith clashing with the arrogance of the church. Its documentation of the frenetic street life of the seaport of Bahia keeps things alive while the peasant stolidly waits permission to bring his huge wooden cross, as a thank-offering to the town's patron saint, into the church. He makes it at the end, on the cross himself, which is the usual way the good and the innocent make it. The Soviet *Peace To Him Who Enters* careens in a truck behind the lines, during a long night of the last weeks of the late holocaust on the Eastern front, to deliver a shell-shocked Russian soldier and a German girl about to have a baby to an army base hospital. After a harrowing journey they arrive, the child is born and proceeds to urinate promptly on a pile of rifles on the floor. Russian in humor but universal in meaning. The audience was jubilant. *Il Posto* ("The Job") from Italy, critics' prizewinner of the 1961 Venice Festival, is Ermanno Olmi's second feature and with the purity of *Umberto D*. A young boy looks for a job, gets it and faces an appalling future in humdrum work. Quietly but mercilessly, details of his road to the calvary of his miserably drab job sear one with their noxious verity. To be so desperate as to be beyond

---

* Even Mae West came close to this idea in her film, *Lady Lou*. Most recently a new Spanish film starring Sarita Montiel premiered in Madrid. It is called *La Belle Lola*. And Robert Rossen's new film is to be called after the gal who started it all, *Lilith*.

consciousness of humiliation—this is the film's exacerbating overtone, until the sudden shock at the end (which for the boy is really the beginning) when the rhythmic drone of an office mimeograph machine underscores the frantic look in his eyes when he realizes that he will probably end his life here. Of course, King Vidor did it all a generation ago, in *The Crowd* of hallowed memory—even to the chilling institution of the "office party," *Il Posto's* best scene and right out of hell. The Czech *Baron Munchhausen*, by the maker of last year's charming fantasy, *The Wonderful World of Jules Verne*, lacks both the charm and felicitous inventiveness of the latter, hélas. A good try by a virtuoso but, unfortunately, this time it's not enough. Godard's *Une Femme est Une Femme,* pairing that ubiquitous duo of the French "new wave"—Brialy and Belmondo—with the director's wife, Anna Karina, is fast, breezy and brazen. With much the same plot as *The Love Game* (a girl wants a baby, her husband doesn't), the film darts all over Paris, mostly in and out of a small side-street strip-joint, where the heroine works, and violates all the accepted canons of current movie-making, which is all to the good. Godard, with Truffaut, is certainly possessed of the nimblest and most agile mind of the French "new wave." And there was, of course, *Yojimbo,* a Japanese "western" by Kurosawa, but *what* a Western, and with the reliable Toshiro Mifune to carry the whole production on his magnificent back. Another illustration of Mercutio's "A plague on both your houses!" It may be *High Noon* with grunts but it's a rousing good show, tho' not in a class with *The Seven Samurai*. I missed *Accattone* which, I was told, was pretty grim, and a couple of others. These (including *Viridiana*) were the most notable, and many interesting shorts were shown. The crown of the festival was, of course, the reprise of Dovzhenko's *Earth,* a complete original print (even to the Russian titles). The years have not dimmed its glory.

Good cinema is where you find it, just as good painting is. Didn't Delacroix say that one of the finest "paintings" he had ever seen was a particularly handsome Persian rug he once came across? It was at a street fair in New York's "Little Italy" honoring St. Gennaro, its patron saint, during a passionate rendition of a Neapolitan folksong on the bandstand by an expatriate overwhelmed by nostalgia for "bella Napoli," that I saw a woman's arm suddenly emerge from an upper-storey window of the house opposite in a gesture of solidarity and understanding salute to his fervor. In its own way it was as good "cinematically" as the arm of the mother in *The Birth of a Nation* coming out of the doorway to embrace her returning son.

Did you know that MGM asked Jacques Feyder to direct Garbo in a film of Shaw's *Saint Joan* and Dreyer to do a remake of *The Passion of Joan of Arc* with her and both declined? Either work was to have served as her sound-film debut. Instead, she made *Anna Christie*.

And that the Queen's banishing Prince "Wild" Wolfram to German East Africa in the original script of Stroheim's *Queen Kelly* to break up the Prince's romance with Kitty Kelly had its real-life inspiration in Kaiser Wilhelm's banishment of the Crown Prince to the same place to break up his romance with the operatic diva, Geraldine Farrar?

And that Katherine Anne Porter's story, *Hacienda* (1934), is a thinly disguised recounting of Eisenstein, Alexandrov, and Tissé at work on the Maguey episode of *Que Viva Mexico?* (She was there.)

And, finally, that René Clair's first task as an academician among the "Forty Immortals" of the current Académie Française to which he was recently elected in France was to define, for the revised dictionary of the French language on which the Academy is working, the word "cinema"? Forty years ago Clair wrote: "That which makes cinema cannot be defined."

Preston Sturges' devastating prologue for *The Great Moment* (on the discovery of anesthesia) has been cut from all TV prints and a vapid, mealy-mouthed, "polite" prologue substituted for it. Good old TV—the snug refuge of all flat-footed orthodoxy, moralistic sheepdip and gutless cowardice, with its great potential for so much good.

Here it is:

"One of the most charming characteristics of Homo Sapiens —that wise guy on your left—is the consistency with which he has stoned, crucified, burned at the stake and otherwise rid himself of those who consecrated their lives to his further comfort and well-being so that all his strength and cunning might be preserved for the creation of ever larger monuments, memorial shafts, pyramids, and obelisks to the eternal glory of generals on horseback, tyrants, usurpers, dictators, politicians and other heroes who led him, usually from the rear, to dismemberment and death."

I find it odd that many regard Buñuel's parody of Da Vinci's "The Last Supper" in *Viridiana* as blasphemous. The painting is a secular object, not a holy one, despite its religious subject matter. It is a figment of the artist's imagination. Buñuel, therefore, indulges in an intellectual joke, not a religious one, an "in" joke in art. There was no special reason in the story of Viridiana for the beggars' orgy to have exploded into a joke at the expense of religion. (In real life, the chances of this parody happening are of such astronomical odds as to be absurd.) Nor was there any special reason why the heroine had to be a nun (or, at least, a novitiate). The story could have played against any other background and have made its same point, i.e., the corruption of innocence. Buñuel doubtless chose to do it this way because the polarity of religion and sex made for an especially vivid way to make such a point. (But such things happen: I read recently of a stripper who became a novitiate only to leave the convent, before taking her vows, to become a liontamer.)

Actually, blasphemy is very rare in films. Buddhists have claimed that a recent Japanese film-biography of Buddha is blasphemous, and one could doubtless make a case on this ground for many well-meaning but idiotic Hollywood biblical spectacles, but with the possible exception of the last scene of *L'Age d'Or*,* there is no blasphemy in Buñuel's films. The sex-hysteria of the nuns in the Polish *Mother Joan of the Angels* is not blasphemous because it is factual (see Lecky's *History of European Morals*). Stroheim, Pabst, and Buñuel combined, couldn't have thought up some of the goings-on among the nuns and monks in convents and monasteries, those bastilles of God. Even the alleged "parody" of the Virgin Birth in Rossellini's *The Miracle* was not deemed blasphemous by the Vatican nor even by the courts here, where the Roman Catholic hierarchy is more Catholic than the Pope. The parody of the raising of the American flag on Iwo

---

* "There is no limit to the extent of error, or of horror, to which logic may lead when it is applied to matters not pertaining to pure reason." (Bergson)

Jima in that famous news photo as done in Ron Rice's "beat" film, *The Flower Thief*, is not blasphemous *per se*, either, because Rice is indirectly indicting the sentimental aspects of war because he despises war.

There are many films, however, that could be said to be blasphemous, or immoral, because their ideational content makes their motives suspect, to put it mildly. Such films degrade both cinema and art; most of all they degrade those who make them. If the so-called "remake" of *Caligari* by Lippert which Fox released ("released" in its bathroom sense) was not such an abysmal piece of turd, I'd call *it* blasphemous for having the gall to call itself by the name of that epochal film.

The greatest performance by an actress I've seen since Falconetti's in Dreyer's *Joan* is given by Anna Synodinou of the Greek National Theatre in *Electra* by Sophocles, a film produced by James Nicholas and Ted Zarpas, shot at the fourth century B.C. Theater of Epidaurus in Greece, a 14,000 seat amphitheater whose acoustics are unmatched in the world. (Are you listening, Lincoln Center?)

Re-seeing Orson Welles's polyphonic and stunningly "orchestrated" *Mr. Arkadin* recently, I was reminded of the apotheosis of the single entendre achieved by most films despite all their huffing and puffing. Not only are they not orchestrated, they are composed for just the treble clef for the right hand of the piano, for all the lushness of their musical scores to "hop them up" or on which they lean like a crutch, trying desperately to make up for the deficiencies of the director. And the most *chic* of them, with their double entendre, are as much double as those mirrored pianos you see in the movies and on TV which reflect the keyboard and the pianist's hands . . . very *dans le vent, à la page* . . . which is supposed to induce a state of euphoria in the spectator like that induced by those hallucinogenic mushrooms of the Mazatec Indians of Mexico.

As for the recent spate of sexual frankness in films in which each director tries to see how much more he can get away with than his colleagues (the latest example being Dassin's *Phaedra*), and which in Roman slang is called *"cinematografaro,"* I am reminded of Chesterton's "Art like morality consists in knowing where to draw the line." (Machaty in *Extase* knew and that's what makes it still unequalled in this genre).

Erwin Panofsky makes an unconscious parallel between the best films of today and yesterday when he says: "In today's art, modern symbolism is too much the private affair of the artist. In the older arts, the symbolism was the common knowledge of the people and their society. That doesn't exist anymore. It is lost and I mourn its passing."

"Cinema—the white man's opium." (Marcel L'Herbier)

After the appearance of Saint-Saëns on the musical scene, it was inevitable that the cinema should be invented.

Now that Darryl Zanuck has put off Fox's proposed filming of Joyce's *Ulysses,* it might be recalled that Joyce and Eisenstein once discussed its filming, E. being particularly fascinated with such challenges in the book as the "interior monologue" of Molly Bloom's soliloquy.

Eisenstein explaining his method of composition within the frame: "Hewing out a piece of actuality with the axe of the lens."

Again re all the well-meaning biblical films: I'm reminded of that line in Brendan Behan's *The Heritage:* "Do you think you're doing God a good turn by speaking well of him?" Or of Gretchen's "Do-It-Yourself Crucifixion Kit."

Better-Dead-Than-Alive Dep't: "MM's Phenomenal Postmortem B.O. . . . : Almost every one of the approximately 885 prints of various Marilyn Monroe pix in the vaults of 20th-Fox domestic (U.S.-Canada) exchanges have been in constant use during the last three weeks, a 20th exec. report . . ." (Variety, Sept. 5th).

Again from Variety, same issue: "At his press conference here yesterday, 20th prexy Darryl F. Zanuck was asked whether he thought that Hollywood was 'responsible' for the death of Marilyn Monroe. Prexy put his answer this way: 'To attend this press conference today, I had to delay my return to New York by one day. Now, if my plane tomorrow should happen to crash, and if I were killed, would you people be responsible for my death?" (My answer—yes.)

On p. 16 of the last FILM CULTURE, Patrick Bauchau says "1962 marks the lowest ebb in U.S. Cinema" and on p. 25 Peter Bogdanovich says *"Hatari* is among the best pictures of 1962." Dubious distinction, what? Bogdanovich also says, "Anyone who does not see the beauty and brilliance of this picture

(*Hatari*) is either a fool or a snob, and both are really the same." Put my name, like Abou Ben Adam's, Peter, at the top of your list, and leave plenty of space underneath for others. I'll regard it as an honor roll when all the names are in.

What did the two greatest American still-photographers do when they wanted to make a film? Alfred Stieglitz chose as his subject the horizon, studies of the meeting of earth and sky. Edward Steichen chose as his subject the growth of a tree. "All art is fake that hasn't its roots in nature," said Rodin. "*N'oubliez pas la nature!*" cried the *douanier* Rousseau as his parting advice to Max Weber, running alongside Weber's train as it started to leave.*

Painting and cinematography are sister arts, with painting, naturally, the older of the two; hence, though many rules of the latter do not apply to the former, all rules of the former apply to the latter. (You can make a fortune in the movies ignoring this maxim but it doesn't change it an iota.)

Such very "precious" things are sometimes said when people get carried away with themselves, as witness the comment of Julian Beck and Judith Malina on Marie Menken's *Visual Variations on Noguchi:* "It blinds! It deafens! There is no greater praise!" (Isn't there?)

Or Miss Menken's description of her own *Dwightiana*: "Animated film shot while watching over an ill friend." (That's a hell of a way to watch over an ill friend. I've been worrying ever since as to whether the friend died or recovered.)

My two favorite Antonioni films are the brooding *Il Grido* and the quasi-Chekovian *Le Amiche*. But that's all.

Truffaut is quoted by the N.Y. Film Bulletin as saying that Renoir's *La Règle du Jeu* ("Rule of the Game") "was the first psychological film in which the notion of a good and bad personage had been entirely eliminated." A statement contradicted forty years ago by Chaplin's *A Woman of Paris*. Its foreword even explicitly stated the case: "Humanity is composed not of heroes and traitors but simply of men and women." (I

---

* What Rodin and Rousseau meant was postulated earlier in another way by Jean-Jacques Rousseau in *The Social Contract,* whose overriding and all-embracing theme is: God is good, man is good, nature is good; evil becomes possible when the natural order is perverted.

quote from memory.) "And the passions that move them, good or bad, were given them by nature. They err in blindness. The ignorant condemn their mistakes, the wise pity them."

Following upon my epochal discovery of someone smoking on the set of *Caligari* (Wiene's not, ugh, Lippert's!) in one scene, described in an earlier column, I now offer the equally epochal discovery of someone (maybe DW himself?) smoking during the scene in *Birth of a Nation* where Walthall brings Mae Marsh's body into the house after her suicide. Left of the screen, puffing away nonchalantly as if cinema history wasn't being made that day. And that was four years before *Caligari*—Griffith seems to have been first in everything.

"Art is the art of leaving out," said Debussy. Hence my fascination with the elliptical styles of Lubitsch, Sternberg, and Welles. *How* you say it is *what* you say.

One of the greatest openings of an American film was the short but frenzied prologue (before the credits and long before this gimmick became a chi-chi vogue) of the blind street evangelist exhorting people to stop hating each other in Cy Endfield's *Try and Get Me*, (ex—*The Sound of Fury*) cauterizing the lynch-mob mentality with searing fury. Frank Lovejoy and Lloyd Bridges were featured.

And a film for which I retain a fond memory as a work of patrician style is *Thunder in the East* by Nicholas Farkas with Boyer, Loder, Oberon, and Inkijinoff, from Claude Farrère's novel, *La Bataille*. (Why alla time *Four Sons* and *Mr. Moto's Gamble* on TV and not this?) Speaking of patrician style, I recommend to your attention a minor British item, *Glory at Sea*, by Compton Bennett with Trevor Howard, which you *can* see on TV. Flawless exposition of why "there'll always be an England."

Mekas' blank screens at the close of each section of *Guns of the Trees* reminds me of Sadakichi Hartmann's "Judicious silences are important in any work. . . ."

I once suggested three films that would personify the cinema: *Greed, Potemkin,* and *City Lights*. I'd choose to personify painting: Watteau's *Embarquement pour l'Ile de Cythère* (to me the highest point reached by Western civilization in art), Daumier's "Sancho Panza Wringing His Hands" (Don Quixote series) and Goya's two men flaying each other as both sink into the mire.

Art, art, always art! Like Danton said of audacity, as a means of achieving a goal. *"L'Arte, a Dio quasi nipote."* (Dante) (Art is to God like a granddaughter.)

Norman McLaren, cognizant of the fact that many people blissfully sleep at the movies while others, doubtless insomniacs, don't, is going to try to lend the latter a helping hand by devising, with an assisting psychologist now working at the National Film Board of Canada, a film to put audiences to sleep, thereby achieving a total state of bliss. What could be more salutary? *"Toujours de l'audace!"*

End of fireworks.

Autumn, 1962

COFFEE, BRANDY & CIGARS

What ho! what ho! this fellow is dancing mad!
He hath been bitten by the Tarantula.
          POE: *The Gold Bug*

Through the courtesy of the Museum of Modern Art, I was recently able to see some 50,000 feet of footage shot by Eisenstein for *Que Viva Mexico*—7000 feet put together by Bell & Howell for *Zapotec Village* and *Mexican Symphony* and 43,000 feet printed up from the original negative by Jay Leyda which didn't get used in his four-hour study material from the film prepared under a special grant. It is of this 43,000 feet that I'd like to speak briefly. There are scenes of the flora and fauna of Mexico (pumas, monkeys, pelicans, parrots, etc.) so rapturously photographed as to make one feel this is the way it must have been in the Garden of Eden before man fell from grace. Here is the purest pantheism. There are the white cathedrals (dazzlingly white) as if sculptured by some half-mad master pastry chef out of spun sugar, so frenetic is the Mexican baroque which makes even the most extravagant European baroque pale by comparison. (Though Eisenstein photographed countless churches, he never filmed a single church interior—it was the incredible façades as architecture that fascinated him.) There are the flower boats of Xochimilco, floating gardens gliding through quiet lagoons carrying señoritas and their caballeros, lazily strumming guitars, flirting and kissing in the late afternoon sun as the oarsmen, as in Venice, paddle them along. There is the deep jungle and the tides of the gulf lapping the shoreline at dusk with the sudden starlike bursts of a maguey plant silhouetted in the moonlight. On the plains and plateaus are the ruins af Aztec, Mayan and Toltec temples, silent monoliths of an ancient grandeur with the old stone gods waiting for sacrifices which never again will be made—and seen in these gloriously photographed images as they will never be seen by any tourist.

Endless fiestas, ritual dances, village and city life, the idyllic life of tropical Yucatan and Tehuantepec, bull-fights, thousands of feet of bullfights whose barbarism was never more murderously depicted, more scenes of the *Calaveras,* or Death Day celebrations, even more visually intoxicating than the ones we know from the Sol Lesser short, *Death Day,* made from this material, scenes supplementing the footage used for *Thunder Over Mexico* and *Time in the Sun,* every bit as magnificent, but "born to blush unseen" as a poet once said. There is the great Independence Day parade in Mexico City—the army, police, fire-fighters resplendent in their uniforms, the sun glinting off their sabers and helmets, the dignitaries reviewing them, these dignitaries who will be shown as skeletons under their gold braid and frock coats on the holiday of Calaveras when the Mexican peon laughs at death, having lived and suffered so long in its shadow. And so the footage goes. There is hardly an aspect of Mexico that Eisenstein didn't cover.

How did he plan to use all this material in a single film? That remains the great and forever to be unanswered question. There are candid shots of Upton Sinclair, too, he who made this great and, as it turned out, sad venture possible; shots of Alexandrov at dusk looking out over the Gulf of Mexico, a statement by Upton Sinclair defending *Thunder Over Mexico,* intended as a prologue to the film which was never used; there is even a shot of Eisenstein, himself, on the porch of Sinclair's home in California, smiling shyly as he sits down in the half-light of early evening to a conference with Sinclair on the project for the Mexican film. And there are the still-to-be-printed-up thousands of feet of negative reposing silently in the Museum of Modern Art vaults in Long Island City. What of them? What do they contain? Will Alexandrov really, as he recently stated, go through with his plan to "reconstitute" *Que Viva Mexico?* He has Eisenstein's script and notes. Will the Soviet Government negotiate for this material with the Museum of Modern Art which has it on permanent loan from Upton Sinclair? Whatever the ultimate answer, it will not change the glory of this footage an iota. It remains as a silent memorial to a shattered dream that, had this really been the best of all possible worlds, could conceivably have resulted in one of the greatest works of art of the Twentieth Century, alas, alas. . . !

The dance known as the twist is nothing new. In 1925 Flaherty's *Moana*, filmed in Polynesia, contained a dance, the "siva," which is the twist in its purest form.

When *Potemkin* was first shown in Sweden it was recut, by government decree, in such a way as to show the mutiny by the sailors put down and its perpetrators shot.

Titling a foreign film gives you a chance to study it to the nth degree since you comb every foot of it slowly and carefully, over and over. My recent assignment to title *Sundays and Cybele,* starring a 12-year-old French charmer, Patricia Gozzi, convinced me that the French consistently make the best films about children—*Visages d'Enfants, Poil de Carotte, La Maternelle, Forbidden Games, The 400 Blows,* etc., and now this latest example of a great Gallic tradition. We make *Lolita* and the French make *Sundays and Cybele.* . . .

Add to the honor roll of great Russian cameramen (Tissé, Kabalov, Demutski, Golovnia, Moskvin, Bobrov, Kalatozov, etc.) the name of Urusevsky, most recently for his virtuoso work in *The Letter That Was Not Sent.* The long, harrowing sequence of the forest fire is surely one of the most amazing scenes ever filmed. Kalatozov, the director, is Russia's ciné-poet of the wastelands. His 1930 *Salt of Svanetia* documented a bleak area of the Caucasian Mountains with a ferocious realism that became surreal . . . and his rendering of an environment as in the desolate Siberian landscapes of *The Letter That Was Not Sent* seems offhand to be scarcely less an achievement than what Stroheim and his cameramen accomplished in Death Valley for *Greed*.

Hollywood is so obsessed with money as the supreme goal and end-all of human happiness that it becomes delirious in depicting the things that money will buy. Did you ever notice how silken the photography becomes, how lush the music (mostly shimmering strings, *bien entendu*) suddenly cascades, in such scenes? Like diving nude into a pool of whipped cream.

Was there ever a fantastic movie-set that could match the incredible fantasy of the temple atop the sheer cliffs of the sacred city of Lhasa in Tibet?

Someone ought to do a piece called, "The Turd Kickers," tracing this venerable institution in the movies from Charles Ray and Richard Barthelmess to its most recent practitioners like James Stewart and Gary Cooper (except in *Morocco*) including those females in direct line of descent like Judy Garland, etc.

Was ever anything sadder and sweeter (both at the same time, and aside from Chaplin) than that moment at the beginning of *Lady With a Dog* when Anna Sergeyevna (exquisitely played by Iya Savvina) says to the handsome stranger who has just been approached by her little white dog, "He won't bite."? The mixture of loneliness, half-hope that the incident might lead to an acquaintance, assurance that the pup would in truth not bite—all this distilled into a single glinting drop of dialogue like the mystery of the human heart refracted by a prism.

If this column ever becomes famous, it'll surely be, among whatever other reasons, for touching on items that probably would never have occurred to anyone else, to wit: Did you know that when Ventucci (Cesare Gravina) shows Prince Karamzin (Stroheim) the picture of his deranged daughter's dead mother in *Foolish Wives*, it is a photo of Stroheim's wife?

When Darryl Zanuck fired Mankiewicz from *Cleopatra*, preventing him from editing it, I was reminded of the gallant tribute paid Zanuck by Mankiewicz in the latter's *All About Eve* and of "the years like black oxen that trample us under foot."

I've been asked why I singled out so difficult a picture as *Guns of the Trees* as the best film so far of the American "new wave." Because it was made from principle. A cinema without principle is as alien to Jonas Mekas as life without principle. When you think about it, very few films are ever made from principle ... and I hope you know the kind of principle I mean. Many excellent films have also been made outside this persuasion, but if you don't start with a principle you have to substitute something else salutary instead. After all, from what principle did *The Last Laugh*, say, or *The 39 Steps*, or *The Devil Is a Woman* spring? What was substituted was very salutary, indeed, but even this substitution wouldn't have been salutary to the degree that is was in works like these if their creators hadn't been men of principle. In short: art isn't possible from an unprincipled man. It is one of the grandest things about art.

The movie press-agents don't seem to care (or don't know) what they say, hence *Boccaccio 70* is heralded as "the first 3-act motion picture ever made" when, in sooth, as far back as 1924 Leni's *Waxworks* was a "3-act" film and there have been many since, including the comparatively recent Maugham trilogy, *Trio* (how short memories are!).

I urge all those who see or plan to see *Sodom and Gomorrah* to try to see a half-hour short, *Lot in Sodom*, made in the early thirties by J. Sibley Watson and Melville Webber, on the same subject. It is not only one of the high points of the American cinema but there's no pussy-footing about the subject. It also contains the greatest prismatic cinematography I've ever seen ... and a remarkable musical score by Louis Siegel that is among the most original (in its best sense) scores ever done for a film. (Prints are at Brandon Films, Audio Films, and the George Eastman House.)

One of the best American gangster films is all but forgotten today and hasn't been seen in a generation—Roland Brown's *Quick Millions*. And will we ever see Sternberg's *Dragnet* again?

Why doesn't someone do a piece on Tod Browning, director of the famous *The Unholy Three* (the first version)? Who was he? Where did he come from? From what bizarre brain came an output of such diablerie as would give Dr. Caligari himself the shakes? No adulterated bogey-man stuff but pure red-eye guaranteed to make the viscera go into conniptions.

"*Ulysses* I've killed completely but whatever other Jerry Wald properties are suitable we'll activate and, of course, Connie Wald and the estate will have equities in these. Jack Cardiff, who was to have directed the James Joyce opus (*Ulysses*) agreed to a year's postponement because he knows that we're trying to "insure" ourselves and he's not going to be given any 'dog' property." (Darryl Zanuck, *Variety*, Sept. 12, 1962.)

Joris Ivens, the Dutch *cinéaste*, who began his career with a film on rain over thirty years ago, has come full circle. After documenting the civil wars in China, Spain, Cuba, he has returned to his first love, as true artists always do (some never even veer from it) and will do next a film about wind—the *mistral*, that heady air current that originates in the Alps and blows through the south of France to the Mediterranean. (Where is the present day Lubitsch or Preston Sturges, or at least Mal St. Clair or Harry d'Arrast, who'll do a satirical comedy about the effects of the *mistral*, the *fon*, or the *sirocco*, on a heterogeneous group of people caught in their devastating paths? Renoir came close in *Picnic on the Grass* but there it was attributed fancifully to the pipes of Pan. But Renoir was on the right track, as he always is no matter what track it is, and he always returns to nature, as befits the son of the great Auguste Renoir.)

The arms coming out of the walls holding candelabras in Cocteau's *La Belle et la Bête* were antedated over a century ago by Theophile Gautier in his sepulchral story, *One of Cleopatra's Nights*, and two centuries before that by an unknown Italian sculptor of a bronze torch-bearing arm. Cocteau's twist was to make out of these purely decorative arms, *real* arms.

A Reuters dispatch from Geneva in a recent issue of *The New York Times:* "Hollywood sometimes spends more money on a single film than the Food and Agricultural Organization and the World Health Organization in an entire year, according to the magazine *World Health*."

Apropos *Greed:* "Wife Rated Tops As Penny Pincher—Chicago, UPI—One study shows it is the wife who is the tightwad in most families. . . . A pilot study by the Public Relations Board shows that most ladies are ready to cut out their husband's beer and cigar money when the budget runs low. . . . Most of the husbands studied wanted more labor-saving household appliances for their wives, but the women saw little need for such husband-savers as power lawn-mowers." (*N.Y. Times*, March 30, 1962.)

Apropos *Potemkin:* "Prisoners in Riot Over Stew; Sheriff says

It Stays on Menu—San Antonio, Tex., UPI—Prisoners at the Bexar County jail here rioted and set mattresses afire today in protest against being served stew for lunch. Four were injured. . . . Wax bullets and high-pressure water hoses were used to break up the riot which involved 130 men and lasted two hours. Sheriff William Hauck ordered stew to be served again for the evening meal. 'The food is good,' he said. (*N.Y. Times*, Sept. 6, 1962.)

Again, before you think the style of *Last Year at Marienbad* is original, read Christopher Morley's *Thunder on the Left*.

I like to think of Proust arriving at a party and, as he takes off his coat, asks his hostess, "What's new?"

I like the introduction of Bette Davis in *Fog Over Frisco* (a good title wasted)—three balloons in front of the camera lens go plop, two, three and there she is.

I like the narrated chariot race in the James Nicholas-Ted Zarpas' *Electra*, after Euripides, starring Anna Synodinou, far better than the one literally acted out in *Ben Hur*.

I like the "F" nudging the "U" in the word "FUN" on the animated electric sign in Times Square when it "showed" Norman McLaren's delightful film advertising travel in Canada last summer. It brought back memories of the Siamese girl in the bordello nudging Prince Nikki in Stroheim's *The Wedding March* when he says he has to leave to visit a nice girl. The Siamese beauty digs him in the ribs with her elbow. "At this hour?" another girl asks. "That's when her parents snore the loudest!" laughs the Prince. Ah, *The Wedding March* . . . ! Most wistful of all films about sacred and profane love . . .

> *After a night of spree*
> *I have come to purify myself*
> *Under your window*
> *As if it were an altar.*
>
> (Old Flamenco song)

Now who else would associate those two films? The most surprised person doubtless would be McLaren himself. (If this is not a bengal-light or roman candle, it is at least a small sparkler which I hold to keep the lights going for MM . . .)

I like Jim Card's music scores for Pabst's *Pandora's Box* and *Diary of a Lost One*, they are in fact perfectly splendid, and the curator of the George Eastman House, that marvelous film archive in Rochester, has turned out a real labor of love. Who wouldn't be inspired by such a lovely creature as Louise Brooks, the star of both films, was at the time she appeared in them? You'd have to have a heart of stone not to be.

Speaking of *Pandora's Box*, every would-be director today ought to study it, among other such purely "director films" of the great classic age of the cinema. What a marvel of subtlety and cinema sophistication it is! It contains one of the best sequences ever filmed—the frenzied preparation backstage of an opulent musical extravaganza just before curtain-rise. Broken up into a thousand details, each dovetailing into the next (Pabst was a master at this) it literally takes your breath away with its choreographed movement. The effect is ravishing not only to the eye but to the vasomotor system.

An Italian film company which announced a motion picture on Mohammed was warned by the spiritual leader of Iran that if they persisted they would bring on a "Holy War" against Italy. (The Moslem religion forbids any pictorial representation of the Prophet of Islam, Allah's missionary on earth.)

What happened to the art of stylized acting (exaggeration to put across an idea, in which the style blends with every detail of the work, even to the *decor*)? Don't tell me, I know—it's disappeared. But I keep remembering Catherine Hessling in Renoir's *Nana,* Elena Kuzmina in the Soviet *The New Babylon,* Roy D'Arcy in Stroheim's *The Merry Widow,* Sam Jaffe in Sternberg's *The Scarlet Empress,* John Barrymore in *Twentieth Century,* not to mention Krauss in *Caligari,* Kortner in *Backstairs,* Jannings in *Waxworks* . . . I'd better stop this.

Who will cast Brigitte Bardot in the title role of Stroheim's gypsy novel, *Paprika?* And do, *but really do,* films on the lives of those odd fish—Bernhardt, Paganini, Diaghilev?

Winter, 1962

COFFEE, BRANDY & CIGARS

Someone once said you could tell more about a man from the letters he receives than the ones he writes. Leafing through the accumulation of years, I select these few fugitive pieces at random, excerpts presented in no particular order—sometimes informative or revelatory, sometimes whimsical or facetious, sometimes sentimental or nostalgic—all bound together by the garland of the arts.

A poem from novelist Joseph Freeman, "On Hearing Herman Weinberg in His Film Class," at which René Clair's *Sous les toits de Paris* was shown:

It's all true; we were there
When Spring came on with rain on a Renoir street
And Eros telegraphed on cobblestones
With lovers' feet.
Faces were innocent,
Weapons small,
Even the apache was magnanimous
Before the Fall.
The roaring smoke and glare of a passing train
Obscured the inconclusive fight;
No blood was shed that night.
Death was not yet despot of the world;
Right knew limits, so did wrong;
And under all the roofs we heard,
Above the self-delusion and the cant,
The golden phoenix chant
His ever-recurring song.
Both rivals lost the girl
To the faithful, astonished friend;
This was the Happy End.
The bombs drove underground to wait
For the next turn of the wheel of fate
When the Spring rains
Will come again.

A note from Ben Hecht commenting on an earlier installment of this column in which he reminisces wistfully about his own youthful walks through the garden of the arts: "It was the best time of all."

A "fan letter" commending me for my titles for *Sundays and Cybele* but adding fretfully, "Why do you insist on spelling 'all right' as one word?" Which reminds me of the late Sherwin Cody's frantic missives to me on the same subject. I hope that in Heaven, where he surely is, he finds both usages tolerantly accepted, else what is Heaven for?

ORSON WELLES

A letter from Orson Welles: "By long practice, I generally refrain from reading reviews of my own movies or plays. Through the years I've found an uncomfortable majority of my critics to be the opposite of encouraging, and I have a weakness in this matter: I tend to be very impressed by almost any reasoned attack on my work which may get into print. But I did read your review (in *Film Culture*). You kindly lulled my suspicions by sending it to me and, besides, there has been so very little written about *Mr. Arkadin* in English at all. The result was a very happy surprise. Unluckily for my professional ego, I have never been able to take a good review quite as seriously as a bad one but I must tell you that your generous appraisal was deeply appreciated. What really pleased me was not so much that you liked *Mr. Arkadin,* but that you liked it for what I take to be the right reasons. This, of course, is the ultimate compliment...."

From Symon Gould, a pioneer in the art cinema movement in the United States back in the Twenties, on the launching of *Potemkin* here: "... As I remember it, those present at the premiere of *Potemkin* in Gloria Swanson's penthouse at 58th and 6th Ave. were Mal St. Clair, Adolphe Menjou, John S. Cohen, Jr., Dick Watts, Lewis Milestone...."

TOM CURTISS AND VON STROHEIM

From Tom Curtiss, *Variety* correspondent and entertainment editor of the Paris Tribune: "How can I apologize for the long silence? ... Whenever Denise, Erich (von Stroheim) and I are together we speak of you and, in the Kipling phrase, 'raise our glasses towards you' ... The Tribune work goes on and widens. I now do theater, films and night-clubs, as my colleague, Art

Buchwald, is concentrating on his N. Y. column. . . . Von is working on the synch score of *The Wedding March*. . . . I haven't seen it in years now. Is *The Honeymoon* print still available? . . . I went to London last week to see some shows and Dick Watts, who is there for the opening of *The Moon Is Blue*. Diana Lynn, his (then) current girl friend, has the lead and has made the play into a hit. She's charming but I wish she was playing something else. Ward Morehouse gets to London tomorrow for a week and I may go back to see him and a few more plays. The London theatre is fine but London life is dreary after Paris. . . ."

From Tony Richardson: "I've been meaning to write you ever since I got back (to London) but my life has been in even more chaos than usual. This has been largely because an uncompromising girl with a child and two lovers (for use and pleasure respectively) has been sitting in my flat. In the meantime I've had to sit on the doorsteps of all my friends. However, she's gone now."

From Karl Freund: "One of the interesting stories about Murnau's life was his friendship with Walter Spies, who lived on the island of Bali. Spies was an excellent painter and musician, handsome, the son of a very fine Baltic family. 'Civilization' at the end of the First World War proved too much for him, so he decided to run away from it and start a new life in the Dutch East Indies. Murnau, however, could never forget Spies, and many times attempted to persuade Ufa to make a South Seas picture so he could see Spies again. While he came quite close to fulfilling that desire during the filming of *Tabu* in Tahiti, I don't think Murnau actually ever did see Spies again. Spies, who was known to all travellers to Bali, including Noel Coward, Vicki Baum, Miguel Covarrubias, died as a prisoner when the boat on which he was being transported to a concentration camp was torpedoed during the Second World War."

'WICKEDEST EYES IN THE WORLD'

From Anielka Elter, the masked girl-musician in Prince Danilo's seduction scene of Stroheim's *The Merry Widow*, once publicized as "the girl with the wickedest eyes in the world": "What a shame that one gets to be old and the wicked eyes are not so wicked anymore. I was a Hollywood girl when the going was good and the most interesting or the craziest people were

Coffee, Brandy & Cigars (January, 1963)

always interested in me. I was a musician in *The Merry Widow*, a girl with a mask, which Stroheim saw as a temptation of evil. I wore what in those days we used to call 'A couple of flowers and nothing to pin them on.' As always in Stroheim films, I was also a face on the cutting-room floor. He shot a cigaret out of my mouth in that picture. I was insured at Lloyds for one day but the scene wasn't shown. I knew 'Von' very well, really well. Some of the parties, with lots and lots of drinking which he enjoyed enormously, were just terrific. Once he told how, in Austria, officers, after a night of spree, would hop out of the windows into the deep snow, their batmen holding up sheets for them. There were always some in the wild party scenes who, being well loaded, tried the same. There were broken legs, blood flowing—a wonderful mess.

"Once he decided my hair needed washing and broke a dozen eggs on my head and poured champagne on it as fast as he could. I could tell stories like this 'till the cows come home. But later he would not have it and did not like to speak about it. There was a wedding in Vienna's Stephansturm (St. Stephen's Cathedral), for instance, a real wedding of his cameraman, Hal Mohr—the church being one of the sets for *The Wedding March*. I was the bridesmaid, Stroheim was best man, but we all had so much 'developer' out of the glass basins where they developed the film that none stood straight during the ceremony. I was one of Elinor Glyn's pets and she was quite a type, too. . . . During the war I became some sort of a Mata Hari but someone slipped up, not me, and I went to prison. It was pretty tough. I was actually in front of a firing squad at one point. My prison experience left me physically ruined by dysentery and infections and my health is very precarious but since I've travelled a great deal and studied a bit I can now make a living as a writer. . . . 'The wickedest eyes in the world' . . . good old Hollywood! 'She prays daily to a god of love.' What nonsense was perpetrated in the name of publicity. Old father De Mille wrote me recently saying, 'I shall never forget how beautiful you were and how brave.' Well, I was by no means ravishing, I think. But look at my generation today . . . Garbo . . . I remember the days when she was in love with Jack Gilbert; she looked as if she had a light shining from within. Don't think me sentimental, I'm quite down to earth now. It's only that old scrapbook. . . ."

From S. T. Carrier: "I do not know whether or not my wife, Anielka Elter, answered your last letter. It is with very great regret that I have to tell you that she died two weeks ago."

Again from Tom Curtiss: ". . . I covered the Venice film festival and saw a great deal of von Sternberg which was very pleasant. In fact I was booked to go to Vienna to spend a few days there with him but he wired he was leaving immediately and later wrote that he was disappointed and depressed by the sight of the postwar Vienna. . . . *The Devil is a Woman* in the retrospective at Venice was the best film to be seen at the festival. Denise is well and happy and we both wonder when—if ever— you are coming here. Do so before we're put in bath-chairs. . . . You should have been in Venice. The festival films were mediocre but the weather was glorious and von Sternberg was a wonderful companion. We dined and shopped and drank a marvelous new beverage called the 'Bellini' (peach juice, orange, and champagne). . . . He talked of a story he has optioned and wants to film—I guess he's the greatest of the directors still with us."

From George Pratt of the George Eastman House in Rochester in reply to my inquiry about Louis Siegel, composer of the score for *Lot in Sodom*, one of the most remarkable music scores for a film ever written: "He died, apparently of cancer, in 1955. He was born in Rochester and when 11 was taken to Belgium where he studied under the violin virtuoso, Ovide Musin. At 16 he graduated with honors from the Royal Conservatory at Liége. He was a close associate later, in Vienna, of Leopold Godowsky. . . . His obituary mentions only one composition, a short symphony (sic) called 'Nocturnal Rouge.' There is no word about his score for *Lot in Sodom*. In 1933 he was decorated by the government of Yugoslavia where he'd gone to conduct Bach, Beethoven and the violin concerto of the American composer, John Alden Carpenter. Hildegarde Watson (who played Lot's wife in the film) recalls listening to his rehearsals in Yugoslavia, which she was able to do as she was touring and singing in Europe at the time. 'He could play any instrument,' she told me on the phone yesterday. 'He was the finest violinist I ever heard, and his performance of the Bach Chaconne was unsurpassed.' In spite of the fact that he was a recluse, 'because he was almost pathologically shy,' Hildegarde said, 'he was a very, very great man.' Hildegarde recalled that he was a great friend also of Casals and at one time had gone to Spain and lived and worked with Casals, 'who was very fond of him.' Hildegarde said, 'Louis Siegel had the most marvelous musical mind I ever met.' She also recalled that the music for *Lot in Sodom* had so impressed someone in Rome that he requested the score separately so that it could be performed there in concert."

And from Ben Abrahamson, the legendary Chicago bookseller: "Pale hands I loved beside the Shalimar. . . . Where are they now?"

January, 1963

COFFEE, BRANDY & CIGARS
(In collaboration with Gretchen)

But each spectator looked in himself for
the miraculous child
Century O century of clouds.
  —*Guillaume Apollinaire*

In case you ever wondered how *Vampyr* by Dreyer came out looking so eerie, now it can be told. The entire cast and crew unknowingly ate horse meat while quartered at the Château de Courtempierre during the filming. "We were being served delicious meals," said Baron Nicolas de Gunzberg (who as Julian West played David Gray in the film) recently over lunch. "And everyone was saying how good the food was. Whereupon the local chef, obviously proud of his prowess, made the startling revelation."

The animal sounds in *Vampyr* (cat, dog, rooster, etc.) were all done by people specially engaged to record them. They were professional imitators.

Potemkin had no greater admirer than John Grierson, but at the Museum of Modern Art last year he said (smilingly), "The reason *Potemkin* was cut so fast was because the Russians were short of film." Then chuckling, "And they called it art."

There is a *Passion of St. Matthew* by Bach, a *Passion of Joan of Arc* by Dreyer, and a *Passion of Charlie Chaplin,* a book by Edouard Raymond, Paris, 1929.

While on the subject of dialogue in motion pictures, most of it sounds like what T.S. Eliot meant when he complained, "I've got to use words when I talk to you."

"Everything which touches upon death," said Champfleury, "is of an astounding gaiety." This bizarre statement nevertheless finds its echo in *Monsieur Verdoux* and *La Règle du Jeu,* especially in the "Danse Macabre" scene in the latter where the piano keys play the piece by themselves while the big fat lady pianist looks on in disbelief (it is a pianola). One of the best moments in all of Renoir. Dio Cassius tells of the Emperor Domitian, who would invite his friends into a room draped from floor to ceiling in black. At the head of the couches were pillars like tombstones with the guests' names written on them. Naked boys, painted black, danced among them, and while the terror-stricken guests looked on, the silence was broken only by the aging Emperor recounting savage stories. . . . The "wild" parties in *La Dolce Vita,* indeed!

Robert Payne, in his book on Chaplin, speaks of the little tramp surviving because he possesses a magic talisman, a flower. The man with the flower—what's happened to him in the movies? Are they really better off without him? Vide Fairbanks in *The Gaucho,* the young Indio in the *Zapotec Village* sequence of *Que Viva Mexico,* Gary Cooper in *Morocco,* Chaplin in *City Lights,* etc. "What secrets does the flower possess?" asks Payne. "Some clue, perhaps, was provided by Coleridge: 'If a man could pass through Paradise in a dream, and have a flower presented to him as a pledge that his soul had really been there, and if he found this flower in his hand when he awoke—Ay! and what then?'"

Speaking of Fairbanks, Sr., was there ever a more magical one-shot introduction to a screen character than the first appearance of the languid Don Diego galvanized into the mercurial Zorro? (*The Mark of Zorro*) that flat black hat, black domino mask and black cape held chin-high, the whole apparition in black suddenly flecked with a puff of white smoke from his cigarette.

They tell a true story of the Hollywood producer studying a

screenplay by Maxwell Anderson for a South Seas picture and complaining to Anderson that no one would know the meaning of the word "buffoon" that was in the dialogue. To prove it, he called the head of the studio, hung up, and smiled approvingly at Anderson. "It's OK," said the producer. "You can keep it in. J. B. knew what it meant— it's what they call those storms they have in the tropics."

Do you know where Renoir and his scenarists got the title of *La Grande Illusion?* From a book by Norman Angel, English pacifist and 1933 Nobel Peace Prize winner. The book was published in 1908 and was called, "The Great Illusion."

In the Homage to Stroheim Brazil Film Festival brochure of Feb. 1954 (a copy of which is in the Stroheim file at the Museum of Modern Art) is reproduced a still of *Greed* illustrating the line in Norris' *McTeague* describing the beating up of Trina by McTeague to get her hoard of goldpieces: "Then it became abominable." The still shows the dead Trina on the floor, her face pitifully swollen out of all recognition by bruises—the most harrowing still I've ever seen.

The French film, *Monkey in Winter,* regarded in some quarters as a comedy, is ineffably sad and wistful and therein lies its merit, not in its surface risibilities which are all too obvious. It is feverish with an ache for youth, its brazenness, for far off horizons and distant shores, for nostalgic memories of what Kay Boyle called "days worn savagely, like parrot feathers." This is its *raison d'être*, not the clowning between Gabin and Belmondo. It is a threnody of lost love and the long dark night of resignation.

T. E. Lawrence, before undertaking a flamboyant escapade like blowing up a railway or making an attack, would announce he was putting on a "cinema show." (Incidentally, the glasses left dangling after the motorcycle accident that killed Lawrence [in *Lawrence of Arabia*] was, of course, a conscious or unconscious echo of the ship's doctor's glasses in *Potemkin* dangling from the rigging after he's been thrown overboard.)

When John Huston commissioned Jean Paul Sartre to do a screenplay on Freud, Sartre spent eight months in research and came up with a script of 450 pages. Huston returned it, asking Sartre to cut it. Sartre then returned a revised script of 870 pages. Returned to him again, Sartre revised it further and this time it came to a thousand pages. Sartre admitted a film of this script would run at least seven or eight hours. It was not used, naturally, but in that word, "naturally," lies much of the lost hopes and shattered dreams of what the cinema might have been. . . .

Both Anna and Ernst Freud, children of Sigmund Freud, protested to Huston against making the film, but received no reply from the director. (Anna Freud is Vice-President of the International Psychoanalytical Society.) The only true "Freudian" film is still Pabst's 1926 *Secrets of a Soul*, made with the master's approval from an actual case history, supervised by two of his assistants.

When Huston shows the young Freud at a class of the French physician, Charcot, who first demonstrated the use of hypnosis in treating diseases of the nervous system, he reproduces a well-known painting of that historic moment—exactly what Griffith did almost a half century before in composing shots after famous historical paintings. Huston also repeats one of the dream sequences from *Secrets of a Soul*, the man returning to the womb, but does come up with one startling and original scene, the revelation by the girl-patient under hypnosis that it was not a hospital where her father died but a brothel. Pictorially this is very effectively done.

From *The N. Y. Times* review of Stroheim's *The Devil's Passkey* (the least known of all his films), August 9, 1920: "Nevertheless his work, in many of its details, is different and new, if compared with that of the great majority of directors, for he has realized that the substance of the photoplay is the dramatic motion picture, not the subtitle, nor the spectacular scene, nor the beauty or tricks of any star, nor the sentiment or surprises of any story, but images that have meaning, that are what they are in a photoplay because they are an integral part of it, telling in themselves some essential incident of the story, exposing suddenly some unexpected, but consistent, or anticipated, but not obvious, side of the character of one of the people in the plot. It is by his accomplishments in his images, therefore, that his story is unfolded forcefully and his characters are definite and comprehensible individuals." And this, mind you, after only two films, for only *Blind Husbands,* made the year before, had preceded *Devil's Passkey.*

Riccoboni, the authority on the *commedia dell'arte*, stated, "The good comedian marches in the middle of the road; the great comedian wanders along the edge of a precipice." Chaplin's statement on the occasion last summer of his being made a Doctor of Letters by Oxford University: "I am finishing the script of a new comedy. It's something I've had in mind for many years. It has, in fact, been half-written for the last ten years. It's real slapstick burlesque. I have some very funny business which I've been keeping and cooking up. . . . I have no bitter feeling about America now. It is not a thing one can carry on. Some of my best friends are Americans. I like them. They come off very well in my book. Writing a book is like developing a photograph, and they come out very well. What happened to me, I can't condemn or criticize the country for that. There are many admirable things about America and about their system too. I have no ill feeling. I carry no hate. My only enemy is time. . . . Nuclear weapons? I think the scientists are more irresponsible than the politicians. They have created this Frankenstein monster and placed it in the hands of third-rate men. It is outrageous, yet we stand for it. That goes for the whole world."

Oscar Levant on the Jack Paar show . . . obviously still suffering the effects of his recent illness, tried gallantly to be the mordant wit he was expected to be on the program but it was sad to hear the old jokes about his hypochondria from a man in so dolorous a physical state. (He kept shaking throughout the eight or ten minutes he was on.) Then Paar asked him to play and the audience vociferously applauded. He sat down at the piano and gave them what he thought they also expected from him—a blues by Gershwin, the ubiquitous cigarette dangling from his lips. Then he suddenly stubbed out his cigarette, cast off the mantle of clown and jazz pianist, ignoring the audience, and was alone with himself. The shaking momentarily ceased and he played a brief canon by Bach, paused a second, and now entirely alone with himself, the real Oscar Levant, which is to say an extraordinarily genial and civilized human being, went immediately into the *lentement* passage of Mompou's *Jeunes Filles au Jardin,* which the composer describes in the score: *"Chantez avec la fraîcheur de l'herbe humide . . ."* He played a dozen or so bars, got up and without a word left. But he had turned his appearance, which might have been a difficult few minutes for all concerned, into something exquisite.

There is a line in Kipling's *Kim* that perfectly characterizes

Norman McLaren at his worktable: "A man with a green shade over his eyes sat a table and, one by one, with white hands picked up globules of light from a tray before him, threaded them on a glancing silken string, and hummed to himself the while."

The current plethora of "midlands" films from England are not as new in theme as they seem to be. A decade ago, the excellent *Hobson's Choice* by David Lean provided the prototype. It even contained the prophetic line: "There's always room at the top."

In Memoriam: Monte Blue, 73. He was half American Indian and began his movie career in westerns. Once he even played Danton in *Orphans of the Storm*. Then Lubitsch cast him in a trio of silken comedies, *The Marriage Circle, Kiss Me Again,* and *So This is Paris,* in which he was perfectly at home in the sophisicated comedy of manners, the delightful roles for which he will be remembered. His last years were spent doing publicity for a circus. *Ave atque vale!*

One of the best movie songs was Friedrich Hollaender's "The Ruins of Berlin" from Billy Wilder's *Foreign Affair,* sung by Dietrich in it. Strangely, it never got much of a play and was never recorded. It has that indefinable *morbidezza* of the best of its kind that once heard is not forgotten.

And, of course—*The Trial,* the new Orson Welles film. That someone had the courage to do it at all is the first miracle. The second is its overall faithfulness to an unrelenting book, by now too familiar to require recounting here. Updating it has made it an attack on the police state as we have come to know it, a "contemporary nightmare," as Welles puts it. It will certainly be called a nightmare of Wellesian brainstorm and worse in some quarters, where to be different than the norm is to be subversive or eccentric. But why expect a film like any other film from Welles? Who is experimenting more with the medium than he? Who plays it safe less than he? (We refer to film makers over the last two decades.) Antonioni? Resnais? Bergman? They are makers of *chic* films, for after-dinner conversation. Welles' films, whatever they are, are never *chic*—they never have been popular enough for that. They are the work of the most individual new cinema talent since the days of the cinema's first individualists— Griffith, Stroheim, Eisenstein, Clair, Lubitsch, Lang, Sternberg,

Murnau, and all the rest. (Those same hostile quarters smirk at the word cinema.) Withal, we do not think *The Trial* is a fully realized work by Welles. Perhaps it is impossible to do it within the confines of a film of normal length. Perhaps it is impossible to do it in a film directed at a wide audience through the usual commercial channels like, say, *Freud* or *Long Day's Journey into Night, Marienbad* or *Eclipse*. There are other things, too. For once the faces in a Welles film are not so uncannily right as usual. (Unfortunately, Anthony Perkins least of all. He suited *Psycho* better.) There is virtuosity for its own sake (unusual for Welles) but, of course, eye-smiting, delirious virtuosity, even if the mind is not enthralled. Yet there is one right face in it—that of Jeanne Moreau, as Welles sees her in the role. And why should one even cavil at virtuosity for its own sake in a medium, particularly today, when any kind of virtuosity is so rare? But a film of *The Trial* should leave us as shattered as the book does. Why else did Kafka write it? But Welles is too much of an artist not to know what he is doing and what he is up against. Thus, there are frightful things in the film, terrible to see, disquieting things, too, that bother one, and bizarre things, and some withering humor, too, all of which take place in the arcanas of today's world, the faceless, anonymous structures, the hideous conglomerations of bureaucracy, business, law, religion and mean dwellings housing people cowed and afraid. For the most part, outside the thread of the story involving the principals, there are either masses of people or none at all and for long stretches the story seems to be taking place in some kind of awful vacuum which, as far as Joseph K. (Kafka himself) is concerned, is certainly the truth. These effects are all perfectly realized. So, as a valiant try to do something no one else would have the guts to do, *The Trial* should absolutely be seen, as well as for those parts of it that are truly Kafka's nightmare world which history has shown us is only too true. Finally, we're told that all the voices of the male characters in the story, other than those of Perkins and Tamiroff, are those of Welles himself.

The amount of film disintegration appears to be less at the Cinémathèque Française than anywhere else. Says Henri Langlois, its passionately dedicated curator: "You can't just keep them in cans in the vaults. You must take them out of the cans periodically, let them "breathe," put them on a rewind and loosen them up by unwinding them. In short, love them and they will respond . . . they will respond."

In reviewing *Love at Twenty*, Jonas Mekas mentioned the "weightlessness of Truffaut's direction"—a felicitous image to which we heartily subscribe. Films can be divided into those that would float and those that would sink. The flight of the human spirit is weightless, and the more winged this flight the surer its immortality.

After seeing *Love and Larceny* in which Vittorio Gassman is so perfectly wonderful in half a dozen larcenous roles, we are convinced that he is the one to rescue Monica Vitti from the dour Antonioni. Monicelli or De Sica to direct from some wacky scenario by Di Filippo, or one of those other long suffering but irrepressible comic spirits with which the Italian cinema is so rife, which would give the Vitti a real chance to display her high comic gifts. Gassman and Vitti, *vis à vis*, what a combination!

Following upon the vogue for books of old (usually silent) movie stills with facetious captions to titillate morons comes word that Desilu, the TV producers, will release a series, "Fractured Flickers," consisting of silent film classics cut to 3 minutes to which have been grafted lip synchronized "topical" soundtracks. Among the twenty-six films acquired for this gruesome and witless operation are the Lon Chaney *Hunchback of Notre Dame*, Barrymore's *Dr. Jekyll and Mr. Hyde*, Valentino's *Blood and Sand*, Fairbanks' *Mark of Zorro*, Keaton's *The General*, etc.

The late eminent American violinist, Albert Spalding, once said, "The rhythm should be going on inside the mind of the player long before he puts the bow down on the string to play the first note." The sun-drenched vision of Monet facing an empty canvas, the sad laughter of Cervantes facing a blank sheet of paper, the ardent fervor of the youthful Eisenstein intoxicated by the October revolution. . . . All art is a fever in which the heart beats faster and this overstrained beating starts *before* the first brush stroke, *before* the first word is put on paper, the first note set down on a score, the first line written for a scenario . . .

May, 1963

COFFEE, BRANDY & CIGARS

"*A good picture is one that earns money at the box-office.*"
—Melvin L. Gold, chairman,
Associated Motion Picture
Advertisers (I.F.I.D.A.)

"*The theatre is a moral institution.*"

—Schiller

Charm is one of the rarest qualities to be found in films, as it is in people. Full of raffish charm is the National Film Board of Canada's short, *Beaver Dam*, a trifle concerned solely with an eager beaver's building a dam. "So what?" you will ask. So this—the sound track consists at one point of the busy little beaver humming to himself as he goes about his task; the humming, of course, being technically provided by some wag at the NFB, but indubitably coming from someone who is thoroughly enjoying his work.

The degree to which an almost completely unknown director, Paul Bern, was a thousandfold more talented than Cecil B. De Mille, than whom hardly any director was more known, can be illustrated by comparing the stupor with which De Mille handled Jetta Goudal in *The Coming of Amos* (an incredible piece of Twenties tripe) with how Bern handled her in his wise and witty *Open All Night* (after "The Six Day Night" of Paul Morand). A real French beauty, she played in the latter with ingrained *esprit gaulois* and intelligence.

Still, I can defend De Mille when it comes to something he understood—*Cleopatra*. Any movie on this subject is made as catnip for the mob, so be it. But if you're going to do it, *some* mystery, *some* witchery has to be there. There is not a moment of these qualities in the Mankiewicz version, but there is even more than a suggestion of it in passages in the De Mille version (with Claudette Colbert), especially in the sequence where Cleopatra entertains Marc Anthony on her barge floating down the moonlit Nile. You can say what you want about De Mille's meretriciousness, his frenzied opulence by Sid Grauman's Egyptian Theatre in Hollywood out of an ancient Egypt that never was, his vulgarity, even, but even honest vulgarity will get you closer to true voluptuousness than the slick modern Hilton Hotel-like Egypt (with its glossy antiseptic sex like a double-page color spread in *Harper's Bazaar*) does in Twentieth Century Fox's current super-duper epic, the apotheosis of the single entendre. De Mille's barge scene has it all over Mankiewicz' for enchantment—the same thousandfold over which Bern had it over De Mille in directing Jetta Goudal.

Where does that leave Mankiewicz—below even De Mille? Nonsense! It still leaves Mankiewicz where he was before he embarked on that misguided (for him) venture . . . at the very top of the directorial hierarchy in America, the brilliant author-director of *Letter to Three Wives* and *All About Eve,* whose incisive psychological delineation of women would have earned him an approving smile from Remy de Gourmont, who knew all about women, and I daresay from the old master, Balzac, himself. Besides which, Mankiewicz has that rarest (with charm) of all qualities in the cinema—a sense of irony, which De Mille totally lacked.

While we're comparing films, let's match Hawks's much vaunted *Hatari* with *Serengeti Shall Not Die,* a straight documentary made with a love for the animals it depicts that shames the fictional film with John Wayne *et al which* exploits them for the cheapest "thrill" effects. And let's compare Garbo in George Fitzmaurice's *Mata Hari* with Dietrich in von Sternberg's *Dishonored.* Two spy pictures (about the same spy), two *femmes fatales,* two directors, two different worlds. How they ever got away with such balderdash as *Mati Hari* is unbelievable, while *Dishonored,* after more than thirty years, is as beautiful and affecting as ever. Granting Garbo's beauty, she was really a very limited actress who played within the smallest possible range. Dietrich (under Sternberg, *bien entendu*) out-played her the same thousandfold previously referred to.

Curious coincidence: the end of Adolfas Mekas' *Hallelujah the Hills* is almost exactly the same, in a sense, as the end of Godard's *Vivre Sa Vie.* But there could be no two films more dissimilar, except in their elliptical styles. The former is an exhilarating comedy about youth, touched with poetry, and the latter is a harsh, clinical study of a prostitute, with details that might have made Maupassant shudder. I prefer the former because it says "Yes!" to life as against the latter that says, "No!" Not because I have anything against so-called "downbeat" themes or dislike unhappy endings, but because there's such a paucity of good comedy around that we should be grateful when one appears.

Whatever happened to Orson Welles' pilot film for a television series made for Desilu ten years ago called, "The Fountain of Youth"? I'm told it's extraordinary.

Did you know that Luis Buñuel studied to be a Jesuit priest? And that before deciding to make Mirbeau's sardonic *Diary of a Chambermaid* as his next film he had plans for a film whose heroine was a one-legged nymphomaniac? Which brings to mind one of the characters (or would it be two?) of Stroheim's novel, *Poto Poto,* set in an African bordello wherein among the available girls was a pair of "Siamese twins." Stroheim, too, once told me he wanted to do *Diary of a Chambermaid.* Only Renoir, till now, has done it . . . and not badly, considering. . . . Buñuel also once wanted to do Pierre Louÿs' *Woman and Puppet,* that devastating, sado-masochistic trifle of Oscar Wilde's favorite French novelist, which Sternberg did so brilliantly and which Duvivier muffed so utterly. Buñuel and Stroheim had many affinities (along with the early Renoir and Sternberg—what a quartet!). *L'Age d'Or* shows a mass of feathers becoming a snowbank; in *The Merry Widow* of Stroheim a mass of feathers becomes a snow-fall.

You can do anything with grace (said amid a plethora of films that have everything but grace)—you can even *carry* a film with grace. When Sternberg brought the print of *Anatahan* from Japan it was encased, not in the conventionally ugly metal film crate, but in a sailor's white canvas duffle bag. (The picture was about sailors.) Looked very handsome, too, and jaunty, and very sensible, being much lighter to carry.

The Treasure of Sierra Madre, reputedly John Huston's best film and often referred to as a classic of American screen realism, is undeniably a good film but it is replete with "cute" scenes and has a soft interior (what Henry James called "a squashy texture") for all its surface toughness. Compare it with *Greed* and its stature shrinks alarmingly. It compromises with its terrible theme—

the lust for gold—for the sake of a happy ending, and *Greed* does not. There are no heroes or villains in *Greed*, only some pitiful people. Pity—perhaps the rarest quality of all, again in art as in human beings.

Few directors can survive unscathed a retrospective of their complete work, and the recent Hitchcock retrospective at the Museum of Modern Art is an eloquent illustration, perhaps because he was so prolific. It was a valuable and fascinating show but it also glaringly showed up so much mediocrity in Hitchcock's work (like *Secret Agent,* etc.) that the really good works (*The 39 Steps, The Lady Vanishes,* etc.) took on the nature of surprising exceptions—but *what* exceptions, of course! *The 39 Steps* is a minor, but flawless, masterpiece of film making.

One of the many definitions of art could be: the ordered and disciplined arrangement of vignettes from life, since art is a highly condensed organization of life. Degas could synthesize the chaos of a nineteenth century cotton market in New Orleans into a painting that had the stylization of a pavane, the grace of one of his ballet classes . . . and yet was true to the *essence* of what the ambiance of such a place was like. It was painted ninety years ago and it still hasn't been improved on as sheer painting. *Les Dames du Bois de Boulogne* is a film that achieves a similar feat in its own medium. There is something enduring, as in the Degas painting, about its serenity.

I think the movies are wrong about having actors or actresses keep saying the line, "I love you!" In real life, people really in love seldom if ever say it. It sounds banal, rhetorical. I was infatuated several times and found myself married twice without ever having said that line once.

Did you know that Stroheim once played a Chinese general in a French film?

That in Hudson's Bay there is a Flaherty Island?

That in the Moving Picture World of March 15, 1919, a YMCA reporter in Russia reported that Russia was virgin territory for the motion picture business and that big business would be done there "once order was again restored"?

That the genesis of *The Cabinet of Dr. Caligari* was a suggestion by Carl Mayer's then girl friend, Gilda Langer, to Hans Janowitz, Czech journalist, that he and Mayer concoct a film story in which she could be starred?

They found the germ in Janowitz' book, *Three Chapters from Hamburg*, in the Holstenwall tale of a young woman who had been murdered by an unknown sex-fiend —a headline story Janowitz had himself reported in October, 1913. And although it was Janowitz who originally recorded the incident, it was Mayer's intuition to conceive it in filmic terms. The central character of the mountebank-hypnotist, who forces his somnambulist to commit murder under cover of darkness, stemmed from Mayer's deeply rooted disgust for a psychiatrist who had tested his sanity in an attempt to prove that he was fit to serve in the armed forces. The name "Caligari" was borrowed at random from "Unknown Letters of Stendhal," merely for its catching sound. (It was the name of an Italian officer whom Stendhal had once known.) Janowitz and Mayer wrote their treatment in six weeks, during February and March of 1919. Gilda Langer, meanwhile, made her screen debut in Fritz Lang's *Der Herr der Liebe*. Just before *Caligari* went into production, she jilted Mayer to become the fiancée of Paul Czinner, then died in less than a week. The part of Jane, originally written for her, now went to Lil Dagover. Disillusioned by Gilda's inconstancy and deeply affected by her untimely death, Mayer cherished his only love, a love that remained platonic to the end of his days. Mayer's early films reflect his loneliness as well as his frustrated and incurable unhappiness. (From *Carl Mayer: A Forgotten Master of Screen Writing*, by Herbert G. Luft.)

Carl Mayer, whose film scripts read like impressionistic poems in blank verse, or ballads, wrote the scripts for *Caligari, Scherben* ("Shattered"), *Hintertreppe* ("Backstairs"), *Vanina* (after Stendhal), *Sylvester* ("New Year's Eve"), *The Last Laugh, Tartuffe, Sunrise* . . .

In Memoriam: Clifford Odets—

'More light!' Goethe cried on his death bed, not 'More profits!' He, of course, was not faced with the temptation of a private Gallup poll, calling itself 'Audience Research Inc.,' which told one studio to whisk away from my desk four months' work on Dreiser's great novel, 'Sister Carrie,' because as a film it could end only in financial disaster.

When I reported this piece of commercial prescience to the old but yet magnificent Dreiser, he growled: 'But they're really cocaine sellers out there. Are you surprised? Life is all in the icebox for Hollywood.' He said other things, too, but they make nasty reading of a Sunday.

Autumn, 1963

COFFEE, BRANDY & CIGARS

"Everybody likes things they don't understand; that's what God's for."
—Gretchen in conversation about the current cult of unintelligibility in the movies.

The latest cinema "discovery" appears to be *"cinéma vérité"* (*vide, Joli Mai, Hitler, Connais Pas*, etc.)—a discovery made forty-three years ago by Dziga Vertov via his *Kino Pravda* (Russian for "cinéma vérité"). These were a series of newsreels edited by him in the Twenties to give this documentary footage its maximum effect before an audience.

I have seen two reels of the African footage Stroheim shot for *Queen Kelly* that survived the years (It will become part of the archives of the Cinémathèque Française following a "gala world premiere" there.) It begins after the arrival of Kitty Kelly in Dar es Salaam in German East Africa at the bordello of her Aunt, who's sent for her, as the Aunt is dying and wishes Kitty to marry the degenerate, crippled and whiskey-swilling trader, Jan (Tully Marshall), because he is very rich and her future will be assured. The footage comprises the meeting of Kitty with her Aunt, two of the bordello girls (one black, one white) preparing Jan for the frightened Kitty, the marriage of Jan and Kitty and the death of the Aunt, after last rites (in Latin) by a black priest (and his black acolytes) who also performs the wedding ceremony.. Readers curious as to where this fits in the entire original story as conceived by Stroheim are referred to the first number of *Film Culture* where I reprinted a synopsis by Stroheim of the complete *Queen Kelly*. Some details: the white girl inmate of the bordello is tattooed, very pretty, and so tough as to make all previous screen female tough gals look like nuns in comparison. The Aunt is *in extremis* and can't talk, so she writes what she has to say on a slate. In the absence of a bridal veil, the white mosquito netting of a bed serves Kitty for the wedding ceremony. The photography is like velvet, the purest kind of painting with light. The direction shows that Stroheim hadn't given in an inch, even at that late date, even after all the disappointments and frustrations . . . stubborn but wonderful to the end.

That's the Way They All Laugh Dep't: "His (Sol Lesser's) closing remark, which dealt with his experiences with Eisenstein's *Thunder Over Mexico*, left his audience laughing. 'Have you ever tried to edit 50,000 feet of clouds?' " (*Daily Variety*, Hollywood, Oct. 2, 1963, reporting a symposium, "Editing Reality," of the American Cinema Editors in cooperation with the Hollywood Museum and hailed by Mr. Lesser as "the first historical contribution to knowledge in which the Hollywood Museum has taken part.")

Ricky Leacock on the photography of *Hallelujah the Hills:* "That's how you make love with a camera."

Everyone dotes on the song *Autumn Leaves* (by the talented gnome-like Joseph Kosma), but who remembers the Carné film, *Les Portes de la Nuit,* from which it comes? A sad and wistful idyll that came and went and is probably all but lost to film history. Yet it was this bitter little film that inspired this haunting and unforgettable song.

Did you know that the genesis (conscious or not) of the episode in *Queen Kelly* where Swanson as a convent student loses her underpants is from Carl Sternheim's *Die Hose*, a turn-of-the-century German satirical play recently revived off-Broadway? Hans Behrendt made an incisive silent film of it in Germany with Werner Krauss as the dumb cluck German husband (a withering comment on the German bourgeoisie) and Jenny Jugo. Its story of the 100 percent *echt*-Deutsche model of respectability who is made to wear horns by the reigning Duke of a small

German principality in the early years of this century, and how the horns fit him so well that he shows them off, irritated the Nazis so that they killed both Behrendt and Sternheim, which goes to show how right Behrendt and Sternheim both were. So, if you want to live, play it safe, laugh at the idea of cutting "50,000 feet of clouds," Hollywood's contemptuous reference to *Que Viva Mexico*, and throw your lot in with the establishment . . . the guys in the saddle.

I'd like to pack someday the way they do in the movies . . . two or three items flung in a valise and, *voilà*, it's done, and they're off to the door, only they seldom make it, that's the only thing. Something invariably happens and they seldom get through the door.

Did you know that the *mystique* of the pyramid is Heaven, Earth, Man? They symbolize its three corners. Michelangelo's notes contain this observation and it is no accident that the entire design of *Que Viva Mexico* is based on this ancient concept.

Talk About *Wuthering Heights:* "Inhabitants of the island of Mykonos, Greece, have decided to erect a monument in memory of Alphonso, the American pelican who died after a long hunger strike induced by his distress over his wife's infidelity. Alphonso and his wife, Omega, came from Louisiana to serve as companions for Peter, a famous pelican of Mykonos. But Omega fell in love with Peter. Alphonso went on a hunger strike in protest and died as a result. Now the inhabitants of the island will erect a monument on which they will place a small statue of the unlucky bird and carve his tragedy in three languages on the marble. Meanwhile, Peter and Omega are honeymooning happily, unconcerned by the grief over Alphonso's death." (A recent Reuters dispatch in *The N.Y. Times.*)

What to me is the mystery of *Muriel* as against the revelations made possible by the archaeologist-physicist, Lerici, who has invented instruments which "see" through the crust of the earth and which has made it possible to discover ancient buried tombs of the Etruscans, thereby uncovering a whole culture and its art (often scarcely less beautiful than ancient Greek art)? Or as against the wistful smile of Nikolai Kolin at the end of *Secrets of the Orient* (Ufa-Wolkoff-1928) in which is revealed the nostalgia of the world for its most rapturous moments? What Lerici and Wolkoff were concerned with was mystery, too, but mystery that contained within itself revelation. Such "mystery" as *Muriel* contains is imposed on it, it is not what is inherent in it.

Did you know that Luis Buñuel wanted to do Golding's *Lord of the Flies?*

El Angel Exterminador, however seemingly formidable a film to encompass at first encounter, is actually no difficult "mystery" film or symbolic work at all, it turns out, but essentially a comic film. "Though with a very strong corrosive interior," writes Juan Buñuel in a letter I received from the director's son. "It's just a repetition of themes he's used in all his films before, *obsessions* would be the correct word. . . . The problem of why these people are caught in this room is of no importance. . . . The doors are wide open, there's no reason why they can't leave, or why the people outside cannot go in. We never know if they can't leave because they can't or because they don't want to. It's not important. The fact is: they are there. Once this is established, the film can go on in its development. It's as if they are shipwrecked. Without food and water they react as you'd expect which allows for satirical barbs at human beings and their social structure. . . . As to the repetitions, we repeat ourselves every day, doing more or less the same things, often saying the same things. . . . As to the ending, well, the Exterminating Angel is like a plague; first it starts with a small group of people, then with a churchful, then on to the rest of society. . . . We've gotten ourselves into a mess and are staying in it either because we want to or think we can't help ourselves. . . . As for the sheep at the end entering the church, what's more logical than to have some thirty sheep enter the church because there are a greater number of people to feed than were in the house: three sheep for twenty persons, thirty sheep for three hundred persons?" In short, Buñuel is half kidding, half in earnest (like Stroheim) in this film. He kids details of his basic idea (the Old Testament God of Wrath, *vide* the parable of the judgment of Sodom and Gomorrah) but he's in earnest about his basic idea. There is a quick shot of the terrible visage of the Exterminating Angel (in a nightmarish montage sequence). You'd better see this film; Buñuel still makes most other directors currently working look very little indeed.

The more I think about *Hallelujah the Hills,* the more I like it. I use it as my current acid or litmus paper test to determine for myself the perceptive from the non-perceptive. After some score or more of films seen during the recent First New York Film Festival at Lincoln Center and the Museum of Modern Art, and now that the euphoria of the festival is calmed down, I find myself having liked three without any reservations; *El Angel Exterminador*, *Hallelujah the Hills*, and, of course, *Lola Montès*. (Runners up: *I Fidanzati* by Olmi and *The Terrace* by Torre Nilsson, the former full of sensibility and truth *sans* a single concession to the box office [its exquisite ending won't add a dime to its box-office potential, I'm afraid, being such an ordinary shot that only a true poet could have thought of it], and the latter having a sinister edge stronger than anything I have thus far found in Nilsson's work. I liked *Electra at Epidaurus*, too, for Anna Synodinou's performance in the title role.)

Monsieur Verdoux, which I saw again recently, is still the most emotionally exhausting film since the sound-film that I have seen. And *Wuthering Heights* still has its old witchery, too, to move one. Where are the counterparts of such films today? At the most we are enthralled, dazzled even, but never moved. Is this part of film-making really over? . . .

Added reflection on *El Angel Exterminador:* It is a comic work in the sense that Joyce's *Ulysses* is a comic work; it is cinematically kidding but thematically serious. With Stroheim it was almost the reverse; cinematically he was always serious but thematically he was half serious, half kidding. (Except *Greed*, of course; he wasn't kidding then.)

Two cinematic dreams of Gretchen: (a) a feature starring Roger Vadim, Tony Richardson, John Huston, François Truffaut, Laurent Terzieff, Roman Polanski, Michel Auclair and Monica Vitti; (b) another feature adapted from Oscar Wilde's *Salome* starring Henri Langlois as Herod, Mary Meerson as Herodias, Brigitte Bardot as Salome, Anthony Perkins as Iokanaan, Michel Auclair as Narraboth, Kenneth Anger as the young guard, Guy Glover as Tigellinus, directed by Orson Welles.

In Memoriam: that Harlequin, Ariel, and eternal spring of the arts—Jean Cocteau.

Winter, 1963

COFFEE, BRANDY & CIGARS

"Humor is the only test of gravity and gravity of humor, for a subject which will not bear raillery is suspicious and a jest which will not bear serious examination is false wit."
—Lecontinus

WE CARPING MORTALS

André Maurois, one of the Forty Immortals of the French Academy, once rebelled at the biologic injustice that allows a carp to live three hundred years while Byron and Mozart died at thirty-five.

Consider the child poetess Margaret Fleming (known as "Pet Marjory") (born 1803, died 1811), who was a dear friend, during her eight brief and brilliant years, of Sir Walter Scott. A great lifter of low spirits was Pet Marjory. According to the English Dictionary of National Biography, Pet Marjory showed "extraordinary precocity." Her reading matter included Shakespeare, Swift, Newton and Ossian. She wrote diaries and poems. Apparently, she showed none of the morbid tendencies associated with prodigies; on the contrary, her work reveals vivacity and humor —and human limitations: "I am now going to tell you the horrible and wretched plaege that my multiplication gives me; you can't conceive it. The most devlish thing is 8 times 8 and 7 times 7; it is what nature itself can't endure." Robert Louis Stevenson believed her to be "one of the noblest works of God," said Harvey Breit, to whom I am indebted for this item. So must we, after reading her epitaph on three young turkeys and their mother (who is the "she" in the third line of the poem):

> *A direful death indeed they had,*
> *That would put any parent mad;*
> *But she was more than usual calm,*
> *She did not give a single dam.*

"GARBO LAUGHS"

Short Memory: Never underestimate the power of high-pressure publicity. "Garbo laughs!" was the banner under which Lubitsch's *Ninotchka* was released, with everybody forgetting that six years before she laughed just as heartily (in the scene where she first encounters her *vis-à-vis*, John Gilbert) in *Queen Christina*.

OF BLESSED RECALL

One difference (among many) between today's films and yesteryear's is the lack of colorful "second string" and bit players we used to have, that zany lot that lent, for a moment, such zestful seasoning to so many pictures that would have been that much less without them—and that much was often considerable. Well, such as: Franklin Pangborn, Tommy Mitchell, William Demarest, Robert Greig, Hank Mann, Sig Rumann, Felix Bressart, Eric Blore, Paul Porcasi, Eugene Pallette, Walter Catlett, Akim Tamiroff, Edward Everett Horton, Walter Connolly, Sig Arno, Alison Skipworth, Ernest Cossart, Basil Radford, Naunton Wayne, Mischa Auer, Warren Hymer, Andy Devine, Laura Hope Crewes, Frank McHugh, Matt Moore, Guy Kibbee, Jack Oakie, Ronald Squire, George Barbier, Raymond Cordy, Lionel Stander, Michael Chekov, André de Beranger, Ford Sterling, J. Farrell McDonald, etc., etc. Where, indeed, are the snows of yesteryear?

BASIC DRAMA IS TWO

A psychiatrist wrote to the *N. Y. Times* not so long ago, describing Roman Polanski's *Knife in the Water* as a perfect example of the Oedipus complex. It was symptomatic of the current tendency to see "things behind things" in the new spate of European films. Not so, says Polanski, the young Polish director of this film. "It doesn't involve three people at all, despite the presence of the trio, but two." He quoted Rainer Maria Rilke: "All that I have written up to now has been very bad because I was dealing with three people and not two. If I had the courage I would write only about two people because the conflict is between two people, not three—the third person is just an excuse." The quarrel in *Knife in the Water*, said Polanski, is just between the husband and wife—the boy, who intrudes in their life, is just an excuse.

Which reminds me of what Alexandre Dumas once said in another context: "The chains of matrimony are so heavy that it takes two to carry them, sometimes three." (A whole Lubitsch comedy concentrated into one sentence.)

RESIDUE OF FRIGHT

Josef von Sternberg once made a film called *The Last Command* in which Emil Jannings, as a Czarist officer, manhandled by a mob during the Russian Revolution, develops a tic from the shock of his maltreatment. In case anyone ever thought this was an invention of a lurid imagination, it might be interesting for them to know that physiologically it was sound. The scion of one of the oldest and most aristocratic families in Russia, Prince Galitzine, developed a bad stutter as a result of the shock of the Russian Revolution. Eventually, he fled to Paris and got a job as a chauffeur. (In Sternberg's film, the Russian general drifts to Hollywood where he gets a job as a movie extra. This, too, actually happened.)

SANS PRESCRIPTION

In the memoirs of Lydia Sokolova of the original Diaghilev Ballets Russes, she recounts this anecdote: "One evening when I was giving my pupil, a rich and handsome Frenchwoman with a lovely villa on the other side of Cap Martin, a lesson, I complained of a splitting headache. My pupil said she had something which would take the headache away, and she gave me a little box of powder, telling me to take a pinch and sniff it as if it were snuff. I followed her instructions, and she drove me back to my flat in her car. I suddenly felt an extraordinary tension round my face as if my jaw had been bound up, and I could neither eat nor speak. However, the headache disappeared and I went to a rehearsal. By the time it came my turn to dance I was feeling on top of the world: I threw myself into the role as I never remembered doing before or since, and enjoyed myself immensely. Diaghilev was watching, and when I finished dancing, he called me over to sit beside him, saying, 'You seem very excited.' I replied, 'I'm not excited. I just feel very well, and I was enjoying dancing and having a lovely time.' He looked at me for a few seconds in silence and then said, 'Who gave it to you?' I asked him what on earth he meant, but he merely repeated his question. 'Are you going to tell me who gave it to you?' I said, 'I don't know what you mean.' 'Weren't you given some powder to smell?' he asked. 'Yes,' I told him, 'for my headache. And now I feel so much better.' Diaghilev got up and walked away. From that day onward I neither gave that lady another lesson, nor did I ever speak to her again. The 'Old Man' had diagnosed the effects of cocaine. . . ."

REAL CRIME AND FICTION

Fritz Lang built his reputation as a director of the first rank on two types of films, the spectacle (*Siegfried, Metropolis*, etc.) and the crime film (*Dr. Mabuse, Spies*, etc.). A favorite theme of his in the latter category was the character, and its variations, of Dr. Mabuse, the master criminal. This sinister idea, which appears to have had its actual modern counterparts in organizations like the Black Dragon Society, the Mafia, etc., was set forth by Conan Doyle in his story, "The Final Problem" in *The Memoirs of Sherlock Holmes*, some seventy years ago. Listen to this description of Moriarty-Mabuse: "*He is the Napoleon of crimes. . . . He is the organizer of half that is evil and of nearly all that is undetected in this great city. He is a genius, a philosopher, an abstract thinker. He has a brain of the first order. He sits motionless, like a spider in the center of its web, but that web has a thousand radiations, and he knows well every quiver of each of them. He does little himself. He only plans. But his agents are numerous and splendidly organized. Is there a crime to be done, a paper to be abstracted, a house to be rifled, a man to be removed—the word is passed to the professor, the matter is organized and carried out. The agent may be caught. In that case,* money is found for his bail or his defence. But the central power which uses the agent is never caught—never so much as suspected."

AUTHOR OF *THE LEOPARD*

Those who think of the late and solitary Palermo prince, Tommasi di Lampedusa, whose novel, *The Leopard* (subsequently filmed) attained posthumous world fame, as a dour fellow, will be surprised to learn that he was capable of the most romantic flights of the imagination. What makes his short story (among a group discovered among his effects)—"Ligheia"—a minor masterpiece is the sweetness with which a simple but affecting story is told. A young journalist makes an acquaintance in a café in Turin with an aged, gruff, peppery Italian Senator who is famous as one of the world's greatest Greek scholars. The old man derides the callow youth for his flighty interest in girls and facile love affairs. He, the Senator, one gathers, has never had anything to do with women. Finally, the Senator tells his story. In his youth, having retired to study on a solitary beach in Sicily, the Senator was seduced by a siren, Ligheia, an authentic daughter of Calliope, who flopped out of the sea into his rowboat while he was out fishing. With Ligheia, the future Senator spent twenty solitary, wonderful days. From her he learned the secret of the Greeks, and all he will know. Then she plunged back and left him. . . . A few days later the Senator leaves Turin to go on a cruise with some friends. One morning the journalist reads that the Senator has disappeared at sea, probably fallen overboard when nobody was looking. Only the journalist knows what really happened: Ligheia had beckoned.

January, 1964

COFFEE, BRANDY & CIGARS

"Fame is the sum of all the misconceptions circulating about an individual."
RAINER MARIA RILKE

"Tell Jean Cocteau that I adore him," wrote Rilke shortly before his death. "He is the only person for whom myth opens its gates and from which he returns bronzed as from the seaside."

In Tokyo, on a world tour, Cocteau was given a cricket for a pet. He took it along with him across the Pacific on the S.S. *President Coolidge* on which Chaplin was also a passenger, with Paulette Goddard. The cricket, named Microbus by Cocteau, carried on like crazy, buzzing like a saw-mill in full blast, a thousand rattles turning. "I'm going to find Charlie Chaplin," wrote Cocteau in his diary. "On his shoulder, Microbus hasn't a care in the world. He just sings." One day Cocteau noticed his cricket's antennae crossed which he interpreted to mean whatever is awful for crickets. Alarmed, he set it free in Los Angeles.

Cocteau before the great Sphinx, a soliloquy by the Sphinx as recorded by Cocteau in his diary: "I am here . . . I used to guard the tombs when they were filled and I still guard the tombs now that they are empty. But it matters little. The will to be beautiful, the fire of genius, the human phoenix continually rising from its ashes, is what matters." Visited at night, the Sphinx can be illuminated for a few piastres by a magnesium flare (it reminded Cocteau of the German Verey lights he experienced in the Yser trenches in Belgium in 1916) "revealing its ironic smile like that of a spy caught red-handed in the light of a flash-light. The magnesium flare dies out, but we know the Sphinx is still there, thinking: 'Well, yes, I *am* spying . . . what about it? What does that tell you about me? For what power am I spying? For whom? For what purpose? Which of the two of us does this discovery embarrass most? Take my advice, pocket your flash-light, leave me alone and go to bed as if you hadn't seen anything.' "

Another page in Cocteau's diary:

"'You should see the Acropolis by moonlight, my dear!' So the tourists say. No doubt they are right. But how do you get in there by moonlight? There are iron gates, which are locked. Then what can one do? Climb over the wall? Sit on a marble seat in the temple of Dionysos and wait? Wait for what? The moon, to be sure, the moon. . . . There was a full moon earlier but now it is no longer full. Nothing but closed gates and no moonlight. 'Diana, the chaste Diana, was great with—??!!' But you're mad! Be quiet or you'll be seized by bandits who will bandage your eyes and you'll walk for eight hours without stopping into the mountains of Delphi. It happened four days ago to the Michauds, friends of yours, of the Arts Department of the University of Istanbul. 'Because they said that Diana—?' Hush! Will you be quiet? If the King of Greece were to hear you he'd send along his moustachioed ballerinas and you would have a nasty time of it."

From Japan Cocteau brought a love-philtre (a powder of crushed lizards) which, if you sprinkled some of it on a girl when she wasn't looking, would make her fall violently in love with you. He also brought a monkey's head preserved in charcoal which was a remedy for madness. A photo of him, his traveling companion, Marcel Khill, and the champion Japanese *sumo* wrestler was hung in the principal brothels of the Japanese capital.

Did my eyes deceive me or was there really a palm tree growing on the deck of Cleopatra's barge in the Mankiewicz film? Answer (of a sort): If an evergreen tree can grow on one of the abutments of the RCA building in Radio City, as it does, why couldn't a palm tree grow on the deck of Cleopatra's barge?

Only when you stop to think about it does the contribution of homosexuality to Western Civilization loom as large as it does. Consider just a few: Socrates, Plato, Aristotle, Thucydides, Euclid, Solon, Aristides, Alcibiades, Theocritus, Pindar, Horace, Hafiz, Ovid, Virgil, Anacreon, Hans Christian Andersen, Alexander Humboldt, Verlaine, Rimbaud, La Rochefoucauld, Leonardo Da Vinci, Nijinsky, Diaghilev, Rodin, St. Augustine, Euripides, Sophocles, Michelangelo, Cellini, Aristophanes, Aeschylus, Oscar Wilde, Walt Whitman, Herman Melville, Magnus Hirshfeld, Lord Byron, André Gide, Henry James, etc., and etc.

During World War I, Cocteau used to scare the hell out of

André Gide by imitating the whine and explosion of a shell. (He'd remembered it from his service in the trenches.) It was this sort of thing that probably initiated Gide's subsequent antipathy to him.

Jeanne Modigliani, daughter of the great painter, recently had her first show at the Galerie La Roue in Paris. She paints abstractions. Asked if she had any of her celebrated father's canvases, she replied tearfully that she had not a single one. "And I have not enough money to buy such expensive paintings," she added.

In memoriam: Gustav Machaty, the Czech director of *Extase*, the forerunner of all erotic films and, after more than thirty years, still the most beautiful, the most poetic, still the model of its kind.

The idea of *Hamlet* in modern dress is nothing new. In 1912 there was an American film, *The Last Supper*, derived from the New Testament, played entirely in modern dress in an allegory set in the present day.

In Murnau's ineffably beautiful *Tabu*, after the natives row out to the schooner anchored in the harbor, they clamber aboard in profusion, like children, hanging gaily from her bowsprit, ropes and spars, as if the boat had suddenly sprouted blossoms.

Good old Murnau! There are differences of opinions about many directors, but none about Murnau; there is an absolute unanimity of opinion about him, as there was about Dovzhenko. "They make jokes about Pudovkin and me," once said Eisenstein. "But no one jokes about Dovzhenko."

It took the rough and tumble Douglas Fairbanks, Sr. to give the suave and courtly Adolphe Menjou a lesson in royal manners. During the filming of *The Three Musketeers*, Menjou played Louis XIII and asked Fairbanks how he should act as a King. "Be yourself," said Doug. "It will be by the actions of those around you that you will be recognized as the King."

A suggestion for Tony Richardson and John Osborne, as director and scenarist respectively: Now that they have got the Midlands bawdry and *Tom Jones* out of their system, let them wait with the inevitable follow-ups, *Moll Flanders, Roxana,* etc., and, for a change of pace and as a welcome relief, do Max Beerbohm's jocund masterpiece, that supremely Oxonian novel, *Zuleika Dobson*, about the pretty witch before the last century's turn who devastated the young men of Oxford so that they threw themselves into the Thames out of frustrated love for her. With, of course, Joan Greenwood as the enchantress.

Department of Semantics: Orson Welles dined with the producer, William Goetz. They discussed a film figure and Welles said, "I don't like him, he's vain." At which Goetz smiled and replied, "The great Orson Welles complains that a man is vain?" To which Welles answered, "Of course. I'm conceited, but I'm not vain. There's a big difference."

We can tell a man's character by his boasts, even if they aren't necessarily true; truth is often irrelevant when a point is to be made, as witness the boast of Diego Rivera, the great Mexican muralist, that he was an atheist preacher at the age of four, an accomplished Don Juan at nine, and a cannibal soon after.

Paulette Goddard once sat a whole afternoon alongside Rivera on a scaffold while he was at work on a mural in Mexico City. They didn't exchange a single word for five hours, following which Paulette began to climb down in weariness. "I see," said Rivera sadly as he watched her descend, "I'm beginning to bore you."

Overheard in Lindy's: "Have you seen *Cleopatra* yet?" "Oh, I always go to see a Hume Cronyn picture."

The Society for Film History and Research of London has just discovered a five-hour version of Gance's *Napoleon* (though *sans* the triple-screen passages) on 17.5 mm. For further details contact Rosemary Heaword, the secretary, Flat 12, 70-72 Westbourne Terrace London, W.2.

The reason why the girl disappears at the beginning of *L'Avventura* and is never seen again, nor is her disappearance explained, is more physical than metaphysical, despite all the soul-searching on the part of so many ciné-analysts. She (Lea Massari) was to have been the heroine of the film until Antonioni, the director, spotted a girl playing a secondary role (Monica Vitti). He was so smitten by her that he "arranged" for Massari to disappear. Vitti then became the heroine, and they are soon to wed. Very simple, as many "profound" things usually are.

Art (substitute beauty, if you wish) is where you find it. Would you believe it possible for it to be found in New York's Fire Department Museum in lower Manhattan, near the City Hall? They have an exhibit there of old fire-engines, handsome, shining relics of a bygone era. Among them is a hand-drawn hose-carriage, made in 1853 and designed and built with such grace and harmony of its component parts as to be as delicious to the eye as a passage by Mozart is to the ear. A Mozartean hose-carriage—now who would have thought that possible? I urge you to see it. It's the black one on the right as you enter from the front.

At the recent UCLA tribute to Fritz Lang, he mentioned a piece of advice Erich Pommer had once given him: "Never have an affair with your leading lady until your film is finished. And remember, this is a medium of the camera; always tell your story with the camera." After which Lang added: "I always adhered to this second piece of advice."

Pare Lorentz confessed recently that he was inspired to make films after having seen Murnau's *Sunrise*. (With Jean Renoir it was Stroheim's *Foolish Wives*.)

Gretchen says that Resnais' feature films make good demonstration films on the uses of the camera for film students, or for sections from them to be shown by shops selling ciné-equipment, or by Kodak, Dupont, Gevaert, or Agfa on one of the uses of celluloid.

Paul Fejos, the Hungarian film director-anthropologist turned officer in the Axel Wenner-Gren Foundation, once made a lovely film in France with Annabella called *Marie*. It dealt with a kitchen maid who is seduced by the son of the family she works for and when she is found to be pregnant is thrown out of the house. She rails against the Madonna in church: "If you could have your child, why can't I have mine?" She has her child and to support it enters a brothel. Years later her child is now grown to young womanhood and Marie, her mother, has died. In Heaven, which is a glorious kitchen full of pots and pans and things to do, Marie is happy again. But looking down on earth one day she sees a young man talking to her daughter, flirting with her, in the garden before the house. In a panic, to keep her daughter from becoming the victim of the young man, as once happened to her, she looks around desperately and finally sees a kitchen pail with scrub water. She empties the pail on the garden which causes the couple to separate, he running away and the girl running into the house to escape the sudden shower. And Marie smiles happily.

That's the way movies once were, O tempora, etc. . . . !

From *Ruggles of Red Gap* to *The Long Hot Summer,* American film comedy has a fine tradition. We ought to do more of it, we do it so well. We've never had enough good comedies and never was such a lack and need of them as now . . . comedies of that crazy ecstasy seasoned with sweet aloes from *The Immigrant* and *The Marriage Circle* to *Twentieth Century* and *All About Eve* to *Hallelujah the Hills* and all those marvelous epiphanies in between.

No one seems to have mentioned that the physical characterization of the ex-Nazi rocket expert, somehow transmogrified into an American citizen, so devastatingly played by Peter Sellers in *Dr. Strangelove,* is taken from two screen characters created by Fritz Lang—Rotwang of *Metropolis* (the black-gloved artificial hand) and Haighi of *Spies* (the wheelchair).

After the mordant humor and Swiftian satire of *Dr. Strangelove,* which leaves certain hallowed local institutions (which were in dire need of unhallowing) reeling against the ropes, and the grotesque comic truculence of McCarthy exposed so searingly in *Point of Order,* there is no longer any reason for withholding the showing here of Chaplin's *A King in New York,* whose implied criticisms of McCarthyism are positively timid by comparison.

Summer, 1964

COFFEE, BRANDY & CIGARS

"From three anecdotes about a man I can tell you his character." —Nietzsche

When Orson Welles presented his version of *Faust* on the Paris stage, he cast Eartha Kitt as Helen of Troy. When Michael MacLiammoir, who was to play Mephisto, objected that it was an odd bit of casting for Miss Kitt to play Helen, Welles retorted, "What do you mean? Everybody knows Helen of Troy was colored."

Welles' *Mr Arkadin*, loosely based in part on that fabulous character, Sir Basil Zaharoff, the mysterious munitions king (the other character from which his portrait of Arkadin is derived being the banker, Lowenstein, who mysteriously disappeared in a plane over the English channel), becomes even more intriguing when it is known that Eisenstein once planned a film on Zaharoff. (He also planned one on Ivar Kreuger, the "match king.")

Sudden thought: Why do so many people in the movies, who live in fine houses, have so much trouble?

Eisenstein's projects for films on Zaharoff and Kreuger were at one stage to have been integrated into a single epic, *The Twilight of the Gods*, predicting the end of capitalism, with such capitalists as Zaharoff, Kreuger, Lowenstein, etc., prominent in the ultimate debacle. (Now we learn that the Soviets will finally embark on a filming of Karl Marx's "Das Kapital," which started the whole thing. Of course, Eisenstein had planned once to do this also.)

Did you know Kurosawa played a girl in the Japanese film, *The Bronze Christ*?

And that Charles Laughton once wanted to direct a remake of William K. Howard's fine film, *White Gold*, which he'd remembered but wanted to see again before doing it? He didn't do it because he couldn't find a print anywhere.

One of the many differences between American and French attitudes could be illustrated by the subtle difference between the title of the forthcoming French film, *Les Plus Belles Escroqueries du Monde* and its American title, *The World's Greatest Swindles*, e.g., "Plus Belles" vs. "Greatest."

There is some incredible dialogue in Mankiewicz's *Cleopatra*. At one point Octavian says to Anthony, "That speech you gave, with your 'Friends, Romans, Countrymen' . . . and inflaming the crowd by holding up Caesar's bloodstained toga!" thus anticipating Shakespeare by no less than 1650 years.

In Mankiewicz' *Cleopatra*, Richard Burton takes a bath, whereas in De Mille's *Sign of the Cross*, Claudette Colbert (as the Empress Poppea, wife of Nero) took a bath. O tempora, O progress!

Also, whoever did the music for the De Mille *Cleopatra* (again with Claudette Colbert) knew infinitely more what he was doing than the composer for the Mankiewicz version.

Especially during the marvelously evocative barge scene, which makes the Mankiewicz barge scene look like it was staged by the drama coach of Wellesley College for the annual senior prom.

You have to hand it to De Mille. He may not have been the cinema genius he thought he was, but he always knew what he was doing, even when it was absurd. In the movies, absurdity doesn't matter—it's natural to the medium which is, basically, one of fantasy and the flight of the imagination through clever tricks of the camera, natural suspension of belief, etc. (Besides, where are there so many good-looking people except in the wonderful never-never land of the movies?)

I've never seen a comment anywhere about the perfect classic Grecian profile of Barbara Stanwyck though *Esquire* once likened Paul Newman, full face, to the Hermes of Praxiteles.

Gretchen suggested that Audrey Hepburn would have made a perfect Cleopatra for the screen and could have played Cleo's effeminate brother, Ptolemy, too. (Didn't Mankiewicz once plan to cast Hepburn in a dual role, as both Viola and her brother, Sebastian, in Shakespeare's *Twelfth Night?*)

Luis Buñuel's pet parrot, which had the run of the house, flew away one day and the heart-broken director inserted the following notice in the "Lost and Found" column of a newspaper: "Lost—a red-yellow parrot, answers to the name of Pizarro. Talks and whistles. However, the political views of this parrot, which is a gift from a friend, are not shared by me."

Rafael Buñuel, youngest son of the director, told this department that when his father was viewing the rushes of his latest film, *The Diary of a Chambermaid*, Octave Mirbeau's sombre look at human duplicity, papa Buñuel laughed throughout, saying, "I think it will be very amusing!"

There exists a recording of James Joyce reading from the "Anna Livia Plurabelle" section of his *Finnegans Wake*, that marvel of prose music, which has to be heard to be believed as one of the most exquisite auditory experiences possible in our time. Joyce's voice was a high tenor (like John McCormack), and very gentle, with the purest Irish brogue. (He was an amateur singer, too, delighting in Italian opera.) These brief five minutes makes the complexities of the text "visible" as nothing else could, recalling Paul Klee's dictum, "Art does not reproduce the visible, it makes visible." In the same way did Rimsky-Korsakov make visible the Invisible City of Kitezh in his famous opera of that name. In the same way did Jean Vigo make the ecstasy of childhood visible in *Zéro de Conduite*.

That great still photographer, Edward Steichen is, at eighty-five, filming a feature he calls, *A Tree Sonata*, consisting entirely of the growth of a single tree through the seasons and through the years, with natural sounds only (wind, rain, rustling leaves, etc.)—no music, no narration. Art from Nature, it will be pure cinema at its purest. (Which reminds me of what Galli Curci, the equally great coloratura soprano of a generation ago, said when she retired to her California farm. When asked what she would do now, after her long career of triumphs, she replied, "I will commune with my old friends, the trees.")

Unaccountably missing from all prints of Dreyer's *Joan of Arc* circulating in the U.S. is a brief scene where at the moment of incision by a physician of Joan's arm for blood-letting, to reduce her fever, an extreme close-up is shown of a priest's foot stepping (pressing) down into her cell. The camera moves back and we see who it is—the hypocrite priest (Maurice Schutz) who pretends to befriend Joan. In the original this had the effect of making it seem as if the weight of the priest was forcing the needle into her arm.

Recommended reading: Robert Flaherty's ribald anecdote of Bozo the Bear in Calder-Marshall's fine biography of him, *The Innocent Eye* (W. H. Allen, London, 1963). Its charm is that tall as it is, Flaherty tells the tale as a "true occurrence" which he and a French-Canadian guide experienced in the sub-Arctic tundra. It's exactly the kind of innocent ribaldry you'd expect from the genial Bob.

From Aldous Huxley's essay, "Faith, Taste and History," a delicious bit sent this department by the irrepressible Louise Brooks: (It's from a section on Salt Lake City.) "Next morning, in the enormous wooden Tabernacle, we listened to the daily organ recital. There was some Bach and a piece by César Franck and finally some improvised variations on a hymn tune. These last reminded one irresistibly of the good old days of the Silent Screen—the days when, in a solemn hush and under spotlights, the tail-coated organist at the console of his Wurlitzer would rise majestically from the cellarage, would turn and bend his swan-like loins in acknowledgement of the applause, would resume his seat and slowly extend white hands. Silence, and then boom! The Picture Palace was filled with the enormous snoring of thirty-two-foot contra-trombones and bombardes. And after the snoring would come the Londonderry Air on the *vox humana*, 'A Little Grey Home in the West' on the *vox angelica*, and perhaps (what bliss!) 'The End of a Perfect Day' on the *vox treacliana*, the *vox bedroomica*, the *vox unmentionabilis*."

The version of Milestone's *All Quiet* . . . currently showing on TV here omits the scene of the young German soldiers fraternizing with French girls and the panic of Himmelstoss, the martinet schoolmaster now a sergeant, under fire.

Re-seeing Ozep's *Der Moerder Karamazov* recently, I was again struck, after more than thirty years, with its masterful blend of image and sound, the subtlety of its cutting, its gleaming photography, its exquisitely balanced acting (by Kortner, Sten, Rasp and everyone else in it), the irony of its dialogue (so meaningfully adapted from Dostoievski, culled for its highest concentration) and, above all, for its direction, which combined all these elements into a stream of image strengthened light. What a beautiful film! It is the closest thing to Von Sternberg I have ever seen from another director. Compare the ravishing (and meaningful) close-ups of Anna Sten in it with the inane and vapid close-ups of Millicent Martin in *The Best of Everything*, one of the most chi-chi of the recent films and you'll see the difference between direction and non-direction.

Nuance: In *Variety*, Jannings hurls a marble-topped café table to the floor in a rage, breaking it to pieces. In *Potemkin*, an equally enraged sailor hurls a plate to the deck but, as the plate is a metal one, Eisenstein breaks up the action itself into pieces. In both instances, the dramatic-power of the scene hinged on the fact that something had to be broken. You can do it literally or figuratively —many are the roads to Parnassus. This is what I teach my film history classes at City College—to train them *to see*, not just to look.

In the old days you used to see candid shots of directors editing their own films with film entwined around them like the *tfilim* (phylacteries) used by orthodox Jews during prayer. You don't see this anymore.

Two great openings of recent films were that of *Flaming Creatures*, with its wailing Oriental music (and its roguish promise that "Ali Baba will come tonight" murmured by the lovely *houris* under the credits) which makes a mockery of the sly amalgamation of sex and the bible and the genteel evasions of so many would-be erotic film-epics with their flat-footed sexual-innuendos—and *Guns of the Trees,* which opens with the majesty of a film by Dreyer. In the best sense of the word (and how rare that sense is evident nowadays), *Guns of the Trees* is a religious film. Another thing I liked in *Flaming Creatures,* aside from its amazing intransigent pantagruelism, is its delicate and witty parody of the odalisques of Delacroix and Ingres. It is many things but not an immoral film, as has been charged. *The Best of Everything,* whose hero is a cold-blooded murderer (who gets away with it) with the ethics of a piranha, and who is glorified as an example of success in a covetous, rapacious world, cynical producers baiting the cupidity of their audiences, *is* an immoral film.

Among several projects Luis Buñuel is considering for future production is Dalton Trumbo's *Johnny Got His Gun,* that most devastating of anti-war novels, about a soldier who returns from war as a "basket" case—a quadruple amputee, deaf, dumb, and blind.

Booby prize for the most idiotic statement of the year in a film book is contained in Jörn Donner's *The Personal Vision of Ingmar Bergman*—"We are today on our way toward something new, which breaks radically with most in the film's past. We are on the way toward a film art where the personality of the individual artist puts its stamp on the work. It has now learned to write. It is now learning to create form and to compose poetically."

And from The Master himself: "I do not think motion pictures is a healthy form of artistic work. It is inhuman, and one is too tense." Whereupon, after having martyred himself by writing seven screenplays for other directors and directing twenty-six films himself, Ingmar Bergman announced he would not make more than eight or ten more pictures before quitting for good. Reminds me of the classic story of the simple-minded farm girl who said while she was being seduced by the new hired hand, "I know whot you're tryin' to do! You look here, I'll give you exactly forty minutes to git off'n me!"

"He (Chekhov) liked to paint his characters and his scenes

in a very few strokes. He could conjure up a whole landscape with one carefully observed detail. 'You can get the effect of moonlight by saying that a scrap of broken glass was glittering like a tiny star on the path by the mill.' Movie directors have made peculiarly their own his method of creating atmosphere by concentrating the camera on the unusual and significant detail."—André Maurois in *The Art of Writing*.

A gentleman has been defined (by Hemingway) as one exhibiting grace under pressure. This quality is inherent in many good films, too. I think immediately of *The 39 Steps, Glory at Sea* (a minor British item by Compton Bennett but flawlessly made), *Maskerade,* and, of course, *Docks of New York*, in which George Bancroft as a stevedore moves with the grace of a Nijinsky through the violence of a waterfront dive. Here where you would least expect it is the most marvelous grace with which a melodramatic tale is told. But then, that's the greatness of Von Sternberg as a film poet. I think, too, of the English version of Farkas' *La Bataille, Thunder in the East*, with Charles Boyer, Betty Stockfield, Inkijinoff, Merle Oberon, and John Loder, from a story of the Russian-Japanese war by Claude Farrère—another example of little known but perfect film making, like *Glory at Sea*. And there's always that classic example, King Vidor's unforgettable *Hallelujah*.

And how well Hemingway's definition fits the marvelous African Watusi dancers, those tall, strikingly handsome natives of Kenya. Adorned with plumes, carrying spear and shield, they dance to tom-toms, the tinkle of bells around their ankles, and the intermittent chant of their leader with such irresistible verve that the idea of music to accompany a dance for once is not only superfluous but silly. That's how good their dancing as dancing is.

"The cinema," wrote Jung, "can with impunity give free rein to the instincts, appetites and passions that must be restrained in normal existence."

The hopped-up ads of many movies show the distributors' contempt for the mentality of their audience. They bait their ads with sex knowing what will lure these makers of so-called "community standards" to the box-office—in short, the world as a trough.

Mid-summer magic: New York's Central Park Shakespeare

season at the Delacorte Theatre. A dreamy site, overlooking the lake and *Hamlet-like* tower on the far shore, dusk melting into darkness pierced by the multi-colored spotlights that softly illumine the stage, all levels and arches, steps and sweeps of platform. . . . The level of acting and direction is generally so high that it compares with the best Shakespeare performances offered anywhere. The costuming is always a delight, as are the interpolated ballet-like roundelays that set the ambiance for a scene (a felicitious idea!). The best *Twelfth Night* and *Tempest* I ever saw I saw there. (The only miss I remember was *A Midsummer Night's Dream*.) It's the chief compensation for having to endure a New York summer—but worth it.

I remember a poetically lyric image in, of all films, William S. Hart's *Tumbleweeds,* in which a roving cowboy (Mr. Hart) is finally corralled by a winsome lass into marriage and a rolling tumbleweed, seen as a *leit-motif* through the film, becomes itself caught in a corner of the corral, to cease its rolling.

Seeing Ronald Colman in *The Light That Failed* on TV recently reminded me of a silent film Colman once appeared in with Vilma Banky for Sam Goldwyn, in which he played a similar role, a man blinded in the war. It was beautifully written and played, and it was called *The Dark Angel.*

I like what Tretiakov (Soviet playwright of *Roar China,* etc.) said of Eisenstein's *Ten Days:* "From its mistakes alone, three generations of film-makers can learn!"

Autumn, 1964

COFFEE, BRANDY & CIGARS

SILENCES, AND ANSWERING SILENCE

Charles Chaplin's recent autobiography is as chockful of names as a Christmas fruit cake is of fruits but, alas, some of the names of those who were closest to him and who worked with him are missing, such as Harry Crocker, Harry d'Arrast, Monta Bell, Eddie Sutherland, Robert Florey, Carter de Haven, Jean de Limur, Max Linder, Jim Tully, Josef von Sternberg (who even made a film for him, *The Sea Gull*, which Chaplin never released, though John Grierson called it "the most beautiful film ever made in Hollywood"), John Decker, etc.

It was Robert Florey, associate director on *Monsieur Verdoux*, who provided Chaplin with his last line of dialogue and the scene accompanying that line in that devastating film. Originally, the scene called for Verdoux to be taken straight from his cell to the guillotine, but Florey reminded Chaplin that in France a condemned man is offered a glass of rum just before his execution. So Chaplin wrote the scene in, with a nice twist of his own.

VON STERNBERG'S RECALL

Speaking of Josef von Sternberg, the title of his autobiography, to be published by Macmillan in March, is *Fun in a Chinese Laundry*. While it is true that working in Hollywood might be akin to that, he got the title from one of the earliest Edison films ever made, a brief slapstick comedy that appeared shortly after the turn of the century when he was a child and did not even know of the existence of such a thing as the movies.

CONFEDERATE GALLANTRY

I wonder if it is generally known that D. W. Griffith in *The Birth of a Nation* poeticized an actual incident of the Civil War in the scene of Pickett's charge at Gettysburg. Armistead led a hundred men in a desperate though hopeless gesture in this charge, scaled the Union fortifications and planted the Confederate flag within the Union lines. Griffith used poetic license with marvelous dramatic effect when he has the "Little Colonel" (Henry B. Walthall) as Armistead, ram the Confederate flag down the mouth of a Union cannon.

LIFE IMITATES ART

A dispatch from Bonn dated October 8, in *The N.Y. Times* was headed, "Bonn 'Buys' Release of Eight Hundred Held by Reds' and went on to say: "The West German Government quietly bought the release of eight hundred political prisoners in recent months in a men-for-butter swap with East Germany, a Government spokesman announced today." Exactly what happens in Eisenstein's *Alexander Nevsky* when Alexander Nevsky swaps the German cur-knights he has taken prisoner for soap.

ORIGIN OF "GLAMOUR"

The word "glamour," so often applied to the most mysteriously beautiful of our screen stars, especially the ones who played sirens or devastating *femmes fatales*, has an intriguing and doubtless little known aspect when you examine its roots, as I did one rainy afternoon. It derives from the Scottish "glamer," meaning "magic," a corruption of the old English "glamarye," meaning a charm or spell. In the Middle Ages certain women were supposed to be able to cast such a spell on men, a power of bewitching them that rendered the male organ "invisible" and even "intangible." Two Dominican secret policemen of Pope Innocent VIII drew up a handbook (*Malleus Malleficarum*) to supplement the Papal Bull, *Summa desiderantes*, a tract against pathological sex phenomena. Their example of a man who, wishing to break off an affair with a girl, became the victim of a spell of "glamour" cast over him by the unhappy lass in revenge (so he claimed), and of how he forced the girl to "break" the spell, reads like something out of Boccaccio.

After a half-century of intensive film making (the cinema is really a densely concentrated art), it's hard to be original. Even such a strange and offbeat work as the Japanese *Woman in the Dunes* had its basic theme—the triumph of habit over adversity and the conquering of fear through this victory of mind over matter—antedated a generation ago by Victor Seastrom's *The Wind*, starring Lillian Gish and Lars Hanson.

IN SPITE OF STALIN

Harrison E. Salisbury of *The N. Y. Times* and Dwight Macdonald of *Esquire* have said that Stalin stifled the arts in Russia but this isn't entirely true. Under Stalin the Soviet cinema flourished as it has not since—comprising the entire "golden age" from *Potemkin* to *Ivan the Terrible*.

O TEMPORA! O MORES!

Morality used to be equated with the rationale: "As long as you don't do it for money." Today the rationale is that you're only doing it for money.

LENIN THE PICASSO

Before World War I, Lenin lived in Paris, on the Rue Marie-Rose in the artists' quarter of Montparnasse. He used to foregather at the Café Rotonde with other Russian exiles like Trotsky, Lunacharsky, Ilya Ehrenburg, where they'd read the papers, drink tea and play chess. It was said he even posed as a model (being so distinguished looking) to augment his meager resources. He painted also and from time to time would indulge in his free, bold style on canvas, employing a well-known model of the period, the Negress, Aicha la Noire, as she was called. When Lenin became the chief of the newly instituted Soviet regime, Aicha hoped she would now be handsomely paid by him for all the hours she served as his model. She is still waiting.

January, 1965

COFFEE, BRANDY & CIGARS

Tout ça ne vaut pas l'amour...
—Old French Song

The many criticisms of Chaplin's autobiography on the grounds of omission and commission leave me cold. It's like criticizing a painter for his self-portrait. "He shouldn't have put that brush stroke in—he should have left that brush stroke out. Anyway, that's not the way I see him." Everything anyone does is part of a sef-portrait, artists and critics alike. Even the layman paints his self portrait by the way he speaks and reacts. The popular conception of a man is not necessarily a true likeness. But if the man says, "This is the way I am," then that's the way he is. Your own opinion of that (if different) is your self-portrait, it has less to do with him than with you. Let's make that distinction. Let's know whose portrait you're talking about. Maybe both are involved—his and yours. Let's not lose sight of that. The way a man sees himself is part of what he is. You cannot cavil with that.

Biography is something else—and very treacherous ground it is just because it is *not* autobiography, *viz.*, Roger Wild, an old denizen of Montparnasse who knew Modigliani, on the subject of that painter. "One could throw up watching Jacques Becker's well-meant film on him with its false sentimentalities. They show Modi stealing sugar because he was hungry. He was never hungry. Whenever he had any money he spent it for drink. Besides, he was too much of an aristocrat to steal sugar or anything else to eat. He wouldn't steal anything."

An old art-collector friend of mine, C. Philip Boyer, who knew Pascin told me he used to sit with him for hours at the Rotonde or Dome cafés watching Pascin sketch the girls that passed as they would appear without their clothes. Nothing, he said, was ever to him any crueller.

Excerpts from an interview with Fritz Lang at the last Cannes Film Festival:

Q—"Have you any projects you're currently working on?"
FL—"I'm working very hard on my next mistake."
Q—"Have you any bad habits?"
FL—"I have only bad habits."
Q—"Have you any favorite actors or actresses with whom you worked?"
FL—"No comment. I've already got enough enemies."
Q—"Have you any special memories of *Le Mépris* in which you played?"
FL—"Top secret."
Q—"You mean the *bellissima* Brigitte Bardot?"
FL—"*Bellissima!*"
Q—"Which do you prefer, your German expressionistic period or your Hollywood period?"
FL—"I don't understand what you mean by my expressionistic period."
Q—"Are you afraid that with so many films to be shown at the festival, you may fall asleep through some?"
FL—"I generally sleep very badly. Your question gives me hope."

Did you know there was a period of twenty years during which Buñuel did not make a single film? (1927–47).

Buñuel: "I have always been true to my surrealist principle: 'The need to eat never excuses prostituting one's art.' In nineteen or twenty films I have made three or four which are frankly bad, but in no case have I infringed on my moral code. To have a code at all is childish to many people, but not to me. I am against conventional morality, traditional sacred cows, sentimentality and all that moral filth of society which comes into it. Obviously, I have made bad films, but always morally acceptable to me." And that is what counts.

A generation ago Mamoulian etched a brief satiric scene of a deadly dull gathering of socialites in his witty *Love Me Tonight*, introducing it casually, then, in the parlance of the theater, "throwing it away." Today they'd stretch this out to a whole film, as indeed was done in *El Angel Exterminador*. (And Mamoulian's brief comic scene was every bit as sinister as the melodramatics of the Buñuel film. Films used to be more highly concentrated.)

In honor of the forthcoming Sternberg autobiography, I reprint for the first time since it originally appeared in 1936 in the London Bystander an excerpt from a cameo pen-portrait of the director by Charles Graves: "Josef von Sternberg walks like a cat, looks like a fallen archangel, wears Mongolian moustachios and black Chinese pyjamas, is never seen out of doors without a walking-stick, craves cornflowers, and always expects head-waiters to bring, unasked, seven iced black grapes when he enters a restaurant. He has wavy grey hair, steel-blue eyes, a horror of the cold, and a consequent love of the tropics. He talks epigrammatically, paints admirably, and has already sculptured his own tombstone—a brooding monkish figure holding its head with one hand. The only thing he has not yet done is to write his own epitaph or to direct Charles Laughton. And he is beginning on the latter early in the New Year. Mr. von Sternberg lives at the Splendide, resents being put under the slightest obligation by strangers, always refers to Marlene Dietrich as "Miss Dietrich," visits lunatic asylums whenever he can find them, and has built himself an all-steel house in the San Fernando Valley. Here he has a valuable collection of paintings by Utrillo, as well as by Van Gogh, Picasso, Modigliani, and most of the other leading modern painters. . . . He is ultra-sensitive to noise (he once told Miss Dietrich to stop her teeth chattering), secretive, cynical, and certain of himself. He says truthfully that he is neither morbid, sinister, nor particularly decadent. He is merely a realist. He thinks deeply, never evades issues, and enjoys trying to disconcert you. Quite incidentally, he is the greatest living director."

(The above was written shortly after Sternberg's arrival in

London at the invitation of Alexander Korda to direct Laughton in *I Claudius,* from the Robert Graves historical novel. Two remarkable reels were shot—"As beautiful as anything I have ever seen on the screen," said Korda—after which Sternberg, not being able to manage Laughton, who was exhibiting odd quirks (and an ensuing motor accident which incapacitated his co-star, Merle Oberon), gave up and returned to America. (The two reels are currently in the National Film Archives in London.)

Films We Can Do Without: The projected remake of Lang's epochal *Nibelungen* to be also called, *Siegfried's Death* and *Kriemhild's Revenge*—"in color and in the original locales," according to the publicity blurb issued by the producer, Arthur Brauner of the Berlin CCC film company. The original, you will recall, was *not* filmed in color nor in the "original locales" (wherever that may be in this mythological story), but shot in the old Ufa studios, a work of such incontestable grandeur as to make Herr Brauner's announcement not only pitiful but insolent.

One of my favorite films is a little known Mexican opus, *Enamorada,* with Pedro Armendariz and Maria Felix, directed by Emilio Fernandez, that unpredictable Indio of the native Mexican cinema. Unpredictable because he vacillates between pedestrian stuff that goes down as easy as *pulque* for the Mexican peon and wild outbursts of the highest lyricism. There is a love scene played without a word of dialogue—just a magnificent close-up, covering the screen, of Maria Felix' face as she lies in bed listening to the Trio Leones singing beneath her window that *Malagueña* from the Huasteca that has been playing havoc with girls' hearts south of the Rio Grande for a long time now. And at a moment when one of the singers goes into an intense falsetto in the melody, Fernandez cuts to a very long shot of her lover Armendariz, astride his horse rearing up in the moonlight on the deserted plaza, letting out that spine tingling cry of ecstasy with which Mexicans slash through a song to give vent to their solidarity with it (well, you know what I mean). He then returns to the face of Maria Felix as the *Malagueña* ends, by which time Fernandez has built up such a nimbus around her that the scene haunts the rest of the film so that everything else is blotted out. That "Indio," Fernandez, certainly could get worked up.

Chaplin used to buy his canes, called "whangees" and made from Chinese bamboo, for $1 each from Uncle Sam the Umbrella Man, still carrying on after all these years on West 45th Street in New York.

Spring, 1965

COFFEE, BRANDY & CIGARS

"All things are literally better, lovelier and more beloved in the imperfections which have been divinely appointed, that the law of human life may be Effort, and the law of human judgment, Mercy."
—John Ruskin

The Montreal International Film Festival continues to maintain an ambiance of charm, and last summer's was no exception. The high quality of the films shown, the exquisite courtesy of the festival staff, the real helpfulness accorded visiting journalists, and the efficiency with which the whole thing operates, like the meshed gears of a Rolls-Royce, under the direction of Rock Demers and Pierre Juneau, make it a model for all other festivals. There is less esthetic pretension, far less of the *faux bon* and the cocktail-party mask, than you will find elsewhere save in a very few other similar celebrations. In sum, less preening for effect. The result is refreshing. The accent is on the films, but the peripheral events—like the Kino Club, receptions, press interviews, etc.—do not overwhelm you. Everything is done with grace and that indefinable seasoning of Gallic zest.

"The film is a sword without a blade, a banner without a staff, an arrow without a head." (Sean O' Casey)

Good old Handel! Three recent films used his "Hallelujah" chorus from "The Messiah" to bolster them: *Viridiana, The Greatest Story Ever Told,* and *One Way Pendulum*—the first at the beginning, the second in the middle and the third at the end. No matter what the filmmaker's problem is, Handel can solve it for him.

In case you think Chaplin was kidding with his feeding-machine in *Modern Times,* there is such a thing, a machine-feeder that monitors food intake electrically. When a button is pushed, the machine dispenses single mouthfuls of a liquid diet formula, through a mouthpiece. (Reported in *The Journal of the American Dietetic Association.*)

O tempora, etc! In *Potemkin* the sailors mutinied because they were fed maggoty meat. Recently seventeen Chinese sailors on a Dutch tanker mutinied because they weren't seeing as many films as other members of the crew, especially a Gina Lollobrigida film the others saw and they didn't.

Rossellini, that most erratic and unpredictable (and therefore one of the most intriguing) of modern directors, has announced a feature documentary on the history of food.

Gallic wit: Guillaume Apollinaire said the Germans aways had been avid Francophiles, the goal of every German being a visit to Paris. When the war of 1914 started it was only because they all decided to come over together.

One reason for the scarcity of even library prints of old films in the vaults of the major studios is that they are being processed for the silver content in them. A recent *Variety* report stated that some $2,000,000 per year is salvaged from prints in use or of library status and this is barely 7 percent of the potential. Maybe this explains the disappearance of so many films, like the complete *Greed,* the entire Universal silent film library, and other similar victims of this kind of *auto da fe.* A buck in the hand is worth etc. . . .

The best comedies use humor to mask the uncertainty of living in a hostile world. It is the secret of the great success of Chaplin's work. "Cure folly with folly," as Israel Zangwill put it.

Film-making today is almost entirely bereft of nuances and this is what makes Godard's *Contempt* (*Le Mépris*) such a special thing. It is a film almost entirely composed of nuances.

Said Pirandello at the time of the transition from the silent film to sound: "The film is the language of images and images don't speak." (*Vide* Malraux' definition of art: "The voices of silence.")

Coffee, Brandy & Cigars (Autumn, 1965)

"Voyeurism and cinema have become synonyms."—Edmond T. Greville.

Elsewhere I have spoken of "our daily bread" of movies. Say rather "our daily betel nut."

Thirty years ago, Von Sternberg wanted to film Franz Werfel's *The Forty Days of Musa Dagh,* about the Turkish massacre of the Armenians in 1915, but the Turkish government objected. Today MGM, apparently no longer caring what the Turkish government thinks, has decided to film it. This year is the fiftieth anniversary of the martyrdom of a million and a half Armenians, though I don't think that's why they're doing it. (Editorial note: They've since changed their mind.)

Thirty years ago, also, when I first saw the Hecht-MacArthur *Crime Without Passion,* I thought it ten or fifteen years ahead of its time. I was optimistic. Seeing it recently again I feel we still haven't caught up with it. For that matter, we haven't caught up with the best of Sternberg or Welles either, or in spectacle with Lang. "The trouble with progress," said Oscar Wilde, "is that it looks forward, not backward."

Speaking of *Crime Without Passion,* it had a real Nietzschean opening (following the allegorical prologue) with Lee Gentry (Claude Rains), the criminal lawyer, looking down contemptuously at the antlike people below his tower office, crawling along the foot of the skyscraper canyons. "One must be skilled in living on mountains," wrote the author of *Beyond Good and Evil,* "seeing the wretched ephemeral rabble beneath one's self."

No one seems aware that the print of *Variety* circulating here has three cuts: The thirty-minute erotic transition from the opening carnival scenes to Jannings and De Putti as trapeze artists; Jannings putting the stocking back on De Putti; the rape of De Putti by Warwick Ward.

Two underrated films, *The Misfits* by John Huston and Arthur Miller and *Death of a Salesman* by Laszlo Benedek and Miller. A good collaborator to have, Miller. *The Misfits* was especially underrated.

I still think of the devastating pan from the genial face of the mother talking to her son during a visit to the reform school to a close-up of her cold eyes while she is talking—in Truffaut's excruciatingly right *400 Blows*—the pan used as eloquently as it ever has been used.

I also keep thinking of the use made of pigeons in flight by Stroheim at the close of *Foolish Wives*, Alexandrov at the close of *Romance Sentimentale*, and Dreyer at the close of *Joan of Arc*. The unifying force of poetry that binds the world and makes all its artists kin.

Another film I remember fondly: Duvivier's almost forgotten *Un Carnet de Bal*.

Billy Bitzer, cameraman for Griffith, once said that towards the end of both *The Birth of a Nation* and *Intolerance* the speed of the action suddenly increases because he got tired hand-cranking his camera and slowed down with the resulting speed-up of the action.

Jiri **Trnka,** the jolly Czech film puppeteer, has recently completed *Archangel Gabriel and Mrs. Gans*—a retelling of that delightfully wicked story, *Putting the Devil Back Into Hell*, from Boccaccio's *Decameron*.

Luis Buñuel, who was enthusiastic over the Beatles' *A Hard Day's Night*, has abandoned the idea of doing Dalton Trumbo's horrendous *Johnny Got His Gun*.

Cuts I remember fondly: From the shot of Guinness reviewing his troops imprisoned by the Japanese, while the Col. Bogey march jauntily plays, to a close-up of the raggedly shod feet of the soldiers marching followed by a cut back to Guinness (this time also in close-up) with an almost indescribable look of mixed pride and compassion. The cut from the French Foreign Legion officer calling out in the desert during the sudden sandstorm for his colleague, gone off to retrace his steps to Atlantis (in Pabst's *L'Atlantide*), to the shot of the Negro spahi holding two camels down during the storm and, over the sound track, the rising music, howling wind and the Legionnaire officer's cry, "Saint Avit! Saint Avit!" Best of all, in *Crime Without Passion*, after Eddie White (Stanley Ridges) has hit Lee Gentry (Claude Rains) backstage of the night-club outside Carmen Brown's dressing room, the cut to a close-up of Lee Gentry as he tries to regain his composure but still smarting from the humiliation of the blow—for a moment all the savor of life has gone out of the usually ebullient Gentry and he has the taste of ashes in his mouth. Where do you see this kind of subtlety anymore?

"You complain of lack of culture in this amusement arcade world. I wonder what you'd say to the world in which I nearly die of disgust," wrote Arnold Schoenberg once to Oskar Kokoschka. "I don't only mean the movies. Here is an advertisement by way of example: There's a picture of a man who has run over a child who is lying dead in front of his car. The man clutches his head in despair, but not to say anything like 'My God, what have I done!' The caption underneath the picture says, 'Sorry, now it is too late to worry—take out your policy at the XX Insurance Company in time.' And these are the people I'm supposed to teach composition to!"

To those who think *The Umbrellas of Cherbourg* is something special as a "sung film," I recommend Reinhold Schuenzel's *Amphitryon* as a *true* sung film, filmed in Germany in 1933 in two versions, French and German, and a thousand times the better film. There are so many plugs for Esso Gasoline in *The Umbrellas of Cherbourg* ("inadvertent," *bien entendu!*) that I agree with Bosley Crowther who called it a "singing commercial."

There is no screen credit in *The Greatest Story Ever Told* for Handel (who doesn't need it) but there is for Alfred Newman (who does).

Anton Rubinstein, the great nineteenth-century Russian pianist, was famous for his "grand style," let-the-wrong-notes-fall-where-they-may. "With the notes I dropped under the piano tonight," he once joked after a recital, "I could give a second recital." Eventually, he wrote an "Etude on Wrong Notes."

The juvenile, trivial, meretricious content of some of the most popular films is incredible. With all the unresolved issues that burn to be told in the modern world, with all the great backlog of marvelous stories available to the screen, *Casablanca* has the gall to show a scene where the café-owner, Bogart, asks his Negro pianist to play "their song" (Bogart's and Ingrid Bergman's) and when the loyal Negro demurs, "No, boss, you don' wanna hear that song!" (shades of "Massah's in de cold, cold ground"!) "Anyway, I forgot it!" the whiskey-sodden Bogart says, "Go on play it—if she can stand it, I can!" The issue of whether Bogie can stand to hear "their song" is the trash level of most Hollywood "heroics."

But *Casablanca* triumphed at the box office and *The Misfits,* which had at least some positive things to say about the human condition, flopped. Mencken was right: "No one ever lost money underestimating the American public."

Who speaks today of Antonin Artaud? I do. He was visible briefly as Marat in Gance's *Napoleon* and played the priest who befriends Joan in Dreyer's *Jeanne d' Arc,* the priest with the fine, young, noble face—the only one among all those gargoyles. Most of all Artaud was a poet, though addicted to nervous seizures during which he became so strong he could bend iron bars. "Me," he once wrote, "I want to live in refusing what is around me: family, religion, institutions, country. Nothing is true, either in us or outside us. All is a lie, all is false: the world, life, laws, love, God. All is polluted—lawyers, ministers, deputies, morality, the theatre, actors, authors . . . everything, I say! Even our whores are false; even our homosexuals, our lesbians. We all swim in the same polluted waters. Society, this paradise, this paragon of morality, I submit to it, but it doesn't have any meaning for me. I say *merde!*" He wrote a study of Van Gogh to prove that Van Gogh was not crazy, that he killed himself because he could not stand to live in such a terrible world. He, too, killed himself, in 1948, at the age of 52.

Pabst hated violence in real life but loved to put it in his films. He loved the pure women in his films but was bored to death with them in real life.

The true artist permits himself the widest latitude in implicitness, but the utmost restraint in explicitness.

Cocteau's two favorite films were *Storm Over Asia* and *Hallelujah.*

Ave atque vale! Rudolph Maté, prodigious cameraman of Dreyer's *Jeanne d'Arc* and *Vampyr* . . . And Linda Darnell . . . who brightened every movie she was ever in . . . And Ary Barroso, composer of those intoxicating love songs to Bahia and Brazil, *Bahia* and *Aquarela do Brasil,* the latter of which Disney used so felicitously in *Saludos Amigos.* Ave, ave. . . !

What did Magali Noel, René Clair, Norman McLaren, Robert Flaherty, Jayne Mansfield, Albert Einstein, Marlene Dietrich, Betty Compson, Ben Hecht, Joseph Wechsberg, Chaplin, and Mistinguette have in common? (They all played the violin.)

Why is it that the infamous distortion of Feuchtwanger's *Jew Süss* by Veit Harlan survives and that honest and powerful filming of it by Lothar Mendes (with Conrad Veidt in the title role) has not survived?

A couple of years ago a brief visit to the Soviet Union left

Shirley MacLaine so frustrated she said she would like to go back and "dance the can-can naked on Red Square every May Day." Unfortunately for United States–Soviet relations, it didn't happen. We'll have to manage it the hard way.

Cary Grant was to do a tour of Army bases and a USO public relations office, gathering biographical data on him in advance of his appearance, wired his studio, "How old Cary Grant?" To which his studio wired back, "Old Cary Grant fine. How you?"

And, in case you heard that one before, allow me to make it up to you with the following excerpt from the March 17 *Variety*, which deserves further circulation:

> Mexico City, March 16. "The Mexican motion picture industry is corrupted by the commercialism and the bad influence of the French and North American pictures," declared Emilio "Indio" Fernandez, visiting Cartagena, Colombia, as a member of the Mexican delegation to the film festival there. Fernandez, co-director with John Huston on *Night of the Iguana*, blasted the entire Mexican film industry. "The producers and the Union which have a tight hold on the Mexican motion picture industry are only interested in profits," said their critic. "If they could make money selling pornographic postcards, they would." Asked by the press if he was not afraid that his statements might hurt him, Fernandez said that he had been boycotted in Mexico for the past ten years for refusing to go along with the "new tendencies." He added: "The producers who control the industry are not concerned with cinema art and culture. Pictures can be made as educational and cultural vehicles just as easily as corruptors of the current generation."

Autumn, 1965

COFFEE, BRANDY & CIGARS

"*Therefore at this fair are all such merchandise sold, as houses, lands, trades, places, honors, preferments, titles, countries, kingdoms, lusts, pleasures, and delights of all sorts, as whores, bawds, wives, husbands, children, masters, servants, lives, blood, bodies, souls, silver, gold, pearls, precious stones and what not. And, moreover, at this fair there is at all times to be seen jugglings, cheats, games, plays, fools, apes, knaves, and rogues, and that of every kind. Here are to be seen, too, and that for nothing, thefts, murders, adulteries, false swearers, and that of a blood-red color.*"
—John Bunyan, *Pilgrim's Progress*

WHO SAYS "EXAGGERATED?"

Erich von Stroheim used to be criticized for the opulence and *bizarrerie* of his productions but no screen fiction can outdo reality in these respects. At the elegant Bad Homburg spa in Germany towards the close of the last century, an aged arthritic Russian countess, accompanied by a Nubian giant bearing a sack of gold coins, used to be carried to the gaming tables by two servants, playing daily from 2 P.M. to 2 A.M. (Shades of Pushkin's "Queen of Spades."!)

Artists often think alike. Thus Scriabin, that mystical Russian composer, wrote two piano sonatas, one called, "The White Mass" and the other, "The Black Mass." Stroheim had a white semi-nude orchestra in his orgy scene for *The Merry Widow* and a black semi-nude orchestra for *The Wedding March*. (Both were cut from the films.)

HOMILY ON THE VALUE OF MONEY

I like Jimmy Durante's homily about money. "Can it buy happiness?" he asked. "Can it buy friendship, affection, love, true loyalty, the joy of an idyllic family life? Can it buy good health, if you don't have it?" He meditated silently for a moment, sadly shook his head and walked slowly off. Before leaving, he turned for an instant and added, "Of course, I'm talkin' about Confederate money."

Apropos money, it has doubtless made as many differences for the worse as for the better. Especially in the arts. Examples are legion. Take the case of the first and second versions of Lehar's overture to *The Merry Widow*. The original is clear, lucid, and to the point. The later and "improved" version, written after the operetta became a hit, all tricked up and flossy, "candy-assed", like the army used to call parade horses, frilled like a high-class *fille de joie* on Easter Sunday showing off her finery. (Like Vladimir Horowitz's arrangement of Sousa's "Stars and Stripes" march, like a $1,000,000 barbershop, or his arrangement of Liszt's "Second Hungarian Rhapsody"—Old Home Week, the Fourth of July and a presidential election pow-wow rolled into one. But, of course, *what* a pianist! The artist, however, should be able to resist his own stimuli.)

REMEMBRANCE OF MATA HARI

Film-buff readers of this once-a-year column may be interested to learn that Josef von Sternberg's *Dishonored*, starring Marlene Dietrich and Victor McLaglen, was based loosely on incidents in the life of Mata Hari, known as H-21, a clumsy spy for the Germans in World War I. (Dietrich is called X-21 in the film and is a spy for Austria.) Mata Hari was a prostitute before becoming a spy (as was the character played by Dietrich); Mata Hari had a liaison with a Colonel Suvarsky of the Russian Secret Service whom she met at the gaming-tables (exactly what happens in the film); Mata Hari was eventually apprehended and shot (so was the Dietrich character in the film). Another character in the film, the Austrian Colonel (played by Warner Oland) who was in the pay of the Russian Secret Service and who shot himself when exposed, had its real-life counterpart in the famous case of Colonel Redl.

MORE MELODRAMATIC MAYERLING

Now that they are going to re-film the story of what happened at Archduke Rudolph of Hapsburg's hunting lodge at Mayerling the night he was found shot, together with his mistress, the Baroness Vetsera, and of the events leading up to that fateful night—all supposedly based on "newly discovered evidence" —it might be pertinent to summarize the equally supposedly true story of what happened as told by Frau Schratt, the Austrian Emperor's best-known mistress, to Raoul Gunsbourg, director of the Monte Carlo Opera, during the time she sojourned near Monaco. George W. Herald and Edward D. Radin report it in their fascinating history of Monte Carlo, *The Big Wheel.*

Franz Josef had his love affairs while the Empress Elizabeth, nicknamed "Sissy," had hers. Her first lover was Hungarian Count Andrássy, and court circles always considered him the actual father of Archduke Rudolph, the heir to the Hapsburg throne, who later mysteriously died at Mayerling. . . . She (Frau Schratt) told Gunsbourg that Franz Josef knew of his wife's infidelities, but for reasons of state had to remain silent. He hated Archduke Rudolph, the heir who was not his son, and the young man in return heartily disliked him. The Archduke was also a notorious woman-chaser, rather indiscriminate in his choices. He picked what pleased his eye, a countess one night, a scullery maid another. But most of the women he pursued had one thing in common: they were usually married. The archduke got a special delight out of cuckolding husbands.

According to Frau Schratt's story, two members of the palace staff, a coachman and gamekeeper, requested an audience with the Emperor. Both men complained to him that the Archduke had seduced their wives. The gamekeeper was particularly bitter and is supposed to have exclaimed, 'If I were a nobleman, I would know how to avenge myself.'

Franz Josef was said to have replied, 'I don't think this is a matter of social rank.'

A few weeks later they shot Rudolph in the head through an open window of his hunting lodge at Mayerling. Marie Vetsera, his mistress of the moment, was killed when she threw herself against his body in a vain attempt to save him.

The death of the couple was long considered by the public a suicide pact. To substantiate her story, Frau Schratt pointed out that the Pope would not grant absolution to a suicide, but when the Emperor gave his word to the Pontiff that it had been a case of murder, absolution was given. She said the coachman and the gamekeeper later received a large sum of money from

Franz Josef to leave Europe for South America. All this is rather different from the romantic fairy tale of Litvak's *Mayerling* with Charles Boyer and Danielle Darrieux, of fond memory, but dubious fact. How close to this harsh version will the new one be?

FOOTNOTE ON WEDNESDAY

Apropos the current stage hit, *Any Wednesday*, there is an old Viennese proverb, "Women were placed on this earth to serve their husbands except on Wednesdays."

FILM SHOT IN ONE HOUR

The rarest film in the world—the one-reel Oriental burlesque turned out by Eisenstein to win a bet that he couldn't make a film in an hour. (Everyone involved must have been drunk.) Together with his assistants, Alexandrov and Tissé, a Persian rug, a few potted palms and a cooch dancer, he shot this parody of all "exotic" films. It happened shortly after the enormously successful premiere of *Potemkin* in Berlin.

NUANCE OF CONSOLATION

I saw a Greek film once consisting of several episodes (like *Trio, Quartet*, etc.), one of which told of a beggar into whose cup someone had dropped a large coin. It made such a loud clink that the beggar examined it and discovered it to be a gold sovereign. Trying to cash it in a bank, he learned it was a counterfeit. Still, it shone and looked impressive. Deciding to palm it off on a *nymphe du pavé* who worked his street, he propositioned her, she accepted, and they spent the night together. Next morning he reached into his trouser pocket for the coin and found there a hole instead. He had lost the coin. When he broke this dire news to the girl, she began throwing things at him in her rage. "Calm yourself, calm yourself!" he said to her, "The coin was a fake anyway!" Ah, those Greeks.

UNRECOGNIZED GREATS

Did you know that Jacob Stainer, the great violin maker, Smetana, the great composer, and Semmelweis, the great pioneer in medicine, all lived and died like dogs because of lack of recognition? Smetana once wrote a pitiful letter to Liszt, asking for a loan, for which he promised to dedicate a composition to the enormously successful Hungarian piano virtuoso and fellow-composer, to which he got an elegantly couched letter of refusal.

THE MORE DIFFICULT ART

I think that what André Gide said in his foreword to Antoine de Saint-Exupéry's *Night Flight* applies most cogently to today's novels, theater, and screen. "Too well we know man's failings, his cowardice and lapses, and our writers of today are only too proficient in exposing these; but we stand in need of one to tell us how a man may be lifted far above himself by his sheer force of will."

TRUE REVERENCE!

Jean Cocteau once told of soirées of chamber music held at his grandfather's at which the violin virtuosi Sarasate and Sivori (only pupil of Paganini) frequently played. One night Sivori, who was practically a dwarf, saw the maid as usual gathering a pile of scores for him to sit on so he could reach the level of his music stand. "Not on Beethoven!" he cried out. "Not on Beethoven!"

January, 1966

Judex (France, 1917) Scenario by Arthur Bernede, Louis Feuillade. Directed by Louis Feuillade. Photography: Guérin. A Gaumont Film with René Cresté, Musidora, Yvette Andreyor, Lebas, Marcel Levesque, Mathot. A serial in 12 episodes.

Judex (France, 1964) Scenario after the original by Bernède and Feuillade. Directed by Georges Franju. With Channing Pollock, Edith Scob, Francine Bergé. An "hommage" to the Feuillade film.

JUDEX

1911 . . . La Belle Epoque is drawing to a close, that florescence of *joie de vivre* that made Paris the gaming grounds for all the high living princes and cocottes of Europe, the kings and crooks and dandies and their ladies, artists, bohemians, nobles and riffraff, flocking to Maxim's or the *bals tabarins* . . .

The Revolution of 1848 and the abdication of Louis Philippe may have marked the end of the Bourbon-Orléans monarchy but it did not stay the Parisians in their lust for pleasure despite the warning of the socialist pamphleteer Proudhon, "You are dancing on the edge of a volcano!" It came—the Franco-Prussian War of 1870, when Paris felt the iron fist of Bismarck, and the *communards* died on the barricades in its wake. . . . But nothing could stem *les dancings* and the delirium of the populace bent on its frenetic gaiety. . . . Dazzling expositions rose, the Eiffel Tower rose, Yvette Guilbert sang nightly at the Divan Japonais or the Moulin Rouge and Aristide Bruant at Le Mirliton, in Montmartre, with Toulouse-Lautrec ever in attendance at both, sketching them and the denizens that quickened their haunts with swift and acid strokes that were to become immortal. Proust chronicled the *haut monde* in his epic *recherches,* while Offenbach and the rest of the raffish composers set its dancing feet to music, the can-can and the quadrille, the waltz and innumerable *chagrins des amours.*. . .

In short, there was never a time like Paris before the First World War. Proudhon was righter than even *he* imagined, for even he did not envision those feverish July days of 1914 when the *poilus* entrained from the Gare St. Lazare for the front while *les boches* similarly entrained from Berlin for an "en masse tourist expedition to France," as Guillaume Apollinaire facetiously put it, *Gott mit uns* engraved on their belt buckles. But the war was regarded as even a greater lark than any that had gone before . . . it would be over in three months, six at the most, and everyone would return to the gay life.

And it was among these pre-war entertainments, in 1911 to be exact, that a new kind of literature began appearing in Paris to regale the populace . . . a *série noire*, adventure stories of dark deeds involving super-crooks and super-detectives, ravishing heroines, sinister nuns carying concealed daggers or hypodermics, catlike creatures of the night in black who could scale sheer walls and lose themselves in the darkness after their nefarious deeds. Parisians read these stories popeyed and could not wait for their sequels, avid for these penny-dreadfuls that sprang from the sewers and dead-falls of Eugène Sue's *Mysteries of Paris* and the like.

Foremost among these lurid paperbacks was the *Fantomas* series, celebrating the exploits of this super-criminal. For three years, from 1911 to 1914, every month, a new volume appeared from the inexhaustible pens of Pierre Souvestre and Marcel Allain, their fecund authors. And what was more logical than that these highly colored tales should have attracted one of the pioneers of that new miraculous toy that was amusing Parisians— the cinematograph—Louis Feuillade? In 1913 Feuillade made his own adaptation of some of these tales, filming them in the form of five feature-length super-serials—*Fantomas, Judex vs. Fantomas, Fantomas vs. Fantomas*, etc. Filmed mostly out of doors, *in toto* they documented Paris and its environs of that day as surely and as vividly as did Atget with his lumbering still camera. Both Apollinaire and Max Jacob attested to the serials' lyric poetry, their marvelous sense of the fantastic, but above all to their documentation of the old France before it emerged, after the First World War, into the glossy twentieth century that was the 1920's with its new jazz delirium.

Not only were the *Fantomas* films an enormous success in France and Europe, but also in Russia and the United States. In the latter they gave impetus to our own serials starring such erstwhile notable exponents of deeds of derring-do as Eddie Polo, Ruth Roland, and Pearl White.

So successful were the *Fantomas* serials that Feuillade, after a brief interruption caused by the outbreak of the war, soon followed them with a new series, *Les Vampires* ("The Vampires"— as he called a notorious gang of criminals). Filmed in ten feature-length episodes, they appeared first as *romans-feuilletons* published daily in the great Parisian daily *Le Matin* one a week, followed each week by the film version of the preceding week's serial. Even the intellectuals were taken by the breathless action and incredible invention of these works, with such spokesmen of surrealism as André Breton, Paul Eluard, and Louis Aragon proclaiming, "It will one day be understood that nothing is more real and poetic than the evocation of our yesterdays in such improvised *ciné-feuilletons* with their joy in our cities and landscapes and the human graffiti that people them. It is in *Les Vampires* that one will find the true reality of the twentieth century, behind the current fashion, behind the curent taste." And they were especially rapturous of Musidora, the actress who incarnated the formidable female leader of The Vampires. "The Tenth Muse" they called her. She was later to be reincarnated on the screen in the person of Francine Bergé in the role of Diana in Georges Franju's *Judex,* inspired by the films of Louis Feuillade. But while Musidora reigned on the French screen, there was no match for her, both as a siren and formidable adversary, and she can be said to have made a personal triumph in her long and arduous roles through the ten episodes of *Les Vampires* which, itself, was the sensation of the 1965 New York Film Festival at Lincoln Center, when *Les Vampires* was presented in its entirety at a single five-hour sitting.

Les Vampires was produced by Feuillade over a period of two years, 1915-16. That most terrible of battles in all the world's lamentable history of bloody battles—Verdun—was being fought in 1916, the year of the apogee of the popularity of *Les Vampires* —the year of Diaghilev and the Ballets Russes, the year of D. W. Griffith's *Intolerance.*

An episode of *Les Vampires* where a group of invited guests in a large salon find themselves unable to leave the room because of some strange miasma that settles over them was subsequently to be used by Luis Buñuel as the key scene of his *The Extermi-*

nating Angel. Indeed, in a dedicatory preface to his film, Buñuel acknowledges his indebtedness to the work of Feuillade whose films he admired profoundly.

And then came the *Judex* series, 1916-17, in twelve feature-length episodes, followed by *La Nouvelle Mission de Judex,* in twelve additional episodes in 1918. Now the heroes were no longer the criminals but Judex himself, a Latin word meaning "judge" or "righter of wrongs" or "champion of the right." In his flying black cape he was the true precursor of today's Batman and even of Superman. Diabolic in their cunning as his adversaries might be, Judex invariably outwitted them. Again the streets of Paris and the pastoral environs and countryside served to document a quickly vanishing era and the alliance of the fantastic and the real served again to all but obliterate its demarcation, for the new century was getting more sophisticated and electronics were coming in, ingeniously made use of by the ever fertile imagination of Feuillade, itself wedded to the latest scientific gimmicks of the days. If possible, *Judex* was an even greater success than its predecessors. The French historian Georges Sadoul speaks of those "divine puerilities" that rose above the physical action to an unconscious poetry which, though involuntary, achieved a unique candor and freshness.

The new *Judex* by Franju, made "in homage to Louis Feuillade," is set in 1914, on the eve of the First World War. One may even feel that the grotesque masked ball, with the principal figures attired in enormous bird heads (Favraux, the villainous banker, wears a vulture's head, Judex an eagle's) is a *danse macabre,* precursor to the horrors of Verdun. That is why the film ends with the phrase "a souvenir of an unhappy time—1914." But it is still the era of social amenities, at least outwardly, and so the rhythm is that of a slow waltz, like the sinister music at the ball. For behind this outward show of grace are murderous sirens disguised as nuns, or female creatures accoutered in black leotards and dominoes, a stiletto strapped to the thigh, and sliding panels and tombs and electronic two-way mirrors or "eyes" like the kind that watch us today in banks, steel clamps springing from locked drawers, handcuffing would-be pilferers, together with all those good old standbys of yesterday, chloroform, homing-pigeons carrying desperate messages, hi-jacking ambulances, the ubiquitous hired detective, or "Hawkshaw," in his Sherlock Holmes get-up, those lovely old cars (so chic then!) with their gas-burning headlights pursuing each other down country lanes at dusk, and kidnappings, the spidery scalings of sheer walls and hurdling of balconies, rooftop fights with the victim sliding down to the edge, grasping an inch of ledge above a six-story drop. . . .

"Judex" has them all, and more, for this is not only a tribute to the cinema's innocent youth, the dear old days of the past, but also almost a compendium of this past, with its lights and shadows, its violences as facile as its graces, its sense of right and wrong (as white is different from black—no psychological or sociological nonsense here!) and always lurking, even where the shadows are darkest, the fluttering white shafts of romance and true love, like the fluttering white doves that Judex releases, harbinger of better days to come.

May, 1966

COFFEE, BRANDY & CIGARS

"Love art in your own selves, and not yourselves in art."
—Stanislavsky

Purist Dep't.: Commented Debussy when told Nijinsky had choreographed *The Afternoon of a Faun*, "Why?"
What the eye rejects, the mind also dismisses.
"Art," said Renoir, "should be inimitable and indescribable." ("You cannot describe *Potemkin*," said Pudovkin. "You must see it.")
"There is no excellent beauty that has not some strangeness in the proportion." (Bacon)
Genius is not necessarily the axiomatic "infinite capacity for taking pains." *Candide* was written in three days.
The only values left are the values of the market place.

I see the new independent cinema rife with visual neologisms but lacking the play of mind. Joyce invented new words to illuminate his themes, and his devastating puns to make them crackle with irony or shimmer with poetry. Their play of mind is the joy of *Ulysses* and *Finnegans Wake*. But all this mindless cinematic virtuosity, save for an occasional exception, springs neither from the heart nor from Nature; it's aesthetically on a par with those colored gelatins that projectionists used to put in front of the projector lens in the old days to lend the picture on the screen "tone." There is nothing more powerful than an honest camera eye, one devoid of chi-chi or fustian. Adolfas Mekas has it, *The Brig*, heaven knows, has it. Emshwiller and Godard have it. So does Truffaut, so did Mizoguchi. Pasolini has it. Ron Rice, Jack Smith, Bresson, Rossellini, Dreyer . . . Chris Marker sometimes has it. . . .

I think of the charming passage in Marker's *Koumiko Mystery*, the overhead shot of a wet Tokyo street with a bevy of girls carrying colored umbrellas in the rain as they cross the street to Michel Legrand's music-theme from *The Umbrellas of*

Cherbourg . . . a brief echo-tribute from Marker that is better than the whole of Demy's "opera" itself.

Carl Dreyer was interviewed all over the place, during his recent visit to New York, about *Joan of Arc,* about *Vampyr,* etc. He courteously answered all the obvious questions put to him and yet, when it was all over, we knew not a whit more about the mystery that made *Joan of Arc* and *Vampyr* the ineffable works they are than we knew before. It's always like that with real artists. Asked to explain their method, they'll tell everything except what we most want to know and that, I'm afraid, is not tellable, and yet it is only that which matters.

Dreyer says he used close-ups in *Joan of Arc* because it was primarily a film of questions and answers, so it was logical. But Bresson, who gave as the reason for his doing this subject again the fact that he would go to the original questions and answers of the trial (as if Dreyer didn't), felt it unnecessary to use closeups. It's exasperating, but it's marvelous . . . the eternal mysteries of art.

Virtuosity isn't enough, you've got to have something cogent to say, even if what is being said is not necessarily very profound—indeed, usually the less "profound" the better, since the cinema isn't the best medium for expounding ideas, even though this has been done on exceptional occasions. Thus, all the virtuosity of Kurosawa's *Red Beard* and Kobayashi's *Kwaidan* cannot save them from being unsatisfying as cinema experiences. One or two more bombastic duds like these, and the Japanese cinema will go right down the drain. Although *Gate of Hell* had a plot (like the corny one of *Red Beard*) right out of the old Tomashevsky Yiddish Art Theatre, *olavasholem,* there was a real poet behind the camera, Kinugasa, an old-timer from the Japanese cinema's silent days. The visuals in *Gate of Hell* had a plangent splendor that makes *Kwaidan* look very self-consciously "artistical" indeed. And I don't forgive Kurosawa for the ambivalent scene (in *Red Beard*) where the nude girl-patient is spread-eagled for an operation, with both her voluptuous breasts and her guts bared. Really, Mr. Kurosawa!

Ichikawa's *Tokyo Olympics* is better. What lenses those Japanese cinematographers have! But a lot of the *panache* and almost all the poetry have been cut from the truncated American release version. Among the missing sequences is the very moving closing ceremonies of the Tokyo Olympiad, which we even saw on television (good old television!). Despite the grafting of a typically American frenzied sportscaster's sound-track, this is worth seeing, even tho' Leni Riefenstahl's Olympic film of 1936 is an infinitely greater work.

Is it possible that a *petite bourgeoise* like the wife Giulietta Masina plays in *Juliet of the Spirits* could have the "sophisticated" dreams and hallucinations depicted in this film? Weren't they all in Fellini's and his oh-so-clever co-scenarists' minds? And what appalling minds! I award this paroxysmic mess my "blue ribbon with palms" (in color) for the cinema diarrhea of the year.

One of the penalties of having a long memory is that it often prevents you from concentrating entirely on the new film you're seeing because something in it reminds you of an old film you once saw. Thus, watching the scene in Machaty's *Ecstasy* where the hero and heroine are brought together by the horse running off with her clothes while she is bathing, I kept thinking of having seen that contretemps before in, of all films, one as opposite to *Ecstasy* as could be imagined—*Tol'able David*. There a dog steals the hero's clothes while he is bathing and thereby brings him and the heroine together. Only the sexes of the nude bathers changed over the years, Hedy Lamarr certainly being more interesting to look upon in the nude than Richard Barthelmess. Ah, for those lost days of innocence. . . !

One of the many things I like about Gloria Swanson is the anecdote she once told me about having seen Lamorisse's *The Red Balloon* and bursting into tears when the balloon exploded.

"Works of art are of an infinite loneliness," wrote Rainer Maria Rilke, "and with nothing to be so little reached as with criticism. Only love can grasp and hold and fairly judge them."

At least the new, young, independent American cinema is trying, and with so much work going on, there are bound to emerge some real talents just as the whole French "new wave" was worth it for the two pearls it cast up—Truffaut and Godard. But the commercial cinema, by and large, is still taking the easiest way by goosing the bourgeoisie with its *sottises,* violences, religious spectacles, and the like, with all their catch-penny devices, a morality compounded of "God-is-looking-at-you" tinctured with Spanish fly.

I have seen the footage Sternberg shot for his uncompleted *I, Claudius* and you will see it, too, when it is released on television in the form of a 75-minute film, *The Epic That Never Was*, produced by the incredible BBC. The film interviews Sternberg, Merle Oberon (who played Messalina), Emlyn Williams (Caligula), and Flora Robson (Claudius' grandmother, the dowager empress); also the costume designer and Robert Graves, author of the book from which it was adapted. Each comments on the abortive project and tries to give his or her reasons why it was never finished. Alas, that Laughton could no longer be interviewed, for he played the title-role, nor Alexander Korda, for whose London Films Sternberg embarked on the film. A half hour of unedited rushes are shown intermittently and every time a Sternberg shot comes on, the contrast of the steely grey BBC-TV photography with the witchery of Sternberg's chiaroscuro is breathtaking. I mean this literally. What a film it could have been, how magnificent Laughton was in the part, and yet it was Sternberg's difficulties with Laughton that made it difficult to continue with the film, just as it was an accident sustained by Miss Oberon that finally brought it to a halt altogether. But those shots, boys and girls, those shots. . . !

August, 1966

COFFEE, BRANDY & CIGARS

They tell of that afternoon in Madrid when Sir Alexander Fleming was recognized sunning himself on a bench in a park. When word buzzed around that he was the discoverer of penicillin, which had saved so many lives, the Madrileños in the area rushed to the flowercarts, scooped up their contents *in toto* and, just as he got up to leave, made a path of blossoms for him to walk upon.

The Tahitians say that coconuts have eyes to see and fall from their high perch in the kava trees only on the heads of mean people, and, as there are no mean people in Tahiti, there is nothing to worry about.

"The strength of the prohibition," said Freud, "shows the strength of the attraction."

All the countries behind the Iron Curtain are rife with jokes about the political situation in which they find themselves. In Bucharest they tell of the teacher who asked her class of boys to relate good deeds that they performed. Said Popescu, "I helped a little old lady cross the street." "Very good," said the teacher. Said Ionescu, "I helped Popescu help the little old lady cross the street." "That's even better," said the teacher, "it shows the collective spirit." Said Constantinescu, "And I helped Popescu and Ionescu help the little old lady cross the street." "Excellent!" exclaimed the teacher, "'a truly collective action!" "And I," said Manescu, "helped Popescu, Ionescu and Constantinescu help the little old lady cross the street." "Great," said the teacher, "but, tell me, why did it take four strong boys to help one little old lady cross the street?" "Because," said Manescu, "she didn't want to cross."

The reason the late Raymond Duncan, "eccentric" brother of the famed dancer, Isadora, wore togas instead of modern dress dates back to 1903 when he presented himself one evening at a soirée with his valet, who was refused admittance because the valet was not properly accoutered in evening dress. Angry, Duncan returned home, changed into a toga and gave his valet his own evening dress. They returned to the ball. This time, the valet was admitted, but not the master. As a reproach to this snobbery, Raymond Duncan never again wore modern clothes.

During the filming of *A Countess from Hong Kong*, the cameraman is reported to have said to Chaplin, "How about an unusual angle for this shot?" To which Chaplin is said to have replied, "I don't need an unusual angle, I am, myself, unusual."

Said the son of Theodore Van Gogh, brother of the famous Vincent, during an interview: "Picasso? He is good, he has done some excellent things. He is a great draftsman. But I also think he is afraid, something in him is afraid, so that he never culminates anything. He comes to the point of discovery and then turns away and does something else." Van Gogh's nephew, himself an art critic, shook his head sorrowfully. "I like him but I think there is something he doesn't want to face."

Maurice Utrillo was engaged by Sacha Guitry for a brief role, as himself, painting a street scene in Montmartre for Guitry's film, *Si Paris M'Etait Conté*. When told the scene was finished and that he could stop, Utrillo replied, "But I am not finished." He continued to paint until he had completed the street scene.

At the time of the Nazi-Soviet nonaggression pact, Von Ribbentrop came to Moscow. The Russians wanted to decorate Moscow with pictures of Hitler but couldn't find any. They didn't want to offend their new ally and were very anxious to put on a show of solidarity. Then someone remembered that they were currently making an anti-Nazi film, *Professor Mamlock*, whereupon they went to the studio, gathered up the supply of Hitler pictures that were being used in the film, and decorated Moscow.

Sergei Eisenstein's letter to Paramount accompanying the screen treatment of Dreiser's *An American Tragedy*, written by himself and Alexandrov, his assistant, and which project was to have served as Eisenstein's American directorial debut:

Oct. 5, 1930.

Gentlemen:

So here we see the miracle accomplished—*An American Tragedy* in only 14 reels.

Still, we think the final treatment must not be over 10.

But we withdraw from the final "shrinking," leaving it for the present "in extenso," so as to have the possibility of making this unpleasant operation *after* receiving the benefit of notes and advice from:

1. The West Coast Magnates.
2. The East Coast Magnates.
3. Theodore Dreiser.
4. The Hays Organization.

Accordingly, gentlemen, we have the honor to submit to your "discriminating kindness":

The Enclosed Manuscript

And . . . *Honi soit qui mal y pense!*

(Signed)
Sergei M. Eisenstein
Grigori Alexandrov

An anecdote straight out of a Lubitsch comedy was recounted in, of all places, the August 24–31, 1775, issue of the weekly *New England & Essex Chronicle*, an early Colonial newspaper. It reported the story of a tanner who came home late one night, undressed and was about to settle down in bed in the darkened bedroom when his wife suddenly got up and complained of a severe migraine headache, asking him to go to the grog shop for some aniseed water to relieve it. The dutiful husband dressed and proceeded to the grog shop, asked for the aniseed water and, reaching into his trousers pocket, brought forth a gold sovereign. Not having owned a gold sovereign in his life, he wondered how it got there, thought it over, and in the process noticed that the trousers were not his own. After a moment's deliberation, feeling that his wife was well taken care of, he sat down, placed the sovereign on the table, and bade the grog shop owner to keep bringing him hot rum toddies to fortify himself against the cold night air. Befuddled from the long night of rum-guzzling, he returned home nigh unto dawn, having left the bottle of aniseed water for his wife in the grog shop. He had forgotten it, but this was of little account, for so had she.

January, 1967

COFFEE, BRANDY & CIGARS

"The cinema was not born to serve humanity—it was born to make money. It relies therefore on those very emotions (with the exception of the comic) that are most suspect." —André Malraux

If film-makers had to swear to a "cinematic Hippocratic oath," how many film-makers would there be? . . . Yemeni tribesmen, who love a good battle of their own, have a taste for American westerns. They take their movie-going seriously. Many like to attend in the afternoon, when they customarily chew *kat*, a mild narcotic leaf that brings on a dreamy euphoria. Yemenis say movies go well with *kat*. . . . Said Jean Genet of French critics: "They're very impressive, very intellectual. I rarely understand what they're saying, so I know it must be intellectual." . . . Did you know that the duo who made the devastating *Nana* of Zola— Jean Renoir and Catherine Hessling—once also made a short, *Little Red Riding Hood?* . . . Two hundred twenty young French musicians and ninety of their German colleagues combined to give a concert before the war memorial at Douaumont, Verdun, to honor the memory of the hundreds of thousands of French and German soldiers who died in the long and bloody carnage there during World War I. They played Brahms' *German Requiem.* The sense of ritual is never lacking, but the sense to avoid the blood-letting that precedes these rituals is always lacking. Boy, what a funeral we gave President Kennedy; wasn't that a humdinger?

D. W. Griffith is where you find him, even in Samoa where the Samoans built a winding trail to the grave of Robert Louis Stevenson and named it "The Road of the Loving Heart." . . . Louise Brooks has sent me her epitaph: "I never gave away anything that I wish I had not kept; nor kept anything that I wish I had not given away." . . . Did you know there are at least two depictions of medicine in music? One is "Concert d'Esculape" for orchestra by a composer named Lalande, the other is a tenor aria, "Gall-Stone Operation," by another named Marais. . . . The swinging metallic spheroid in Léger's *Ballet Mécanique,* so symbolic of the twentieth century's age of the machine, was already thought of a century before by Turner in his canvas, "Metallic Spheroids," painted in 1820. . . . Stroheim's character of Roulette Masha in his novel, *Poto-Poto,* about a Russian adventuress who used to work the boats in their gaming rooms, betting herself against her opponents' cash, had a real-life counterpart in the Contessa Rattazzi, cousin of Napoleon III. She reportedly would appear, accompanied by a well-groomed, impeccable escort who offered to bet her against the house, providing the wager was matched in kind. Businesslike croupiers invariably declined the offer. . . . What a year 1905 was! Einstein's Theory of Relativity was published, the foundation stone on which the development of energy rested, resulting eventually in the splitting of the atom; Lehar's *The Merry Widow* had its world premiere at the Theater An der Wien in Vienna; and the abortive Russian Revolution which was to sow the seeds of the October Revolution in 1917, which changed the whole course of history, took place.

One of the many ways of illustrating the greatness of Murnau's visual sense is to compare his image of The Four Horsemen of the Apocalypse that appears at the beginning of his version of *Faust,* with Albrecht Dürer's, engraved in 1498. Murnau's is infinitely more powerful. . . . And speaking of unforgettable images, two of the most beautiful ever on the screen appeared in Rex Ingram's *Mare Nostrum*, from the Blasco-Ibáñez novel: the goddess, Aphrodite, riding the waves of the sea on a dolphin during a luminous night, watched by Neptune hiding behind a rock on the shore—and the epilogue of the drowned lovers meeting again and forever in the depths of the sea. . . . Who has preserved the great tradition of allegories on the screen, save Luis Buñuel? *Mare Nostrum* also contains a rendezvous in an aquarium before a tank containing an octopus (overtonal montage within the frame) which was the progenitor of Orson Welles' rendezvous of the lovers in *Lady from Shanghai*, also in an aquarium, this time before a tank containing a huge predatory fish.

Did you know that the Armed Forces Pathological Institute in Washington, D.C., is reputed to contain in its archives Goebbels' collection of pornographic films, confiscated by the United States Army in Berlin after the war? . . . What's in a name? Burroughs the naturalist, Burroughs the adding machine, Burroughs the pornographer. . . . There is no vibrato in Bresson. But then you don't need vibrato to play Bach, either. . . . Did you know there are over 80,000 different dishes in the vast realm of Chinese cuisine? . . . And do you know where Gregory Markopoulos got the title for his trilogy, *Du Sang, de la Volupté, et de la Mort?* From the nineteenth century French novelist Maurice Barrès . . . *Ave atque vale*—Seena Owen, whose regal beauty graced *Intolerance* as the Babylonian Queen and *Queen Kelly* as the mad Queen. Two of the greatest directors cast her as the *alpha* and *omega* of Queens and that made her a *real* Queen of the cinema. *Ave, ave . . . !* It is reported that Chaplin doesn't know how to operate the 16mm projector in his home; Oona has to run it. . . . Which reminds me that Fritz Lang once told me Rudolph Klein-Rogge, who played the scientist, Rotwang, in *Metropolis*, who creates the robot-woman in his fantastically complex laboratory, couldn't even operate an electric toaster in real life . . . "Ah, good taste! What a dreadful thing! Taste is the enemy of creativeness." (Picasso). . . . When this column began, about fifteen years ago, its epigraph was a quotation from Stendhal, "Truth is to be found only in details." Details are important, they make comments. Thus, in *Ten Days that Shook the World*, Eisenstein shows a close-up of Lenin's foot mounting the hub-cap of a car to reach a platform during the early days when he was exhorting the workers and soldiers. Later, during the storming of the Czar's Winter Palace, Eisenstein shows another close-up, this time of a soldier's foot stepping on the royal crown of the palace's iron gate to break into the palace.

"Men are wise," said Shaw, "not in their experience but in their capacity for experience." . . . Half the world lives on rice. In some places the word for rice is the same as that for food. The Balinese believe that rice has a soul and they use human terms, such as "mother," in referring to it. Some Indonesian harvesters try to spare the feelings of rice by hiding their knives. In Ceylon, astrologers and geomancers pick the most auspicious time and place for sowing rice. They even tell the planters what clothes to wear. The Japanese consider wasting rice a mortal sin. A common Chinese greeting is "Have you had your rice today?" . . . There are parts of Asia (I'm told Afghanistan is one of them) where the food is so bad that the common greeting is "How is your digestion?" . . . Pop art is nothing new. Marcel Duchamp was doing it in 1917. . . . Ron Rice always looked to me like John Wilkes Booth might have looked, or a Southern gentleman of the antebellum days with a derringer in his vest. He also looked like a poet, which he was. . . . Said Karl Freund, one of the world's great cinematographers: "When I say that certain technical developments, such as the color process, were not necessary, I mean it with regard to the artistic development of the film. . . . In this connection, I state that technical developments have impeded artistic ones. . . . I don't know of a single color film in which the possibilities of color reproduction have been really utilized as artistic means. . . . The overwhelming majority of color films are nothing more than pretty-pretty films—on the level of postcard *kitsch*. The color is used to get the audience to say 'Ah' and 'Oh' and basically this is done to conceal the miserable quality of the film—in short, color is used to throw sand in the eyes."

You have to hand it to Orson Welles: from Kafka's *The Trial* to Shakespeare's *Falstaff* (*Chimes at Midnight*) to Stevenson's *Treasure Island*, all the while working on (and now reportedly finishing) Cervantes' *Don Quixote*. What a range! Also reported, that he will direct a companion featurette to the Buñuel featurette, *St. Simon of the Desert*, so that the two may go out as a single feature "package." There was a time not too long ago when the old guard French directors like Delannoy, Autant-Lara, etc., were regarded as "old hat" by the young men of the "new wave." Today there is an underground French cinema in which the present young men regard Truffaut, Godard, etc., as "old hat." Ah, youth!

Directors who used famous non-film people in their films to preserve their image for posterity: Murnau's *Faust*—Yvette Guilbert; Pabst's *Don Quixote*—Feodor Chaliapin; Gance's *Napoleon* and Dreyer's *Joan of Arc*—Antonin Artaud; Feyder's *Carmen*—Raquel Meller; Ben Hecht's and Charles MacArthur's *Once in a Blue Moon* and Eugene Frenke's *The Girl in the Case*—Jimmy Savo; Renoir's *Nana*, Pabst's *Dreigroschenoper*, *Joyless Street*, and *Diary of a Lost One*—Valeska Gert; André Cayatte's *Lovers of Verona*—Marianne Oswald; Ben Hecht's *Specter of the Rose*—Michael Chekov; Carné's *Drôle de Drame*—Maurice Duhamel; Pabst's *White Hell of Pitz Palu*—Ernst Udet; Pabst's *Dreigroschenoper*—Lotte Lenya; Yevgeni Slavinsky's *The Girl and the Hooligan*—Mayakovsky; Clair's *Entr'acte*—Man Ray, Picabia, Marcel Duchamp, Darius Milhaud; Hans Richter's *Vormittagsspuk*—Darius Milhaud, Paul Hindemith; Hans Richter's *Dreams that Money Can Buy*—Max Ernst, Peggy Guggenheim, Fernand Léger; Richter's *Passionate Pastime*—Marcel Duchamp, Larry Evans; Richter's *Dadascope*—Marcel Duchamp, Yves Tanguy, Jean Arp, Richard Hulsenbeck; Richter's *8 x 8*—Jean Arp, Duchamp, Tanguy, Hulsenbeck, Calder, Max Ernst, Jean Cocteau, Paul Bowles, José Sert, Frederick Kiesler; Marcel L'Herbier's *Gallery of Monsters*, Man Ray's *Etoile de Mer* and Léger's *Ballet Mécanique*—Kiki; Gance's *Lucretia Borgia* and *Mater Dolorosa*—Antonin Artaud; Arnold Fanck's *S.O.S. Iceberg*—Ernst Udet; Marcel Carné's *Jenny*—Joseph Kosma, etc., etc.

Did you know that G. W. Pabst almost made the film from Heinrich Mann's novel, *Professor Unrat*, that Von Sternberg subsequently made as *The Blue Angel*? . . . "The brain does not have to be cudgeled to think of something that might be beautiful to one person while revolting to another," writes Von Sternberg in his autobiography, *Fun in a Chinese Laundry*. He quotes Emerson, "All thoughts of a turtle are turtles, and of a rabbit, rabbits." . . . "There are problems enough without sin." (Hemingway) . . . Did you know that Mata Hari kept a personal scrap-book of her exploits? . . . Do you know the dish, *poule en demi deuil,* chicken in half-mourning? You haven't really eaten until you've had this. It was the favorite of Sir Basil Zaharoff, *olavasholem.* . . . "You should hear my Oriental music, it's still in manuscript," wrote George Antheil to me once. "Parodying Near-Eastern music is what I like doing best but I get so few opportunities to publish it, alas!"

The first story: Adam in the Garden of Eden watches, for the first time, the setting sun. He is apprehensive. When it disappears and it grows dark he weeps. Exhausted from weeping, he falls asleep. He awakes the next morning to find the sun high in the heavens. A smile breaks out on his face, for he knows now it will always be like that. (The first fear, the first tears, the first sleep and the first smile.)

"There are trivial truths and great truths. The opposite of a trivial truth is plainly false. The opposite of a great truth is also true." (Niels Bohr) . . . The beginnings of the cinema were ominous enough: among the major pioneers, Uchatius, an Austrian, the first film projectionist, shot himself, as did the American, George Eastman. Friese-Greene of England ended in a debtors' prison; the Frenchman, La Prince, mysteriously disappeared on a journey, and Reynaud, also of France, went mad. . . . Not to speak of Louis Lumière's observation. "The cinematograph is an invention without a future."

The importance of the right actor for the role was alarmingly illustrated for me recently when I saw the French version of *Extase* by Machaty, made with a French actor in the role originally played by Aribert Mog, a Czech, as a result of which the whole picture was ruined because the miscast French player looked like a jerk. On the other hand, the French version of Schuenzel's *Amphitryon* is infinitely better than the original German version because the players (Garat, Boitel, Moreno, Bernard, and Florelle) had a tradition of the *opera-bouffe* in their playing that the heavy German cast utterly lacked. And those marvelous French faces! In my last column I stated, "What the eye rejects, the mind rejects also." I find this to be true over and over again.

One of the most beautiful of all films is the 22-minute ciné-poem, *Notes on the Port of St. Francis* by the late Frank Stauffacher, made in 1948 (you can rent it for only $7.00 from the

Audio Film Center in Mount Vernon, N. Y.—another instance of the relative value of money). Never has a sound-track been used with more sensitivity, with more intense lyricism. It is worth any dozen Academy Award features.

Spring, 1967

Written for the Souvenir Program of the 1967 Montreal Film Festival, at which Fritz Lang was guest of honor.

WELCOME, FRITZ LANG!

There are individuals who, by virtue of the body of their exemplary work, a life work encompassing many years, even the peaks of which, however touched with nobility and the hosannas accorded them at the time, have for so long been taken for granted that they wear the mantle of legend like the mantle of the dwarf Alberich in *Siegfried* that rendered him invisible. We hardly think of them as living presences. Were they suddenly to appear in our midst, we would be at a loss for words. What do you say to a living legend?

Well, you can say, "Welcome!"

Welcome, indeed, is Fritz Lang who has come from the mists of the past to join us in celebrating this year's film festival.

How fitting it is that one of the Giottos of the cinema, one of the pioneers who blazed the first trails through the wilderness that was the cinema in the immediate post—World War I years, graces our festival with his presence.

In this commanding figure, the past and present unite, for he is representative of both, not only of the early history of the cinema, and even of its pre-history, having written his first film scripts as far back as 1916 while convalescing from war wounds in a hospital in Vienna, but he is also the contemporary author in our own time of *The Thousand Eyes of Dr. Mabuse* (1960) and even as an actor, playing himself, in Jean-Luc Godard's *Le Mépris* (1963).

He has, indeed, encompassed a span of years, having been born in Vienna in 1890 before the motion pictures were even invented. He watched the effusions emanating from this miraculous toy, the cinematograph machine, develop and grow, and witnessed its flowering through the golden years of its florescence in the twenties and thirties, spanning the peaks of the silent and sound eras, and become an integral part of that florescence himself.

He had first studied architecture (prophetic of the *Metropolis*-to-come), then painting in Munich and Paris, followed by his *Wanderjahre* in Africa, Asia Minor, Russia, China, Japan, the South Seas, then back to Europe where he supported himself painting post-cards, selling pictures, and drawing cartoons for newspapers. Caught in Paris at the outbreak of World War I, he managed to escape to Vienna and, as a reserve officer in the Austrian Army, soon found himself at the front. Otis Ferguson, an American critic, puzzled by Lang's early interest in motion pictures, posed this intriguing observation: "And here comes a factor that neither Lang nor any other of the old line first-class men can explain. . . . (That) when the movies were just a clumsy, struggling art, there were men everywhere who knew somehow that this was the work they wanted to do. . . . So when peace came, when other intellectuals were spending their time being 'bohemians,' if nothing else, he went where he could get his chance to make movies." This was, of course, Berlin, the film center of Germany, where he met the protean producer, Erich Pommer, who was to become the mentor of so many film talents.

Lang's German period was rooted in expressionism, that hallucinatory art movement that flourished with especial fecundity in Germany even before Germany in effect declared war on the world in 1914. The nightmare carnage of Verdun, 1915–16, and the chaotic post-war years of inflation were reflected with special vividness in the first films of Lang with their spectral figures of Death, Woman as Siren Incarnate, the Super Criminal (as in *Die Spinnen*—"The Spiders"—a mafia or cartel of master gangsters bent on world domination through the fabulous buried wealth of the Incas, the precursors of his *Mabuse* series). For

"That monument to the cinema...."* Fritz Lang, 1968. (Photo by Gretchen Berg)

*Georges Sadoul, in *Dictionnaire des Cinéastes*, Microcosme/Editions du Seuil, Paris, 1965.

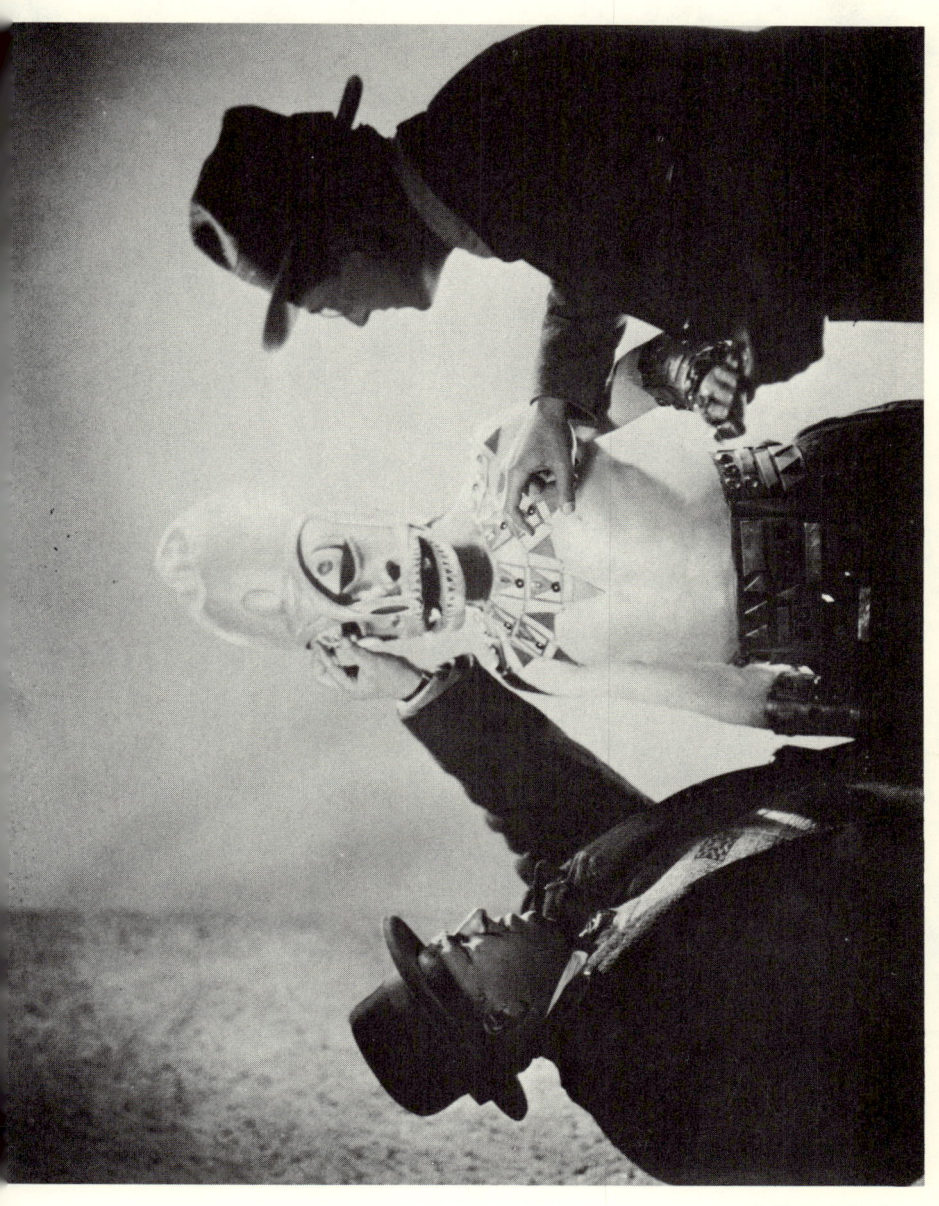

One of the characters cut from the American released version of *Metropolis* being given his finishing touches by cameraman Karl Freund (left) and director Fritz Lang (1926).

Another character cut from the American version of *Metropolis*, the robot woman (Brigitte Helm) as siren of the Yoshiwara, the great brothel of Metropolis.

The Yoshiwara on the "morning after the night before." A Chinese porter sweeps away the debris of the merrymakers as young Fredersen (Gustav Fröhlich) disconsolately leaves the now empty place. Cut from the American version of *Metropolis*.

Siegfried (Paul Richter) is speared by Hagen Tronje. A remarkable reconstruction of nature in the studio, testament to the witchery of the golden age of Ufa. Fritz Lang's *Siegfried*, Part One of *The Nibelungen Saga* (1923–24).

Attila (Rudolf Klein-Rogge) showering gold on the pagan children of the North in celebration of the birth to his wife, Kriemhild, of a son. But behind the witchery is the witch, in this case Lang, another of the screen's great camera eyes. *Kriemhild's Revenge*, Part Two of *The Nibelungen Saga*.

five years after the armistice of 1918 this cinema of demoralization mirrored the frenzied post-war era.

Two years after he started directing, he achieved his first international success with the allegorical fantasy, *Der Muede Tod* (released here as *Destiny*).

Then, after eight months of work between 1923 and 1924, he produced his *Nibelungen* saga, consisting of two parts, *Siegfried* and *Kriemhild's Revenge,* the beginning of the glory that was to become Ufa's, the great studio where it was made. Derived from ancient Teutonic myths and Norse sagas which served as a source for Wagner's *Ring* cycle, this extraordinary achievement in cinema wizardry stunned the world.

How do you follow a work like that? If you have the apocalyptic visions of a Fritz Lang, you display your range and counter an epic of the past with one of the future, and so we were vouchsafed *Metropolis*—that terrifying vision of the year 2000 with its triumph of the machine over man, against which philosophers and socio-economists have warned. It was the last gasp of expressionism in Germany, and one can say that the movement went out in a blaze of pyrotechnics such as will probably never be seen again on a screen.

Then what? Well, *Spies,* that vertiginous echo of the early anarchistic *Mabuse* films, *The Woman in the Moon,* which prophetically pretold manned flights by rockets into space. . . .

Then *M*—his first sound film, and *what* a first! Bridging the treacherous chasm between the silent and the sound film with masterly ease, it brought universal fame to its young star, Peter Lorre, playing with uncanny veracity the child-killer, as well as new honors as a master of the psychological film to its director, who was not "just" a cunning manipulator of highly colored melodrama or impresario of spectacle, but a detective of the human soul.

It is 1932, Lang follows *M* with the demonic *Testament of Dr. Mabuse* and for the first time turned a film thriller into a political weapon by putting the Nazi philosophy into the minds of the now crazy Mabuse and his henchman, the director of the asylum which now holds Mabuse. Goebbels bans the film but offers Lang the post of *gauleiter* of the German film industry. That same afternoon Lang flees to Paris where he finds Pommer, already fled. Then comes Hollywood and *Fury,* that savage indictment of lynching and mob rule, a brave film for a foreigner to make his debut in America with. He follows it with another social document (*You Only Live Once*) on the theme of the rehabilitation of criminals. During the war years, he makes five violently anti-Nazi films, one with the poet Bertolt Brecht (*Hangmen Also Die*). A dozen or more violent films follow in which he pursues a favorite theme, documenting the damned. The German film industry, floundering for lack of artists since the Second World War, asks him to come back to make films in the "old Lang style," with memories of what that once meant. They want a remake of Joe May's *Tiger of Eschnapur* and *The Indian Tombstone*, melodramas for which Lang wrote the original scripts back in 1920. He even goes to India for the exteriors. Back in Berlin he gives them another Mabuse film ("I had to reincarnate him in another man as I had already killed him off in the last Mabuse film!" Lang says wryly)—this time, *The Thousand Eyes of Dr. Mabuse*, inspired by a diabolic plot of Goebbels to spy on foreign diplomats through photo-electric cells serving as television "eyes" monitored to a central control room. Then the call to Rome and Capri to play himself in the Brigitte Bardot film about film-making, *Le Mépris*, in which a mellow Fritz Lang quotes Hoelderlin.

And now he is among us, with his tired smile, but eager as ever for new experiences. He plans next to embark on a film in defense and in praise of today's misunderstood American youth —a far cry and a long way from his own demon-haunted youth. The only director to have received both the Commander Cross Order of Merit from the Federal Republic of Germany and the Order of Arts and Letters from the French Government, he comes as our honored guest, full of years and memories of a schizophrenic mankind, capable of such grandeur and such baseness, and of an exultant and clamorous life, such as is given to few men, as a chronicler of this mordant *comédie humaine*.

Summer, 1967

COFFEE, BRANDY & CIGARS

MERELY UNDERSTANDS HIS TIME

At Picasso's birth, he didn't utter a sound and hardly breathed. They thought he was dead. His uncle, Dr. Salvador Ruiz, who attended him at his birth and who was smoking a thick black cigar afterwards, blew a mouthful of smoke right in his face which caused the infant to make a pained expression and which exploded into a loud (and jubilant) cry.

Picasso at 85: "Today I am, as you see, a rich and famous painter. But when I'm alone with myself, I don't think of myself at all as an artist in the old and great sense of the word, like Giotto, Titian, Rembrandt or Goya. I'm just one who understands his time. This is bitter to contemplate, but it's the truth."

FRANZ KAFKA AS TO FILMS

"Franz Kafka always gave a look of surprise when I told him I had been to the cinema. Once I reacted to this change of expression by asking, 'Don't you like the cinema?' After a moment's thought Kafka replied, 'As a matter of fact, I've never thought about it. Of course it's a marvelous toy. But I cannot bear it because perhaps I am too "optical" by nature. I am an eye-man. But the cinema disturbs one's vision. The speed of the movements and the rapid change of images force men to look continually from one to another. Sight does not master the pictures, it is the pictures which master one's sight. They flood one's consciousness. The cinema involves putting the eye into uniform, when before it was naked.'

" 'That's a terrible statement,' I said. 'The eye is the window of the soul, a Czech proverb says.'

"Kafka nodded. 'Films are iron shutters.' "

(*Conversations with Kafka by Gustav Janouch*)

JAPANESE & HAPPY ENDINGS

"I have become aware that men are unhappy," said Kon Ichikawa, the Japanese film director, recently. "You can even say that they are in anguish and so the only way to show a real man is to show an unhappy one. Oh, I look around for some kind of humanism, but I never seem to find it. People are always complaining; the ending of the Olympic film (*Tokyo Olympiad*) is an example—why show all that strain and pain, they say. They want happy endings. But doesn't this desire for a happy ending show how unhappy they really are?"

DANGER OF OVER-EDUCATING HORSES

Archaeologists are convinced they have finally found the exact site of Sybaris, whose pleasure-seeking living was unmatched in history.

For the last one hundred years, archaeologists have been searching southern Italy for the sixth century B.C. city which was danced to doom in 510 B.C. by its trained performing horses. The city's luxury-loving ways had made Sybarite a synonym for lavish living.

A dozen possible sites around the Gulf of Taranto have been probed inconclusively in the last twenty years. Then archaeologists and experts from the University of Pennsylvania and Italy's Lerici Foundation went to work on a site a mile and a half inland from the delta of the Crati River sixty miles southwest of Taranto.

Dr. Giuseppe Foti, superintendent of antiquities for Calabria, said subsoil tests in 1965 proved conclusively that this was the site. Many of the buried structures of the city have been traced. But uncovering the ruins and bringing the city of sweet life back into view are expected to be harder than it was to find it.

When the jealous Crotonians attacked wealthier Sybaris, the Sybarites galloped into the fray with their crack cavalry. But a Crotonian band began blaring a catchy dance rhythm. The Sybarites charge broke up in a chaos of prancing horses. The Crotonians killed the men, enslaved the women, burned the town and diverted the river to cover the city, and wiped Sybaris from the map for all time.

IT PAYS TO BE IGNORANT DEPARTMENT

What did Tolstoi, Ibsen, Heine, Maupassant, Nietzsche, Gogol, Voltaire, Stendhal, Schumann, Van Gogh, Toulouse-Lautrec, Semmelweis, Hölderlin, Tausig, Ruskin, Smetana, Tasso, and

Alexander the Great have in common? Answer: They all died insane.

ALIBI FOR A "LOST WEEKEND" DEPARTMENT

The ancient Greeks were a very orderly, rational and logical people, having invented reason, philosophy, and geometry. "Every man," they said, "owes five days to Dionysus, five days a year in which he should get drunk and foolish and dismiss the cold forces of logic and reason."

COMFORTING

"The daily challenge," said Dr. Charles Huggins, co-winner of the 1966 Nobel Prize in medicine for cancer research, "lies in pitting one's wits against apparently inscrutable Nature. She can refuse to speak but she cannot give a wrong answer. It is the genius of research to frame a question so simply that a conditional answer is prohibited."

OVER-SIMPLIFYING ART

If one is to believe one school of thinking, the great mystery about the Mona Lisa is no mystery at all or, at least, can be explained very simply. Da Vinci, being a homosexual, had one of his young boy friends pose for the portrait and the "in-joke" between them resulted in the irrepressible smirk on the young boy's face.

January, 1968

Thunder In The East (1934) English version of "La Bataille," directed in French and English versions by Nicholas Farkas. English version adapted by Robert Stevenson. Both versions from the novel by Claude Farrère. Music by André Gailhard. With Charles Boyer (Marquis Yorisaka), Merle Oberon (Mitsoukou, the Marquise), John Loder (Commander Fergan), V. Inkijinoff (Hirata), Betty Stockfield (Betty), Miles Mander (the painter).

THUNDER IN THE EAST

A Forgotten Masterpiece.

There is a genre of film that, although it achieves perfection of form, and may even stir the critics to paeans of praise for a brief moment, is somehow quickly forgotten and relegated to that limbo between Olympus and oblivion where so many worthy films languish. I would place them on a high level, indeed, which is to say, along with such meritorious works of the class of *Crime Without Passion*, *The 39 Steps*, and *The Story of a Cheat*, not world shaking masterworks, surely, but brilliant examples of cinema craftsmanship that did achieve lasting fame and are enshrined in the cinema pantheon. In this genre of all but forgotten works that deserved a better fate at the hands of film historians (not to mention that fickle, hydra-headed animal, the public) are such films as the Hecht-MacArthur *The Scoundrel*, Reinhold Schünzel's *Amphitryon* (French version), Fedor Ozep's *Der Mörder Karamazov*, Pabst's *L'Atlantide* and even Compton Bennett's *Glory at Sea*. Perhaps the most striking of them all, however, is Nicholas Farkas' ardent *Thunder in the East*, the English version of his *La Bataille*, produced in 1934 in France from the novel of that name by Claude Farrère.

Hark to the American reviewers when it was premiered here in the spring of that year:

"It crashes over New York like a clap of thunder. . . . An

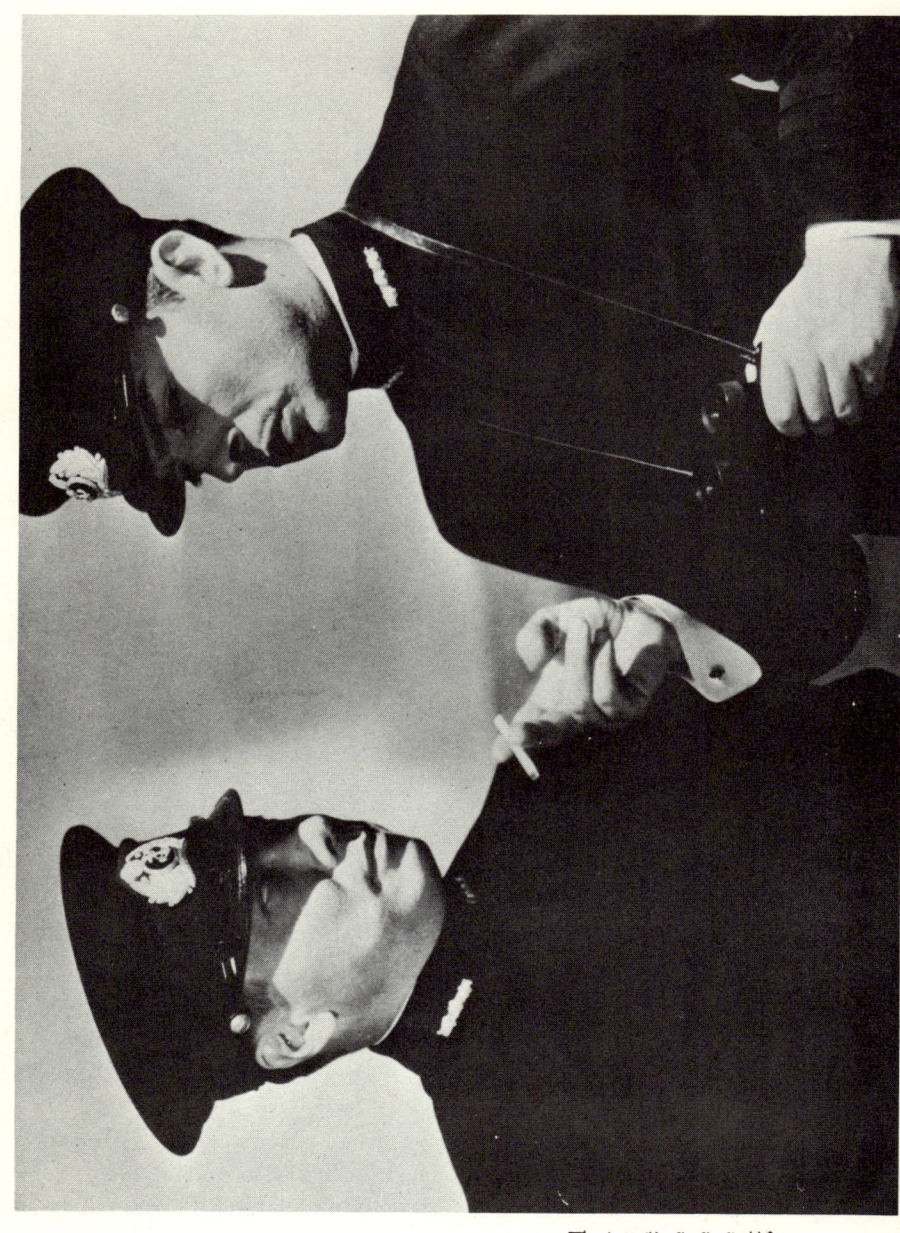

Hirata (Inkijinoff) and Commander Yorisaka (Charles Boyer) in Nicholas Farkas' *Thunder in the East* (1934), after Claude Farrère's *La Bataille*. "We have the same ships as the English," says Yorisaka, "but we have not the same men." (Lost)

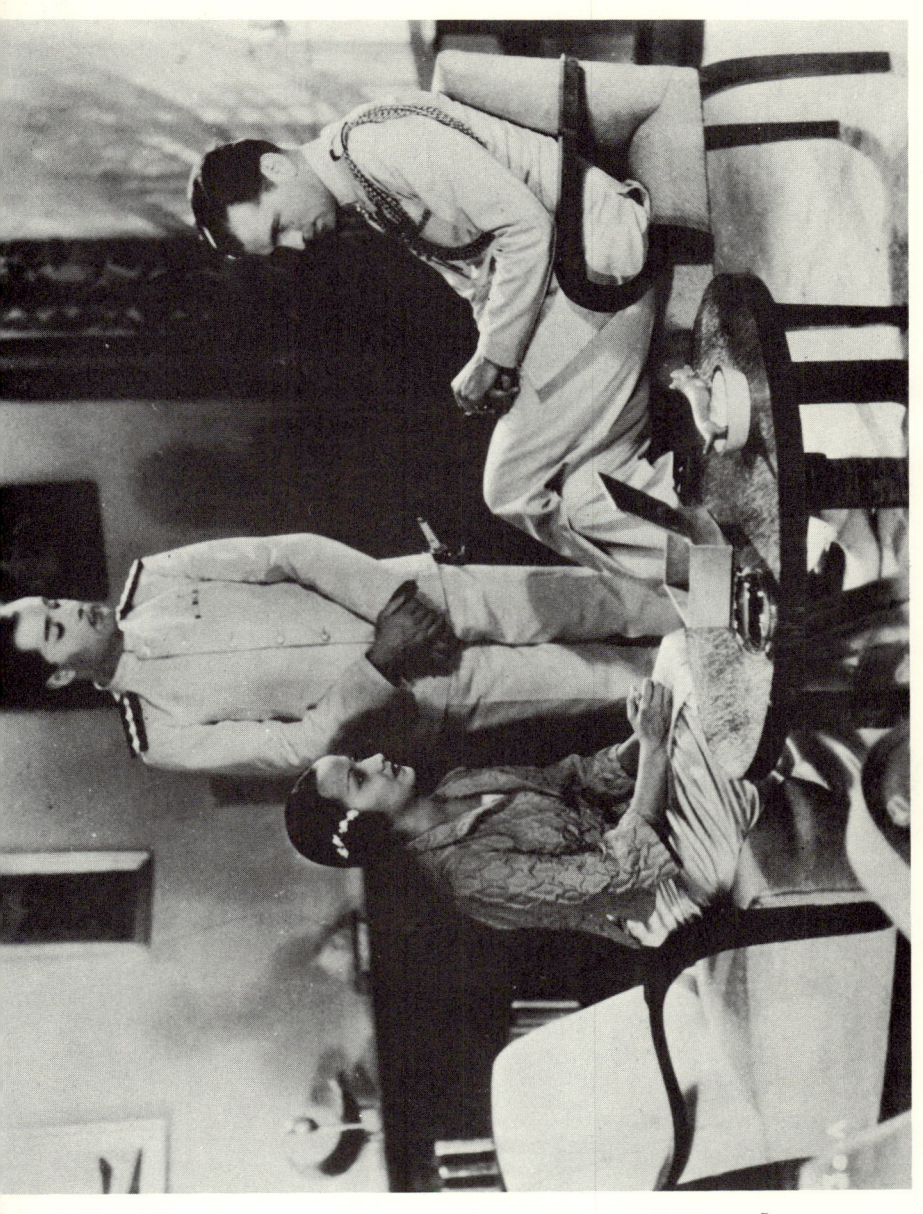

Mitsoukou, wife of Yorisaka (Merle Oberon), and Commander Yorisaka (Boyer) receive Commander Fergan (John Loder). *Thunder in the East.*

important cinema event . . . more acutely touching than any screen drama of the year. . . . Charles Boyer gives an extraordinarily moving performance. . . . In every way this is a screen drama of enormous power" *(N. Y. Times)*

"A beautifully directed motion picture. . . . Charles Boyer and Merle Oberon act with an originality new to the screen." *(N. Y. Herald-Tribune)*

"Very nearly the perfect picture." *(Time Magazine)*

"An immense and powerful film . . . bursts forth in a tremendous climax." *(N. Y. Post)*

"This production, which created a sensation abroad, will make even more of a stir here. The direction is masterful." *(N. Y. Daily News, 4 stars)*

"The finest motion picture in years." *(Picture Play Magazine)*

"No praise is too high, no superlative too lavish, for this picture. Yet one hesitates to smother it in adjectives and phrases that have taken on a tinsel glitter from being used too often in describing films that have never approached the artistry and the exaltation of this striking masterpiece." *(The Philadelphia Inquirer)*

Voilà . . .

How is it possible, you will think, for such a work to fall into oblivion? How, indeed? Besides Boyer and Oberon, the cast included John Loder, Valerie Inkijinoff, Betty Stockfield, and Miles Mander. Robert Stevenson worked with Farkas on the script and dialogue of the English version. (Boyer and Annabella were featured in the original French version.) But it was Boyer and Oberon who, this once in their respective careers, played with such incandescence as to beggar description. The reviewer of *The Philadelphia Inquirer* was all but beside himself: "Charles Boyer gives one of the most remarkable performances the screen has ever seen. . . . Genius is not too powerful a word to describe both Boyer's and Merle Oberon's magic playing in this film, and authentic genius is not something to be met with every day."

Farkas, the director, was a Hungarian cameraman who had distinguished himself particularly with his luminous photography for Pabst's *Don Quixote,* filmed in Spain. *La Bataille* (called *Thunder in the East* in its English version) was his first directorial effort, made the following year and released in the United

States by United Artists. In 1935 he did a remake of Dupont's *Variety*, with Jean Gabin, Fernand Gravey and Annabella, and in 1936 another film in the same milieu as *La Bataille, Port Arthur*, this with Danielle Darrieux and Anton Walbrook as the Japanese counterparts of Merle Oberon and Charles Boyer. I did not see his *Variety* but I did see *Port Arthur*—it was no match for the earlier film. What few references there are to Farkas in the film histories and encyclopedias, and there are very few, indeed, are of the briefest and most perfunctory. *Sic transit.* . . .

In 1934, Farkas had been chief photographer for Alexis Granowsky* for the latter's satirical comedy, *Le Roi Pausole*, after the novel by Pierre Louÿs, a luxurious "super-film" shot on a rocky isle in the Mediterranean about a jolly sybaritic king (played by Emil Jannings) who had 365 wives, one for every night in the year. Financed by a wealthy woman in Paris, the cast and crew were "living it up" to such a high degree during the filming, sending for more champagne, more delicacies, more money and more of so much else that the poor woman saw no end in sight to her misguided investment and, in despair, committed suicide. Everybody connected with the film was now out of a job. Farkas then decided he would organize a film production of his own and managed to raise the backing for the project he had in mind (Farrère's *La Bataille*) from both French and Czechoslovak financiers. Nothing could be further away in theme or treatment from the facetious *Roi Pausole* than Farrère's sombre and tragic story. (The film's producer and general manager was a White Russian émigré living in Paris—Leon Garganoff.)

Claude Farrère (1876–1957) was one of that coterie of French diplomat-writers, like the Comte de Gobineau, Paul Claudel and Paul Morand. He entered the French Naval Academy in 1894 and served as an officer, attaché, and observer in the naval service from 1899 to 1919, emerging from many sea battles during the First World War with the rank of captain. Farrère was particularly attracted to the extreme Orient, and like his compatriot,

---

*Granowsky came from the Jewish Art Theatre in Vilna to Berlin where he staged a number of experimental plays, turning later to films, his *Das Lied vom Leben* ("The Song of Life"), whose climax utilized actual footage of a Caesarian section, having been one of the most original early German sound films.

Pierre Loti,* published a number of exotically flavored works including a volume of bizarre short stories, *Black Opium* (1904), and the novels, *Les Civilisés* (1905), which Stroheim once told me he would have liked to film, *La Bataille* (1909), *Les Hommes Nouveaux* (1923), *La Marche Funèbre* (1929), etc. In 1935 he was elected to the Académie Française. He died at the age of 81 in 1957.

It was not the first time *La Bataille* had been filmed, but to compare the earlier silent version starring Sessue Hayakawa and Tsuru Aoki (Mrs. Hayakawa) in the Boyer–Oberon roles with Farkas' film is like comparing Ferdinand Zecca's account of the *Potemkin* mutiny made in 1906 with Eisenstein's.

The era with which *Thunder in the East* (we will henceforth refer to *La Bataille* under its English version title, which is the version under discussion) deals is that of Puccini's *Madame Butterfly* (1904) but, apart from a high caste Japanese woman falling in love with an English (in the opera, American) naval officer, any similarity stops right there. The Japan of the film is on the surface the exotic Nippon encountered by the American violinist-composer, Henry Eichheim, who "painted" a delicately impressionistic tone poem, *Japanese Nocturne*, which Stokowski has recorded with the Philadelphia Orchestra. It is also the Japan of Cyril Scott's *Lotus Land* and William Gerhardi's novel, *The Polyglots*. In short, "The Japan of yesterday," as the Marquis Yorisaka (the Japanese naval commander played by Boyer), says with light sarcasm to the English naval officer, Commander Fergan, played by John Loder. "A land full of little bridges that don't lead anywhere."

But what the film deals with is much harsher—the Russo-Japanese War of 1904–05—although the enemy is not named and we never see him. A brief précis of the political background of this war might be in order here:

1904. The Japanese military clique was angered because Russia and other powers had obliged Japan to get out of Port Arthur, the chief seaport of Manchuria. (Japan had taken Port Arthur from China in 1895.) The presence of Russian and other allied troops in Manchuria after the Boxer Rebellion of 1900 had

---

*Loti's *Mme. Chrysanthème*, also set in Nagasaki, has in its central love story many points of similarity with *La Bataille*.

been insupportable to the Mikado's officer and after four years of seething resentment, Japan struck without declaring war. The Tokugawa Shogunate had learned from the "gunboat diplomacy" of Commodore Perry. The protoype of the Marquis Yorisaka, the Japanese naval commander in the film, was Heihachiro Togo, Japan's naval hero, the speed and efficiency of whose battle cruisers were to startle the world before the war was finished. Togo had studied naval science and navigation in England (1871–78). (There is a reference in the film's dialogue to this when Yorisaka says to Commander Fergan, "Last year, when I was an observer on one of your ships . . ." The Japanese had great respect for the secrets of English naval strategy and her superiority as a naval power. The plot of the film turns around just this.) The victory of the Japanese army on land at the River Yalu was also the first victory of the modern "yellow men" over white men. The subsequent victory of the Japanese naval forces at sea was the second. With Port Arthur retaken by the army, Admiral Togo now encountered the Baltic Russian fleet, sent to redress the Eastern naval balance, as it entered the Strait of Tsushima in May 1905. But the Japanese so outmaneuvered, outsped, outgunned Admiral Rozhdestvensky's flotilla that only two cruisers and two destroyers could escape to Vladivostok. The Czarist battleships *Korgez Suvorov, Tsar Alexander III,* and *Borodino* were all sunk. It is this battle at Tsushima which forms the climax of the film. (It was in that same summer of 1905 that the crew of the Russian armored cruiser, *Prince Potemkin,* mutinied during maneuvers in the Black Sea, which was to become the subject of another film twenty years later.)

As Schumann said of the music of Chopin, there were guns behind the flowers. There were heavy guns and armor plate from Mitsubishi (the Krupp of Japan) behind the chrysanthemums and the cherry blossoms of the "golden flower kingdom." The Emperor Meiji still reigned (until 1912) and the fanatic military and admiralty had set upon a path of conquest with an arrogance and sense of destiny that was to have far reaching results. To borrow from Sternberg's narration for *Anatahan,* "some were Buddhists, some were Shintoists, others believed only in Japan."

The Marquis Yorisaka was one of the latter. It is his story that is told, his passion according to the code of *bushido*° which is told, like an ancient saga. . . .

°The code of Japanese knighthood (*samurai*) and chivalry.

From the opening credits a sense of doom is already present and hangs heavily over the events as they unfold like a miasma. André Gailhard's score senses what this tale is about from its ominous opening cadence:

. . . over which sound wind and waves and a ship's prow cutting the sea.

To the port of Nagasaki has come Commander Fergan of the British Navy as an observer attached to the flagship of the Marquis Yorisaka in the early months of the Russo-Japanese War. Fellow officers of their respective admiralties, they reminisce about their exchange as observers—the year before Yorisaka had been an observer attached to Commander Fergan's squadron in the Mediterranean when it was based at Malta. And Fergan has not escaped noticing the beautiful wife of Yorisaka, the Marquise, who glides silently around the house in the background in her smart Western gowns, in her Western coiffure, for Yorisaka does not want foreigners to look upon him and his wife as exotic "savages," but as Western, as European and modern as Commander Fergan, himself. And so Yorisaka finds himself ever fawning on Fergan, to win his friendship, his easy, unstrained friendship, which will efface the barrier of race between them. Secretly the Marquise has noticed the favor she has found in the eyes of Fergan, and as secretly she is pleased. Only Hirata (V. Inkijinoff) Yorisaka's aide-de-camp, objects to the state of affairs in the Yorisaka ménage. He resents Yorisaka's fawning on the Englishman. But Yorisaka persists. "We have the same ships," he says, "but we have not the same men."

"I do not understand you, Commander Yorisaka Sadao. You put too much faith in the English," says Hirata. "We are yellow, they are white—gold is better than silver."

Yorisaka smiles. "Now you despise me. Can you tell me why?"

"Certainly," answers Hirata, and leaves.

There is a party aboard a yacht owned by an English heiress (Betty Stockfield). The yacht is moored to the quay and lights have been strung beneath the tarpaulin that protects the aft deck where couples are drinking and dancing in the balmy summer night. The ship's orchestra plays a waltz. From a distance we see Betty talking to Fergan aboard, and we hear a tinkling reedy melody spiralling through the night. . . .

Closeup of Betty and Fergan by the gangplank. Fergan is bored with the party and wants to leave to visit the Marquise.

Betty is jealous and tries to joke with Fergan about his new Japanese sweetheart (Betty and Fergan are old friends).

"Is she a real Marquise?" asks Betty, wryly.

"Yes, Betty," answers Fergan, impatient to be going. But she holds him.

"Was her mother a Marquise?" persists Betty.

"Yes, Betty," answers Fergan, this time disengaging himself and scudding down the gangplank to a waiting rickshaw.

"Yes, Betty . . . Yes, Betty," repeats Betty with a knowing smile as she watches Fergan scurry away to his rendezvous.

Yorisaka informs Mitsoukou that they will receive Commander Fergan in their home in Western attire. She is not to wear the traditional kimono and obi, "So that he may see," says Yorisaka sarcastically, "that we are no longer savages."

Another day, another rendezvous. But the Marquise has dressed in the traditional Japanese costume, kimono and obi. She is playing the koto for Fergan and singing a sad Japanese love song. Enter Yorisaka. He is stunned but tries to cover it, and smiles as he comes forward, greeting Fergan. Still smiling, he turns towards his wife, who is visibly shaken.

"You must forgive her," he says to Fergan. "She's just a little girl who likes to dress up."

"In ancient times," says the Marquise, "I would have been locked in a tower, but now . . ."

"Now," finishes Yorisaka, "now you are free to do as you please, aren't you?" And the smile fades from his lips in contradiction to his utterance.

Fergan apologizes and excuses himself, saying he has reports to write. He leaves.

Alone with the Marquise, Yorisaka's rage now vents forth.

"How dare you profane that sacred costume before the eyes of a foreigner?" he says. "If I cultivate his friendship, it is because I need him, but you . . ." The Marquise is weeping softly. "*You?*" he continues "What did *you* hope to gain by it?"

"Nothing," she murmurs brokenly.

The next day, Yorisaka visits Fergan in his quarters, interrupting him as he is writing his report to the British admiralty of a recent naval engagement he observed. Seeing Yorisaka enter, he quickly takes the papers from his desk, puts them in a drawer and locks it, which action is not lost on Yorisaka, who is still smiling. They greet each other affably and Fergan jokingly says:

"Sorry, I didn't know you were coming."

"I purposely didn't tell you," says Yorisaka, "in order to catch you in the act of writing your report on my mistakes." Then, "Tell me," he continues, " would your Lord Nelson have done what I did?"

Fergan offers Yorisaka a cigarette, takes one for himself, and lights them. Yorisaka glances at the desk drawer which contains Fergan's report. "What is it you want?" asks Fergan. Yorisaka smiles broadly and confesses, "I just want to know the secrets that enable the British navy to win battles at sea."

Fergan smiles at his candor. "You take the British navy very seriously, don't you?" he says wryly.

The smile now fades from Yorisaka's face and the joking is over. "The British navy," he says slowly and quietly, ". . . is very serious . . ."

Cut to the forward turret guns on a battleship gliding through the sea. . . .

". . . and very silent . . ." he continues over the above shot.

". . . and so . . ." he concludes, still over this shot, ". . . next time it will be the same." (There is no sound of the sea, only the voice of Yorisaka.)

There is another confrontation between Yorisaka and Hirata. The savor of life is not in Yorisaka's mouth and Hirata tries to encourage him. "Our men," he exclaims with passion, "can perform miracles!" To which Yorisaka replies, "Possibly," and before turning to go, "but a naval staff should not rely on miracles."

A day comes when Yorisaka receives news that the enemy squadron has been sighted and that preparations are to be made to engage his combined fleets.

Yorisaka breaks the news to Fergan aboard his flagship. They will set forth in twenty-four hours. "All leaves have been canceled," says Yorisaka.

"Still," smiles the genial Fergan, "another night ashore . . ."

Yorisaka smiles wanly and makes a gesture that does not belittle another night ashore.

That night, Yorisaka changes from his Commander's uniform to shabby civilian clothes which he has obtained. Confronting his wife in this outfit, topped by a disreputable looking cap, all of which makes him look like a gangster, she is shocked. He tells her to ask no questions but to receive Fergan when he comes, as he has suggested that the Marquise would be glad to wish him well on the eve of the big battle. She does not understand and is about to remonstrate.

Yorisaka cuts her off abruptly with, "The woman of our country does not argue, she obeys!" He leaves through a window for he has already heard the *amah* receiving Fergan at the door.

Fergan enters and sees the troubled Marquise. He approaches her and repeats, "The woman of our country does not argue, she obeys . . ."

The Marquise is startled. He apologizes. "I'm sorry," he pleads, "I couldn't help overhearing."

The Marquise recovers her composure. "My husband loves me very much," she says.

A moment's heavy silence between them.

"Tomorrow there'll be a battle," Fergan says. "I'll be returning to England when it's over." The Marquise is troubled at hearing this. "But without you," Fergan continues, "there won't be anyone there for me."

She dares not look at him but says, "There'll be someone in Japan . . ."

And while Fergan is with the Marquise, Yorisaka has stolen into Fergan's quarters and is rifling the drawers of his desk. Finally he finds what he has been looking for—Fergan's reports to the British admiralty. With a smile of triumph he reads them and carefully replaces them. Then he leaves.

On Betty's yacht, steaming out of the harbor, she is only half-listening to one of her guests on the cruise, a French painter (Miles Mander) who is doing a portrait of her. Her thoughts are far away, perhaps of Fergan? "The Japanese," the painter remarks without taking his eyes from his canvas as he applies his brush strokes, "one never knows where one is with them. They say one thing and mean another. They smile at you, but behind the smile . . .?"

Morning of the battle. Fergan is aboard the flagship watching through his binoculars. Yorisaka is giving orders. The enemy is approaching. He calls down to the forward turret guns to open fire. A salvo explodes, then another, and another. The aft turret guns swing around to get in range. They, too, open fire.

It is a fierce battle, a terrible battle. Perhaps the enemy, too, has his secrets? One turret has been knocked out by the enemy's answering fire, and another is badly damaged. Yorisaka is desperate. With his present knowledge it would be unthinkable if anything went amiss. He decides to take personal charge of the still functioning starboard turret. Entering the steaming interior, he sees the gunners swathed in damp rags against the insufferable heat. He spurs them on. They are not in proper range; they are not hitting the enemy with deadly enough accuracy. He directs them:

"Range . . . Deflection . . . Fire!"

A direct hit. Yorisaka is beside himself with joy. Again:

"Range . . . Deflection . . . Fire!"

Another hit. The enemy warship catches fire and begins to list badly.

Again:

"Range . . . Deflection . . . Fire!"

A second enemy vessel, when the smoke clears away, reveals a gaping hole in her side at the water line. Yorisaka is delirious with joy. Again and again and again—all afternoon he spends in the turret directing the attack, the dead and wounded sprawling all around.

At dusk the firing from both sides has ceased. The battle is over. The enemy has been sunk and routed.

The next morning, along a row of bodies covered with the banners of the Land of the Rising Sun, Commander Yorisaka, with the mien of one who had transcended an inferno, a white patch over one eye, his mouth set grimly, reviews the casualties spread out along the deck, accompanied by his aide, Captain Hirata. Yorisaka stops suddenly as he sees one body covered with the British Union Jack.

"Commander Fergan of His Majesty's Navy," says Hirata.

Yorisaka salutes, expressionless, and continues the desolate review of the casualties.

There is a final scene between Yorisaka and his wife. He has come to say goodbye to her. He tells her of his hurt at realizing the bond of affection that had grown between Fergan and her.

"But I loved you first, Mitsoukou," he says softly. She breaks down and weeps. And then he tells her why he must leave her, because he had dishonored himself by using her to attain his ends. "I did it all for my country," he says, "and for that I lost you." "No!" she whimpers, but Yorisaka is adamant. "Yes, I have lost you."

Next morning, Hirata, responding to a call from Yorisaka, comes in with the greeting, "Victory! Victory!" scarce on his lips, when he is startled to see Yorisaka garbed in the ceremonial white of the *hara kiri* ritual.

"Commander Yorisaka!" he exclaims, incredulously.

"Yes, a great victory," replies Yorisaka, "bought at the price of my honor. I have no further excuse for living."

Hirata is aghast.

Yorisaka kneels and draws the *seppuku* knife from its sheath.

"It is time for me to join my ancestors," says Yorisaka. "Please be good enough to assist me."

Hirata sees the samurai sword and grasps it, raising it above his head. Yorisaka takes a last look at a portrait of Mitsoukou that the French artist had painted while Betty's yacht was in port. He thrusts the blade into himself and then draws it up, looking once more at the portrait of Mitsoukou which is now a blur in his eyes, and Hirata's sword comes down as the crowd on the jetty at Nagasaki greets the victorious Japanese fleet with bunting flying and joyous shouts of:

"*Banzai!* . . . *Banzai!* . . . *Banzai!*"

Boyer with his heavy-lidded eyes made a perfect Yorisaka physically, while Merle Oberon, already a Eurasian beauty before she essayed the role, was exquisite as the delicate Mitsoukou.

Remains merely to sum up the felicities that joined to make this work a rather special thing—the screenplay which was structured like a Greek tragedy, the dialogue which was sparse, almost reticent, and frequently more eloquent than words can express. The spare use of music, too, or musical sounds, which were part of the whole orchestration of sounds, of voices, the hiss of a ship's prow cutting the waves, the blow of a hot wind, a distant waltz, guns booming, *banzai, banzai*. . . . The pacing, the unerring cutting, the sudden appearance of a character, like the entrance of a passage in a music score, everything was thought out for maximum effect through minimal means, so that everything moved with effortless grace, one scene fused into another so that one was never conscious of separate "big scenes" or any conscious wish to "impress" by *any* means. . . .

There are films (as there are plays) that exist without an audience*— they don't need an audience to react, to complement their effects, because such works are without "effects" as "effects" —they exist as consummations of the work of an artist or artists when they have been completed. No audience, however receptive, or critical, can add or detract from them. This is always true of the top rung masterworks and is sometimes true of the second rung masterly works. Of the latter it is true to a greater or lesser degree. It was the "happy accident" of *Thunder in the East* to be blessed with that rare thing, that syncope between consciousness and unconsciousness that sometimes results in an artist's achieving more than he realized he was achieving, even surprised to be told after the work's completion of perfervid qualities touching the sublime.

Autumn, 1968

---

*One audience this film never had was a Japanese one. It was banned in Japan.

H. D'ABBADIE D'ARRAST—IN MEMORIAM

You will look almost in vain for the name of H. d'Abbadie d'Arrast in film histories or encyclopedias. With a few, a very fleeting few, exceptions—cursory at best—it is almost as if he had never existed. Certainly he occupies no niche at all in the cinema pantheon, where he belongs, and one had to delve into the forgotten files of the past, long since consigned to archival darkness, to bring to light again the original reviews of his films which reveal, only too vividly, why he belongs in this pantheon. To be sure, that amazing compendium of scholarship, the ten volume *Enciclopedia dello Spettacolo*, published in Rome in 1954 under the editorship of Silvio D'Amico (the entries under the letter "A," alone, take 1198 pages!), gives d'Arrast a brief paragraph; Paul Rotha mentions him in passing, during a recital of names of directors influenced by Lubitsch (in *The Film Till Now*); and Dwight Macdonald, in his 1933 piece in *The Symposium*, takes notice of him—but search long and assiduous has failed to reveal anything more.* This for a life's work, for a life's salutary work.

It is to make up for—if it can be made up for at so late a date—this neglect and to give d'Arrast his rightful place in film history that I address these remarks to the film scholars and historians of the future.

Of course, d'Arrast had a short career, hardly spanning seven years, from 1927 to 1934, during which he managed to make eight films. In a quantitative sense, this was, perhaps, not much, though by movie standards it was rather more than is usually the case with stubborn artists up against equally stubborn

---

*Nor was any film of d'Arrast mentioned by Henri Langlois in his harrowing recital of films lost or destroyed through neglect or wanton callousness, on the occasion of the twentieth anniversary of the founding of the Cinémathèque Française in 1956, although the most *recherché* titles appeared in his list. The fact is, that, so far as can be determined, the only d'Arrast films that still exist are *Laughter* and *Topaze*. (In the 1970 *Dictionnaire du Cinéma Universel* of René Jeanne and Charles Ford, d'Arrast is given a brief paragraph.)

financial backers. In much longer careers, Flaherty and Stroheim hardly managed five films, and Eisenstein six. Qualitatively, however, they were very much indeed, these eight by Harry d'Arrast (as he was popularly known at the time of his florescence)—eight of the loveliest films ever made by anyone. Not world-shaking masterworks of social and political comment, to be sure, not filled with big scenes and thundering dramatics, not even probings into the mysteries of the human heart, and surely *sans* the bravura of cinematic fireworks and the whole panoply of dazzling virtuosity with which those names that have been enshrined in this pantheon have enthralled us. Just eight quiet, witty comedies, sometimes edged with satire but always with elegance, made by a civilized gentleman (what we used to call "a man of the world") who thought that it was something, too, to dedicate oneself to laughter (indeed, one of his films is called just that, *Laughter*) as Chaplin and Lubitsch did, as René Clair did ("It is easier to make melodrama than to make Mack Sennett," wrote Clair to me once, lamenting the decline of comedy in today's cinema world, grim with sex and violence, in which facetiousness poses as comedy)—and as d'Arrast did so felicitously in five silent films and three sound ones.

Nor did d'Arrast eschew the niceties of film technique, for all that, for he cloaked his urbanity in a silken sheen, his photography being so incandescent that it was said he could not photograph even a telephone in close-up without making it a thing of beauty. (Of course it would usually be a French cradlephone in a lady's boudoir, when ladies were still ladies and had boudoirs.) This was especially true of d'Arrast's quintet of silent films, where the physical aspect of the scenes (as the choice of words in a story by, say, Katherine Mansfield) was a part of what the films were about. A master (I would say, an instinctive one) of pace and cutting, with never a frame too much, in which the slightest gesture counted and the human face—most important of all—reflected that joy of living that seems today to have gone out of the world. D'Arrast was a gentle spirit of what certainly was a gentler time, celebrating the raptures of young love, with a light and airy grace celebrating the epiphanies of winsome romance (how archaic and obsolete such phrases sound in our cynical world today!). His films were comedies of *mœurs*, comedies of manners (whatever happened to good manners and *noblesse*

Harry d'Arrast (left) and his scenarist, Ernest Vajda, 1928.

oblige and all the rest of what once constituted cultured and civilized behaviour?) done in high comic style—as if the cinema were not a mass medium but a patrician one, an aristocratic and cerebral one. His films were like a string quartet, in which the subtlest effects are obtained in the least ostentatious manner, for an audience that brings to the work its own worldly wisdom, its own capacity for appreciation for what is being done, its own delight in meaningful nuances. And though the celebration of laughter was what the films were all about, one rarely heard guffaws of physical laughter in an audience during the unreeling of his films. But if you looked in the penumbral darkness about you at the faces of the spectators you would see that they were all smiling. At the most, occasional delighted murmurs or chuckles might be heard, and when it was all over and the lights went up, every countenance was wreathed in beatific smiles. In short, d'Arrast celebrated that most evanescent of virtues—charm.

D'Arrast's seven Hollywood films were *Service for Ladies, A Gentleman of Paris, Serenade, The Magnificent Flirt, Dry Martini, Laughter,* and *Topaze. It Happened In Spain,* adapted from Alarcón's *The Three Cornered Hat,* was the only film he made outside of Hollywood—in Spain.

Of course, d'Arrast was a disciple of both Chaplin and Lubitsch—he served an apprenticeship as assistant to Chaplin on both *A Woman of Paris* and *The Gold Rush;* and he was one of that short-lived glittering galaxy that had learned their Lubitsch lesson well and had set forth on their own to emulate the "Sultan of Satire," notably Malcolm St. Clair, with whom he had much in common. Both d'Arrast and St. Clair made films the way Heifetz plays the violin—flirtatious, coquettish, cool, feminine in the best sense of the word, their sense of timing and *rubato* and punctillio as full of exquisite sensibility as his—I think especially of the first four silent films of d'Arrast and of St. Clair's *Are Parents People?* and, of course, *The Grand Duchess and the Waiter.* Chaplin, while we're at it, may be said to have possessed the full-blooded grandeur of Ysaye, while Lubitsch certainly had the ineffable warmth and juiciness of Kreisler.

Many of the characters who drifted to Hollywood in the early days and subsequently became directors were rough and ready fellows. And some of these became very good directors, too, after serving their apprenticeships. But who was H. d'Abbadie d'Arrast? Where did he come from, this director with a name as fancy as a souvenir pillow? This genial patrician. . . .

Kirk Bond has traced for me the origin of the d'Arrast family, and I condense here some of the findings of his scholarly research:

"D'Abbadie is a fairly common name throughout Gascony, the French Pyrenees,* and into Languedoc. It comes from *abbadie*, which is both Gascon and Languedocien for abbey, the French *abbaye*. In particular it seems to signify what was an institution peculiar to the region—the lay abbot or abbé who was not a clerical person but a patron who was responsible for parish appointments and tithes, though he did not take the place of the lord of the manor. The immediate line of the film director d'Abbadie d'Arrast goes back to Michel d'Abbadie, who was born in Arrast in the 1770's. Arrast is a small village in the old vicomte of Soule, one of the three territories that comprise the French Basque region.

"The third of Michel's three sons, who took part in his brothers' early explorations in Ethiopia, died at the château of Echaux, which the family now held in the village of St. Etienne de Baigorry, further west in the Basque country; he is presumably Harry's great-grandfather. His name was Jean-Charles, and he, and apparently one of his brothers also, received permission to add 'd'Arrast' to their name." Bond then traces the genealogy of this family to the ancient Spanish house of Aguirre, *circa* 850. "What would appear to tie d'Abbadie d'Arrast definitely to this family is that another branch, the Agüero family, has a name that means 'irrigation ditch,' and the name Echaux, which in modern times the d'Abbadie d'Arrast family gave to its château, *also* means 'irrigation ditch.'" Finally, Bond concludes, Harry isn't the only one: Daguerre must have the same origin. "What ties it all up is the fact that the director was interred at the family château of Echaux at Etienne de Baïgorry in the Basses-Pyrénées."

The New York Times and *Variety* on March 17, 1968 briefly noted d'Arrast's death in Monte Carlo, where he had been living in seclusion for many years. Richard Watts Jr.—he alone of all the critics in America, and one of d'Arrast's early appreciators

---

*This doubtlessly accounts for the director's having been referred to frequently as a Basque.

during the years when Watts was film reviewer of the *New York Herald Tribune*—paid him a recent tribute in his column in the *New York Post*: "The late Harry d'Arrast was one of the distinguished directors from the great days of the silent cinema."

For all his French Basque background, d'Arrast was born in Argentina, educated at the Lycée Janson-de-Sailly in Paris and at Bradford University in England (he spoke French, Spanish and English perfectly), was badly wounded and decorated during the First World War as a subaltern in the French army, and following the Armistice met the Irish director, George Fitzmaurice, in Paris. Fitzmaurice urged him to come to Hollywood. In the spring of 1922, d'Arrast arrived there. A charming young fellow, handsome, debonair, very "high society," a Count, clubman, who had already met many famous Americans in Deauville, Monte Carlo, and such places, d'Arrast was received everywhere. Chaplin, taken with the elegant young man, offered him the post of technical advisor on his *A Woman of Paris*, which d'Arrast gladly accepted. Chaplin also kept him on as his assistant on *The Gold Rush*. By that time d'Arrast knew everyone in Hollywood and even made the "inner circle" that was regularly invited by Marion Davies and William Randolph Hearst to their Xanadu at San Simeon, out of which contact came d'Arrast's first contract to direct a picture—for Hearst's Cosmopolitan Productions, then releasing through MGM. Harry was delighted; but no assignment developed, so when Adolphe Menjou, who had co-starred in *A Woman of Paris*, went to Paramount, Harry followed him there and got a four-picture contract from that studio. The year was 1927.

D'Arrast's first picture, which starred Menjou, was *Service for Ladies*, and few directorial debuts have been more auspicious. From a delectable truffle by Ernest Vajda and Benjamin Glazer, d'Arrast had spun a completely winning tale of a *maître d'hôtel*, so expert as a concocter of sauces that he was the confidant of kings and princes, who falls in love with a visiting American debutante and follows her, incognito, to the Swiss Alps. "Fully as bright, fully as charming as *The Grand Duchess and the Waiter*," wrote John S. Cohen, Jr., critic of the *New York Sun*. "The chief assets of the film are its romantic charm and generally congenial and mature atmosphere. All the scenes at the resort in the Swiss Alps, at the height of the sporting season, impress one with their holiday spirit, and all the scenes in Mr. Menjou's domain, a Parisian hotel restaurant, impress with their genuine Continental touch. The settings are tasteful and handsome and the direction of Harry d'Arrast is admirable in every detail." And what was the "Act Two" contretemps that was to be resolved?—a characteristically Molnaresque bitter-sweet situation wherein the *maître d'* woos and wins the lovely creature only to break off the affair because he considers his social position as a headwaiter beneath hers; while she, poor girl, thinks he has left her because he is of a higher station in life, for had she not seen him palling around with the visiting king of a Balkan country? "A deft and engaging light comedy," wrote Richard Watts, Jr., in the *Herald Tribune*, "skillfully directed by Harry d'Arrast and brilliantly acted, it stands in the high and select company of *The Grand Duchess and the Waiter* and the Lubitsch comedies. . . . Throughout the mood of deft high comedy has been skillfully and tastefully maintained and to this has been added just a touch of half-ironic sentimentality that is delightful. About the entire production is an air of good breeding and charm that is a tribute to both the director and actors."

Not only had d'Arrast learned his Lubitsch lesson well, but also his Chaplin lesson, particularly from the epochal *A Woman of Paris*, some of whose most incisive scenes occur in a swank Paris restaurant, like that presided over by Albert, the headwaiter (played by Menjou, of course) in *Service for Ladies*. Guests who patronize this place prefer to have their dishes suggested by Albert, and on one such occasion he embarks on a description of a house specialty, *canard bigarade flambé*, so rhapsodically, accompanying his ode to this delicacy with the appropriate gestures that both he and the guest are almost moved to tears. But a minute later, when Albert instructs the waiter what to bring the party, it is summed up briefly and perfunctorily in the simple word, "Duck." And the carving of a duck by Albert is an artistic proceeding wherein he reveals his thorough knowledge of the bird's anatomy, and, for performing this task, he is wont to stick a monocle in his eye. "There are a thousand little touches throughout which may be attributed in part to the scenarists, Vajda and Glazer, and certainly in even greater part to the director, Harry d'Arrast. *Service for Ladies*," wrote Mordaunt Hall in the *Times*, "in fact seems to be the natural result of the

Bliss . . . *Service for Ladies* (1927)—d'Arrast's enchanting directorial debut, all snowflakes and sunbeams. Adolphe Menjou and Kathryn Carver in the sleigh. Do people ride in sleighs any more? Where, indeed, are the snows of yesteryear? (Lost)

"When Hollywood was Camelot and beauty was enough." *Service for Ladies.*

combined intelligence of a number of intelligent people—an unusual event in the studios."

Of such felicities was d'Arrast's first film. Clearly a new star was in the directorial firmament, one that twinkled brightly, for that year was to witness not jut one but three films by him, all as felicitous, one right after the other.

The second was *A Gentleman of Paris*, a sort of denatured *Affairs of Anatol* with a harsh touch of *Daybreak*—indeed, if Schnitzler could ever have compromised with Hollywood and lent his talents as a writer to the film capital, the result might have been something like *A Gentleman of Paris*, for though this, too, was a gay and scintillating comedy of a charming roué, eternally "on the make," it also had sombre glints when the "gentleman of Paris" is framed by his valet to appear as a card cheat and is faced with the only honorable way out—a gun. But the Hollywood of 1927 was not the pre-World War I of Vienna, and so an ironic twist at the end preserves the happy ending. However, in the *Times* opinion of André Sennwald *A Gentleman of Paris* "fell far short of *Service for Ladies*, a work as close to perfection as any screen or stage audience has a right to expect." Again Menjou was the star, and again he showed how beautifully he could respond to intelligent direction; while Nicholas Soussanin as the faithful valet—faithful, that is, until he learns that one of his master's light o'loves is his own wife—showed that the director could elicit sterling performances even from his secondary players, as he had elicited the much talked about performance by Lawrence Grant as the Balkan monarch in *Service for Ladies*. D'Arrast, obviously, was at home with valets as he was with kings, and he knew the psychology of both. "The picture is a delight," again complimented Cohen in the *Sun*, "a charming bit of sophistication. . . . The scenes following the discovery of Menjou at a card game with an ace up his sleeve are about as adroitly amusing as anything the screen has to offer." The "gentleman of Paris" is left alone with the gun offered him by a fellow player. The rest of them wait to see if he will or will not shoot himself. Suspense. Finally they hear a shot—and it is here that d'Arrast has sport with *noblesse oblige*, the code of the duello, "honorable way out" and the whole part and parcel of such things, not to mention happy endings for the sake of happy endings, and, in a kidding denouement, he provides his audience with a catharsis that is both plausible, sensible and very satisfying. In Schnitzler's remarkable novella, *Daybreak,* the Lieutenant shoots himself because he is too cowardly to fight a duel. But why should "the gentleman of Paris" shoot himself? Merely because he was offered a gun to preserve punctilio? Pish posh! After all, he wasn't *really* guilty.

"The very fine hand of Harry d'Arrast is again evident in *A Gentleman of Paris,*" commented Watts in the *Herald Tribune.* "It is a work of sophisticated allure, of imaginative direction and intelligent fun." When the noble night-hawk, the Marquis (the gentleman of Paris) comes home from a rendezvous early one morning to learn from his valet that his fiancée and her impatient father are waiting for him, the Marquis quickly undresses, jumps in a shower and pokes his head through the curtain to greet his intended bride and her father with a cheery "Good morning!" as if he had just gotten up. Another time, when the Marquis inadvertently learns, while being shaved by his valet, that one of his mistresses is the wife of this valet, he shows concern as to what the valet might do with his razor. But the valet, who knows how necessary he is to his master, declares as he wipes the soap off the razor blade, that there is more than one way of cutting a throat. They both laugh it off, but the valet has already decided on his own means for revenge. Only the valet reasons as a valet —the "come-uppance" suffered by his master accused as a card cheat would have been revenge enough—he does not reason as a gentleman, however perfect a valet he is; and so he is shocked when his "plot" takes a very dramatic turn, indeed, that might cost him the life of his master.

Thus, a director who has reasoned everything out for himself has no need to indulge in extravagances. Common sense is frequently the best dramaturgist, and consistency within the characterization is the best actor. Harry d'Arrast was that *rara avis* among directors, a perfectly disciplined mind beneath the seeming frivolous exterior, whose characters were rational beings because they acted that way; one did not have to take them at face value merely because the director had imposed that value on us.

His third picture, *Serenade,* again deriving from a gossamer fluff by Ernest Vajda and again starring Menjou, this time as an operetta composer in Vienna, was termed by one critic "the individual achievement of Harry d'Arrast, who is by way of being very near the top of Hollywood megaphone wielders, for it is his direction which lifts the picture to the heights it attains. It is crammed with subtle wit. Here is one director who will have no truck with the humdrum, the bromidic, the stereotype . . . throughout one was startled by the injection of wholly unexpected and therefore highly engaging twists. Its story isn't much, about a successful composer whose music lacks feeling until he falls in love with his flaming star, whereupon his music becomes very emotional, indeed. His patient and loving wife gets him back on the track, however, by making him jealous and all ends in sweet harmony. Nothing much, is it? But you should see what Mr. d'Arrast has done with it." "A silken production," rhapsodized Cohen in the *Sun*, "Superbly done. . . . Harry d'Arrast is clearly the most intelligent and the cleverest director in the jungles of Hollywood. Taste, charm, a flair for romance and exquisite humor, all these are revealed in *Serenade*. Moreover, photography, lighting, camera placement and tempo, all of the techniques of the difficult business of making photoplays, are of the highest order. And if adjectives, hats and superlatives were tossed high in the air over the advents of Lubitsch, Vidor, Mal St. Clair and Monta Bell and their ilk, they should be tossed a little higher for Mr. d'Arrast. A graduate of Chaplin's salons in Hollywood, an obviously cultivated and talented man, he brings a new note to movieland. One feels that, for the first time, an adult intelligence, an adult sense of humor, a fine sense of cultivation, have at last been discovered who is also a practical technician." The aristocratic style of the director is reiterated. " So brilliant is Mr. d'Arrast's direction of *Serenade* that it becomes a thoroughly charming, tasteful and adult cinema comedy," wrote Watts in the *Herald Tribune*. "Possibly this new director's finest gift is his good taste. Every scene in *Serenade* gives the impression of being the work not only of a brilliant man, but also of a gentleman. One of the quaintest things in the cinema is usually the effort of the films to create the atmosphere of breeding, culture and what we reviewers love to call 'sophistication.' In *Serenade* the mood is achieved with perfection and a proper lightness of touch." Even the staid *Times* opined that the director "had blossomed into one who may prove a boon to motion pictures."

How often have you seen in the movies someone hailing a

taxicab? It is always going in the direction the person wishes to go. In *The Magnificent Flirt*, the cab is going in the opposite direction and has to make a turn to pick up its passenger. This is such a little detail as to be almost not worth mentioning, save for the fact that even in these most minute details, d'Arrast was fresh and original in his approach. This last of his incomparable quartet of silent comedies for Paramount was a dream to watch. "Everything is expert, charming, brilliantly directed," extolled Cohen in the *Sun*. "Soft, velvety photography catches up the sheen of exquisite gowns, the steely surfaces of modernistic settings and furnishings, and turns them into eyefilling spectacles. The director can actually photograph a telephone in close-up and make it a thing of beauty. Even Florence Vidor is photographed so that she seems younger and lovelier than ever. Everybody behaves nicely, subtly. In short, Mr. d'Arrast proves again that he is the only director in films who combines impeccable taste with a highly cultivated camera sense. . . . The film presents as close an approach to physical beauty as a camera can record." This time Albert Conti (character actor in Stroheim films) replaced Menjou as the ubiquitous "gentleman of Paris" in this folderol about a beautiful lady of Paris whose pretty and nubile daughter disapproves of mama's flirtations. When the daughter's marriage plans are interfered with because of mama's behavior, mama reforms and herself weds the uncle of the very boy who becomes her daughter's husband. Miss Vidor was mama, Loretta Young the daughter, and Mr. Conti the uncle. The film derived from a French farce, *Maman*, by Germaine and Moncousin. The adaptation and scenario were by d'Arrast and his erstwhile colleague on *A Woman of Paris*, Jean de Limur. "It is a sparkling affair," said the *Times*, "and while the story is no weightier than the bubbles in champagne, it is fashioned so delightfully that yesterday afternoon it kept its audience in a constant state of high glee." The critic went on to extol the charming dissolves, the roguish acting, "the artistic highlights and shadows, coupled with an intelligent and natural development of the various incidents."

It is 1928. D'Arrast quits Paramount to accept a contract from the old Fox company for which he makes *Dry Martini*, about a middle-aged expatriate American who hies him to Paris, with the advent of Prohibition, there to pursue the "hobby" of indulging in his favorite beverage, dry martinis, at Harry's American Bar, the while administered to by a bevy of complaisant Parisian ladies. This bliss is rudely interrupted by the sudden arrival of his daughter, herself in search of adventure like papa. How her quest leads to an affair with a French artist whose intentions are somewhat less than honorable, much to papa's alarm, and of her encounter with a nice but fatuous American whose concern for her honor gets him beaten up by the villainous French artist for his pains, but thereby winning the sympathy and heart of the girl, is the stuff of the plot, such as it is. Papa returns to his stool at Harry's bar, after this moment's agitation, and life resumes its serene course for him.

Once again the critics were taken with that very special aspect of d'Arrast, a quality in all screen annals not singled out so acutely of any other screen director. "Among all the current cinema directors," began Watts in the *Herald Tribune,* "there is no one who, so completely as Harry d'Arrast, gives you the impression that the film comedies he makes are the work of a gentleman. And he is one of the finest of film makers." Watts is delighted that the director flouts one of the hoariest of plot clichés, wherein the hero beats up the villain. "Mr. Arrast offers here an innovation that is not only pleasant, but unparalleled." What d'Arrast had done, of course, is to have the villain beat up the hero, and a foreign villain beating up an *American* hero at that, and no come-back on the American hero's part, either. "Blithe . . . deft . . . sly . . ." said John Hutchins in the *Post.* Cohen in the *Sun* found it "more satisfying than *The Wind, Ten Days that Shook the World* and *Show People*"—all playing the week that *Dry Martini* opened, which may or may not have surprised the Messrs. Seastrom, Eisenstein, and Vidor, had they seen it. "This imaginative Frenchman is just simply proving again what a master of cinematic expression he is, one to whom triteness and banalities are poison." "It is rendered cheerful," said André Sennwald in the *Times,* "by the happy faculty of refusing to take seriously such worthy items as the Younger Generation, the Divorce Question and the Kept Woman. It should be stated at once that the greater attributes of the picture are those given by the deft directo l touch of Harry d'Arrast. The story itself dates back to when ... Victorians themselves were the Younger Generation. But Mr. d'Arrast, by a carefree juggling of sense and nonsense, has turned out an hour's high amusement out of it." (Albert Gran, Mary Astor, Albert Conti, and Matt Moore were featured.)

Could d'Arrast keep it up with the advent of the sound film? For it was now 1929, and movies were beginning to talk. D'Arrast's old friend, Monta Bell, who was also a Chaplin disciple (from *The Pilgrim* to *The Gold Rush,* as assistant) was now a producer at Paramount's Long Island studio. He sent for d'Arrast and asked him to make his first sound film under his aegis for Paramount. The result was *Laughter,* a wry comedy about an ex-chorus girl (Nancy Carroll) who marries a millionaire (Frank Morgan) only to find that she prefers one of her erstwhile "bohemian" friends, a struggling composer (Fredric March). A typical Hollywood fairy tale, you will say. But all true love stories are fairy tales.

Out of the smallest things d'Arrast made a delight; when Nancy Carroll puts out her hands to receive several diamond bracelets from her maid, she places her wrists together with a tired smile as if she were to be handcuffed, for that's what her jeweled bracelets are, handcuffs that keep her tied to her dull millionaire. An encounter between the butler and the ebullient young composer begins with all the hoity-toitiness of class distinctions and ends in a charming duet at the piano with them playing the allegro movement of Beethoven's *Moonlight Sonata*—the level on which all classes meet. An excursion into the country—March and Nancy Carroll are driving in an old jalopy—ends when the motor suddenly stops. March gets out to see what's wrong. "If this were only a piano," he says. To which Nancy replies, "I've never been out with a piano." A storm breaks and they take refuge in a house whose occupants are out. Two bearskin rugs on the floor soon have them gruntling and growling under the bearskins at each other, then one of the bears is in the kitchen having a snack that Nancy is preparing. Only when the police, investigating prowlers, enter the house does March doff his bearskin. They're arrested, of course, but a quick phone call from the local jail by Nancy to her rich and powerful husband gets them a police escort back to the city, with sirens wailing to clear the way. "That noise," says March to Nancy, "that's money, that's power." He looks at her. "But you, you're dying, you're dying for lack of nourishment, life, laughter!" And so Nancy leaves her bewildered rich husband and we next see her with Freddie March at a café

table in Paris. Her eye catches an elegantly dressed woman at a nearby table fondling her diamond bracelet. March watches her wistfully watching the woman. Then Nancy turns back to him and breaking into an innocent smile says, "I didn't say anything." And they both laugh. End.
It was one of the most delicious moments in the cinema.

D'Arrast then took a short vacation abroad, France and Spain. He returned to Hollywood and around 1937 married the beauteous Eleanor Boardman, the ex-Mrs. King Vidor. Robert Florey, director and film historian, knew them both well, in Hollywood and abroad, and reminisced long and fondly to me about those blithe days.

On d'Arrast's return to Hollywood, he was assigned to direct Al Jolson in *Hallelujah, I'm a Bum,* which didn't sound like a d'Arrast picture to begin with. A fight between the director and Joseph Schenck, the film's producer, settled it: d'Arrast was fired. Florey remarks on d'Arrast's sensitivity; he couldn't stand being dictated to, no matter how high and strategic the studio mogul was. But in 1933 an opportunity came at RKO to direct John Barrymore in *Topaze,* from the satirical comedy by Marcel Pagnol, in an adaptation by Ben Hecht. Pagnol had already filmed it, himself, the year before, with Fernandel. This bitter-sweet harlequinade on the fruits of chicanery was an ideal subject for d'Arrast. Barrymore was superb as the meek professor of a boy's lycée who taught his students that "honesty is the best policy" only to find that in real life it was just the reverse. Myrna Loy made a charming vis-à-vis playing opposite him—first the mistress of the professor's tycoon friend who wishes to exploit him, then as the lady-love of the professor himself, when he turns tables on the tycoon and takes full advantage of the irresistible situation in which he finds himself. The professor and his lady go out one night to celebrate, to a movie on whose marquee is *Man, Woman and Sin.* "Fancy that!" exclaims the now very elegantly accoutered professor, amusedly, and, arm in arm, they go into the show.

Next came an offer from Samuel Goldwyn to direct *Raffles.* This quickly ended in a fight with that producer and, once more, d'Arrast found himself dismissed. Disgusted, he went back to France. Meanwhile, *Topaze,* like *Laughter,* scored a big success with the critics and there seemed no question that he would make as distinguished a career in the sound medium as he had done in the silent.

In 1934 d'Arrast went to Spain again, and with a release contract with United Artists he made *The Three Cornered Hat*, based on the nineteenth-century tale by Pedro de Alarcón that had already served Manuel de Falla so well for the heady and irrepressible ballet he composed in 1919. D'Arrast accomplished hardly a whit less.

"A jovially sardonic story, based on an eighteenth century poem, of a dignitary who has the tables turned on him while attempting to seduce the miller's wife," wrote the London exhibitors' trade paper, *The Cinema News*.

"Rare humorous savour achieved by brilliant and sensitive handling of simple and hearty comic situations, culminating in mistaken belaboring of the elderly would-be Don Juan by crowd under his own window. Pervasive lyric quality mingled with rich and delicious touches of humor and characterizations, enhanced by superb pictorial compositions of authentic Spanish sun-drowsy village and pastoral scenes, and effective musical background, lift film out of the ordinary box-office class. Excellent leading portrayals and sure minor characterizations; clever dramatic use of spontaneous rhythmic dances; sparing use of well-written English dialogue. Possible booking venture for very intelligent patronage and outstanding fare for halls specializing in Continental product. D'Abbadie d'Arrast is a director who exemplifies Shakespeare's dictum that the hand of least employment hath the keenest touch; every one of the new films he has made has been worth seeing. But none of them is so worth seeing as this exquisite picturization of Alarcón's poetic farce. The pity of it is that its appeal resides so much in beauty of setting, pictorial perfection, rich characterization and a pervasive lyrical quality; it is so much above the heads of the average patrons as to be definitely out of the popular box-office class. But for specialized halls, it cannot be too strongly recommended."

The English actor, Allan Jeayes, played the licentious corregidor, Victor Varconi was the miller, Hilda Moreno, the volatile and provocative Rosarita, the corregidor's wife, and Eleanor Boardman, d'Arrast's wife, played, of course, the miller's beautiful wife who was the cause of it all. The film was made in three versions—English, French and Spanish, and it was released as *It Happened in Spain*. As the *Cinema News* predicted, it did not do well at the box-office.

In November of 1935, d'Arrast, again back in Hollywood, was engaged by the newly formed Pickford-Lasky Productions but nothing came of it. Early in 1937 he tried to promote a film based on his treatment of *Cyrano de Bergerac* by Rostand. He seemed to have interested 20th Century Fox in it. Robert Kane was assigned as the producer and Ben Hecht as the screenplay writer. The film was to have beeen shot at the Alexander Korda studios in London that year. It didn't happen.

D'Arrast returned to France, and when the war broke out he came back to America, this time on a Spanish vessel by way of Havana, where his wife met him. Together they returned to Hollywood. For five or six years he idled in the film capital, unable to obtain work. In 1946 he returned again to France. It was to be for the last time. Florey reports seeing him there then at their apartment in the Rue du Bac. D'Arrast was discouraged. "He seemed to have lost his ambition, he was not the same old Harry. . . . He tried again in England and France and spent several months in Madrid with Barney (Benjamin) Glazer, an old friend of his, trying to promote a deal on Glazer's script for a two-version film. The Spaniards were not interested. Glazer returned to the States and died not long afterwards." As if things weren't sad enough for "good, old Harry," he and Eleanor Boardman parted, though, as Florey assures us, "they were still devoted to each other."

But Harry d'Arrast lived now alone "in a hotel room in Monte Carlo," as Florey described it, ". . . the Hotel de Paris, where he would write me a couple of times each year—reminiscing about the old days. I got his last letter about six weeks ago"—the date of Florey's letter to me is April 11, 1968—"and I'm looking at it now. It was short and he said that he would write again soon, but now he never will. Poor Harry."

Harry d'Arrast died in Monte Carlo on March 16, 1968.

I have two items to add. . . .

One is Paramount's 1927 "sweepstakes": a ten-thousand dollar bonus to whichever Paramount director made the most successful (at the box office, naturally) picture of the year. D'Arrast hoped, after the ecstatic reviews of *Service for Ladies* and *A Gentleman of Paris*, that he would win it. An equally new director at Paramount decided he would win it. His name was Josef von Sternberg. He got it for *Underworld*.

The second is a personal note—three communications I had from d'Arrast in 1965 and 1966. I had written him, saying I would like to do an article on him (the article you have just read) to show him that he was still remembered and to show the world how unjustly he had been neglected. I wanted his help in filling in "the lost years" and anything else he had to say.

His first reply is dated February 27, 1965, and is written on the stationery of the Hotel de Paris, Monte Carlo:

> A note in haste—for the moment—as I will write you at length in a few days, as I didn't want your very touching letter to remain unanswered more than ten minutes! As Florey will have told you, I am possibly the world's worst correspondent. A friend in America wrote five years ago—he has since written about seven times—his last was a card with a question of no importance—he wanted me to answer if I was still alive? This has still remained unanswered as I think with delight how happy he will be to hear I am—to say nothing of my pleasure in answering such a question! As we say in France, "I'll be seeing you!" Yours, d'Arrast.

Christmas of 1965 I received a picture post-card of Monaco from him:

> Please, please pardon me—no ill will, believe me. I have had so many different problems—after all, I only have two heads! Believe me, you are part of my plans and I will get around to it—with order in my house and in my head—there is plenty of order in my heart. Best wishes for 1966 (fancy!) et la suite. Harry d'Arrast.

Alongside an outline of a dachshund, printed on the top of the correspondence side of the card, he had written: "Ya! Dat iss der sausage dog! I don't know how or why he got there but I suppose there is a reason!"

The following Spring, April 8th, 1966 a letter came, again on Hotel de Paris stationery:

> I would be inexcusable were it not for the following fact: My sister was operated on in Nice November 15th after which she was given two months to live. As she wasn't to know about this, on any account, I couldn't tell even my very best friends about it. My wife, Eleanor Boardman, in California, doesn't even know about it!! Since that date I have been going every day to Nice and, as you can well imagine, living a nightmare. She is still alive and I'm having her come over to Monte where I hope she will have happier last days. Please pardon me—I *did* receive the clippings and I was extremely touched by your kindness and the trouble you went to. I haven't a single recent photo of myself except passport photos and a rather good photo (taken in 1922 with my ex-friend Chaplin). I will have it photographed and send it to you just as soon as I find time. I had a very good and original idea for T.V. in the U.S. which is at a standstill as I receive letters scolding me for my so called "procrastination" (A $1000 word!) P. S. Also excuse this letter, "edited" and ever so messy. If I read it a third time, you will never get it!! Harry.

He added another postscript on the side: "I will have more time after my sister's arrival and will write you at length. Best regards."

I never heard from him again.

This is the story I wanted to tell.

Summer, 1969

THE PARALLEL WITH GEORGES FEYDEAU*

Originally written for the author's The
Lubitsch Touch *but completed too late for
inclusion in the book.*

Lubitsch can be said to have been the closest to a farceur of the stature of Georges Feydeau that the cinema ever achieved, "the Shakespeare of the boulevard farce" and the greatest comic dramatist after Molière.

(Chaplin? But he *was* the cinema's Molière!)

They had many things in common. Feydeau not only wrote and directed his own plays but was never seen without chomping, when not smoking, a cigar. And he, too, began as an amateur actor, and by the merest chance (the tardiness of a theater manager) became a playwright. He, too, had to make his farces as hilarious as it was physically possible to make them, and he, too, wrote every bit of action down, leaving nothing to chance. Everything had to count and be accounted for.

Marcel Achard's description of Feydeau's method sounds exactly as if he were describing Lubitsch's:

> It is impossible to cut anything in Feydeau's plays. The most amazing thing about them is the infallibility with which all things are regulated, explained, justified, even in the most extravagant buffoonery. There is not a single incident, once introduced, of which we cannot say, "Yes, that's true—it could not have happened any other way."
>
> There is not a single detail, not one, which is not necessary to the action as a whole; there is not a single word

---

*The extracts from Marcel Achard on Feydeau are from Eric Bentley's *Let's Get a Divorce! and Other Plays* (Hill and Wang, 1958), originally the introduction to Feydeau's *Théâtre Complet,* copyright by Editions du Bélier, 1948. The translation of the Achard passages is by Mary Douglas Dirks.

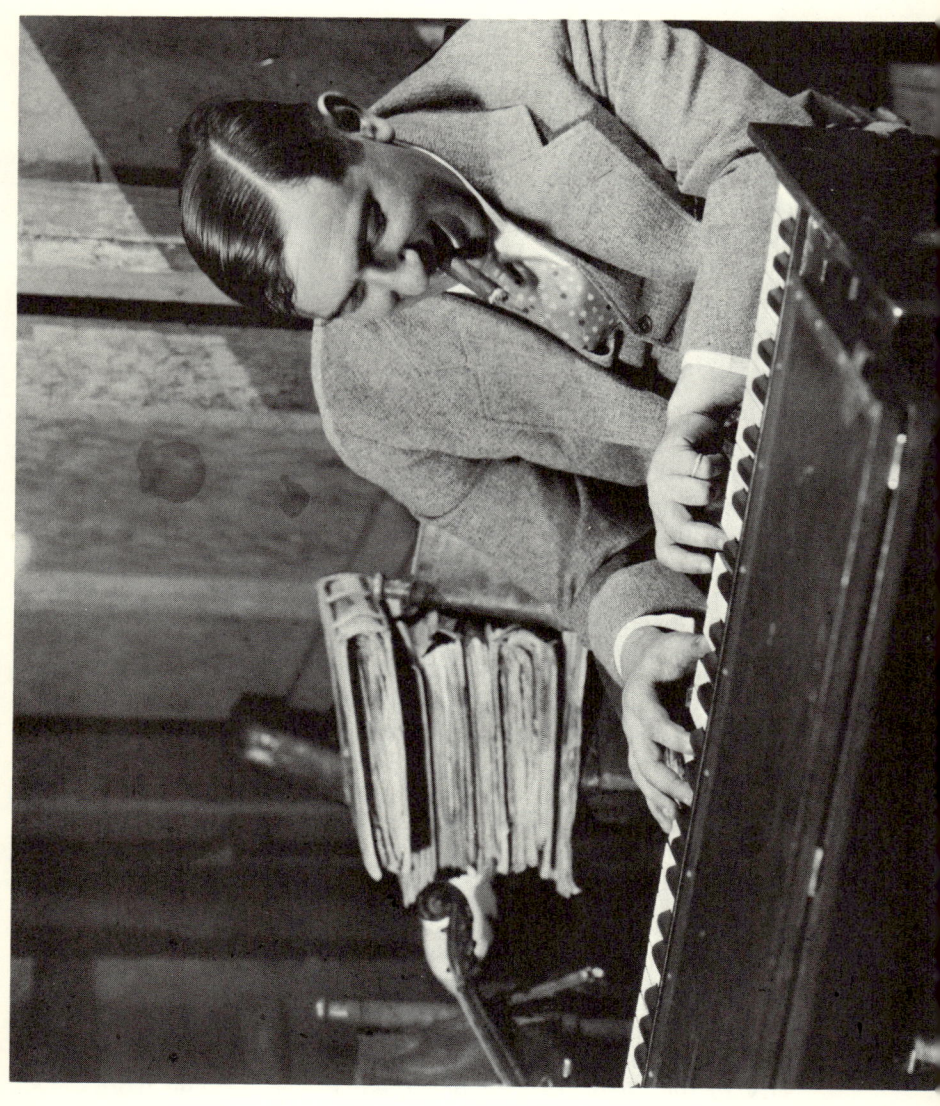

"Beat me, daddy, eight to the bar!" The one, the only, the unique—Ernst Lubitsch takes time out for a solo jam session between scenes of *The Patriot* (now lost) at the Paramount Studios in Astoria, Long Island, 1928.

Flaherty's "official" favorite film was Dovzhenko's *Earth* but "unofficially," he told me, it was that miracle of calculated art and malice, Lubitsch's *Kiss Me Again* (1925), a favorite also of Edmund Wilson, and also of the author of this book. The concluding scene—husband (Monte Blue) and wife (Marie Prevost) decide to "make up." (Lost)

which, at a given moment, does not have its repercussion in the comedy—and this one word, I have no idea why, buries itself into our subconsciousness, only to issue forth at the precise moment when it most illumines an incident we were not anticipating but which we find entirely natural, and which delights us because it sounds improvised—and because we realize that we should have foreseen it.

(*Vide* the last shot of Lubitsch's *So This is Paris*, of M. Lalle trudging in the prisoner's line, an explosively hilarious moment that had been casually planted much earlier when he was mistakenly arrested for his inamorata's husband and about which we had all but forgotten until Lubitsch springs it for his final guffaw.)

Achard goes on to describe a characteristic example of the meticulous care with which Feydeau insured even the most minute of his desired effects:

It happens in *Occupe-toi d'Amélie* that two actors have to say in relation to each other and twice over:
"Ah-hah! That's it!"
Obviously, "Ah-hah! That's it!" can be said in any number of different ways, any one of which may be funny.
But we have reached the third act of a Feydeau play. By this time the audience is convulsed with laughter. It is now a question of getting bigger laughs than ever. Feydeau has no intention of leaving this problem to the possibly faulty inspiration of the actor.
There is a way of saying, "Ah-hah! That's it!" the right way—Feydeau's way. And I beg you to realize that it is not exactly the easiest way. He gave directions for it. He wrote it down—on a stave with notes: he made his "Ah-hah! That's it!" into music.

Achard concludes by quoting Jean Richepin's amazement that a brain could give birth to so many buffooneries, so much sensible nonsense, without bursting. "It happened at dawn, June 5, 1921," he says. "He died from his desire to make us laugh, killed by his own genius."

As did Lubitsch.

Winter, 1969

Foreword to the re-issue of the complete
run of *Close Up* Magazine. Arno Press, 1970.

FOREWORD TO *CLOSE UP*

It was still the Twenties when *Close Up* first appeared, the wonderful giddy Twenties which celebrated for an entire decade the blessed cessation of the cannons' boom on that never-to-be-forgotten November 11, 1918. It was July 1927, to be exact, that Winifred Bryher and Kenneth Macpherson presented to the film world their modest little magazine, that soon to become familiar beige pocket-size affair, which was to flourish for six and a half years, first as a monthly, then as a quarterly, to the end of 1933. In short, the period coinciding with the peak achievements in both silent and sound films during the "golden age" between the two world wars—1927 through 1933. What a time it was!

The cinema was still new enough to be full of experiment and light-headed with rapture over the new medium, which suggested possibilities enough to make one swoon. It was still the beginning (scarcely a dozen years old was the cinema in 1927 if we date its parturition from *The Birth of a Nation*) and beginnings are like first loves—there can never be anything like them again. That's the best thing about first times—their originality and uniqueness.

It was a time of great ferment in all the arts (the post-World War II aftermath saw no such florescence) and "little magazines" proliferated everywhere. In America we had *The Dial, Broom, Contact, Secession, This Quarter, Transatlantic Review, Hound and Horn, Pagany* and, from abroad, *transition*, and of course, *Close Up*, which was for us at the time as much a literary magazine as a film one for it had a distinguished roster of contributors including Havelock Ellis, André Gide, Osbert Sitwell, H.D., Dorothy Richardson, Gertrude Stein, Marianne Moore, René Crevel, Jean Prevost, and Arnold Bennett, among others. Heading the film writers were V. I. Pudovkin and Sergei Eisenstein (his essays, "The Dynamic Square" and "Principles of Film Form," appeared here in their English versions for the first time), Harry Alan Potamkin, Oswell Blakeston, Robert Herring, Marc Allégret, Pera Attasheva, Man Ray, etc.—names that were to join their French, German, Soviet and American colleagues to form the first body of serious film criticism. In America, spanning a good part of *Close Up*'s existence was *Experimental Cinema*, edited by Seymour Stern and Lewis Jacobs, of which five issues appeared between February 1930 and June 1934. In France, *La Revue du Cinéma*, under the editorship of Jean-Georges Auriol, lasted from July 1929 to October 1932 during its first florescence and may be said to have been the closest thing to a French *Close Up* that we had. And, of course, there was the *Filmliga* of Holland, edited by L. S. Jordaan and Henryk Scholte (1932–35) that easily qualified as the Dutch *Close Up*. *Close Up*, the brilliant model for all, was five years old when *Sight and Sound* appeared on the scene in 1932, and Martin Kamin's quarterly, *Film*, edited by Lincoln Kirstein, Jay Leyda, Mary Losey, Robert Stebbins and Lee Strassberg, was not to make it debut until 1939. (Only four numbers covering one year appeared.)

That was what the "little magazine" world was like at the time *Close Up* made its initial bow.

And the films? The films! It was, perhaps the best time of all. In finely reproduced copper cuts on coated (enameled) stock, we were vouchsafed our first glimpses of *Potemkin, The End of St. Petersburg, Storm Over Asia, Mother, Earth, Ten Days, Old and New,* and *Turksib* from the new Soviet nation whose birth we all thrilled at. And from Germany, Pabst's exquisite *Die Liebe der Jeanne Ney*, that ardent paean to young love with its nostalgic Paris vignettes, *Pandora's Box* and *The Diary of a Lost One, Westfront 1918, Die Dreigroschenoper* (fresh from its triumph at the Theater am Schiffbauerdamm in Berlin), *L'Atlantide*—all Pabst, who was an especial favorite of the magazine (Murnau and Dupont having been lured to Hollywood), not to mention the Czinner-Bergner idylls, *Ariane, Der Geiger von Florenz, Der Träumende Mund.* . . . From France, René Clair's *Sous les Toits de Paris, Le Million,* and *A Nous la Liberté, Vampyr* (albeit from the Danish Dreyer), the Gide-Allégret *Voyage au Congo*, Cavalcanti's *Rien Que les Heures* and *En Rade* with the bewitching Hessling, Gance's *La Fin du Monde, Don Quixote* (Pabst's

Foreword to Close Up

cosmopolitan transmogrification of the Spanish genius of Cervantes via an Austrian director, Russian Quixote, English Sancho, French composer and scenarist, and only the backgrounds Spanish)—and from Hollywood, Stroheim's mordant *The Wedding March*, Eisenstein's defense of his version of *An American Tragedy* (and subsequently the achingly beautiful stills of his ill-starred venture, *Que Viva Mexico*), the manifesto attacking Upton Sinclair for the vandalization of *Que Viva Mexico*, Roy del Ruth's Freudian and very Lubitschean *Wolf's Clothing*, and *Sunrise*, which the editors found unworthy of Murnau for its "*Edelkitsch*. . . ."

The mind reels from the riches we harvested in these pages—features, documentaries, shorts, from every nation producing good work, illuminated by the clarity of the accompanying text, as lucid as the films themselves. Articles, reviews, interviews, of the sharpest observation, all of them illustrated by the rarest stills—it is no wonder that each next issue of *Close Up* was looked forward to with the keenest anticipation. What of Wiskowski's *Black Sunday*, reputedly more realistic even than *Potemkin*? And Granowsky's *jeu d'esprit, Le Roi Pausole*, with its 365 beauties and Jannings? And *Salt of Svanetia* from Kalatozov, which had stunned those who'd seen it? And Room's *Bed and Sofa*—the *Potemkin* of domestic comedies? And Part Two of *The Wedding March*? Who could wait to read what *Close Up* would have to say about them, let alone wait to see them? Patience cannot abide in the heart of a lover, says an Arab proverb. That's the way it was with us, in those days, when we and the cinema were young. (May I at this point set my own position in this milieu by saying that Harry Alan Potamkin, Seymour Stern, Alexander Bakshy [who was also the American translator of Gorky] and I formed a kind of "three musketeers" [with me a hopeful d'Artagnan] of the cinema at that time? And for those who remember the period, let me also recall two names that were involved with us in those blithe days—Joseph Fliesler of the Fifth Avenue Playhouse and Symon Gould of the fondly remembered Films Arts Guild that first brought Leni's *The Waxworks*, Lubitsch's *So This Is Paris*, and gave us the chance to see Chaplin's legendary *A Woman of Paris* again. . . .)

What eventually happened was, I suppose, inevitable under the circumstances.

"The little magazines died off rapidly in the early 1930's," as Granville Hicks described it recently, "the obvious explanation being the Depression, which was death on angels. The Depression had another and in the long run probably more important consequence: the creation of an atmosphere unfavorable to the doctrine of the supremacy of art. Hungry, jobless, desperate men could not be deeply interested in the subtleties of James Joyce and T. S. Eliot, to say nothing of the more obscure writers. . . . The Revolution of the Word did not seem to be anything much when it was possible that there might be barricades in the streets. The new little magazines were intensely political, and often enough the esthetes of the 1920's became the fanatics of the 1930's."

Experimental Cinema and *Film* especially reflected this. (Who can, once having read it, ever forget James Agee's scenario for the execution of the Communists by the Kuomintang from his script for a film of Malraux's *Man's Fate* that appeared in *Film?*)

And so, *Close Up*, too, at the close of the year that saw Hitler's ascendency as chancellor of the Third Reich, gave up. Perhaps that isn't the right phrase for it. In any case, it was a different world now. How different was to be spelled out slowly but inexorably until the Nazi hydrophobia could contain itself no longer.

But the Third Reich is dead (we hope) and *Close Up* still lives, phoenix-like risen from the ashes of the holocaust. Here, in these pages, miraculously (there is really no other word for it) restored to our view, since the magazine has long since been out of print, individual copies being among the rarest of cinema incunabula, here that old enchantment, that "old black magic"— whatever it was—lives again. And if you say, "Well, it's the past, after all. . . ." I can only remind the gentle reader that so are we (as the poet said, "with Yesterday's Sev'n Thousand Years"), so are we. . . .

Winter, 1969

A TRIBUTE TO WALT DISNEY

They say that Toscanini's favorite film was Disney's *The Band Concert* in which Mickey Mouse conducted the definitive performance of the "William Tell" Overture, despite the blandishments of a kibitzing Donald Duck, playing a fife, to seduce the band into joining him in "Turkey in the Straw." When the band's playing of the storm movement kicks up a real storm—what do I say, storm?—a real blow, a twister, a cyclone—lifting the players up into its center and whirling them around, without Mickey and the band losing a single note, the Maestro is said to have been beside himself with joy. This was conducting, this was the way a conductor maintained control over an orchestra! Boy, would he give it to the Philharmonic boys at the next rehearsal... !

My own favorite among the Disney short films is one whose name I have forgotten but whose delight remains eternally green in my memory: the one about the wolf playing the fiddle for coins on a cold Christmas Eve, the passersby scurrying homewards with their packages and trees in the darkened dusk, occasionally dropping a coin in the tin cup dangling from the violin's neck, then hurrying on as gusts of wind send the snow flurries swirling about the huddled figure playing so forlornly....

Bitter it is to have to beg on this most joyous of eves. . . .
Bitter it is to have to go to someone for something. . . .
What is it he is playing, with its wild gypsy wail, echoing a half-forgotten song remembered from flickering campfires on the *puszta*? A song whose plaint will not be stilled . . .

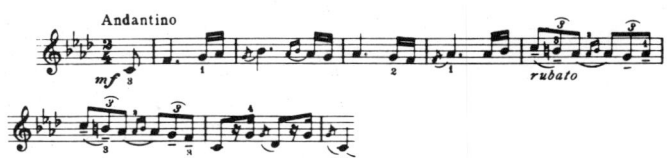

Ah yes, of course, a Hungarian Dance of Brahms, in the Kreisler arrangement no less ... well, well ... he's an accomplished fiddler, all right, to be able to negotiate this virtuoso piece, but hark, how beautifully he sings along with Kreisler and Brahms on his violin ...

And then, passionately, as if one string were not enough on which to pour out his grief, *a due corde* ... the dirge-like *lassan* in the doleful key of F minor. ...

It is difficult for a hunchback to play the violin—did we forget to note that the poor wolf is afflicted not only with a lack of this world's goods but with a hunchback too? What then, like the poet asked, did the hand of the Potter shake? A cloak covers up his hunchback but does little to protect him from the cold, which has turned his fingers blue. Although he is wearing mittens, he has cut out the fingers of the left mitten to enable his fingers to touch the strings, and they are blue with the cold. Still, it does not prevent him from playing, *mirabile dictu*, as if Ysaye himself were holding the bow, the fabulous, legendary Ysaye. ...

Clink!
Close-up we see the wolf with a pained smile look up as a coin is dropped in his cup of sorrow. ...

Clink!
Another coin is dropped in his cup of affliction and again in close-up we see all of life's hurt in his eyes as, with the faintest nod, he acknowledges the largess visited upon him so generously this hallowed night of nights . . . this night that celebrates the largess visited upon a child in a manger (certainly little better than a cold street corner) by three kings guided there by a star . . .

Oh, but it is bitter cold and the night grows dark and the wolf is now but a deeper shadow in the night, while the song grows more disconsolate, more plaintive, as the lights in the people's homes begin to go on and seem to twinkle in their snugness as they did for the starving man wandering the city of Christiania in that story about a man who was hungry. The people of Christiania didn't care and let him starve, but tonight, here, the people are generous. Is it because it is Christmas Eve? Is it because he is playing so well? Is it because people are basically good? No matter—enough that the wolf's tin cup clinks merrily . . .

Good will towards men . . .

And then it happens—a gust of wind lifts up the wolf's cloak and reveals a portable phonograph strapped to his back, on which a record is playing (and which continues to play during this unmasking) the music we have just heard and which has moved us so deeply.

When the passersby see this, some laugh, others are outraged at the deception. . . .

"Faker! Bum!" they cry after him, for he has panicked and started to race down the street. Stones are flying after him. His tin cup now lies in the snow, its coins spilled out around it.

And the wolf, now a speck in the distance as he runs to escape the devils, disappears as the camera irises out.

Winter, 1969

SOME THOUGHTS ON VON STERNBERG — IN MEMORIAM

He was concerned with raveling and unraveling psychological skeins in which the characters were merely vehicles for his designs, to adumbrate his personal mythology.

He was a director like Manet and Degas were painters, holding himself aloof from his subject matter. Behind every image one sensed a glacial detachment.

He composed his films with a kind of insolent bravura, employing a technique that was all but invisible. Stupendous care went into the fashioning of every "curve" in the film, every moment on the screen. Every thing that happened, everything that was said, clicked into place like the tumblers in a lock.

Morocco, Shanghai Express and *The Devil is a Woman* are the works of an astonishingly gifted lapidary. Toughness combined with elegance, the whole seasoned, but judiciously, even sparingly, with fruity dialogue, invariably of a sardonic impulse, cast in a kind of dream world that had just enough contact with reality to give substance to his delicate shadows. No one was a better example of the style of poetic realism, of neo-baroque.

In another sense, one might be tempted to describe his style

It was said of Beaumarchais that he had but one character in all his plays —himself. "Madame Bovary is myself!" exclaimed Flaubert. "Marlene is me," said Sternberg. "All my characters are me." Josef von Sternberg, 1939.

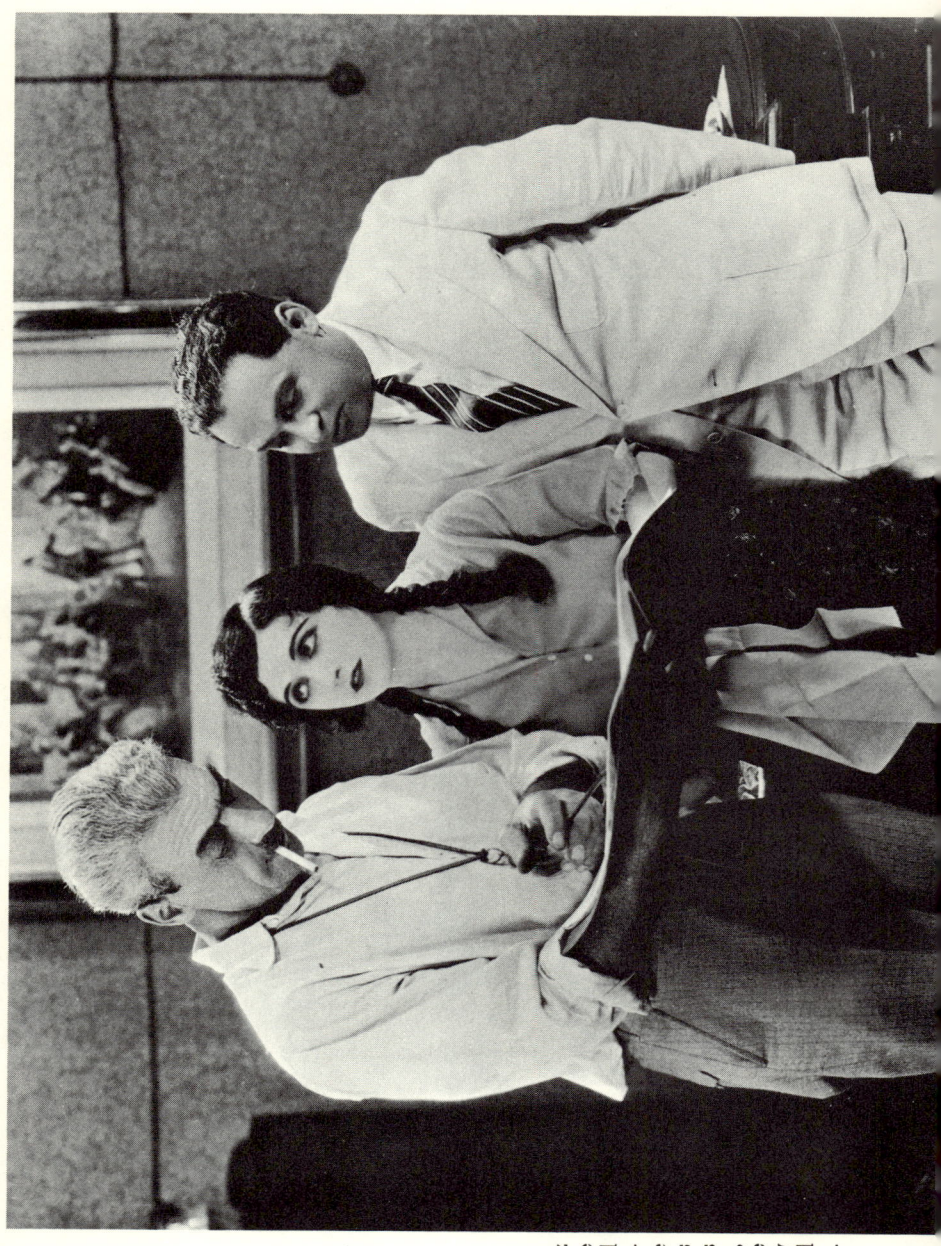

In memoriam... Mauritz Stiller (left), one of the most sensitive and gifted directors, slain with humiliation by Hollywood. Here he is with Pola Negri, his star, and Ufa's fabulous Erich Pommer, his producer, preparing a take for the one memorable film they let him make in Hollywood —*Hotel Imperial* (1927).

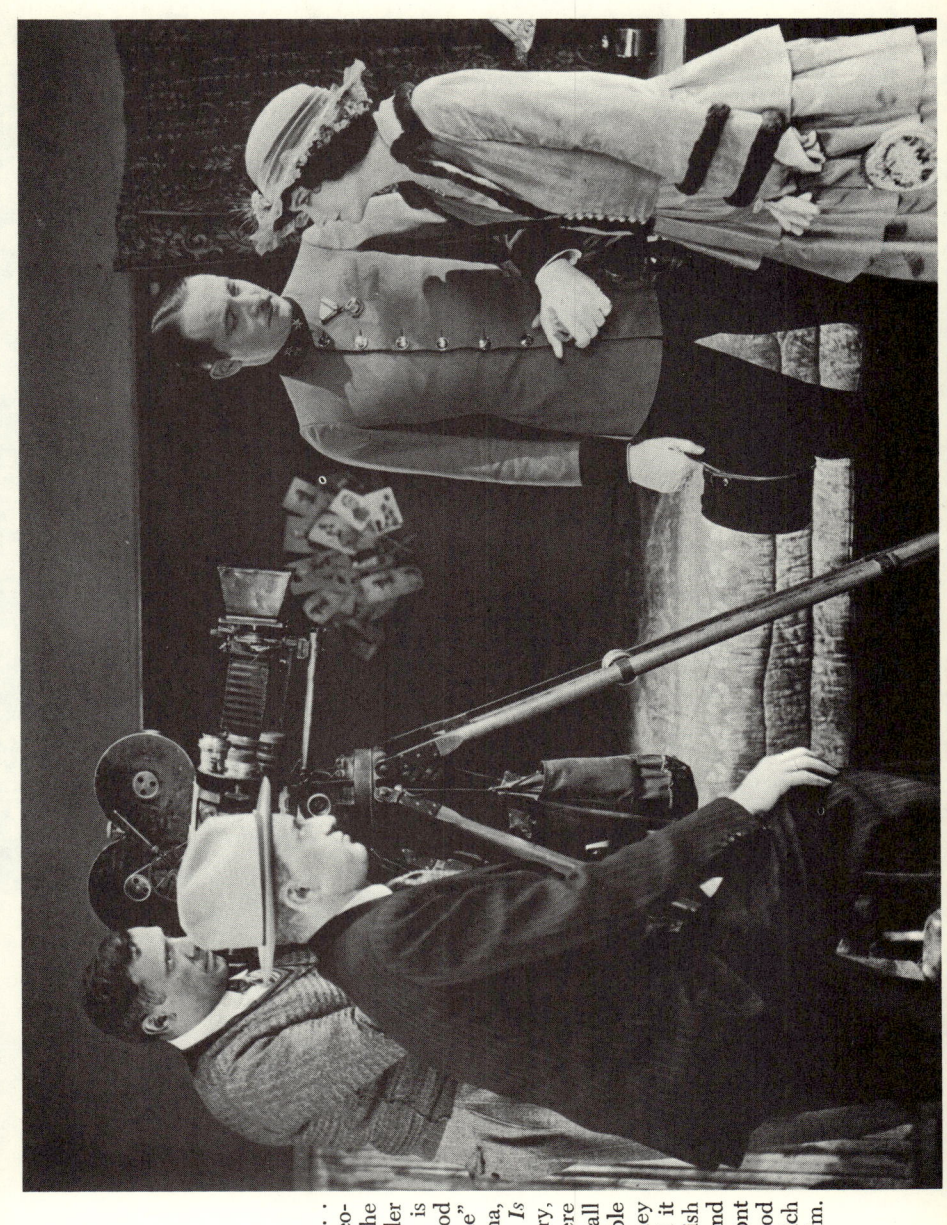

In memoriam... Ewald André Dupont, co-scenarist and director of the great *Variety* (under Pommer at Ufa in 1925) is given for his Hollywood debut a "Stroheimesque" evocation of old Vienna, *Love Me and the World Is Mine* (with Norman Kerry, Mary Philbin—pictured here —and George Siegmann, all from Stroheim's memorable *Merry Go Round*). But they recut and mutilated it and it flopped. After a brief British comeback—*Piccadilly* and *Moulin Rouge*—Dupont ended his days in Hollywood doing trash quickies, which was all they'd give him.

In memoriam . . . When directors used to meet their stars arriving by train with flowers. Paul Bern—scholar, gentleman, brilliant scenarist (of that milestone in screen wit, Lubitsch's *The Marriage Circle*) and director—welcomes to Los Angeles the French star of his new film, *Open All Night*, Jetta Goudal.

If two beers won't settle it, nothing will. Jetta Goudal and Adolphe Menjou in Paul Bern's delightful charade, *Open All Night*, from a story in a book of that name by Paul Morand (1925–blithe year!).

In memoriam . . . Florence Vidor and Adolphe Menjou in the closing scene of Malcolm St. Clair's *The Grand Duchess and the Waiter*.

as imbued with an immense *chic*, if one would not be misunderstood.

Everything counted in his film. There was not a gesture, a word, a shot, anything, that did not add to the whole, contributing its bit to propel the story forward, much like the action of a combustion engine. Anathema to him was that barren fustian or rhetoric that in music is called "passage work" and which, in films, he called "pictorial wasteland."

An idea was refracted by an attitude toward that idea so that it was bent to his purpose. *The Shanghai Gesture*, for example, is a lesson in diffractions, wherein everything that happens has been broken up into its various meanings (tones and overtones), much as rays of light are broken up by interference into all the colors of the spectrum. That "interference" in the making of a Sternberg film was the prism of the director's brain through which his story was filtered and which was refracted into the intellectual glints that made watching a Sternberg film a totally different (and richer) experience than watching most other directors' work.

He was, in a sense, "an old China hand," as the expression has it, but his *chinoiserie* and *japonaiserie* were based less on actual Chinese and Japanese designs than on the Western vision of Cathay. Sternberg had never been to China before he made *Shanghai Express* or *The Shanghai Gesture*, though *Anatahan* was made in Japan. (For that matter, Sternberg was never in North Africa, either, before he made *Morocco*.) All were works of the imagination, of the fantasy of the director, of an idea, a real idea, refracted through the prisms of the director's attitude, his personal vision. A Sternberg film was a very personal thing. (Melville didn't visit Nantucket, either, until after *Moby Dick* was published.)

Remains the matter of Marlene Dietrich . . .

Among those Viennese who attempted to come to terms with Eros were Freud, Schnitzler, and Hofmannsthal—and the Americanized Viennese, Sternberg.

So much has been said on this subject that I will sum it up here by suggesting that she became a prop for his bedizenment fetishes, an object for his sublimative search, a tool for his psychological exorcisms.

In conclusion:

If I were to search for an epigraph to place before an essay which attempted to describe the style of Sternberg as a filmmaker, I don't think I would hesitate to use this from Kafka:

> Leopards break into the temples and drink the sacrificial chalices dry. This occurs repeatedly, again and again; finally, it can be reckoned on beforehand and becomes a part of the ceremony.

Kahlil Gibran once wrote that work is "love made visible . . . if you bake bread with indifference," he noted, "you bake a bitter bread that feeds but half a man's hunger. And if you grudge the crushing of the grapes, your grudge distills a poison in the wine."

Sternberg's works were labors of love. "In a *milieu* with its easy contempt for aesthetic values," I wrote in my book on him, "the hieratic disdain of his style—which ranks with the most patrician filmmaking in the world—is a thrilling thing to see, as it always is wherever work is touched, beyond the call of duty, with the vital grace of art."

Spring, 1970

TRIPTYCH—ITALIAN STYLE

The bars of prisons that keep untold thousands unjustly incarcerated are still up, but the bars of movie censorship are down. . . .

Kyrie eleison!

Our air and waters are polluted, our processed foods tainted with noxious additives, children are dying of hunger or drugs, youths revolting, bombs going off in buildings and airplanes, governments appropriating huge sums for the murder weapons of war including atomic missiles, gasses, bacterial agents, napalm, defoliants that poison sources of food, asphyxiating agents, and war, never-ending war, and the sinews of war, wherever we turn . . . but the bars of movie censorship are down. . . .

Glory hallelujah!

Oil spillage is fouling our seas and coastlines, the last of our natural resources are no longer even slowly disappearing, just as a tin-horn culture has supplanted our historical heritage in our urban centers with loveless and graceless architectural monstrosities. Government appropriations for medical research are cut back, but government price supports to farmers (including rich senator-farmers) continue to subsidize their not growing crops while half the world starves . . . but the bars of movie censorship are down. . . . *Om mani padme hum!*

When one sees the moral cesspool that the Times Square area in New York has become, is one supposed to forget all the above as the background for the offal that is being given public exposure in the name of a "free screen," "free speech," etc?

Moral nihilism has set in, protected by the law (the same law that clubs students) and defended in the newspaper ads with their "hypocrisy of words" (in D. H. Lawrence's apt phrase) when not boasting of the filth, both in sight and sound, that they are now permitted to peddle. So now the screen is polluted, too. Thus is a gullible public (which doubtless gets what it deserves for flocking to these troughs) importuned by the distributors who act as touts for those who have put their money in these wares. We're in a virulent moral inflation.

You could have bet on it. You could have bet on what would happen to the screen once the bars of censorship were down. How could you possibly underestimate the movie producers? How could you underestimate the movie public?

Nietzsche said it in *Thus Spake Zarathustra,* when he has Zarathustra, the superman, report on man as he found him: "They know nothing better than to lie with a woman." And St. Thomas Aquinas said it in the *Summa Contra Gentiles,* when he spoke of those qualities which are most noble in man, which have to do with the intellect and not carnal pleasures. As for Freud, he said nothing else.

"Yonic disturbances," as Ben Hecht called it, or erotic fioritura are one thing, but *tabes dorsalis* is quite another, and the present "free screen" is not only suffering from this disease but is enslaved by it. So much for your "free screen."

Of aesthetic equilibrium there is none. Chesterton said that art, like morality, consists in knowing where to draw the line.

And Cocteau even makes the point by standing it on its head when he refers to the true artist's scrupulous observance of the tenet: to know how far to go too far. The illustrations by Clara Tice for *Woman and Puppet* of Louÿs or by Beardsley for Wilde's *Salome,* for example, are adroit instances of this.

What the new "permissive" films do achieve is, in Christopher Fry's memorable phrase, "the height of depth." They pretend to be profound but they achieve only the apotheosis of the single *entendre*. The makers of so-called "profound" or "deep" films don't realize that film stories are only a pretext, a "hanger" on which a film is hung, so to say. (Just like the subjects of paintings are, for the most part, pretexts to display the art of painting.) In this way, a film differs from a novel or a play. In a film the story, or subject, is only a point of departure, and the extent of the departure connotes the degree of art achieved. Most efforts in films are expended at the arrival at the story idea. By the time the point has been made, the film is over. No thought has been given to the film as film, as an abstraction of itself, which is the only true test of its worth. No matter how valid the subject of a film, it is still only a pretext to create *une matière cinématographique,* a cinematographic subject. The *way* you do it is what it is.

But what Visconti, Antonioni, and Fellini have done in *The Damned, Zabriskie Point,* and *Fellini Satyricon* is not *une matière cinématographique,* but in a phrase they know only too well, they have made *cinematografaro,* which is Roman slang for movie makers who are convinced they can get away with anything. It's a word coined on the Via Veneto and it is as cynical as it sounds.

Each has put things in his film which are unprecedented (consciously or unconsciously following the dictum of Gauguin, "There are only imitators and revolutionaries"?) and in the process of being "novel" (shall we say) they have confused knowledge with wisdom. It is not enough to be "novel," or even "daring," you have to make sense too and, above all, you have to achieve what Aristotle demanded of tragedy, *catharsis,* the purification of the emotions by art. Today we live in a world preoccupied with novelty and the merchandising of a new "avant garde" every Monday morning. Yet despite everyone doing his own thing and that novelty equated with panache, we live in a singularly joyless society. As for style, I don't dare use the word that was once used in connection with Titian, Mozart or, Coleridge . . . except to say that we also live in a singularly styleless society. Worst of all, we live in a society of stupefying vulgarity.

I chose this trio—Visconti, Antonioni, and Fellini—because they are representative of the best filmmaking we have today. Why should I bother with lesser men?

But like the old German hotel manager in Ludwig Bemelmans' *La Bonne Table* used to say when faced with some awful fact:

"Cheeses greised!"

I never expected anything like this. To begin with, Pabst had already graphically portrayed the Nazi inferno in *Der Letzte Akt* (called *The Last Ten Days* here.) fifteen years ago, so *The Damned* (or *Die Götterdämmerung—The Twilight of the Gods*—its original title) is not as novel as all that. And Pabst made a strong, lean film, right to the point, without any of the unedifying sights Visconti feels impelled to foist on his audience (hoping they will be so shocked they will talk about it to others, therefore making for new customers in an endless chain reaction?). A real artist has no need to achieve his catharsis through shock therapy, through literal rendering of atrocities, both homicidal and sexual; a theater, after all, is not an ancient Roman circus arena or even a modern clinic where the goings-on in abattoirs are documented, though that is what our theaters have apparently become. As for the Pabst film, no one mentioned it, and, doubtless, few remember it, in this connection, which is why this book started its foreword with a plaint by Jean Renoir—remember?—"What disturbs me most is the thought that films have such a short life." It is a disturbing thought because the cinema—the good old saintly cinema—is the one art which is not permitted to consolidate its gains. Its history is just a succession of new films, with no roots, and, as a result, no growth and no flowering—only new films. And if no one remembered the Pabst film, who would remember the even older one, the 1923–24 *Kriemhild's Revenge* of Lang—there was a "Götterdämmerung" for you, done with true Wagnerian *Zauberfeuer* by someone who knew what he was doing. It is all well for Signor Visconti to wish to remind us again of the hell the Nazis made of the earth but it is no credit to the director of the noble *La Terra Trema* to be so flat-footed about it and so lacking in imagination. This "House of Atreus" depicted in *The Damned,* whose fortune comes from the blast-furnaces of molten steel in the Ruhr in the early years of Hitlerism, to be turned into Nazi bombs, should not this doomed house have been shown destroyed by the same molten steel become bombs raining down on them from the skies from the R.A.F.? Thus would the biblical prophecy have been fulfilled, as indeed in real life it was: "Those that live by the sword shall die by the sword." This would have been poetic justice. This would have been a true "Götterdämmerung"—this, or its equivalent, would have given the film true visual and ideological form, and form, as Godard has reminded us, is the outside of content. As it is now, *The Damned* has no form. It ends with the same shot of the blast furnace with which it started, which says absolutely nothing. And Pabst's film made a point at the end, which the spectator carried away with him, something, as I recall, about never again saying "Yes" to immoral orders just because they are orders. That is something to remember (here content becomes the inside of form) and is alone a reason to have made the film. If Visconti had not been permitted to indulge himself or his producer with the incredibly gauche incest scene, would he have made the film anyway? He most certainly would not—the picture would then have lacked its central "gimmick," a *sine qua non* at the box office today. There you have the measure of its worth as anything other than a momentary sensation. Q.E.D.

In an androgynous society like today's, where it becomes increasingly difficult to differentiate between girls and boys, a film like *Fellini Satyricon,* which is about homosexuals, hermaphrodites, and other such *goyim naches,* fits, I suppose. It's a humorless (a fault, for a satire) Neronian *"dolce vita"* with but a single joke, and that blasphemes against the dignity of man for the sake of a cheap laugh. Though what can you expect of a society that coins blasphemous jokes like the one about the Roman centurion who is supposed to have snarled, in true traffic-cop style, "I don't care who you are, you can't drag that cross up a one-way street!"

So here it is, human archaeology, i.e., the "jet set" of

Neronian society, with the debonair Signor Fellini as both its Elsa Maxwell (by setting it up) and Lucius Beebe (by telling about it). (Too bad his original idea to cast Mae West, Groucho Marx and Danny Kaye in key roles was bypassed. It might have made the whole thing palatable. As it is, it's like those gargantuan Roman feasts depicted—it looks wonderful but taste it and you get sick.) Perhaps if the voices had been dubbed in Latin, as was also originally planned, the sound track would, at least, have been interesting; as it is, there is nothing in it to regale the ears, nor the mind, for that matter; it is all for the eyes. "And," says Fellini (no director was ever more voluble about himself), "if you see with innocent eyes, everything is divine." But this isn't necessarily so, is it? The child in Andersen's tale, "The Emperor's Clothes," also saw with innocent eyes and, therefore, saw that the Emperor was wearing no clothes. I'm afraid innocent eyes will see Fellini's film the same way. Certainly there is nothing divine about it unless you are playing with words, as Fellini, of course, is—as one woman might have said to another (I know they don't talk that way, anymore) of her friend's new earrings, "My dear, they're simply divine!" Signor Fellini doesn't really wish us to equate his divinity with the divinity of the Sermon on the Mount? "All art is autobiographical," continues Fellini. Does he *really* wish us to equate the porcine peccadilloes of his *Satyricon* with himself? If not, then why say it? Or doesn't it matter what Signor Fellini says? "It doesn't matter," he says. "One mustn't believe too much what I say in interviews. I have a tendency to be rhetorical, to let myself be carried away by my imagination." But he *does* wish us to equate his work and himself for, never at a loss for an apt metaphor, he vouchsafes us, "The pearl is the oyster's autobiography." The world may be, for the moment—O rare, wonderful moment!—Signor Fellini's oyster, but his *Satyricon* is no pearl.

To a public more avid for scandalous anecdote than for balanced historical judgment, *Fellini Satyricon* is just the dish, and I use the metaphor advisedly, there being no concoction around more calculated to sate an appetite for *faisandé* wares. Certainly, if it was the director's intention by drawing on Petronius to depict the Rome of Nero ("before the Christian conscience") as a sewer of iniquity, to arouse horror and revulsion, he may be said to have succeeded. He creates a vivid and lurid picture of life in that city in the first century A.D., partly derived from the cultured Roman cynic who, Tacitus tells us, was both arbiter and friend to the Emperor, and partly from Fellini's own imagination.

Thus do the ancient Roman and modern Italian sophistications meet (does not Fellini assure us that Italians have an innate streak of paganism in them?) but, even more than that, the director justifies his work ("methinks he doth protest too much?") by claiming for it a parallel with today's decadence, today's decline in moral, ethical, and spiritual values. So be it. This has always been claimed for *The Satyricon* itself, in all eras. (And, by the way, I don't accept that "streak of innate paganism in Italians" Fellini says they all have. The most cultured Italian I know hasn't the faintest trace of it and would smile at the thought.) But whereas Petronius looked on the spectacle of human decay with amused and ironic detachment, taking pleasure in describing those passions against nature normally hidden, and those whose only concern is voluptuousness, Fellini wallows in epicene fancies, piling Pelion on Ossa, to make sure we "get" it.

What Pelions and *what* Ossas! There hasn't been such a calorific whoop-de-doo since some of the more recherché Hollywood caliphs' and Chicago meat-packers' saturnalias in the good old days, *olavasholem*, before conglomerates took all the joy out of "doing your thing." Although for Fellini, who is a man who gets around, it's still going on, as witness his further rationale, to wit, "We live in a society today which recalls the Rome just before the coming of Christ, a cynical, perverse, uneasy society, because the old gods had died and the new gods had not yet appeared."

But for all Fellini's sexual didoes, and this aspect of Neronian Rome seems to have intrigued him more than anything else, the work is curiously anti-erotic (although this may have been intentional), being both bold (in some of its explicitness) and skittish (in some of its shyness)—like fake Liszt—so that you end up being exasperated, with the feeling you've been had. With the exceptions of his central characters, the perverts Encolpius and Ascyltus, and perhaps Giton, the object of their affections, his faces, which are so important in successful film dramaturgy, are not evil, they are merely homely. Trimalchio's feast, which made up such a large part of the fragments that survived of what originally were some twenty books, is now just an anecdote among a string of similar baneful anecdotes, each more grotesque than the others, as the raucous and bawdy Graeco-Roman society of the time is paraded before us, a kaleidoscope of zombies which the spectator has to understand as the author-director's excursion into "science fiction," as he calls it— "a journey into the unknown, like describing the life found on the planets Mercury or Mars, but in this case a pagan planet, unknown to the spectator. It was a world in which charity and conscience did not exist, in the Christian sense. The audience will have the sensation of being surrounded by mysterious masks, ghosts and shadows, the like of which they have never before seen."

If someone were to say to me that he found "a diabolic intelligence" behind this film, I would agree, but, on the other hand, if another would call it all rather *fa lal,* or "a bit long in the tooth," as our English cousins say, I would also agree. That's the kind of ambiguous filmmaking we have today. In the end I find myself rejecting all this intelligence put to the service of the moral equivalents of cock fights as a substitute for revelations of the human condition. Aren't such illuminations what every work is obligated to make a statement about? Emotionally the film lacks the satirical center of the book; stylistically it lacks an imperative, that imperative being the poetry and mystery and "bouquet" that would have made it persuasive, even the kind that De Mille knew how to give this sort of thing, so that you *are* persuaded. Of course, the difference is that De Mille believed in his vision of antiquity, Fellini doesn't, and even when it comes to trumpery, it's the believer's vision that will persuade, rather than the unbeliever's, for all the latter's intelligence. I never for a moment felt I was anywhere but in the Cinecittà Studios of Rome or its environs, for all the Bosch-like faces with which Fellini crowded his own canvas. And, of course, the reason why there is no revelation of the human condition for us today is obvious, according to Fellini, because no such revelation in our own terms is possible in the depiction of a pre-Christian world, whose society and mentality are completely foreign to us. This may be true, but you've got to have, in a work of satire, some moral recoil, else where's the satire? The moral recoil remains outside the film, in the director's statement: "I have only the greatest disgust for the orgies in my film. The proof? Each time I pass the Colosseum, where during its peak as an arena they slaughtered more than ten thousand persons a day, I feel like vomiting." But the film as an emetic, like the Colosseum, remains.

Forty-five years ago, out of a *milieu* as convulsive as pagan Rome—post-World War I Berlin—came a truly erotic film, *Variety*, a masterpiece not only of sophisticated film making but of imagery in the delineation of sex (heterosexual, to be sure, which is not quite so recalcitrant for the artist to deal with) that did not play at suttee with one's sensibilities but reinforced them by its veracity—and in its own intellectually measured way it went the whole way. The irony is that Fellini's film, for all its literalness, never really does. Petronius, in any case, was not the bitter moralist that Juvenal was in the latter's own satires, and neither is Fellini, for whom this film, so aptly named (like "Saudi Arabia"), is a veritable "Roman holiday," with all that this dubious phrase implies. The point is: I never read a word by director E. A. Dupont in rationalization of his *Variety*. They didn't have to "protest" so much in those days—they just quietly made masterpieces. Today, the plethora of interviews a director gives, to get publicity for his film, become part of the film; we have to take it all into consideration, in order to fully understand his work. Never has there been such a flood of words for the moviegoer to read. . . .

Life used to be simpler, especially for the filmmaker, like Eisenstein's precept:

> *Primo—the cadre.*
> *Secondo—the shot.*

How about it, Mr. Fellini?

I think of Sternberg's own discreet fragments of *I, Claudius*, in which the accent is on what is *said*, this being a work directed at the mind, in its own incarnation of ancient Rome, the Rome of another monster, Caligula, but portrayed in a film as ordered and stylized as a pavane. For all that appeals to the mind in *Fellini Satyricon*, the dialogue could have been any kind of gibberish. Or I think of the marvelous sense of antiquity of the

Sibley Watson–Melville Webber miracle, *Lot in Sodom* (with its equally marvelous musical score by Louis Siegel, which makes it also something for the ear), which could teach Fellini a lesson in how you portray homosexuality and cruelty and like aberrations, not as catnip for the mob (unless, of course, that's what you set out to do), but with a cauterizing effect, which heals and cleanses as it burns, because it *has* a moral recoil. In this brief retelling of the story of Lot and the wrath of God that was visited upon the cities of the plain is the tact and poetry (and Old Testament fury) of which the Fellini film is completely bereft. I think of how Edgar Saltus put it so succinctly in his *Historia Amoris:* "It was the mission of Rome to make conquests, not statues, not to create, but to quell. Her might reverberated in her name. Roma means strength. It is only in reading it backwards that Amor appears. Love there was secondary. Might had precedence. It was Might that made first the home, then the state, then the senate that ruled the world." Do not these few words say it all?

Sans poetry, literal renderings of sex and/or violence become redundant, and redundancy is a bore.

The French director, Marcel L'Herbier, once called the cinema "the white man's opium." Both the white man's and the "yellow" man's opium are, however, valuable commodities in the market place—in the cinemas of the world on the one hand, and in the warrens and hutches of the world on the other, where drivel of the most stupefying sort makes fortunes at the box-office and a pound of uncut opium selling for $35,000 in the illicit market, has a retail value, cut, of $800,000.

Which is all the more reason why the conscientious director cannot abdicate his responsibility as an artist.

Finally, I wonder how such "sex subjects" as *M, Maedchen in Uniform, Ecstasy, Pandora's Box, The Baker's Wife, Secrets of a Soul, The Blue Angel, The Devil is a Woman,* and, God forbid, *Kiss Me Again* of Lubitsch, would be treated today, on today's "permissive" screen, if they were remade. The mind boggles at the thought. That's the measure of corruption of the screen today.

Anyway, the greatest satire on the *mœurs* of antiquity (it happens to be of Greece, not Rome) is a ravishing film made thirty-six years ago by Reinhold Schuenzel, his French version of

Amphitryon. This is how you do it, how you make the world a better place for your being in it. The director of *La Strada* was such an artist, but for me the director of *Fellini Satyricon* is not.

Remains—the last panel of the "triptych."
Zabriskie Point.

In one of Chekov's plays someone says, "When people don't know what to say, they say, 'Ah, youth!' "

I don't think Antonioni had nearly as much to say as he thinks he did with his cross-cut of some of the things that are wrong with America. Certainly, his two young protagonists, the boy and girl, are as two-dimensional, flat, and characterless, as the billboard or television dummies he shows as indictments of the plastic and plexiglass culture of America. We never know them, they are just symbols of youth, making symbolic, passionless love in the desert (such cardboard figures are they that they never perspire and seem not in the least uncomfortable, groveling on the burning sand in 120° heat), and the words they say don't come from any heart or brain but from the front of the mouth, via a movie script. In short, everything in the film is surfaces—the people, the landscape, and the things that happen, like the opening confrontation of students at a protest meeting in which we never learn what they are protesting.

It is enough for Antonioni to show his audience that he is "with it" by opening his "documentary" with a protest scene to set the tone for his theme—revolt against the Establishment. Now this is a very salutary theme and some great films have come out of such an idea, from *Potemkin, Mother,* and *Storm Over Asia,* to *Zéro de Conduite* and *La Marseillaise.* But you don't achieve revolutionary passion through a succession of posters, which is what *Zabriskie Point* so frequently looks like. (How photogenic Death Valley is! Antonioni admits he chose it as a locale because "it's so beautiful" and he "loves landscapes." Compare this reason for chosing Death Valley with Stroheim's for *Greed.*)

We recognize his "posters" for what they symbolize (I was about to say "advertise," which is the same thing) and have to accept the emotions of his protagonists entirely on the director's say-so. Besides, in a film about revolution, if you want to be convincing, you don't literally muck it up with a long copulation scene (compounded by a reprise from the chorus in which some dozen or twenty additional couples echo the protagonists' frenzy with a balletic abstraction of their copulation—surely the Blue Ribbon With Palms winner of the Idiocy Sweepstakes in film imagery). The viewer begins to wonder: Is this the dog and the rest of the film the tail, or is it the other way around? Which is wagging which? Even Antonioni's Death Valley has no character, only picture-postcard prettiness. His protagonists might as well have been in Palm Springs or any other desert resort. There was nothing of the sense of heat, of burning sun, of blanched salt flats and scrub brush blackened by the murderous fireball in the sky that we felt in Stroheim's *Greed*. Besides which, Antonioni played it safe, he stayed on the edge of Death Valley, photographing the very picturesque Panamint Mountains. After all, the place as such plays no role in his story, as it did in *Greed*, does it?

His humorous flirtation of the young man's plane buzzing the girl's jalopy also doesn't make sense because he couldn't possibly know a *girl* was driving from where he was, but Antonioni is so tickled by the "cuteness" of this scene that he not only doesn't think how it could never happen but he holds it for an unconscionable while. Sternberg achieved wryly amusing "aerotics" in *Jet Pilot* when he has the two planes of his hero-pilot and heroine-pilot briefly "nuzzling" each other in the air—and they *know* who their partners are in this *jeu d'esprit*—but then Antonioni is no Sternberg.

Is there *anything* on the positive side? Yes—a few glints of raffish humor, a couple of real characters the director encounters in the desert and whom he lets speak their own speech, some good (if by now familiar) documentation of garish, gaudy California vs. the bleak but, by contrast, heavenly desert landscapes after the appalling junk culture of urban and suburban America —and, perhaps best of all, at least an attempt to achieve that catharsis we previously spoke of, at the end . . . the senseless killing of the boy, when he comes to return his stolen plane, by the goon cops lying in wait for him, which triggers an allegorical blowing up of the Establishment in reprisal. After all, hasn't a voice no less than that of William Douglas of the Supreme Court in his book, *Points of Rebellion*, advocated revolution if necessary to achieve justice? It's a brave thing for a foreigner to do, just as it was a brave thing for Fritz Lang to make, as his first American film, a savage indictment of American lynch mob psychology in *Fury*. That was in 1936. Thirty-four years later, foreigners are still criticizing America for things so obviously wrong with this country that they cannot be ignored. What's the matter with America?

So *Zabriskie Point* is a mixed bag, of the good and bad. I prefer the Antonioni of *Il Grido*, just as I prefer the Hitchcock of *The 39 Steps* to the director of *Psycho* and *The Birds*, and, as I stated before, the Visconti of *La Terra Trema* and the Fellini of *La Strada*, in the days of their purity, before they became so successful, before they became bloated with that success. ("The artistic health of a director doesn't last long," says Fellini.) There's a fine line in Orson Welles' *The Lady from Shanghai* where Welles, as "Black Irish," the seaman, says to his rich and arrogant employer, "I've always found it sanitary to be broke." There's something sanitary about those earlier films of these men. Someone once described a young child as "fresh from the hand of God." I would describe these earlier films as fresh from the hands of artists, not rich artists. There's a difference.

It is ironic to see that as the youthful discretion of Fellini (*Variety Lights, The White Sheik, I Vitelloni*, etc.) matured into the anarchic creator of miasmic mists like *Giulietta of the Spirits* and *Fellini Satyricon*, the anarchic fury of the youthful Buñuel (*Un Chien Andalou, L'Age d'Or*, etc.) has matured into the mellow creator of so discreet and gentle a work as *The Milky Way*. Despite all the "permissiveness" of the current screen, Buñuel continues to make films the way he has always made them, since 1928, never resorting to explicitness or literalness in sex, and utilizing for some of his most expressive effects one of the great Buñuelian matrices: surrealism. As his colleagues have become more bold and feverish, he has become more circumspect and reflective. Who, would you say, has *really* matured?

My "Italian Triptych" is all but done. Remains only the three men themselves, the men behind the artists. What about them? Why argue with any man's error when it is his error that he is? But who will exorcise the dybbuk that is haunting them? Perhaps the illustrious gentlemen will understand me if I quote their countryman, Metastasio:

> *Se a ciascun l'interno affanno*
> *si leggesse in fronte scritto,*
> *quanti mai che invidia fanno*
> *ci farebbero pietà!*
>
> (*If each one's inner worry*
> *were written on his brow,*
> *how many would we pity*
> *whom we envy now!*)

Do you know Chaplin's *The Adventurer?* It's a twenty-minute trifle he turned out in 1917. It is a miracle of virtuosity and charm. I wouldn't swap it for all three of these super-duper features of Italy's three greatest directors. I'm not even talking about *The Immigrant* and *The Cure.*

Nor Bresson's description of the calvary of a little donkey named Balthazar . . .

What is Visconti's *Götterdämmerung* at the end of *The Damned* as against Captain Ahab, as described by Melville, looking on the dying attempt of a harpooned sperm whale to hold its head toward the sinking sun, and commenting sadly, "Life dies sunward full of faith"?

After glimpsing the eternal bliss of Watteau's *L'Embarquement pour Cythère* or Fragonard's *Girl Reading*, is it possible to be ever satisfied with imagery of less enchantment, in or out of the movies? And what revelation, what illumination, do such pretentious works as the three films we have discussed have to match even the minuscule but immortal line of Heraclitus of 2500 years ago: "When people are awake, they enjoy one world in common, but asleep, each roams a world of his own."

As I write this, there is a rumbling of what may prove to be the next genuine advent in the cinema, following the present half-gods. Over the horizon there is said to be a new young Russian director, Andrei Tarkovski, who has made a film called *Rublèv.* . . .

A friend, recently returned from the Middle East, said that driving from Beirut to Tripoli his car was stopped by children selling tourists daisies and other wild flowers which they had fashioned into necklaces. He bought all they had and left a bevy of smiling faces. It was, he said, the most beautiful day of his life.

Each does what he can. All offerings are equal in the sight of God.

Spring, 1970

Old friends.
TOP: Hans Richter (with George Méliès, at the Château Orly in France, 1937). MIDDLE: Robert Florey (as associate director) and Chaplin during the shooting of *Monsieur Verdoux*, 1946. BOTTOM: Jean Renoir, René Clair and Florey at Clair's home in Beverly Hills, 1942.

Old friends.
TOP: King Vidor, 1953. BOTTOM: Fritz Lang and the author at the Montreal Exposition, 1967.

L'ENVOI

Like the Irish say, there are three sides to every question—mine, yours, and the hell with it.

There is a legend that monkeys really know how to speak, but don't so that men will not put them to work.

"Paintings are not made to decorate apartments or museums—they are instruments of war against brutality and darkness." (*Picasso*)

"It is necessary to know not to be timid with the camera, to do violence to it, to force it beyond its last boundaries, because it is a vile machine. What counts is the poetry." (*Orson Welles*)

The ancient Greeks are said to have designed their alphabet after watching cranes in flight.

"I never made *avant-garde* pictures purposely. Bresson has said that originality is when you try to do like everyone else but don't quite make it." (*Jean Renoir*)

"How wonderful women are," says a character in one of Sacha Guitry's plays. "How tender and sympathetic they are, how they minister to us when we are ill." Then, almost as an afterthought, "But we can't always be ill, can we?"

"What I like about Hollywood is that one can get along quite well by knowing just two words of English—*swell* and *lousy*." (*Vicki Baum*, author of *Grand Hotel*.)

Michelangelo spoke of "removing the excess stone to reveal the figure God had already made inside." And Eisenstein spoke of "hewing out a piece of actuality with the axe of the lens."

"He is dying," said Bourdelle of his sculpture, *The Dying Centaur*, "because no one believes in him."

The thing against pornography is that it is sex without piquancy. It is sexual inflation—valueless. "Cold mutton," in the phrase of Wilde.

Reported by *The New York Times* from Rome, April 10, 1969: "The Vatican City newspaper, *L'Osservatore Romano*, said today that a flood of obscene films portended a dim outlook for the motion picture. The critic, Claudio Sorgi, wrote: 'I don't think there is much hope for the future of the cinema. Shortly, if not already, it will no longer be possible to enter a movie house because the mere fact of stepping in to it, apart from the film actually showing, may mean entering an indecent place, a brothel for maniacs.'"

Of how few of today's films can it be said that they are, as Howard Clurman said of Isadora Duncan's dancing, "as free of prurience as lightning."

"With Rossellini a shot is beautiful because it is just—but with others it becomes just only by dint of being beautiful." (*Jean-Luc Godard*)

Pío Baroja, the Spanish novelist, speaks of those who have not the brains to protest about anything. "Back of all this correctness, this very proper chatter about all the right things, may be divined the optimism of eunuchs."

The right cut in a film is like what Isaac Babel, the Russian novelist, said of writing: "No steel can pierce the human heart so chillingly as a period at the right moment."

And apropos the current rage for nudity in the films, one is reminded of J. K. Huysmans' appraisal of Degas' nudes, women bathing, etc. "Never have works been so lacking in slyness or questionable overtones. They even glorify a disdain for carnality as no artist since the Middle Ages has dared to do it."

"A picture," said Degas, "is something which requires as much knavery, trickery and deceit as the perpetration of a crime. The artist does not draw what he sees but what he must make others see. Only when he no longer knows what he is doing does the painter do good things."

". . . the endearing, misbegotten Egyptian scenery of *Intolerance* . . ." (Herbert Whitaker, *Toronto Globe & Mail*)

Jim Tully, the Irish writer who flourished in the blithe days of Mencken and Nathan, referred to "the torrent that was Stroheim." He went on to say, "For in that far day, when those who follow us will be able to get a perspective on film history, Stroheim is likely to be considered the first one of genuine and original talent to break his heart against the stone wall of cinema imbecility."

With Stroheim it was *"Aut Caesar, aut nihil."* (Caesar or nothing!) Echoed by William Faulkner who said (in *Wild Palms*), "Between grief and nothing, I will take grief."

Of the length of *Greed*—of all long works—one might recall that it was Thomas Mann's cherished conviction that only the exhaustive is truly interesting. So *Greed* (in the 24-reel final cut of Stroheim) would have taken four or five hours to show. It took sixty-seven years to build the cathedral of Notre Dame. A conventional film runs, perhaps, two hours and a conventional modern office building of even sixty storeys is completed in under a year. It's a matter of what your goal is.

"All great people function with the heart. . . . Always remember to think with it, to feel with it, and above all, to judge with it." (Zuloaga, Spanish portrait painter)

The heart, that epicenter of a man's physical as well as spiritual life. At the end, it failed Von Sternberg, as it did so many men. Said *The New York Times* in its eulogy of him, "The director ended his autobiography with a sentence from Goethe that might have been his own:

> The greatest happiness of man is to explore that which is explorable and to revere that which is unexplorable.

How many of our current film directors would have been capable of such a thought, or would have been impelled to utter it? In that you have the measure of Von Sternberg. Or in these lines from his Japanese threnody on the human condition, *Anatahan*:

> The full moon of the autumn equinox is the time for the Ohigan festival, when we pay respect to our ancestors. Our thoughts then go from them to our families. The word *Higan* means the other shore. It is taken from the Buddhist legend that there is a river marking the division of this earthly world to a future one. This river is full of illusion, passion, pain, and sorrow. Only when you cross the river, having fought the currents of temptation to gain the far shore, do you reach enlightenment. . . .

Vale, vale . . !

Finally . . .

Two reflections about mirrors:

"Mirrors do but show us masks." (*Oscar Wilde*)

"Mirrors would do well to think before they cast their reflections back at us." (*Jean Cocteau*)

To which I would add a third:

"What a wonderful world it would be if it were peopled by those we see reflected back at us in mirrors."

Spring, 1970

AFTERWORD

"For this is the journey men must make to find themselves. If they fail in this, it doesn't matter much what else they find. But if a man happens to find himself, if he knows what he can be depended upon to do, the limits of his courage, the position from which he will no longer retreat, the secret reservoirs of his determination, the extent of his dedication, the depth of his feeling for beauty, his honest and unpostured goals —then he has found a mansion which he can inhabit with dignity all the days of his life."

—James Michener,
The Fires of Spring

The main thing is to have patience and to keep shuffling the cards.

Cervantes, *Don Quixote*

AUTHOR'S NOTE

Herman G. Weinberg grew up with the movies, having been born before they were hardly anything more than a side-show entertainment at fairs, or a "peep show" ("Which is what they've become again, coming full circle," he says, "after a half-century of dubious progress.") He was born in New York City in 1908 and in 1923, at the age of 15, he says he saw the film that "started it all" for him—*Foolish Wives*, by Erich von Stroheim. ("The 14-reel version," he emphasizes, "not the pitiful 7-reel fragment that has survived in the U.S.") Like Jean Renoir in France, around the same time, he wanted to become associated with a medium which could produce so remarkably fascinating a work as this. After "flirting" (as he puts it) with the violin for several years as a student of Louis Svecenski at the Institute of Musical Art (forerunner of the Juilliard School), preparatory to a possible concert career, he changed his mind and entered the field of motion pictures, first arranging the music for silent foreign films, then subtitling them when sound came in. He estimates he has titled over 400 French, Italian, German, etc. films, and for a long while held a virtual "monopoly" in this profession here. ("Chiefly," he says, "because no one else seemed interested in entering the field.") He began writing about films in 1929 after seeing Dreyer's *The Passion of Joan of Arc*, his first writings appearing in *Close Up*, that seminal periodical of all film periodicals. Since then he has contributed ("That's the right word, too," he opines, "as they either didn't pay or paid so little as to amount to the same thing.") to most of the leading film journals throughout the world. He has lectured extensively on film aesthetics in the United States and Canada, inaugurated the Index Series on directors for the British Film Institute, as well as a column, *Coffee, Brandy and Cigars* (begun almost two decades ago), comprising "notes for an as yet unwritten history of the motion pictures." In 1960–61 he served as juror at the San Francisco and Vancouver International Film Festivals, and in 1964 mounted an elaborate exhibition, "Homage to Erich von Stroheim," at the Montreal International Film Festival. The following year he delivered a memorial address on Stroheim at the New York Film Festival and in 1966 at the Canadian Film Institute in Ottawa. He translated and edited the American editions of *50 Years of Italian Cinema* and *50 Years of Opera and Ballet in Italy* and has contributed ("Still the right word!" he says) to many anthologies of film writings here and abroad, notably several published by the Venice Film Festival. He was for ten years American correspondent for *Sight & Sound* (London) and served in a similar capacity for *Cahiers du Cinéma* (Paris), among other periodicals. His short film, *Autumn Fire*, an early classic of the first American *avant-garde*, is now in the collections of most of the principal film museums here and abroad. He has been "profiled" in The New Yorker's *Talk of the Town* and in *Esquire* and has been working on a *magnum opus*, *Sin and Cinema*, a moral history of the movies, on and off for the past decade until he recently gave it up because, as he put it, "the subject got out of hand." In 1967 he published a critical study, *Josef von Sternberg*, following it the next year with another, *The Lubitsch Touch*. 1970 saw the appearance of the first edition of *Saint Cinema*. In the Spring of 1972 a reconstruction by him of the original version of Stroheim's masterwork, *The Complete "Greed,"* via 400 stills, was issued by the Arno Press. Since 1960 he has been teaching a course on the history of motion pictures as an art at the City College in New York and in 1973 conducted a seminar on that subject at the Graduate Center of the City University of New York.

INDEX

Only names of persons and films are indexed. Film titles are listed only in the language in which they appear in the text. Credits listings are not indexed. Italic numbers refer to illustration pages.

Abrahamson, Ben, 197
Accattone, 177
Achard, Marcel, 315
Adams, Henry, 89
Adventurer, The, 347
Aeschylus, 221
Aesop, 109
Agate, James, 44
Age d'Or, L', 165, 179, 207, 346
Agee, James, 172, 322
"Aicha la Noire," 235
Alarcón, Pedro Antonio de, 298, 311
Alcibiades, 221
Alexander Nevsky, 145, 233
Alexander the Great, 280
Alexandrov, Grigori, 26, 71, 73, 178, 185, 186, 242, 249, 261
All About Eve, 187, 206, 225
Allain, Marcel, 252
Allégret, Marc, 320
All Quiet on the Western Front, 20, 166, 229
American Tragedy, An, 261, 321
Amiche, Le, 182
Amphitryon, 27, 28, 29, 30, 243, 267, 281, 344
Anacreon, 221
Andersen, Hans Christian, 52, 221, 339
Anderson, Maxwell, 199
Andrássy, Count Gyula, 248
Anet, Claude, 87
Angel, Norman, 199
Angel Exterminador, El, 213, 214, 237, 253, 254
Anger, Kenneth, 214
Animal Farm, 108 - 111
Annabella, 224, 285
Anna Christie, 178

A Nous la Liberté, 164, 171, 320
Antheil, George, 267
Antonioni, Michelangelo, 182, 202, 204, 336, 337, 344, 345, 346
Aoki, Tsuru, 286
Apollinaire, Guillaume, 197, 240, 252
A Propos de Nice, 172
Aragon, Louis, 253
Archangel Gabriel and Mrs. Gans, 242
Archer, Eugene, 168
Are Parents People?, 142, 298
Ariane, 320
Aristides, 221
Aristophanes, 67, 221
Aristotle, 221
Armendariz, Pedro, 238
Armistead, Lewis A., 233
Arnna, Jacques, 12
Arno, Sig, 216
Arp, Jean, 266
Artaud, Antonin, 12, 13, 244, 266
Aspasia, 111
Astor, Mary, 309
Atalante, L', 172
Atget, Eugène, 252
Atlantide, L', 25, 242, 281, 320
Attasheva, Pera, 320
Attila, 84
Auclair, Michel, 214
Auden, W(ystan) H(ugh), 167
Auer, Mischa, 216
Augustine, St., 221
Aumont, Jean-Pierre, 162
Auriol, Jean-Georges, 320
Autant-Lara, Claude, 266
Autumn Fire, 356
Avventura, L', 172, 223

Babel, Isaac, 351
Bach, Johann Sebastian, 196, 198, 201, 228, 264
Backstairs, 107, 191, 209
Bacon, Sir Francis, 256
Baker's Wife, The, 66, 67, 68, 343
Bakshy, Alexander, 321
Balbusch, Peter, 72
Ballet Mécanique, 16, 263, 266
Balzac, Honoré de, 67, 206

Bancroft, George, 231
Bandera, La, 130
Banditti a Orgosolo, 173
Banky, Vilma, 232
Bara, Theda, 174
Barbier, George, 216
Bardelys the Magnificent, 144
Bardot, Brigitte, 191, 214, 236, 277
Baroja, Pío, 351
Baron Munchhausen, 177
Barrès, Maurice, 264
Barroso, Ary, 244
Barrymore, John, 191, 204, 310
Barthelmess, Richard, 187, 258
Bas-Fonds, Les, 130
Bataille, La, 231, 281, 284, 285, 286
Bauchau, Patrick, 181
Baudelaire, Charles, ii
Baum, Vicki, 194, 350
Baur, Harry, xii, 49
Baxter, Anne, 145
Beardsley, Aubrey, 336
Beatles, The, 242
Beatrice (Portinari), 107
Beaumarchais, Pierre Augustin Caron de, 327
Beaver Dam, 205
Beck, Julian, 182
Becker, Jacques, 236
Beckett, Samuel, 171
Bed and Sofa, 321
Beebe, Lucius, 339
Beerbohm, Max, 220
Beethoven, Ludwig van, 133, 196, 250, 309
Behan, Brendan, 181
Behrendt, Hans, 211, 212
Bell, Marie, 50, 51
Bell, Monta, 232, 306, 309
Belle et la Bête, La, 189
Belle Lola, La, 176
Belmondo, Jean-Paul, 177, 199
Bemelmans, Ludwig, 337
Benedek, Laszlo, 241
Ben Hur, 30, 145, 146, 148, 163, 171, 190
Bennett, Arnold, 319
Bennett, Compton, 183, 231
Benoit, Pierre, 25
Bentley, Eric, 315

Beranger, André de, 216
Berg, Gretchen, 167, 181, 210, 214, 224, 227, 270
Bergé, Francine, 253
Bergman, Ingmar, xii, 143, 144, 164, 173, 202, 230
Bergman, Ingrid, 243
Bergner, Elizabeth, 34, 320
Bergson, Henri, 179
Berley, 12
Berlioz, Hector, 44
Bern, Paul, 205, 330, 331
Bernard, Armand, 30, 267
Bernhardt, Sarah, 162, 191
Bernstein, Henry, 55
Best of Everything, The, 229, 230
Bête Humaine, La, 52, 56
Bierce, Ambrose, 162
Bigger Than Life, 171
Big Parade, The, 140, 166, 171
Birds, The, 346
Birth of a Nation, The, 2, 135, 183, 233, 242, 319
Biscuit Eater, The, 130
Bismarck, Otto von, 251
Bitzer, Billy, 242
Black Orpheus, 146, 162
Black Sunday, 321
Blakeston, Oswell, 320
Blanchar, Pierre, 51
Blasco-Ibáñez, Vicente, 264
Blind Husbands, 40, 41, 114, 117, 130, 132, 150
Blinn, Holbrook, 164
Bloem, Walter, 104
Blood and Sand, 204
Blood of a Poet, 92
Blore, Eric, 216
Blue, Monte, 202, 317
Blue Angel, The, 95, 141, 147, 166, 175, 266, 343
Blum, Léon, 65
Boardman, Eleanor, 144, 310, 311, 312, 314
Bobrov, Georgi, 186
Boccaccio, Giovanni, 88, 188, 242
Boccaccio 70, 188
Bogart, Humphrey, 243
Bogdanovich, Peter, 181 - 2
Bohr, Niels, 267
Boitel, Jeanne, 30, 267
Bond, Kirk, 299
Booth, John Wilkes, 265
Bosch, Hieronymus, 341
Boswell, James, xiii
Bourdelle, Emile Antoine, 350
Bowles, Paul, 266
Box of Pandora, The, 20, 25
Boyd, Ernest, 138
Boyd, William, 140
Boyer, Charles, 183, 231, 249, 282, 283, 284, 285, 286, 294
Boyer, C. Philip, 236
Boyle, Kay, 199
Bracey, Sidney, 118, 151, *153*
Brahe, Tycho, 38
Brahms, Johannes, 263, 324
Brauner, Arthur, 238
Breathless, 163
Brecht, Bertolt, 19, 23, 24, 277
Breer, Robert, 168

Breit, Harvey, 216
Bressart, Felix, 216
Bresson, Robert, 256, 264, 347, 350
Breton, André, 253
Breughel, Pieter (the Elder), 43, 104
Brialy, Jean-Claude, 177
Bridges, Lloyd, 183
Brig, The, 256
Britt, Mai, 147
Broken Blossoms, 171
Bronson, Betty, 142
Bronze Christ, The, 226
Brooks, Louise, 191, 228, 263
Brown, Roland, 188
Browning, Tod, 188
Bruant, Aristide, 251
Bryher, Winifred, 319
Buchwald, Art, 194
Buñuel, Luis, 165, 173, 179, 207, 213, 227, 230, 236, 242, 253, 254, 265, 346
Buñuel, Rafael, 227
Bunyan, John, 246
Burke, Thomas, 83
Burroughs, John, 264
Burroughs, William, 264
Burton, Michael, 168
Burton, Richard, 226
Busch, Mae, 118
Bushman, Francis X., 163
Byron, Lord, 215, 221
Byron, Walter, *156*

Cabinet of Dr. Caligari, The, 25, 84, 85, 139, 180, 183, 191, 208, 209
Cadieux, Germain, 170
Caesar, Julius Caius, 352
Calder, Alexander, 266
Calder-Marshall, Arthur, 228
Caldwell, Erskine, 130
Caligula, 342
Candide, 93
Capra, Frank, 130
Card, James, 190
Cardiff, Jack, 188
Carmen, 266
Carné, Marcel, 211, 266
Carnet de Bal, Un, xii, 49, 50, 51, 242
Carpenter, John Alden, 196
Carr, Harry, 113, 118
Carroll, Nancy, 309
Caruso, Enrico, 35
Carver, Kathryn, *302, 303*
Casablanca, 243
Casals, Pablo, 172, 196, 197
Casanova, Giacomo, 149
Castellani, Renato, 106
Cat and the Canary, The, 164
Cather, Willa, 166
Catlett, Walter, 216
Cau, Jean, 143
Cavalcanti, Alberto, 320
Cayatte, André, 266
Cellini, Benvenuto, 221
Cervantes, Miguel de, 204, 265, 321, 354
Cézanne, Paul, 86, 137
Chabrol, Claude, 161
Chaliapin, Fyodor, 266

Champfleury, 198
Chaney, Lon, 139, 204
Chaplin, Charles, 6, 14, *15, 16*, 17, 18, 77, 78, 79, 80 - 82, 103, 116, 124, 127, 130, 144, 146, 148, 149, 164, 182, 187, 198, 201, 220, 225, 232, 233, 235, 239, 240, 244, 260, 264, 296, 298, 300, 301, 306, 309, 314, 315, 321, 347, *348*
Chaplin, Oona, 264
Chaplin, Sydney, 14, 17
Charcot, Jean Martin, 200
Charlot cubiste, 16
Chekhov, Anton, 230, 344
Chekhov, Michael, 216, 266
Chesterton, Gilbert K., 180, 335
Chien, Andalou, Un, 346
Chienne, La, 52, 130
Chimes at Midnight, 265
Chopin, Frédéric, 147, 287
Citizen Kane, 125, 143
City Lights, 15, 183, 198
Civilisation à travers les âges, La, 164
Clair, René, 4, 5, 6, 8, 124, 130, 162, 164, 178, 192, 202, 244, 266, 296, 320, *348*
Claudel, Paul, 164, 285
Cleopatra, 174, 205, 206, 221, 223, 226, 227
Clurman, Howard, 351
Cochrane, Gifford, 142
Cochrane, R. H., 131
Cocteau, Jean, 92, 18?, 214, 220, 221, 222, 244, 250, 266, 336, 353
Cody, Sherwin, 195
Coeur Gros Comme Ça, Un, 167, 176
Cohen, John S., Jr., 105, 193, 300, 304, 306, 307, 308
Colbert, Claudette, 205, 226
Coleridge, Samuel Taylor, 198, 336
Colman, Ronald, 232
Coming of Amos, The, 205
Compson, Betty, 244
Confidential Report, 122, 123, 124 - 126, 140, 141, 166, 180, 193
Connolly, Walter, 216
Conti, Albert, 307, 309
Cooper, Gary, 187, 198
Corday, Charlotte, 62
Cordy, Raymond, 216
Corelli, Arcangelo, 90
Cossart, Ernest, 216
Côté, Guy, 169
Countess from Hong Kong, A, 260
Covarrubias, Miguel, 194
Coward, Noel, 166, 194
Crack in the Mirror, 163
Crawford, Joan, 164
Crevel, René, 319
Crewes, Laura Hope, 216
Crime Without Passion, 241, 242, 281
Crisis, 25
Crocker, Harry, 232
Croisière Jaune, La, 31, 32

Cronyn, Hume, 223
Crowd, The, 127
Crowther, Bosley, 243
Cure, The, 347
Curtiss, Thomas Quinn, 130, 138, 141, 193, 194, 196
Czinner, Paul, 209, 320
Dacheux, 12
Dadascope, 266
Dagover, Lil, 209
Daguerre, Louis Jacques, 299
Dame Blanche, La (script), 154, 161
Dames du Bois de Boulogne, Les, 208
D'Amico, Silvio, 295
Damned, The, 336, 337, 338, 347
Damn Yankees, 175
D'Annunzio, Gabriele, 144
Danton, Georges Jacques, 63, 107, 184, 202
D'Arcy, Roy, 164, 191
Dark Angel, The, 232
Darnell, Linda, 244
d'Arrast, Harry d'Abbadie, xii, 189, 232, 295, 296, *297*, 298 - 314
Darrieux, Danielle, 249, 285
Dassin, Jules, 180
Daumier, Honoré, 183
Davies, Marion, 300
Davis, Bette, 190
Dawes, Charles G., 105
Day in the Country, A, 52
Dead End, 130
Death Day, 185
Death of a Salesman, 241
Debussy, Claude, 148, 183, 256
Decker, John, 233
Degas, Edgar, 208, 326, 351
De Haven, Carter, 232
Delacroix, Eugène, 177, 230
Delannoy, Jean, 266
del Ruth, Roy, 321
Demarest, William, 216
Demazis, Orane, *59*
Demers, Rock, 239
De Mille, Cecil B., 195, 205, 206, 224, 227, 341
Demutzki, Danilo, 186
Demy, Jacques, 257
De Putti, Lya, 241
Derain, Lucie, 11
de Seta, Vittorio, 173
de Sica, Vittorio, 204
Devil is a Woman, The, 99, 165, 188, 196, 326, 343
Devil's Passkey, The, 40, 116, 130, 132, 150, 200
Devine, Andy, 216
Diaghilev, Serge, 172, 191, 217, 218, 221, 253
Diary of a Chambermaid, 207, 227
Diary of a Lost One, The, 190, 266, 320
Diary of Anne Frank, The, 163
Dickinson, Thorold, 137
Dietrich, Marlene, 96, 131, 134, 136, 141, 147, 162, 166, 202, 206, 237, 244, 247, 327, 333
Di Filippo, Eduardo, 204
Dio Cassius, 198
Dirks, Mary Douglas, 315
Dishonored, 145, 206, 247
Disney, Walt, 39, 323 - 326
Döblin, Alfred, 163
Docks of New York, The, 99, 231
Doelle, Franz, 28
Dolce Vita, La, 164, 165, 172, 198
Domitian, 198
Donner, Jörn, 230
Don Quixote, 163, 265, 266, 284, 320
Doolittle, Hilda (H. D.), 10, 319
Dostoievski, Fyodor, 133, 148, 229
Douglas, William, 345
Dovzhenko, Alexander, 144, 169, 177, 222, 317
Doyle, Arthur Conan, 218
Dragnet, The, 188
Drasin, Dan, 169
Dreams That Money Can Buy, 266
Dreier, Hans, 72
Dreigroschenoper, Die, 19, 23, 24, 25, 266, 320
Dreiser, Theodore, 209, 210, 261
Dreyer, Carl, xii, 4, 6, 10, 11, 12, 13, 139, 145, 178, 197, 198, 228, 230, 242, 244, 256, 257, 266, 320, 355
Dr. Jekyll and Mr. Hyde, 204
Dr. Mabuse, the Gambler, 85, 218, 269, 276, 277
Drôle de Drame, 266
Dr. Strangelove, 225
Drunken Angel, 145
Dry Martini, 298, 307
Duchamp, Marcel, 265, 266
Duhamel, Maurice, 266
Dumas, Alexander, *fils*, 143
Dumas, Alexander, *père*, 144, 217
Duncan, Isadora, 260, 351
Duncan, Raymond, 260
Dupont, Ewald André, 106, 285, 320, *329*, 342
Durante, Jimmy, 246
Dürer, Albrecht, 101, 263
Du Sang, de la Volupté, et de la Mort, 264
Duse, Eleonora, 34, 144
Duvivier, Julien, 50, 207, 242
Dwightiana, 182

Eagle, Arnold, 168
Earth, 103, 169, 177, 317, 320
Eastman, George, 267
Eclipse, 203
Ecstasy, 180, 258, 267, 343
Eggeling, Viking, 91
Ehrenburg, Ilya, 235
Eichheim, Henry, 286
8 x 8, 266
Einstein, Albert, 244
Eisenstein, Sergei, 6, 8, 39, 40, 71, 72, 75, 76, 88, 122, 124, 130, 142, 145, 172, 178, 181, 184, 185, 186, 202, 204, 211, 222, 226, 232, 233, 249, 261, 263, 264, 265, 286, 296, 308, 319, 321, 342, 350
Eisner, Lotte, 156, 161
Ekman, Gösta, *102*
Electra, 180, 190, 214
Eliot, T. S., 198, 322
Elizabeth (Empress of Austria), 248
Ellis, Havelock, 319
Elter, Anielka, 194, 196
Eluard, Paul, 253
Emerson, Ralph Waldo, 266
Emshwiller, Ed, 256
Enamorada, 238
Endfield, Cy, 183
End of St. Petersburg, The, 39, 103, 171, 320
En Rade, 320
Entr'acte, 266
Epic That Never Was, The, 259
Ermler, Friedrich, 26
Ernst, Max, 266
Etoile de Mer, 266
Euclid, 221
Euripides, 221
Evans, Larry, 266
Everything Turns!, 91
Exodus, 171
Exquisite Sinner, The, 146

Fa'angase, 89
Fairbanks, Douglas, 8, 162, 165, 198, 204, 222
Falconetti, Maria, *10*, 13, 180
Falla, Manuel de, 311
Fanck, Arnold, 25, 266
Fantomas, 252, 253
Farkas, Nicholas, 183, 231, 281, 282, 284, 285
Farrar, Geraldine, 178
Farrère, Claude, 2, 130, 183, 231, 281, 282, 285, 286
Faust, 26, 99, *100 - 102*, 103 - 108, 263, 266
Fawcett, George, 118, *129*
Fejos, Paul, 224
Felix, Maria, 238
Fellini, Federico, 6, 138, 165, 258, 336, 337, 338, 339, 340, 341, 342, 343, 346
Fellini Satyricon, 336, 338, 339, 342, 344, 346
Fernandel, 51, 310
Fernandez, Emilio, 238, 245
Feuchtwanger, Lion, 19, 244
Feuillade, Louis, 252, 253, 254
Feydeau, George, 315, 316
Feyder, Jacques, 178, 266
Fidanzati, I, 214
Film Study, 91
Fin du Monde, La, 320
Fischinger, Oscar, 92
Fitzmaurice, George, 206, 300
Five Graves to Cairo, 145
Flaherty, Monica, 87, 88, 90
Flaherty, Robert, xii, 85, *86*, 87 - 90, 106, 137, 186, 208,

228, 244, 296, 317
Flaming Creatures, 229, 230
Flaubert, Gustave, 52, 327
Fleming, Alexander, 259
Fleming, Margaret, 215
Fleming, Victor, 130
Fliesler, Joseph, 321
Florelle, Odette, 30, 267
Florey, Robert, 146, 232, 233, 310, 312, *348*
Flower Drum Song, 165
Flower Thief, The, 180
Fog Over Frisco, 190
Foolish Wives, 41, *42 - 44*, 116, 117, 130, 132, 150, 151, 154, 155, 171, 172, 187, 224, 242, 355
Foote, Shelby, 147
Forbidden Games, 186
Ford, Charles, 295
Ford, John, 130
Foreign Affair, A, 202
Forst, Willy, 34, 35
Fort, Charles, 127
42nd Street, 171
Foti, Giuseppe, 279
Fountain of Youth, The, 207
Four Devils, The, 106
Four Horsemen of the Apocalypse, The, 113, 171
Four Hundred Blows, The, 186, 241
Four Sons, 183
Fra Angelico, 10
Fragonard, Jean Honoré, 347
France, Anatole, ix, 67
Franck, César, 228
Franchi, Rudi, 168, 169
Franju, Georges, 253, 254
Franz Ferdinand, Archduke, 160
Franz Josef, Emperor, 34, 151, 248, 249
Frau im Mond, Die, 106, 139
Freeman, Joseph, 192
Frenchman and Love, The, 162
Frenke, Eugene, 266
Freud, Anna, 200
Freud, Ernst, 200
Freud, Sigmund, 20, 80, 199, 203, 260, 333, 335
Freund, Karl, 166, 194, 265, *271*
Friese-Greene, William, 267
Fröhlich, Gustave, *273*
Fry, Christopher, 145, 336
Fujikawa, Jun, *97*
Fuller, Dale, 117
Fury, 85, 276
Fütterer, Werner, *100*

Gabin, Jean, 199, 285
Gabrio, Gabriel, *59*
Gailhard, André, 288
Galitzine, Prince, 217
Gallery of Monsters, 266
Galli-Curci, Amelita, 228
Gance, Abel, 123, 223, 244, 266, 320
Garat, Henri, 30, 267
Garbo, Greta, 144, 178, 195, 206, 216
Garganoff, Leon, 285

Garland, Judy, 187
Gassman, Vittorio, 204
Gate of Hell, 108, 257
Gaucho, The, 162, 198
Gauguin, Paul, 336
Gautier, Théophile, 189
Gay, John, 23, 24
Geiger von Florenz, Der, 320
General, The, 204
General Line, The: see *Old and New*
Genet, Jean, 262
Genthe, Arnold, 173
Gentleman of Paris, A, 298, 304, 305, 313
George, Leila, 140
George, Maude, *43*, 118, *129*
Gerhardi, William, 286
Gershwin, George, 201
Gert, Valeska, 138, 266
Giant, 163
Gibran, Kahlil, 334
Gide, André, 148, 162, 221, 222, 250, 319, 320
Gilbert, John, 144, 166, 195, 216
Giono, Jean, 60, 67, 68
Giotto, 2, 268, 278
Giraudoux, Jean, 30
Girl and the Hooligan, The, 266
Girl in the Case, The, 266
Gish, Lillian, 234
Giulietta of the Spirits, 258, 346
Glazer, Benjamin, 300, 301, 312
Glory at Sea, 183, 231
Glover, Guy, 167, 169, 214
Glyn, Elinor, 195
Gobineau, Comte de, 285
Godard, Jean-Luc, 6, 163, 177, 206, 256, 258, 266, 269, 338, 351
Goddard, Paulette, *79*, 220, 223
Godowsky, Leopold, 196
Goebbels, Joseph, 138, 264, 276, 277
Goethe, Johann Wolfgang von, 81, 99, 100, 101, 104, 209, 352
Goetz, William, 223
Gogol, Nicolai, 148, 149, 279
Golding, Louis, 213
Gold Rush, The, 298, 300, 309
Goldwyn, Samuel, 156, 232, 310
Golem, Der, xii, 36 - 38
Golovnia, Anatoli, 186
Gone With the Wind, 130
Gorki, Maxim, 24, 52, 321
Goudal, Jetta, 205, 206, *330*, *331*
Gould, Gloria, 140
Gould, Symon, 193, 321
Gounod, Charles, 26, 107
Gourmont, Remy de, 206
Gowland, Gibson, 117
Goya, Francisco, 46, 155, 183, 228
Gozzi, Patricia, 186
Gran, Albert, 209

Grand Duchess and the Waiter, The, ii, 298, 300, *332*
Grande Illusion, La, xii, 52, 53 - 57, 63, 65, 130, 199
Grand Hotel, 350
Granger, Stewart, 172
Granowsky, Alexis, 285, 321
Grant, Cary, 245
Grant, Lawrence, 304
Grant, Ulysses S., 166
Grapes of Wrath, The, 130
Grauman, Sid, 206
Graves, Charles, 237
Graves, Robert, 238, 259
Gravey, Fernand, 285
Gravina, Cesare, 117, 119, 187
Great Dictator, The, 77 - 82
Greatest Story Ever Told, The, 239, 243
Great Moment, The, 178
Greco, Juliette, 163
Greed, 39, 45, 46, 107, 112, 113, 114, *115*, 116 - 122, 130, 132, 139, 146, 151, 154, 155, 163, 164, 172, 183, 187, 199, 207, 208, 214, 240, 344, 345, 352
Greene, Graham, 145
Greenwood, Joan, 223
Greig, Robert, 216
Greville, Edmond, 241
Grido, Il, 182, 346
Grierson, John, 167, 197, 233
Griffith, D. W., 6, 116, 122, 140, 164, 183, 200, 202, 233, 242, 253, 263
Griffith, Hugh, 148
Grock (Adrian Wettach), 14, 17, 18
Grosz, Georg, 138
Guarnerius, Joseph, 3
Guggenheim, Peggy, 266
Guilbert, Yvette, 107, 251, 266
Guinness, Alec, 242
Guitry, Sacha, 133, 260, 350
Gunsbourg, Raoul, 248
Guns of the Trees, 187, 230
Gunzberg, Nicolas de, 139, 197

Haardt, Georges-Marie, 31, 32
Hafiz, 221
Hall, Mordaunt, 301
Hallelujah, 231, 244
Hallelujah, I'm a Bum, 310
Hallelujah the Hills, 206, 211, 213, 214, 225
Hammett, Dashiell, 163
Handel, George Frederick, 239, 240, 243
Hangmen Also Die, 85, 277
Hanson, Lars, 234
Hard Day's Night, A, 242
Harlan, Veit, 244
Harris, Jed, 138
Hart, William S., 232
Hartmann, Sadakichi, 183
Harvest, xii, 57, *59*, 61, 67
Hatari, 206
Hauptmann, Gerhart, 107
Hawaii, 163
Hawks, Howard, 206
Hayakawa, Sessue, 286

Hays, Will, 261
Hayworth, Rita, 164, 173
Hearst, William Randolph, 25, 300
Heaword, Rosemary, 223
Hecht, Ben, 138, 193, 241, 244, 266, 281, 310, 312, 335
Heifetz, Jascha, 298
Heilige Berg, Der, 25
Heine, Heinrich, 279
Heliogabalus, 130
Hello, Sister!, 130
Helm, Brigitte, 272
Hemingway, Ernest, 231, 266
Hepburn, Audrey, 227
Herald, George W., 248
Herr der Liebe, Der, 209
Herring, Robert, 320
Hersholt, Jean, 118
Hessling, Catherine, 191, 262, 320
Heston, Charlton, 134
Heydrich, Reinhold, 85
Hicks, Granville, 322
High Noon, 177
Hika, Kazuko, 96
Himmler, Heinrich, 85
Hindemith, Paul, 266
Hirshfeld, Magnus, 221
Hitchcock, Alfred, 208, 346
Hitler, Adolf, 55, 56, 80, 84, 85, 261, 322, 338
Hitler, Connais Pas, 210
Hobson's Choice, 202
Hoffmann, Carl, 108
Hofmannsthal, Hugo von, 333
Hölderlin, Friedrich, 277, 279
Hollaender, Friedrich, 202
Homer, Winslow, 6
Honeymoon, The, 194
Hope, Anthony, 155
Hopkins, Arthur, 140
Horace, 221
Horn, Camilla, *102*, 106, 107
Horowitz, Vladimir, 247
Horton, Edward Everett, 216
Hotel Imperial, 328
Howard, Trevor, 183
Howard, William K., 226
Huggins, Charles, 280
Hughes, Howard, 146, 162
Hugo, Victor, 65, 144
Hulsenbeck, Richard, 266
Human Beast, The, 52
Humboldt, Alexander, 221
Hunchback of Notre Dame, The, 204
Hunter, Ross, 165
Huston, John, 199, 214, 241, 245
Hutchins, John, 308
Huxley, Aldous, 6, 228
Huysmans, Joris-Karl, 351
Hymer, Warren, 216

Ibsen, Henrik, 279
Ichikawa, Kon, 257, 278
I, Claudius, 238, 259, 342
Immigrant, The, 225, 347
Indian Tombstone, The, 277
Informer, The, 130
Ingram, Rex, 113, 118, 171, 264

Ingres, Jean Auguste Dominique, 230
Inkijinoff, Valeri, 183, 231, 282, 284, 288
Innocent VIII, Pope, 234
Intolerance, 164, 242, 253, 264, 351
It Happened in Spain, 298, 312
It's All True, 162
Ivan the Terrible, 234
Ivens, Joris, 189

Jacob, Max, 252
Jacobs, Lewis, 320
Jaffe, Sam, 191
James, Henry, 207, 221
Jannings, Emil, 106, 107, 166, 191, 217, 229, 241, 285, 321
Janouch, Gustav, 278
Janowitz, Hans, 139, 208, 209
Jazz Comedy, 26
Jeanne, René, 295
Jean Paul (Richter), ix
Jeayes, Allan, 311
Jenny, 266
Jessner, Leopold, 19, 107
Jet Pilot, 146, 345
Jew Süss, 244
Johnny Got His Gun, 230, 242
Joli Mai, Le, 210
Jolson, Al, 310
Jones, Idwal, 113, 118
Jordaan, L. S., 320
Jouvet, Louis, 49
Joyce, James, 8, 140, 181, 189, 214, 227, 256, 322
Joyless Street, The, 19, 25, 266
Judex, 251 - 255
Jugo, Jenny, 211
Julian, Rupert, 151, 152, 153, 154, 155
Juneau, Pierre, 170, 239
Jung, Carl, 231
Jutra, Claude, 168
Juvenal, 342

Kabalov, Grigori, 186
Kafka, Franz, 203, 265, 278, 334
Kalatozov, Mikhail, 186, 321
Kameradschaft, 20, 22, 23
Kamin, Martin, 320
Kane, Robert, 312
Karina, Anna, 177
Karno, Fred, 14
Kaufmann, Walter, 100
Kawakita, Nagamasa, 98
Kaye, Danny, 339
Keaton, Buster, 141, 146, 204
Keats, John, 99
Kennedy, John F., 263
Kennedy, Joseph, 47, 159
Kepler, Johannes, 38
Kerensky, Alexander, 62, 142
Kermesse Héroïque, La, 130
Kerry, Norman, 151, *152*, 329
Kessel, Joseph, 139
Khill, Marcel, 221
Kibbee, Guy, 216
Kiesler, Frederick, 266
Kiki, 266
Kilmer, Joyce, 122
King in New York, A, 149, 225

Kino Pravda, 210
Kinugasa, Teinosuke, 257
Kipling, Rudyard, 193, 201
Kirstein, Lincoln, 320
Kisch, Egon Erwin, 37
Kiss Me Again, 202, *317*, 343
Kitt, Eartha, 225
Klee, Paul, 227
Klein-Rogge, Rudolph, 264, 275
Kline, Franz, 140
Knife in the Water, 216, 217
Kobayashi, Masaki, 257
Kohner, Paul, 131
Kokoschka, Oskar, 243
Kolin, Nikolai, 212
Kollorsz, Richard, 72
Korda, Alexander, 141, 238, 259, 312
Korda, Zoltan, 141
Kortner, Fritz, 191, 229
Kosma, Joseph, 211, 266
Koumiko Mystery, The, 256
Kozintsev, Grigori, 163, 171
Krafft-Ebing, Richard von, 176
Krauss, Werner, 191, 211
Kreisler, Fritz, 170, 298, 324
Kriemhild's Revenge, 238, 275, 276, 337
Krueger, Ivar, 125, 226
Kubla Khan, 124
Kurosawa, Akira, 145, 177, 226, 257
Kuzmina, Elena, 191
Kwaidan, 257

Lady from Shanghai, The, 125, 143, 170, 173, 264, 346
Lady Lou, 176
Lady Vanishes, The, 208
Lady with a Dog, The, 187
Laemmle, Carl, 41, 114, 116
Lambert, Evelyn, 168
Lampedusa, Giuseppe Tommasi di, 219
Lang (chancellor), 38
Lang, Fritz, xi - xiii, 19, *85*, 104, 106, 137, 138, 139, 202, 209, 218, 224, 225, 236, 238, 241, 264, 268, 269, *270*, 271, 274, 275, 337, 346, *349*
Langer, Gilda, 208, 209
Langlois, Henri, 156, 160, 203, 214, 295
Lanner, Josef, 33
La Prince, 267
La Rochefoucauld, François de, 221
Last Command, The, 217
Last Laugh, The, 8, 103, 107, 165, 188, 209
Last Supper, The, 222
Last Ten Days, The, 337
Last Will of Dr. Mabuse, The, 84, 85
Last Year at Marienbad, 173, 190, 203
Latzko, Andreas, 77
Laughter, 295, 296, 298, 309, 310
Laughton, Charles, 226, 237, 238, 259
Laurel and Hardy, 171

Laurents, Arthur, 146
Lawrence, D. H., 171, 335
Lawrence, T. E., 199
Lawrence of Arabia, 199
Leacock, Richard, 86, 211
Lean, David, 202
Lecky, William, 179
Lecontinus, 215
Lee, Francis, 92
LeFanu, Sheridan, 145
Léger, Fernand, 16, 137, 263, 266
Legman, Gershon, 140
Legrand, Michel, 256
Lehar, Franz, 33, 247, 263
Leigh, Janet, 134
Lemonnier, Camille, 165
Lengyel, Melchior, 148
Leni, Paul, 164, 188, 321
Lenin, Vladimir I., 234, 235, 265
Lenya, Lotte, 266
Leonard, Robert Z., 131
Lerici, Carlo Maurilio, 212
Lesser, Sol, 185, 211
Letter That Was Not Sent, The, 186, 187
Letter to Three Wives, A, 206
Letzte Akt, Der, 337
Levant, Oscar, 201
Lewis, Marshall, 168
Ley, Willy, 139
Leyda, Jay, 172, 184, 320
L'Herbier, Marcel, 181, 266, 343
Lied Vom Leben, Das, 285
Life Begins Tomorrow, 162
Light That Failed, The, 232
Lilith, 176
Limur, Jean de, 232, 307
Lincoln, Abraham, 166
Linder, Max, 232
Lippert, Robert, 180, 183
Lipsett, Arthur, 169
Liszt, Franz, 147, 247, 340
Little Match Girl, The, 52
Little Red Riding Hood, 262
Litvak, Anatole, 249
Llona, Victor, 140
Loder, John, 183, 231, 283, 284, 286
Loew, Frederick, 170
Loew, Rabbi, 38
Logan, Joshua, 173
Lola Montès, 172
Lolita, 186
Lollobrigida, Gina, 240
Long Day's Journey into Night, 203
Long Hot Summer, The, 224
Lord of the Flies, 23
Lorentz, Pare, 224
Losey, Mary, 320
Lost Squadron, The, 48
Loti, Pierre, 286
Lot in Sodom, 188, 196, 197, 343
Louisiana Story, 86, 87, 90
Louis-Philippe, 251
Louis XVI, 62, 64
Louis XIII, 8, 222
Louÿs, Pierre, 2, 4, 207, 285, 336

Love at Twenty, 204
Love Game, The, 177
Lovejoy, Frank, 183
Love Me and the World Is Mine, 329
Love Me Tonight, 237
Love of Jeanne Ney, The, 20, 25, 320
Lovers, The, 149
Lovers of Verona, The, 266
Lowenstein, Alfred, 124, 226
Lower Depths, The, 52
Loy, Myrna, 310
Lubitsch, Ernst, 6, 46, 106, 124, 127, 130, 139, 148, 183, 189, 202, 216, 217, 261, 295, 296, 298, 301, 306, 315, *316*, 317, 321, 330, 343, 356
Lucretia Borgia, 266
Luft, Herbert G., 209
Lumière, Auguste, 7
Lumière, Louis, 267
Lunacharsky, Anatole, 235
Lye, Len, 92
Lynn, Diana, 194

M, 85, 276, 343
Macao, 139, 146
MacArthur, Charles, 281
Macdonald, Dwight, 234
Machaty, Gustav, 180, 222, 258, 267
Mack, Hughie, 118
MacLaine, Shirley, 245
MacLiammoir, Michael, 225
MacPherson, Kenneth, 319
Madame Bovary, 52
Mädchen in Uniform, 343
Maeterlinck, Countess, 127
Magician, The, 164
Magnificent Ambersons, The, 143
Magnificent Flirt, The, 298, 307
Mainay, 12
Malina, Judith, 182
Malraux, André, 149, 240, 262, 322
Mamoulian, Rouben, 237
Mander, Miles, 284, 292
Manet, Edouard, 4, 326
Mankiewicz, Joseph, 175, 187, 205, 206, 221, 226, 227
Mankowitz, Wolf, 143
Mann, Hank, 216
Mann, Heinrich, 175, 266
Mann, Klaus, 127
Mann, Thomas, 25, 130, 141, 142
Mannes, Leopold, 147
Mansfield, Jayne, 244
Mansfield, Katherine, 296
Man, Woman and Sin, 310
Marat, Jean-Paul, 62
Marc Anthony, 206
Marceau, Marcel, 148
March, Fredric, 309
Marcorelles, Louis, 168
Mare Nostrum, 264
Marie, 224
Marie Antoinette, 62
Marie Antoinette, 62, 64
Marinoff, Fania, 164

Marker, Chris, 256, 257
Mark of Zorro, The, 198, 204
Markopoulos, Gregory, 264
Marlowe, Christopher, 104
Marriage Circle, The, 171, 202, 225, 330
Marriage of the Prince, 46
Marseillaise, La, 62 - 65, 344
Marsh, Mae, 183
Marshall, Tully, 160, 210
Marthe Richard, 132
Martin, Millicent, 229
Maruyama, Michiro, 97
Marx, Groucho, 339
Marx, Harpo, 137, 145, 171
Marx, Karl, 226
Marx Brothers, 149
Masefield, John, 85
Masina, Giulietta, 258
Masked Bride, The, 146
Maskerade, 33 - 36, 231
Massari, Lea, 223
Mastroianni, Marcello, 164
Mata Hari, 191, 206, 247, 266
Maté, Rudolph, 244
Mater Dolorosa, 266
Maternelle, La, 186
Mathias, Archduke, 38
Mathis, June, 117, 121
Maugham, W. Somerset, 144, 145, 163, 188
Maupassant, Guy de, 52, 67, 130, 138, 141, 207, 279
Maurois, André, 215, 231
Maxwell, Elsa, 339
May, Joe, 166, 277
Mayakovsky, Vladimir, 266
Mayer, Carl, 8, 139, 149, 208, 209
Mayer, Louis B., 146
McCarthy, Joseph, 225
McCormack, John, 227
McDonald, J. Farrell, 216
McHugh, Frank, 216
McLaglen, Victor, 247
McLaren, Norman, 92, 167, 173, 184, 190, 202, 244
McTeague, 164, 199
Meerson, Mary, 214
Meiji, Emperor, 287
Mekas, Adolfas, 206, 256
Mekas, Jonas, 168, 183, 188, 204
Méliès, Georges, 92, 164, *348*
Meller, Raquel, 266
Melody of the World, 87
Melville, Herman, 87, 221, 333, 347
Mencken, H. L., 243, 351
Mendelssohn, Felix, 99
Mendes, Lothar, 106, 244
Mendoza, David, 142
Menjou, Adolphe, 142, 193, 222, 300, 301, *302*, *303*, 304, 305, 307, *331*, *332*
Menken, Marie, 182
Mépris, Le, 236, 240, 269, 277
Merry Go Round, 39, 116, 117, 150, 151, *152*, *153*, 154, 155, 161, 329
Merry Widow, The, 39, 46, 130, 131, 132, 140, 149, 160,

161, 164, 191, 194, 195, 207, 246
Merry Wives of Vienna, The, 34
Metastasio, Pietro, 346
Metropolis, 85, 105, 138, 169, 218, 225, 264, 269, *271* 273, 276
Metzner, Erno, 25
Mexican Symphony, 184
Meyrink, Gustav, 36
Michelangelo Buonarroti, 145, 212, 221, 350
Michener, James, 163, 354
Mifune, Toshiro, 177
Milestone, Lewis, 130, 166, 193, 229
Milhaud, Darius, 141, 148, 164, 266
Milky Way, The, 346
Miller, Arthur, 174, 241
Million, Le, 164, 320
Minnelli, Vincente, 171, 172
Miracle, The, 179
Mirbeau, Octave, 130, 207, 227
Misfits, The, 241, 243
Misraki, Paul, 126
Mistinguette, 244
Mitchell, Tommy, 216
Mitsubishi, 287
Mizoguchi, Kenji, 256
Moana, 87, *89,* 103, 186
Modern Hero, A, 19
Modern Times, 164, 240
Modigliani, Amedeo, 235, 236, 237
Modigliani, Jeanne, 222
Mog, Aribert, 267
Mohammed, 148, 191
Mohr, Hal, 195
Molière, 30, 144, 315
Mompou, Federico, 201
Mondrian, Piet, 138
Monet, Claude, 86, 204
Monicelli, Mario, 204
Monkey in Winter, A, 199
Monroe, Marilyn, 174, 181, 190
Monsieur Verdoux, 198, 214, 233
Montaigne, Michel de, 144
Montana, "Bull," 139
Montherlant, Henri de, ix
Montiel, Sarita, 176
Moore, Jerrold, 2
Moore, Marianne, 319
Moore, Matt, 216, 309
Morand, Paul, 8, 205, 285, 331
Mörder Karamazov, Der, 229, 281
Morehouse, Ward, 194
Moreau, Jeanne, 203
Moreno, Hilda, 311
Moreno, Marguerite, 30, 267
Morgan, Frank, 309
Morisot, Berthe, 4, 6
Morley, Christopher, 140
Morocco, 95, 98, 187, 198, 326, 333
Moskvin, Andrei, 186
Mother, 24, 320, 344
Mother Joan of the Angels, 179

Moulin Rouge, 329
Mozart, Wolfgang A., 90, 99, 215, 224, 337
Mr. Arkadin: see *Confidential Agent*
Mr. Deeds Goes to Town, 130
Mr. Moto's Gamble, 183
Müde Tod, Der (Destiny), 276
Munsterberg, Hugo, 104
Muriel, 212
Murnau, Friedrich W., 8, 99 - 108, 124, 143, 145, 165, 170, 194, 203, 222, 224, 263, 266, 320, 321
Musidora, 253
Musin, Ovide, 196
Mussolini, Benito, 25, 55

Nabokov, Vladimir, 175
Nana, 52, 262, 266
Nanook of the North, 87
Napoleon (Gance), 223, 244, 266
Napoleon (Guitry), 133
Nathan, George Jean, 351
Navigator, The, 145
Nebenzahl, Seymour, 24
Nebuchadnezzar, 7
Negishi, Akemi, *94,* 96, *97*
Negri, Pola, 106, *328*
Nero, 226, 338, 339
Never Give a Sucker an Even Break, 171
New Babylon, The, 171, 191
Newman, Alfred, 243
Newman, Paul, 227
Newton, Isaac, 215
New Year's Eve, 107
Nibelungen, Die, 238, *274,* 275, 276
Niblo, Fred, 163
Nicholas, James, 180, 190
Nicholas, II, 62
Nichols, George, 118
Nietzsche, Friedrich, 225, 241, 279, 335
Night of the Iguana, The, 245
Nijinsky, Vaslav, 221, 231, 256
Nikitine, 12
Ninotchka, 130, 148, 216
Noel, Magali, 244
Norris, Frank, 45, 113, 117, 119, 121, 199
Nosferatu, 107, 145
Notes on the Port of St. Francis, 267
Notte, La, 172
Nouvelle Mission de Judex, La, 254
Novarro, Ramon, 163

Oakie, Jack, 216
Oberon, Merle, 183, 231, 238, 259, *283,* 284, 285, 286, 294
O'Casey, Sean, 149, 239
Odets, Clifford, 209
Offenbach, Jacques, 251
Of Mice and Men, 130
Oland, Warner, 247
Old and New (The General Line), 8, 39, 103, 320
Olmi, Ermanno, 176, 214
Olympiad, 258

Once in a Blue Moon, 266
One Way Pendulum, 239
Open All Night, 205, 330, *331*
Ophuls, Max, 141, 170, 172
Ormandy, Eugene, 142
Orphans of the Storm, 62, 202
Orpheus, 92
Osawa, Yoshio, 98
Osborne, John, 222
Ossian, 215
Oswald, Marianne, 266
Our Daily Bread (Murnau), 106
Our Daily Bread (Vidor), 20
Our Town, 130
Ovid, 221
Owen, Seena, *156,* 160, 264
Ozep, Fedor, 136, 229, 281

Paar, Jack, 201
Pabst, Georg W., 19, 20, *21,* 22 - 26, 90, 124, 137, 179, 190, 191, 200, 242, 244, 266, 281, 284, 320, 337, 338
Pagador de Promessa, O, 169, 176
Paganini, Niccolò, 172, 191, 250
Pagnol, Marcel, 59, 60, 66, 130, 310
Pallette, Eugene, 216
Pandora's Box, 190, 191, 320, 343
Pangborn, Franklin, 216
Panofsky, Erwin, 4, 181
Parker, Dorothy, 162
Pascin, Jules, 236
Pasolini, Pier Paolo, 6, 256
Passionate Pastime, 266
Passion of Joan of Arc, The, xii, 5, *10,* 11 - 13, 103, 178, 180, 198, 228, 242, 244, 257, 266, 355
Pasternak, Joseph, 131
Pastrone, Giovanni, 145
Patriot, The, 316
Paxinou, Katina, 125
Payne, Robert, 15, 198
Peace to Him Who Enters, 169, 176
Peasants, 26
Pépé Le Moko, xii, 82 - 84
Perkins, Anthony, 203, 214
Perry, Matthew, 281
Peter the Great, 107
Petronius, Gaius, 339, 342
Phaedra, 180
Philbin, Mary, *329*
Picabia, Francis, 266
Picasso, Pablo, 237, 260, 264, 278, 350
Piccadilly, 329
Pick, Lupu, 107
Pickett, George E., 233
Picnic on the Grass, 189
Pilgrim, The, 309
Pindar, 21
Pinnacle, The, 41
Pirandello, Luigi, 240
Piscator, Erwin, 139
Pitts, Zasu, 117, 118
Plaisir, Le, 141
Plato, 111, 221

Plautus, 30
Plus Belles Escroqueries du Monde, Les, 226
Poe, Edgar Allan, 184
Poil de Carotte, 186
Point of Order, 225
Polanski, Roman, 214, 216, 217
Pollock, Jackson, 140
Polo, Eddie, 253
Polo, Marco, 31, 32
Pommer, Erich, 19, 106, 224, 269, 276, *328*, 329
Poppea, 226
Porcasi, Paul, 216
Port Arthur, 285
Porter, Katherine Anne, 178
Portes de la Nuit, Les, 211
Posto, Il, 176, 177
Potamkin, Harry Alan, 320, 321
Potemkin, 23, 39, 99, 103, 107, 146, 164, 183, 186, 189, 193, 197, 199, 229, 234, 240, 249, 256, 320, 321, 344
Powers, Pat, 47
Pratt, George, 146, 196
Praxiteles, 227
Preminger, Otto, 173
Prevost, Jean, 319
Prevost, Marie, *317*
Private Life of Helen of Troy, The, 130
Private Property, 149
Professor Mamlock, 261
Proudhon, Pierre-Joseph, 251
Proust, Antonin, 4
Proust, Marcel, 144, 190
Psycho, 203, 346
Ptolemy Dionysus, 227
Puccini, Giacomo, 286
Pudovkin, Vsevolod I., 139, 222, 256, 319

Quartet, 249
Quatorze Juillet, Le, 8
Queen Christina, 216
Queen Kelly, 47, 155, *156 - 158*, 159 - 161, 178, 210, 211, 264
Que Viva Mexico!, 40, 69, 70, *71 - 76*, 122, 161, *163*, 171, 173, 178, 184, 186, 198, 212, 321
Quick Millions, 188

Radford, Basil, 216
Radin, Edward D., 248
Raffles, 310
Raimu, 51, 66
Rain, 164
Rains, Claude, 241, 242
Ralleu, 12
Raphael, 99
Rasp, Fritz, 229
Ravel, Maurice, 166
Ravet, 12
Ray, Charles, 187
Ray, Man, 266, 320
Raymond, Edouard, 198
Recznicek, 34
Red Balloon, The, 258
Red Beard, 257

Redgrave, Michael, *123*, 125
Redl, Col., 247
Regina, Joe, 173
Règle du Jeu, La, 182, 198
Reichenbach, François, 167, 176
Reinhardt, Max, 19, 165
Reisch, Walter, 36
Reisenfeld, Hugo, 142
Rembrandt van Rijn, 171, 278
Renoir, Auguste, 171, 189, 256
Renoir, Jean, xii, 1, *52*, 53 - 57, 62 - 65, 116, 130, 182, 189, 191, 198, 199, 207, 224, 262, 266, 337, *348*, 350, 355
Resnais, Alain, 173, 202, 224
Reynaud, Emile, 267
Ribbentrop, Joachim von, 261
Riccoboni, Luigi, 200
Rice, Ron, 180, 256, 265
Richardson, Dorothy, 319
Richardson, Tony, 194, 214, 222
Richepin, Jean, 318
Richter, Hans, 91 - 93, 165, 266, *348*
Richter, Paul, *274*
Ridges, Stanley, 242
Riefenstahl, Leni, 258
Rien Que les Heures, 320
Rififi, 163
Rilke, Rainer Maria, 220, 258
Rimbaud, Arthur, 221
Rimsky-Korsakov, Nikolai, 227
Rivera, Diego, *71*, 223
Rivera, Frida Kahlo, *71*
Robespierre, Maximilien, 62, 63
Robson, Flora, 259
Roda-Roda (Alexander Rosenfeld), 4
Rodin, Auguste, 157, 166, 182, 221
Roi Pausole, Le, 285, 321
Roland, Ruth, 253
Rolland, Romain, 133
Romance Sentimentale, 242
Romeo and Juliet, 108
Room, Abram, 321
Rossellini, Roberto, 179, 240, 256, 351
Rossen, Robert, 176
Rostand, Edmond, 312
Rotha, Paul, 295
Rothko, Mark, 140
Rousseau, Henri, 182
Rousseau, Jean-Jacques, 182
Rozhdestvensky, Zinovi, 287
Rubens, Peter Paul, 145
Rubinstein, Anton, 243
Rublëv, 347
Rudolph, Archduke, 247, 248
Rudolph II, 37, 38
Ruggles of Red Gap, 224
Ruiz, Salvador, 278
Rule of the Game, The, 52
Rumann, Sig, 216
Ruskin, John, 239, 279
Ruttmann, Walter, 87

Sacher-Masoch, Leopold, 160
Sade, Donatien de, 160

Sadoul, Georges, 156, 254, 265, 270
Saga of Anatahan, The, *94*, 95, 96, *97*, 98, 99, 144, 207, 287, 333, 352
St. Clair, Malcolm, ii, 129, 142, 193, 298, 306, 332
Saint-Exupéry, Antoine de, 250
Saint-Saëns, Camille, 5, 181
Salamoun, Jiri, 169
Salinger, J. D., 166
Salisbury, Harrison, 234
Salt of Svanetia, 321
Saltus, Edgar, 175, 343
Saludos Amigos, 244
Sand, George, 147
Sarasate, Pablo de, 250
Sarris, Andrew, 168
Sartre, Jean-Paul, 199
Savo, Jimmy, 138, 266
Savvina, Iya, 187
Scarlet Empress, The, 72, 99, 137, 191
Scarlet Pimpernel, The, 62
Schelling, Ernest, 166
Schenck, Joseph, 310
Schiller, Friedrich, 205
Schlosser, Eve, 168, 169
Schlosser, Peter, 168, 169
Schnitzler, Arthur, 304, 305, 333
Schoenberg, Arnold, 243
Scholte, Henryk, 320
Schratt, Frau, 248
Schumann, Robert, 149, 279, 287
Schünzel, Reinhold, 29, 30, 243, 267, 281, 343
Schutz, Maurice, 11, 12, 228
Scott, Cyril, 286
Scott, Walter, 215
Scoundrel, The, 281
Scriabin, Alexander, 246
Sea Gull, The, 233
Seastrom (Sjöström), Victor, 234, 308
Secret Agent, The, 208
Secrets of a Soul, 20, 25, 200, 212, 343
Sellers, Peter, 225
Semmelweis, Ignaz Philipp, 249, 279
Sennett, Mack, 296
Sennwald, André, 304, 308
Serenade, 298, 304, 305, 306
Serengeti Shall Not Die, 206
Sert, José, 266
Service for Ladies, 298, 300, 301, *302*, *303*, 313
Seton, Marie, 163
Seven Samurai, The, 177
Shakespeare, William, 20, 81, 127, 144, 150, 175, 215, 226, 227, 231, 232, 311
Shane, Ted, 89
Shanghai Express, 72, 95, 99, 326, 333
Shanghai Gesture, The, 333
Shattered, 107, 209
Shaw, George Bernard, 166, 175, 178
Sheehan, Winfield, 130

Sherwood, Robert E., 146
Show People, 308
Siegel, Louis, 188, 196, 197, 343
Siegfried, 218, 238, 268, *274*, 276
Siegmann, George, 329
Sign of the Cross, The, 226
Simon of the Desert, 265
Sinclair, Upton, 185, 186, 321
Siodmak, Curt, 85
Si Paris M'Etait Conté, 260
Sitwell, Osbert, 319
Sivori, Camillo, 250
Skandal um Eva, 25
Skipworth, Alison, 216
Slavinsky, Yevgeni, 266
Smetana, Bedřich, 249, 279
Smith, Jack, 256
Socrates, 221
Sodom and Gomorrah, 188
Sokoloff, Vladimir, 20
Sokolova, Lydia, 217
Solomon and Sheba, 144
Solon, 221
Something's Got to Give, 174
Sophocles, 221
Sorgi, Claudio, 351
S.O.S. Iceberg, 266
So This Is Paris, 202, 318, 321
Sound of Fury, The, 183
Sousa, John Philip, 246
Sous les Toits de Paris, 130, 192, 320
Soussanin, Nicholas, 304
Souvestre, Pierre, 252
Spalding, Albert, 204
Spartacus, 25
Specter of the Rose, 266
Spies, Walter, 194
Spies (Spione), 85, 106, 218, 225, 276
Spinnen, Die, 269
Squire, Ronald, 216
Stage Coach, 130
Stainer, Jacob, 249
Stalin, Joseph, 234
Stander, Lionel, 216
Stanislavsky, Constantin, 256
Stanwyck, Barbara, 227
Starr, William, 168
Stauffacher, Frank, 92, 267
Stebbins, Robert, 320
Steegmuller, Francis, 141
Steichen, Edward, 182, 228
Stein, Gertrude, 319
Steinlen, Théophile, 141
Sten, Anna, 229
Stendhal (Henri Beyle), 80, 209, 264, 279
Sterling, Ford, 216
Stern, Seymour, 320, 321
Sternberg, Josef von, 5, 42, 47, 72, 94, *95*, 96, *97*, 98, 99, 124, 127, 136, 137, 139, 140, 144, 145, 146, 147, 165, 183, 188, 191, 196, 202, 206, 207, 217, 229, 231, 232, 233, 235, 237, 238, 241, 247, 259, 266, 287, 313, 326, *327*, 333, 334, 342, 352, 356
Sternheim, Carl, 149, 211, 212
Stevens, George, 163

Stevenson, Robert Louis, 149, 216, 263, 265, 284
Stewart, James, 187
Stieglitz, Alfred, 182
Stiller, Mauritz, 328
Stockfield, Betty, 231, 284, 288
Stokowski, Leopold, 286
Storm Over Asia, 139, 244, 320, 344
Story of a Cheat, The, 281
Strada, La, 344, 346
Stradivarius, Antonio, 3
Strassberg, Lee, 320
Strauss, Johann, 33, 35
Stroheim, Erich von, xii, xiii, 6, *21*, 34, 39 - 41, *42 - 44*, 45 - 48, *112*, 113 - 122, 124, 125, 126, 127, *128*, *129*, 130 - 133, *138*, 139, 140, 141, 142, 143, 147, 148, 149, 150 - 161, 163, 164, 165, 169, 172, 178, 179, 187, 190, 191, 193, 194, 195, 199, 200, 202, 207, 208, 210, 211, 214, 224, 242, 246, 263, 286, 296, 307, 321, 329, 344, 345, 351, 352, 355, 356
Sturges, Preston, 178, 189
Sue, Eugène, 252
Sunday, 169
Sundays and Cybele, 186, 193
Sunrise, 106, 209, 224, 321
Sutherland, Edward, 232
Suvarsky, Col., 247
Svecenski, Louis, 355
Swanson, Gloria, 47, 155, *158*, 159, 161, 164, 193, 211, 258
Swift, Jonathan, 215
Sylvain, 11, 12
Sylvesterabend, 209
Symons, Arthur, ii
Synodinou, Anna, 180, 190, 214
Szyk, Arthur, 138

Tabu, 106, 194, 222
Tacitus, 340
Tairov, Alexander, 165
Tale of Two Cities, A, 62
Tamerlane, 84
Tamiroff, Akim, 125, 216
Tanguy, Yves, 266
Tarkovski, Andrei, 347
Tartuffe, 107, 209
Tasso, 279
Tausig, Carl, 279
Taylor, Elizabeth, 147, 174, 175
Ten Days That Shook the World, 39, 142, 171, 232, 264, 308, 320
Terrace, The, 214
Terra Trema, La, 338, 346
Terzieff, Laurent, 214
Testament of Dr. Mabuse, The, 137, 276
Thalberg, Irving, 116, 150, 151
Theft of the Mona Lisa, The, 34
Theocritus, 221
Thief of Bagdad, The, 165
Thirty-Nine Steps, The, 188,
208, 231, 281, 346
Thousand Eyes of Dr. Mabuse, The, 268, 277
Three Cornered Hat, The, 298, 311
Three Loves, 141
Three Musketeers, The, 8, 222
Thucydides, 221
Thunder in the East, 183, 231, 281, *282*, *283*, 284 - 294
Thunder Over Mexico, 161, 185, 211
Tice, Clara, 336
Tiger of Eschnapur, The, 277
Time in the Sun, 69, 70, *71 - 76*, 161, 163, 185
Tissé, Eduard, 71, 72, 74, *75*, 76, 171, 178, 186, 249
Titian, 278, 337
Todd, Mike, 87
Togo, Heihachiro, 287
Tokyo Olympiad, 257, 279
Tol'able David, 258
Tolstoi, Leo, xii, 143, 279
Tom Jones, 222
Tone, Franchot, 146
Topaze, 295, 298, 310
Torre Nilsson, Leopoldo, 214
Toscanini, Arturo, 323
Touch of Evil, 134
Toulouse-Lautrec, Henri de, 251, 279
Transatlantic Tunnel, 23
Trauberg, Ilya, 171
Träumende Mund, Der, 320
Treasure Island, 265
Treasure of Sierra Madre, The, 207
Tree Sonata, A, 228
Tretiakov, Sergei M., 232
Trial, The, 202, 203, 265
Trio, 188, 249
Trnka, Jiří, 242
Trotsky, Leon, 235
Truffaut, François, 177, 182, 214, 241, 256, 258, 266
Trumbo, Dalton, 230, 242
Try and Get Me, 183
Tschechowa, Olga, 34, 36
Tully, Jim, 232, 351
Tumbleweeds, 232
Turksib, 320
Turner, Joseph M. W., 263
Twain, Mark, 30
Twelfth Night, 227
Twentieth Century, 191, 225
Twilight of the Gods, The, 226
Two Hearts in Waltz Time, 34

Uchatius, Franz von, 267
Udet, Ernst, 266
Ulysses, 181, 188, 189
Umberto D., 176
Umbrellas of Cherbourg, The, 243, 256
Under Two Flags, 146
Underworld, 313
Une Femme Est Une Femme, 177
Unholy Three, The, 188
Urusevsky, Sergei, 186
Utrillo, Maurice, 237, 260, 261

Vadim, Roger, 214
Vajda, Ernest, 297, 300, 301, 305
Valentin, Albert, 30
Valentino, Rudolph, 171, 204
Vampires, Les, 253
Vampyr, 139, 145, 197, 244, 257, 320
Van Gogh, Theo, 260
Van Gogh, Vincent, 260, 279
Van Hoeydonck, 171
van Horne, Harriet, 6
Vanina, 209
Varconi, Victor, 311
Varèse, Edgar, 137
Variety, 107, 229, 284, 329, 342
Variety Lights, 346
Veidt, Conrad, 106, 172, 244
Venetian Nights, 165
Verlaine, Paul, 221
Vernac, Denise, 132, 193, 196
Verne, Jules, 145
Vertigo, 171
Vertov, Dziga, 210
Very Nice, Very Nice, 169
Vetsera, Marie, 248
Vidor, Florence, *ii*, 142, 307, 332
Vidor, King, 20, 144, 166, 177, 231, 306, 308, 310, *349*
Vigo, Jean, 172, 228
Villon, François, 24
Vinci, Leonardo da, 221, 280
Virgil, 221
Virgin Spring, The, 162
Viridiana, 165, 177, 179, 239
Visages d'Enfants, 186
Visconti, Luchino, 336, 337, 338, 346, 347
Viskovsky, Vyacheslav, 321
Visual Variations on Noguchi, 182
Vitelloni, I, 346
Vitti, Monica, 204, 214, 223
Vivre Sa Vie, 206
Vollmöller, Carl, 165
Voltaire, 162, 279
Vormittagsspuk, 266
Voyage au Congo, 320

Wagner, Fritz Arno, 20
Wagner, Richard, 81, 276, 337
Walbrook, Anton (Adolf Wohlbrück), 36, 285
Wald, Jerry, 188
Walking Down Broadway, 47, 130
Wallace, Dorothy, *153*
Walthall, Henry B., 183, 233
Ward, Warwick, 241
Wassermann, Jakob, 19
Watson, Hildegarde, 196, 197
Watson, J. Sibley, 188, 343
Watteau, Jean-Antoine, 183, 347
Watts, Richard, 193, 194, 299, 300, 301, 305, 306, 308
Waxworks, 188, 191, 321
Wayne, John, 206
Wayne, Naunton, 216
Webber, Melville, 188, 343
Weber, Max, 182
Wechsberg, Joseph, 244
Wedding March, The, 39, 46, 47, 118, *128, 129*, 130, 132, 139, 151, 161, 163, 164, 190, 194, 246, 320
Wedekind, Frank, 20, 175
Weill, Kurt, 19, 23
Weinberg, Herman G., xii, xiii, *349*, 355, 356
Welles, Orson, xii, 115, 122 - 126, 134 - 136, 140, 143, 146, 162, 163, 166, 170, 173, 180, 183, 193, 202, 203, 207, 214, 223, 225, 226, 241, 264, 265, 346, 350
Werfel, Franz, 241
Wessely, Paula, 34, 35, 36
West, Julian, 139, 197
West, Mae, 176, 339
West, Nathanael, 146
Westfront 1918, 20, 22, 23, 320
Wettach, Adrian: see Grock
Whitaker, Herbert, 351
White, Eric Walter, 23
White, Pearl, 253
White Gold, 226
White Hell of Pitz Palu, 25, 266
White Sheik, The, 346
Whitman, Walt, 221
Whitney Brothers, 92
Wiene, Robert, 183
Wild, Roger, 235
Wilde, Oscar, 80, 148, 149, 162, 207, 214, 221, 241, 336, 351, 353
Wilder, Billy, 145, 202
Wilhelm II, 178
Wilhelm (crown prince), 178
Williams, Emlyn, 259
Williams, Tennessee, 149
Wilson, Edmund, 317
Wind, The, 234, 308
Winsten, Archer, 88
Wiskowski, Vyacheslav, 321
Wohlbrück, Adolf: see Walbrook, Anton
Wolf's Clothing, 321
Wolheim, Louis, 140
Wolkoff, Alexander, 212
Woman in the Dunes, 234
Woman in the Moon, The, 276
Woman of Paris, A, 146, 164, 171, 182, 298, 300, 301, 307, 321
Woman of the Sea, 146
Wonderful World of Jules Verne, The, 177
Woollcott, Alexander, 137
World's Greatest Swindles, The, 226
Wray, Fay, *128*
Wurtzel, Sol, 130
Wuthering Heights, 166, 212, 214

Yd, Jean d', 12
Yellow Cruise, The, xii, 31, 32
Yellow Pass, The, 136
Yojimbo, 177
Yoshizawa, 140
Young, Loretta, 307
You Only Live Once, 277
Ysaye, Eugène, 298, 324

Zabriskie Point, 336, 344, 346
Zaharoff, Basil, 125, 226, 267
Zangwill, Israel, 240
Zanuck, Darryl, 175, 181, 187, 189
Zapotec Village, 184, 198
Zarpas, Ted, 180, 190
Zecca, Ferdinand, 286
Zéro de Conduite, 172, 228, 344
Zimmerman, Katherine, 103
Zinnemann, Fred, 163
Zola, Emile, 52, 114, 262
Zuloaga, Ignacio, 352

**A CATALOGUE OF SELECTED DOVER BOOKS
IN ALL FIELDS OF INTEREST**

A CATALOGUE OF SELECTED DOVER BOOKS
IN ALL FIELDS OF INTEREST

AMERICA'S OLD MASTERS, James T. Flexner. Four men emerged unexpectedly from provincial 18th century America to leadership in European art: Benjamin West, J. S. Copley, C. R. Peale, Gilbert Stuart. Brilliant coverage of lives and contributions. Revised, 1967 edition. 69 plates. 365pp. of text.
21806-6 Paperbound $3.00

FIRST FLOWERS OF OUR WILDERNESS: AMERICAN PAINTING, THE COLONIAL PERIOD, James T. Flexner. Painters, and regional painting traditions from earliest Colonial times up to the emergence of Copley, West and Peale Sr., Foster, Gustavus Hesselius, Feke, John Smibert and many anonymous painters in the primitive manner. Engaging presentation, with 162 illustrations. xxii + 368pp.
22180-6 Paperbound $3.50

THE LIGHT OF DISTANT SKIES: AMERICAN PAINTING, 1760-1835, James T. Flexner. The great generation of early American painters goes to Europe to learn and to teach: West, Copley, Gilbert Stuart and others. Allston, Trumbull, Morse; also contemporary American painters—primitives, derivatives, academics—who remained in America. 102 illustrations. xiii + 306pp.
22179-2 Paperbound $3.50

A HISTORY OF THE RISE AND PROGRESS OF THE ARTS OF DESIGN IN THE UNITED STATES, William Dunlap. Much the richest mine of information on early American painters, sculptors, architects, engravers, miniaturists, etc. The only source of information for scores of artists, the major primary source for many others. Unabridged reprint of rare original 1834 edition, with new introduction by James T. Flexner, and 394 new illustrations. Edited by Rita Weiss. 6⅝ x 9⅝.
21695-0, 21696-9, 21697-7 Three volumes, Paperbound $13.50

EPOCHS OF CHINESE AND JAPANESE ART, Ernest F. Fenollosa. From primitive Chinese art to the 20th century, thorough history, explanation of every important art period and form, including Japanese woodcuts; main stress on China and Japan, but Tibet, Korea also included. Still unexcelled for its detailed, rich coverage of cultural background, aesthetic elements, diffusion studies, particularly of the historical period. 2nd, 1913 edition. 242 illustrations. liii + 439pp. of text.
20364-6, 20365-4 Two volumes, Paperbound $6.00

THE GENTLE ART OF MAKING ENEMIES, James A. M. Whistler. Greatest wit of his day deflates Oscar Wilde, Ruskin, Swinburne; strikes back at inane critics, exhibitions, art journalism; aesthetics of impressionist revolution in most striking form. Highly readable classic by great painter. Reproduction of edition designed by Whistler. Introduction by Alfred Werner. xxxvi + 334pp.
21875-9 Paperbound $2.50

CATALOGUE OF DOVER BOOKS

VISUAL ILLUSIONS: THEIR CAUSES, CHARACTERISTICS, AND APPLICATIONS, Matthew Luckiesh. Thorough description and discussion of optical illusion, geometric and perspective, particularly; size and shape distortions, illusions of color, of motion; natural illusions; use of illusion in art and magic, industry, etc. Most useful today with op art, also for classical art. Scores of effects illustrated. Introduction by William H. Ittleson. 100 illustrations. xxi + 252pp.
21530-X Paperbound $2.00

A HANDBOOK OF ANATOMY FOR ART STUDENTS, Arthur Thomson. Thorough, virtually exhaustive coverage of skeletal structure, musculature, etc. Full text, supplemented by anatomical diagrams and drawings and by photographs of undraped figures. Unique in its comparison of male and female forms, pointing out differences of contour, texture, form. 211 figures, 40 drawings, 86 photographs. xx + 459pp. 5⅜ x 8⅜.
21163-0 Paperbound $3.50

150 MASTERPIECES OF DRAWING, Selected by Anthony Toney. Full page reproductions of drawings from the early 16th to the end of the 18th century, all beautifully reproduced: Rembrandt, Michelangelo, Dürer, Fragonard, Urs, Graf, Wouwerman, many others. First-rate browsing book, model book for artists. xviii + 150pp. 8⅜ x 11¼.
21032-4 Paperbound $2.50

THE LATER WORK OF AUBREY BEARDSLEY, Aubrey Beardsley. Exotic, erotic, ironic masterpieces in full maturity: Comedy Ballet, Venus and Tannhauser, Pierrot, Lysistrata, Rape of the Lock, Savoy material, Ali Baba, Volpone, etc. This material revolutionized the art world, and is still powerful, fresh, brilliant. With *The Early Work*, all Beardsley's finest work. 174 plates, 2 in color. xiv + 176pp. 8⅛ x 11.
21817-1 Paperbound $3.00

DRAWINGS OF REMBRANDT, Rembrandt van Rijn. Complete reproduction of fabulously rare edition by Lippmann and Hofstede de Groot, completely reedited, updated, improved by Prof. Seymour Slive, Fogg Museum. Portraits, Biblical sketches, landscapes, Oriental types, nudes, episodes from classical mythology—All Rembrandt's fertile genius. Also selection of drawings by his pupils and followers. "Stunning volumes," *Saturday Review*. 550 illustrations. lxxviii + 552pp. 9⅛ x 12¼.
21485-0, 21486-9 Two volumes, Paperbound $10.00

THE DISASTERS OF WAR, Francisco Goya. One of the masterpieces of Western civilization—83 etchings that record Goya's shattering, bitter reaction to the Napoleonic war that swept through Spain after the insurrection of 1808 and to war in general. Reprint of the first edition, with three additional plates from Boston's Museum of Fine Arts. All plates facsimile size. Introduction by Philip Hofer, Fogg Museum. v + 97pp. 9⅜ x 8¼.
21872-4 Paperbound $2.00

GRAPHIC WORKS OF ODILON REDON. Largest collection of Redon's graphic works ever assembled: 172 lithographs, 28 etchings and engravings, 9 drawings. These include some of his most famous works. All the plates from *Odilon Redon: oeuvre graphique complet,* plus additional plates. New introduction and caption translations by Alfred Werner. 209 illustrations. xxvii + 209pp. 9⅛ x 12¼.
21966-8 Paperbound $4.00

CATALOGUE OF DOVER BOOKS

DESIGN BY ACCIDENT; A BOOK OF "ACCIDENTAL EFFECTS" FOR ARTISTS AND DESIGNERS, James F. O'Brien. Create your own unique, striking, imaginative effects by "controlled accident" interaction of materials: paints and lacquers, oil and water based paints, splatter, crackling materials, shatter, similar items. Everything you do will be different; first book on this limitless art, so useful to both fine artist and commercial artist. Full instructions. 192 plates showing "accidents," 8 in color. viii + 215pp. 8⅜ x 11¼.   21942-9 Paperbound $3.50

THE BOOK OF SIGNS, Rudolf Koch. Famed German type designer draws 493 beautiful symbols: religious, mystical, alchemical, imperial, property marks, runes, etc. Remarkable fusion of traditional and modern. Good for suggestions of timelessness, smartness, modernity. Text. vi + 104pp. 6⅛ x 9¼.
20162-7 Paperbound $1.25

HISTORY OF INDIAN AND INDONESIAN ART, Ananda K. Coomaraswamy. An unabridged republication of one of the finest books by a great scholar in Eastern art. Rich in descriptive material, history, social backgrounds; Sunga reliefs, Rajput paintings, Gupta temples, Burmese frescoes, textiles, jewelry, sculpture, etc. 400 photos. viii + 423pp. 6⅜ x 9¾.   21436-2 Paperbound $5.00

PRIMITIVE ART, Franz Boas. America's foremost anthropologist surveys textiles, ceramics, woodcarving, basketry, metalwork, etc.; patterns, technology, creation of symbols, style origins. All areas of world, but very full on Northwest Coast Indians. More than 350 illustrations of baskets, boxes, totem poles, weapons, etc. 378 pp.
20025-6 Paperbound $3.00

THE GENTLEMAN AND CABINET MAKER'S DIRECTOR, Thomas Chippendale. Full reprint (third edition, 1762) of most influential furniture book of all time, by master cabinetmaker. 200 plates, illustrating chairs, sofas, mirrors, tables, cabinets, plus 24 photographs of surviving pieces. Biographical introduction by N. Bienenstock. vi + 249pp. 9⅞ x 12¾.   21601-2 Paperbound $4.00

AMERICAN ANTIQUE FURNITURE, Edgar G. Miller, Jr. The basic coverage of all American furniture before 1840. Individual chapters cover type of furniture—clocks, tables, sideboards, etc.—chronologically, with inexhaustible wealth of data. More than 2100 photographs, all identified, commented on. Essential to all early American collectors. Introduction by H. E. Keyes. vi + 1106pp. 7⅞ x 10¾.
21599-7, 21600-4 Two volumes, Paperbound $11.00

PENNSYLVANIA DUTCH AMERICAN FOLK ART, Henry J. Kauffman. 279 photos, 28 drawings of tulipware, Fraktur script, painted tinware, toys, flowered furniture, quilts, samplers, hex signs, house interiors, etc. Full descriptive text. Excellent for tourist, rewarding for designer, collector. Map. 146pp. 7⅞ x 10¾.
21205-X Paperbound $2.50

EARLY NEW ENGLAND GRAVESTONE RUBBINGS, Edmund V. Gillon, Jr. 43 photographs, 226 carefully reproduced rubbings show heavily symbolic, sometimes macabre early gravestones, up to early 19th century. Remarkable early American primitive art, occasionally strikingly beautiful; always powerful. Text. xxvi + 207pp. 8⅜ x 11¼.   21380-3 Paperbound $3.50

CATALOGUE OF DOVER BOOKS

ALPHABETS AND ORNAMENTS, Ernst Lehner. Well-known pictorial source for decorative alphabets, script examples, cartouches, frames, decorative title pages, calligraphic initials, borders, similar material. 14th to 19th century, mostly European. Useful in almost any graphic arts designing, varied styles. 750 illustrations. 256pp. 7 x 10. 21905-4 Paperbound $4.00

PAINTING: A CREATIVE APPROACH, Norman Colquhoun. For the beginner simple guide provides an instructive approach to painting: major stumbling blocks for beginner; overcoming them, technical points; paints and pigments; oil painting; watercolor and other media and color. New section on "plastic" paints. Glossary. Formerly *Paint Your Own Pictures*. 221pp. 22000-1 Paperbound $1.75

THE ENJOYMENT AND USE OF COLOR, Walter Sargent. Explanation of the relations between colors themselves and between colors in nature and art, including hundreds of little-known facts about color values, intensities, effects of high and low illumination, complementary colors. Many practical hints for painters, references to great masters. 7 color plates, 29 illustrations. x + 274pp.
20944-X Paperbound $2.75

THE NOTEBOOKS OF LEONARDO DA VINCI, compiled and edited by Jean Paul Richter. 1566 extracts from original manuscripts reveal the full range of Leonardo's versatile genius: all his writings on painting, sculpture, architecture, anatomy, astronomy, geography, topography, physiology, mining, music, etc., in both Italian and English, with 186 plates of manuscript pages and more than 500 additional drawings. Includes studies for the Last Supper, the lost Sforza monument, and other works. Total of xlvii + 866pp. 7⅞ x 10¾.
22572-0, 22573-9 Two volumes, Paperbound $10.00

MONTGOMERY WARD CATALOGUE OF 1895. Tea gowns, yards of flannel and pillow-case lace, stereoscopes, books of gospel hymns, the New Improved Singer Sewing Machine, side saddles, milk skimmers, straight-edged razors, high-button shoes, spittoons, and on and on . . . listing some 25,000 items, practically all illustrated. Essential to the shoppers of the 1890's, it is our truest record of the spirit of the period. Unaltered reprint of Issue No. 57, Spring and Summer 1895. Introduction by Boris Emmet. Innumerable illustrations. xiii + 624pp. 8½ x 11⅝.
22377-9 Paperbound $6.95

THE CRYSTAL PALACE EXHIBITION ILLUSTRATED CATALOGUE (LONDON, 1851). One of the wonders of the modern world—the Crystal Palace Exhibition in which all the nations of the civilized world exhibited their achievements in the arts and sciences—presented in an equally important illustrated catalogue. More than 1700 items pictured with accompanying text—ceramics, textiles, cast-iron work, carpets, pianos, sleds, razors, wall-papers, billiard tables, beehives, silverware and hundreds of other artifacts—represent the focal point of Victorian culture in the Western World. Probably the largest collection of Victorian decorative art ever assembled—indispensable for antiquarians and designers. Unabridged republication of the Art-Journal Catalogue of the Great Exhibition of 1851, with all terminal essays. New introduction by John Gloag, F.S.A. xxxiv + 426pp. 9 x 12.
22503-8 Paperbound $4.50

CATALOGUE OF DOVER BOOKS

A HISTORY OF COSTUME, Carl Köhler. Definitive history, based on surviving pieces of clothing primarily, and paintings, statues, etc. secondarily. Highly readable text, supplemented by 594 illustrations of costumes of the ancient Mediterranean peoples, Greece and Rome, the Teutonic prehistoric period; costumes of the Middle Ages, Renaissance, Baroque, 18th and 19th centuries. Clear, measured patterns are provided for many clothing articles. Approach is practical throughout. Enlarged by Emma von Sichart. 464pp. 21030-8 Paperbound $3.50

ORIENTAL RUGS, ANTIQUE AND MODERN, Walter A. Hawley. A complete and authoritative treatise on the Oriental rug—where they are made, by whom and how, designs and symbols, characteristics in detail of the six major groups, how to distinguish them and how to buy them. Detailed technical data is provided on periods, weaves, warps, wefts, textures, sides, ends and knots, although no technical background is required for an understanding. 11 color plates, 80 halftones, 4 maps. vi + 320pp. 6⅛ x 9⅛. 22366-3 Paperbound $5.00

TEN BOOKS ON ARCHITECTURE, Vitruvius. By any standards the most important book on architecture ever written. Early Roman discussion of aesthetics of building, construction methods, orders, sites, and every other aspect of architecture has inspired, instructed architecture for about 2,000 years. Stands behind Palladio, Michelangelo, Bramante, Wren, countless others. Definitive Morris H. Morgan translation. 68 illustrations. xii + 331pp. 20645-9 Paperbound $3.00

THE FOUR BOOKS OF ARCHITECTURE, Andrea Palladio. Translated into every major Western European language in the two centuries following its publication in 1570, this has been one of the most influential books in the history of architecture. Complete reprint of the 1738 Isaac Ware edition. New introduction by Adolf Placzek, Columbia Univ. 216 plates. xxii + 110pp. of text. 9½ x 12¾. 21308-0 Clothbound $10.00

STICKS AND STONES: A STUDY OF AMERICAN ARCHITECTURE AND CIVILIZATION, Lewis Mumford. One of the great classics of American cultural history. American architecture from the medieval-inspired earliest forms to the early 20th century; evolution of structure and style, and reciprocal influences on environment. 21 photographic illustrations. 238pp. 20202-X Paperbound $2.00

THE AMERICAN BUILDER'S COMPANION, Asher Benjamin. The most widely used early 19th century architectural style and source book, for colonial up into Greek Revival periods. Extensive development of geometry of carpentering, construction of sashes, frames, doors, stairs; plans and elevations of domestic and other buildings. Hundreds of thousands of houses were built according to this book, now invaluable to historians, architects, restorers, etc. 1827 edition. 59 plates. 114pp. 7⅞ x 10¾. 22236-5 Paperbound $3.50

DUTCH HOUSES IN THE HUDSON VALLEY BEFORE 1776, Helen Wilkinson Reynolds. The standard survey of the Dutch colonial house and outbuildings, with constructional features, decoration, and local history associated with individual homesteads. Introduction by Franklin D. Roosevelt. Map. 150 illustrations. 469pp. 6⅝ x 9¼. 21469-9 Paperbound $4.00

CATALOGUE OF DOVER BOOKS

THE ARCHITECTURE OF COUNTRY HOUSES, Andrew J. Downing. Together with Vaux's *Villas and Cottages* this is the basic book for Hudson River Gothic architecture of the middle Victorian period. Full, sound discussions of general aspects of housing, architecture, style, decoration, furnishing, together with scores of detailed house plans, illustrations of specific buildings, accompanied by full text. Perhaps the most influential single American architectural book. 1850 edition. Introduction by J. Stewart Johnson. 321 figures, 34 architectural designs. xvi + 560pp.
22003-6 Paperbound $4.00

LOST EXAMPLES OF COLONIAL ARCHITECTURE, John Mead Howells. Full-page photographs of buildings that have disappeared or been so altered as to be denatured, including many designed by major early American architects. 245 plates. xvii + 248pp. 7⅞ x 10¾.
21143-6 Paperbound $3.50

DOMESTIC ARCHITECTURE OF THE AMERICAN COLONIES AND OF THE EARLY REPUBLIC, Fiske Kimball. Foremost architect and restorer of Williamsburg and Monticello covers nearly 200 homes between 1620-1825. Architectural details, construction, style features, special fixtures, floor plans, etc. Generally considered finest work in its area. 219 illustrations of houses, doorways, windows, capital mantels. xx + 314pp. 7⅞ x 10¾.
21743-4 Paperbound $4.00

EARLY AMERICAN ROOMS: 1650-1858, edited by Russell Hawes Kettell. Tour of 12 rooms, each representative of a different era in American history and each furnished, decorated, designed and occupied in the style of the era. 72 plans and elevations, 8-page color section, etc., show fabrics, wall papers, arrangements, etc. Full descriptive text. xvii + 200pp. of text. 8⅜ x 11¼.
21633-0 Paperbound $5.00

THE FITZWILLIAM VIRGINAL BOOK, edited by J. Fuller Maitland and W. B. Squire. Full modern printing of famous early 17th-century ms. volume of 300 works by Morley, Byrd, Bull, Gibbons, etc. For piano or other modern keyboard instrument; easy to read format. xxxvi + 938pp. 8⅜ x 11.
21068-5, 21069-3 Two volumes, Paperbound $10.00

KEYBOARD MUSIC, Johann Sebastian Bach. Bach Gesellschaft edition. A rich selection of Bach's masterpieces for the harpsichord: the six English Suites, six French Suites, the six Partitas (Clavierübung part I), the Goldberg Variations (Clavierübung part IV), the fifteen Two-Part Inventions and the fifteen Three-Part Sinfonias. Clearly reproduced on large sheets with ample margins; eminently playable. vi + 312pp. 8⅛ x 11.
22360-4 Paperbound $5.00

THE MUSIC OF BACH: AN INTRODUCTION, Charles Sanford Terry. A fine, nontechnical introduction to Bach's music, both instrumental and vocal. Covers organ music, chamber music, passion music, other types. Analyzes themes, developments, innovations. x + 114pp.
21075-8 Paperbound $1.25

BEETHOVEN AND HIS NINE SYMPHONIES, Sir George Grove. Noted British musicologist provides best history, analysis, commentary on symphonies. Very thorough, rigorously accurate; necessary to both advanced student and amateur music lover. 436 musical passages. vii + 407 pp.
20334-4 Paperbound $2.75

CATALOGUE OF DOVER BOOKS

JOHANN SEBASTIAN BACH, Philipp Spitta. One of the great classics of musicology, this definitive analysis of Bach's music (and life) has never been surpassed. Lucid, nontechnical analyses of hundreds of pieces (30 pages devoted to St. Matthew Passion, 26 to B Minor Mass). Also includes major analysis of 18th-century music. 450 musical examples. 40-page musical supplement. Total of xx + 1799pp.
(EUK) 22278-0, 22279-9 Two volumes, Clothbound $17.50

MOZART AND HIS PIANO CONCERTOS, Cuthbert Girdlestone. The only full-length study of an important area of Mozart's creativity. Provides detailed analyses of all 23 concertos, traces inspirational sources. 417 musical examples. Second edition. 509pp. 21271-8 Paperbound $3.50

THE PERFECT WAGNERITE: A COMMENTARY ON THE NIBLUNG'S RING, George Bernard Shaw. Brilliant and still relevant criticism in remarkable essays on Wagner's Ring cycle, Shaw's ideas on political and social ideology behind the plots, role of Leitmotifs, vocal requisites, etc. Prefaces. xxi + 136pp.
(USO) 21707-8 Paperbound $1.50

DON GIOVANNI, W. A. Mozart. Complete libretto, modern English translation; biographies of composer and librettist; accounts of early performances and critical reaction. Lavishly illustrated. All the material you need to understand and appreciate this great work. Dover Opera Guide and Libretto Series; translated and introduced by Ellen Bleiler. 92 illustrations. 209pp.
21134-7 Paperbound $2.00

HIGH FIDELITY SYSTEMS: A LAYMAN'S GUIDE, Roy F. Allison. All the basic information you need for setting up your own audio system: high fidelity and stereo record players, tape records, F.M. Connections, adjusting tone arm, cartridge, checking needle alignment, positioning speakers, phasing speakers, adjusting hums, trouble-shooting, maintenance, and similar topics. Enlarged 1965 edition. More than 50 charts, diagrams, photos. iv + 91pp. 21514-8 Paperbound $1.25

REPRODUCTION OF SOUND, Edgar Villchur. Thorough coverage for laymen of high fidelity systems, reproducing systems in general, needles, amplifiers, preamps, loudspeakers, feedback, explaining physical background. "A rare talent for making technicalities vividly comprehensible," R. Darrell, *High Fidelity.* 69 figures. iv + 92pp. 21515-6 Paperbound $1.25

HEAR ME TALKIN' TO YA: THE STORY OF JAZZ AS TOLD BY THE MEN WHO MADE IT, Nat Shapiro and Nat Hentoff. Louis Armstrong, Fats Waller, Jo Jones, Clarence Williams, Billy Holiday, Duke Ellington, Jelly Roll Morton and dozens of other jazz greats tell how it was in Chicago's South Side, New Orleans, depression Harlem and the modern West Coast as jazz was born and grew. xvi + 429pp.
21726-4 Paperbound $2.50

FABLES OF AESOP, translated by Sir Roger L'Estrange. A reproduction of the very rare 1931 Paris edition; a selection of the most interesting fables, together with 50 imaginative drawings by Alexander Calder. v + 128pp. 6½x9¼.
21780-9 Paperbound $1.50

CATALOGUE OF DOVER BOOKS

AGAINST THE GRAIN (A REBOURS), Joris K. Huysmans. Filled with weird images, evidences of a bizarre imagination, exotic experiments with hallucinogenic drugs, rich tastes and smells and the diversions of its sybarite hero Duc Jean des Esseintes, this classic novel pushed 19th-century literary decadence to its limits. Full unabridged edition. Do not confuse this with abridged editions generally sold. Introduction by Havelock Ellis. xlix + 206pp. 22190-3 Paperbound $2.00

VARIORUM SHAKESPEARE: HAMLET. Edited by Horace H. Furness; a landmark of American scholarship. Exhaustive footnotes and appendices treat all doubtful words and phrases, as well as suggested critical emendations throughout the play's history. First volume contains editor's own text, collated with all Quartos and Folios. Second volume contains full first Quarto, translations of Shakespeare's sources (Belleforest, and Saxo Grammaticus), Der Bestrafte Brudermord, and many essays on critical and historical points of interest by major authorities of past and present. Includes details of staging and costuming over the years. By far the best edition available for serious students of Shakespeare. Total of xx + 905pp.
21004-9, 21005-7, 2 volumes, Paperbound $7.00

A LIFE OF WILLIAM SHAKESPEARE, Sir Sidney Lee. This is the standard life of Shakespeare, summarizing everything known about Shakespeare and his plays. Incredibly rich in material, broad in coverage, clear and judicious, it has served thousands as the best introduction to Shakespeare. 1931 edition. 9 plates. xxix + 792pp. (USO) 21967-4 Paperbound $3.75

MASTERS OF THE DRAMA, John Gassner. Most comprehensive history of the drama in print, covering every tradition from Greeks to modern Europe and America, including India, Far East, etc. Covers more than 800 dramatists, 2000 plays, with biographical material, plot summaries, theatre history, criticism, etc. "Best of its kind in English," *New Republic.* 77 illustrations. xxii + 890pp.
20100-7 Clothbound $8.50

THE EVOLUTION OF THE ENGLISH LANGUAGE, George McKnight. The growth of English, from the 14th century to the present. Unusual, non-technical account presents basic information in very interesting form: sound shifts, change in grammar and syntax, vocabulary growth, similar topics. Abundantly illustrated with quotations. Formerly *Modern English in the Making.* xii + 590pp.
21932-1 Paperbound $3.50

AN ETYMOLOGICAL DICTIONARY OF MODERN ENGLISH, Ernest Weekley. Fullest, richest work of its sort, by foremost British lexicographer. Detailed word histories, including many colloquial and archaic words; extensive quotations. Do not confuse this with the Concise Etymological Dictionary, which is much abridged. Total of xxvii + 830pp. 6½ x 9¼.
21873-2, 21874-0 Two volumes, Paperbound $6.00

FLATLAND: A ROMANCE OF MANY DIMENSIONS, E. A. Abbott. Classic of science-fiction explores ramifications of life in a two-dimensional world, and what happens when a three-dimensional being intrudes. Amusing reading, but also useful as introduction to thought about hyperspace. Introduction by Banesh Hoffmann. 16 illustrations. xx + 103pp. 20001-9 Paperbound $1.00

CATALOGUE OF DOVER BOOKS

POEMS OF ANNE BRADSTREET, edited with an introduction by Robert Hutchinson. A new selection of poems by America's first poet and perhaps the first significant woman poet in the English language. 48 poems display her development in works of considerable variety—love poems, domestic poems, religious meditations, formal elegies, "quaternions," etc. Notes, bibliography. viii + 222pp.
22160-1 Paperbound $2.50

THREE GOTHIC NOVELS: THE CASTLE OF OTRANTO BY HORACE WALPOLE; VATHEK BY WILLIAM BECKFORD; THE VAMPYRE BY JOHN POLIDORI, WITH FRAGMENT OF A NOVEL BY LORD BYRON, edited by E. F. Bleiler. The first Gothic novel, by Walpole; the finest Oriental tale in English, by Beckford; powerful Romantic supernatural story in versions by Polidori and Byron. All extremely important in history of literature; all still exciting, packed with supernatural thrills, ghosts, haunted castles, magic, etc. xl + 291pp.
21232-7 Paperbound $2.50

THE BEST TALES OF HOFFMANN, E. T. A. Hoffmann. 10 of Hoffmann's most important stories, in modern re-editings of standard translations: Nutcracker and the King of Mice, Signor Formica, Automata, The Sandman, Rath Krespel, The Golden Flowerpot, Master Martin the Cooper, The Mines of Falun, The King's Betrothed, A New Year's Eve Adventure. 7 illustrations by Hoffmann. Edited by E. F. Bleiler. xxxix + 419pp.   21793-0 Paperbound $3.00

GHOST AND HORROR STORIES OF AMBROSE BIERCE, Ambrose Bierce. 23 strikingly modern stories of the horrors latent in the human mind: The Eyes of the Panther, The Damned Thing, An Occurrence at Owl Creek Bridge, An Inhabitant of Carcosa, etc., plus the dream-essay, Visions of the Night. Edited by E. F. Bleiler. xxii + 199pp.   20767-6 Paperbound $1.50

BEST GHOST STORIES OF J. S. LEFANU, J. Sheridan LeFanu. Finest stories by Victorian master often considered greatest supernatural writer of all. Carmilla, Green Tea, The Haunted Baronet, The Familiar, and 12 others. Most never before available in the U. S. A. Edited by E. F. Bleiler. 8 illustrations from Victorian publications. xvii + 467pp.   20415-4 Paperbound $3.00

MATHEMATICAL FOUNDATIONS OF INFORMATION THEORY, A. I. Khinchin. Comprehensive introduction to work of Shannon, McMillan, Feinstein and Khinchin, placing these investigations on a rigorous mathematical basis. Covers entropy concept in probability theory, uniqueness theorem, Shannon's inequality, ergodic sources, the E property, martingale concept, noise, Feinstein's fundamental lemma, Shanon's first and second theorems. Translated by R. A. Silverman and M. D. Friedman. iii + 120pp.   60434-9 Paperbound $1.75

SEVEN SCIENCE FICTION NOVELS, H. G. Wells. The standard collection of the great novels. Complete, unabridged. *First Men in the Moon, Island of Dr. Moreau, War of the Worlds, Food of the Gods, Invisible Man, Time Machine, In the Days of the Comet.* Not only science fiction fans, but every educated person owes it to himself to read these novels. 1015pp.   (USO) 20264-X Clothbound $5.00

CATALOGUE OF DOVER BOOKS

LAST AND FIRST MEN AND STAR MAKER, TWO SCIENCE FICTION NOVELS, Olaf Stapledon. Greatest future histories in science fiction. In the first, human intelligence is the "hero," through strange paths of evolution, interplanetary invasions, incredible technologies, near extinctions and reemergences. Star Maker describes the quest of a band of star rovers for intelligence itself, through time and space: weird inhuman civilizations, crustacean minds, symbiotic worlds, etc. Complete, unabridged. v + 438pp. (USO) 21962-3 Paperbound $2.50

THREE PROPHETIC NOVELS, H. G. WELLS. Stages of a consistently planned future for mankind. *When the Sleeper Wakes,* and *A Story of the Days to Come,* anticipate *Brave New World* and *1984,* in the 21st Century; *The Time Machine,* only complete version in print, shows farther future and the end of mankind. All show Wells's greatest gifts as storyteller and novelist. Edited by E. F. Bleiler. x + 335pp. (USO) 20605-X Paperbound $2.50

THE DEVIL'S DICTIONARY, Ambrose Bierce. America's own Oscar Wilde—Ambrose Bierce—offers his barbed iconoclastic wisdom in over 1,000 definitions hailed by H. L. Mencken as "some of the most gorgeous witticisms in the English language." 145pp. 20487-1 Paperbound $1.25

MAX AND MORITZ, Wilhelm Busch. Great children's classic, father of comic strip, of two bad boys, Max and Moritz. Also Ker and Plunk (Plisch und Plumm), Cat and Mouse, Deceitful Henry, Ice-Peter, The Boy and the Pipe, and five other pieces. Original German, with English translation. Edited by H. Arthur Klein; translations by various hands and H. Arthur Klein. vi + 216pp.
20181-3 Paperbound $2.00

PIGS IS PIGS AND OTHER FAVORITES, Ellis Parker Butler. The title story is one of the best humor short stories, as Mike Flannery obfuscates biology and English. Also included, That Pup of Murchison's, The Great American Pie Company, and Perkins of Portland. 14 illustrations. v + 109pp. 21532-6 Paperbound $1.25

THE PETERKIN PAPERS, Lucretia P. Hale. It takes genius to be as stupidly mad as the Peterkins, as they decide to become wise, celebrate the "Fourth," keep a cow, and otherwise strain the resources of the Lady from Philadelphia. Basic book of American humor. 153 illustrations. 219pp. 20794-3 Paperbound $1.50

PERRAULT'S FAIRY TALES, translated by A. E. Johnson and S. R. Littlewood, with 34 full-page illustrations by Gustave Doré. All the original Perrault stories—Cinderella, Sleeping Beauty, Bluebeard, Little Red Riding Hood, Puss in Boots, Tom Thumb, etc.—with their witty verse morals and the magnificent illustrations of Doré. One of the five or six great books of European fairy tales. viii + 117pp. 8⅛ x 11. 22311-6 Paperbound $2.00

OLD HUNGARIAN FAIRY TALES, Baroness Orczy. Favorites translated and adapted by author of the *Scarlet Pimpernel.* Eight fairy tales include "The Suitors of Princess Fire-Fly," "The Twin Hunchbacks," "Mr. Cuttlefish's Love Story," and "The Enchanted Cat." This little volume of magic and adventure will captivate children as it has for generations. 90 drawings by Montagu Barstow. 96pp.
22293-4 Paperbound $1.95

CATALOGUE OF DOVER BOOKS

THE RED FAIRY BOOK, Andrew Lang. Lang's color fairy books have long been children's favorites. This volume includes Rapunzel, Jack and the Bean-stalk and 35 other stories, familiar and unfamiliar. 4 plates, 93 illustrations x + 367pp.
21673-X Paperbound $2.50

THE BLUE FAIRY BOOK, Andrew Lang. Lang's tales come from all countries and all times. Here are 37 tales from Grimm, the Arabian Nights, Greek Mythology, and other fascinating sources. 8 plates, 130 illustrations. xi + 390pp.
21437-0 Paperbound $2.50

HOUSEHOLD STORIES BY THE BROTHERS GRIMM. Classic English-language edition of the well-known tales — Rumpelstiltskin, Snow White, Hansel and Gretel, The Twelve Brothers, Faithful John, Rapunzel, Tom Thumb (52 stories in all). Translated into simple, straightforward English by Lucy Crane. Ornamented with headpieces, vignettes, elaborate decorative initials and a dozen full-page illustrations by Walter Crane. x + 269pp.
21080-4 Paperbound $2.00

THE MERRY ADVENTURES OF ROBIN HOOD, Howard Pyle. The finest modern versions of the traditional ballads and tales about the great English outlaw. Howard Pyle's complete prose version, with every word, every illustration of the first edition. Do not confuse this facsimile of the original (1883) with modern editions that change text or illustrations. 23 plates plus many page decorations. xxii + 296pp.
22043-5 Paperbound $2.50

THE STORY OF KING ARTHUR AND HIS KNIGHTS, Howard Pyle. The finest children's version of the life of King Arthur; brilliantly retold by Pyle, with 48 of his most imaginative illustrations. xviii + 313pp. 6⅛ x 9¼.
21445-1 Paperbound $2.50

THE WONDERFUL WIZARD OF OZ, L. Frank Baum. America's finest children's book in facsimile of first edition with all Denslow illustrations in full color. The edition a child should have. Introduction by Martin Gardner. 23 color plates, scores of drawings. iv + 267pp.
20691-2 Paperbound $2.50

THE MARVELOUS LAND OF OZ, L. Frank Baum. The second Oz book, every bit as imaginative as the Wizard. The hero is a boy named Tip, but the Scarecrow and the Tin Woodman are back, as is the Oz magic. 16 color plates, 120 drawings by John R. Neill. 287pp.
20692-0 Paperbound $2.50

THE MAGICAL MONARCH OF MO, L. Frank Baum. Remarkable adventures in a land even stranger than Oz. The best of Baum's books not in the Oz series. 15 color plates and dozens of drawings by Frank Verbeck. xviii + 237pp.
21892-9 Paperbound $2.25

THE BAD CHILD'S BOOK OF BEASTS, MORE BEASTS FOR WORSE CHILDREN, A MORAL ALPHABET, Hilaire Belloc. Three complete humor classics in one volume. Be kind to the frog, and do not call him names . . . and 28 other whimsical animals. Familiar favorites and some not so well known. Illustrated by Basil Blackwell. 156pp.
(USO) 20749-8 Paperbound $1.50

CATALOGUE OF DOVER BOOKS

EAST O' THE SUN AND WEST O' THE MOON, George W. Dasent. Considered the best of all translations of these Norwegian folk tales, this collection has been enjoyed by generations of children (and folklorists too). Includes True and Untrue, Why the Sea is Salt, East O' the Sun and West O' the Moon, Why the Bear is Stumpy-Tailed, Boots and the Troll, The Cock and the Hen, Rich Peter the Pedlar, and 52 more. The only edition with all 59 tales. 77 illustrations by Erik Werenskiold and Theodor Kittelsen. xv + 418pp. 22521-6 Paperbound $3.50

GOOPS AND HOW TO BE THEM, Gelett Burgess. Classic of tongue-in-cheek humor, masquerading as etiquette book. 87 verses, twice as many cartoons, show mischievous Goops as they demonstrate to children virtues of table manners, neatness, courtesy, etc. Favorite for generations. viii + 88pp. $6½ \times 9¼$. 22233-0 Paperbound $1.25

ALICE'S ADVENTURES UNDER GROUND, Lewis Carroll. The first version, quite different from the final *Alice in Wonderland,* printed out by Carroll himself with his own illustrations. Complete facsimile of the "million dollar" manuscript Carroll gave to Alice Liddell in 1864. Introduction by Martin Gardner. viii + 96pp. Title and dedication pages in color. 21482-6 Paperbound $1.25

THE BROWNIES, THEIR BOOK, Palmer Cox. Small as mice, cunning as foxes, exuberant and full of mischief, the Brownies go to the zoo, toy shop, seashore, circus, etc., in 24 verse adventures and 266 illustrations. Long a favorite, since their first appearance in St. Nicholas Magazine. xi + 144pp. $6⅝ \times 9¼$. 21265-3 Paperbound $1.75

SONGS OF CHILDHOOD, Walter De La Mare. Published (under the pseudonym Walter Ramal) when De La Mare was only 29, this charming collection has long been a favorite children's book. A facsimile of the first edition in paper, the 47 poems capture the simplicity of the nursery rhyme and the ballad, including such lyrics as I Met Eve, Tartary, The Silver Penny. vii + 106pp. (USO) 21972-0 Paperbound $1.25

THE COMPLETE NONSENSE OF EDWARD LEAR, Edward Lear. The finest 19th-century humorist-cartoonist in full: all nonsense limericks, zany alphabets, Owl and Pussycat, songs, nonsense botany, and more than 500 illustrations by Lear himself. Edited by Holbrook Jackson. xxix + 287pp. (USO) 20167-8 Paperbound $2.00

BILLY WHISKERS: THE AUTOBIOGRAPHY OF A GOAT, Frances Trego Montgomery. A favorite of children since the early 20th century, here are the escapades of that rambunctious, irresistible and mischievous goat—Billy Whiskers. Much in the spirit of *Peck's Bad Boy,* this is a book that children never tire of reading or hearing. All the original familiar illustrations by W. H. Fry are included: 6 color plates, 18 black and white drawings. 159pp. 22345-0 Paperbound $2.00

MOTHER GOOSE MELODIES. Faithful republication of the fabulously rare Munroe and Francis "copyright 1833" Boston edition—the most important Mother Goose collection, usually referred to as the "original." Familiar rhymes plus many rare ones, with wonderful old woodcut illustrations. Edited by E. F. Bleiler. 128pp. $4½ \times 6⅜$. 22577-1 Paperbound $1.00

CATALOGUE OF DOVER BOOKS

TWO LITTLE SAVAGES; BEING THE ADVENTURES OF TWO BOYS WHO LIVED AS INDIANS AND WHAT THEY LEARNED, Ernest Thompson Seton. Great classic of nature and boyhood provides a vast range of woodlore in most palatable form, a genuinely entertaining story. Two farm boys build a teepee in woods and live in it for a month, working out Indian solutions to living problems, star lore, birds and animals, plants, etc. 293 illustrations. vii + 286pp.
20985-7 Paperbound $2.50

PETER PIPER'S PRACTICAL PRINCIPLES OF PLAIN & PERFECT PRONUNCIATION. Alliterative jingles and tongue-twisters of surprising charm, that made their first appearance in America about 1830. Republished in full with the spirited woodcut illustrations from this earliest American edition. 32pp. $4\frac{1}{2}$ x $6\frac{3}{8}$.
22560-7 Paperbound $1.00

SCIENCE EXPERIMENTS AND AMUSEMENTS FOR CHILDREN, Charles Vivian. 73 easy experiments, requiring only materials found at home or easily available, such as candles, coins, steel wool, etc.; illustrate basic phenomena like vacuum, simple chemical reaction, etc. All safe. Modern, well-planned. Formerly *Science Games for Children*. 102 photos, numerous drawings. 96pp. $6\frac{1}{8}$ x $9\frac{1}{4}$.
21856-2 Paperbound $1.25

AN INTRODUCTION TO CHESS MOVES AND TACTICS SIMPLY EXPLAINED, Leonard Barden. Informal intermediate introduction, quite strong in explaining reasons for moves. Covers basic material, tactics, important openings, traps, positional play in middle game, end game. Attempts to isolate patterns and recurrent configurations. Formerly *Chess*. 58 figures. 102pp. (USO) 21210-6 Paperbound $1.25

LASKER'S MANUAL OF CHESS, Dr. Emanuel Lasker. Lasker was not only one of the five great World Champions, he was also one of the ablest expositors, theorists, and analysts. In many ways, his Manual, permeated with his philosophy of battle, filled with keen insights, is one of the greatest works ever written on chess. Filled with analyzed games by the great players. A single-volume library that will profit almost any chess player, beginner or master. 308 diagrams. xli x 349pp.
20640-8 Paperbound $2.75

THE MASTER BOOK OF MATHEMATICAL RECREATIONS, Fred Schuh. In opinion of many the finest work ever prepared on mathematical puzzles, stunts, recreations; exhaustively thorough explanations of mathematics involved, analysis of effects, citation of puzzles and games. Mathematics involved is elementary. Translated by F. Göbel. 194 figures. xxiv + 430pp.
22134-2 Paperbound $3.00

MATHEMATICS, MAGIC AND MYSTERY, Martin Gardner. Puzzle editor for Scientific American explains mathematics behind various mystifying tricks: card tricks, stage "mind reading," coin and match tricks, counting out games, geometric dissections, etc. Probability sets, theory of numbers clearly explained. Also provides more than 400 tricks, guaranteed to work, that you can do. 135 illustrations. xii + 176pp.
20335-2 Paperbound $1.50

CATALOGUE OF DOVER BOOKS

MATHEMATICAL PUZZLES FOR BEGINNERS AND ENTHUSIASTS, Geoffrey Mott-Smith. 189 puzzles from easy to difficult—involving arithmetic, logic, algebra, properties of digits, probability, etc.—for enjoyment and mental stimulus. Explanation of mathematical principles behind the puzzles. 135 illustrations. viii + 248pp.
20198-8 Paperbound $1.75

PAPER FOLDING FOR BEGINNERS, William D. Murray and Francis J. Rigney. Easiest book on the market, clearest instructions on making interesting, beautiful origami. Sail boats, cups, roosters, frogs that move legs, bonbon boxes, standing birds, etc. 40 projects; more than 275 diagrams and photographs. 94pp.
20713-7 Paperbound $1.00

TRICKS AND GAMES ON THE POOL TABLE, Fred Herrmann. 79 tricks and games—some solitaires, some for two or more players, some competitive games—to entertain you between formal games. Mystifying shots and throws, unusual caroms, tricks involving such props as cork, coins, a hat, etc. Formerly *Fun on the Pool Table*. 77 figures. 95pp.
21814-7 Paperbound $1.00

HAND SHADOWS TO BE THROWN UPON THE WALL: A SERIES OF NOVEL AND AMUSING FIGURES FORMED BY THE HAND, Henry Bursill. Delightful picturebook from great-grandfather's day shows how to make 18 different hand shadows: a bird that flies, duck that quacks, dog that wags his tail, camel, goose, deer, boy, turtle, etc. Only book of its sort. vi + 33pp. 6½ x 9¼.
21779-5 Paperbound $1.00

WHITTLING AND WOODCARVING, E. J. Tangerman. 18th printing of best book on market. "If you can cut a potato you can carve" toys and puzzles, chains, chessmen, caricatures, masks, frames, woodcut blocks, surface patterns, much more. Information on tools, woods, techniques. Also goes into serious wood sculpture from Middle Ages to present, East and West. 464 photos, figures. x + 293pp.
20965-2 Paperbound $2.00

HISTORY OF PHILOSOPHY, Julián Marias. Possibly the clearest, most easily followed, best planned, most useful one-volume history of philosophy on the market; neither skimpy nor overfull. Full details on system of every major philosopher and dozens of less important thinkers from pre-Socratics up to Existentialism and later. Strong on many European figures usually omitted. Has gone through dozens of editions in Europe. 1966 edition, translated by Stanley Appelbaum and Clarence Strowbridge. xviii + 505pp.
21739-6 Paperbound $3.50

YOGA: A SCIENTIFIC EVALUATION, Kovoor T. Behanan. Scientific but non-technical study of physiological results of yoga exercises; done under auspices of Yale U. Relations to Indian thought, to psychoanalysis, etc. 16 photos. xxiii + 270pp.
20505-3 Paperbound $2.50

Prices subject to change without notice.
Available at your book dealer or write for free catalogue to Dept. GI, Dover Publications, Inc., 180 Varick St., N. Y., N. Y. 10014. Dover publishes more than 150 books each year on science, elementary and advanced mathematics, biology, music, art, literary history, social sciences and other areas.

OHIO UNIVERSITY LIBRARY
FINE ARTS LIBRARY

Please return this book as soon as you have
order to avoid a fine it must

Fine Arts
PN
1994
W39
1973